The Abraham Lincoln
Companion

The Abraham Lincoln Companion

A Celebration of His Life and Times through a Selection of Remembrances, Poems, Songs, and Tributes by Relatives, Friends, Colleagues, and Citizens, Including Important Speeches and Writings by Lincoln, along with a Chronology and Contact Information for Relevant Organizations

Edited by Helene Henderson

Foreword by Douglas L. Wilson
George A. Lawrence Distinguished Service,
Professor Emeritus of English, Lincoln Studies Center, Knox College

P.O. Box 31-1640
Detroit, MI 48231-1640

Omnigraphics, Inc.

Cherie D. Abbey, *Managing Editor*
Helene Henderson, *Editor*
Allison A. Beckett and Mary Butler, *Research Staff*

* * *

Peter E. Ruffner, *Publisher*
Matthew P. Barbour, *Senior Vice President*
Kay Gill, *Vice President — Directories*

* * *

Elizabeth Collins, *Research and Permissions Coordinator*
Kevin Hayes, *Operations Manager*
Cherry Stockdale, *Permissions Assistant*
Shirley Amore, Martha Johns, and Kirk Kauffman, *Administrative Staff*

Copyright © 2008 Omnigraphics, Inc.
ISBN 978-0-7808-0823-2

Library of Congress Cataloging-in-Publication Data

The Abraham Lincoln companion : a celebration of his life and times through a selection of remembrances, poems, songs, and tributes by relatives, friends, colleagues, and citizens, including important speeches and writings by Lincoln, along with a chronology and contact information for relevant organizations / edited by Helene Henderson ; foreword by Douglas L. Wilson.
      p. cm.
   Summary: "Contains over 100 primary source selections including essays, proclamations, letters, eulogies, poems, and songs to illustrate Abraham Lincoln's life, presidency, and legacy. Features include a chronology, bibliography, and contact information and web sites for associations, libraries, museums, and historic sites"--Provided by publisher.
   Includes bibliographical references and index.
   ISBN 978-0-7808-0823-2 (hardcover : alk. paper) 1. Lincoln, Abraham, 1809-1865–Anecdotes. 2. Presidents–United States–Anecdotes. 3. Lincoln, Abraham, 1809-1865–Miscellanea. 4. Presidents–United States–Miscellanea.
   I. Henderson, Helene, 1963-
   E457.15.A153 2008
   973.7092--dc22

                                                                                          2007035407

The information in this publication was compiled from sources cited and from sources considered reliable. While every possible effort has been made to ensure reliability, the publisher will not assume liability for damages caused by inaccuracies in the data, and makes no warranty, express or implied, on the accuracy of the information contained herein.

This book is printed on acid-free paper meeting the ANSI Z39.48 Standard. The infinity symbol that appears above indicates that the paper in this book meets that standard.

Contents

Part 6 – Centennial Celebrations

Part 7 – A Selection of Lincoln's Speeches and Writings

Foreword

When Abraham Lincoln was inaugurated as the 16th president of the United States in 1861, only one person qualified as the foremost American. Honored for his crucial role in winning the nation's independence and establishing a viable national government, George Washington was universally revered. The story of his seemingly exemplary life was often retold and eventually assumed the proportions of a legend. Lincoln, by contrast, was not even well known. He had been elected by virtue of divisions in the opposition party, and even leaders in his own party feared that he lacked the skills and experience necessary to deal with a great national crisis. But when Lincoln was assassinated just four years later, the outpouring of admiration and affection from his fellow countrymen was unprecedented, and he was already being widely compared to Washington. Since that time, his stature as a great national hero has only increased and his story has become even better known and more legendary than George Washington's, as shown in the many selections gathered here in *The Abraham Lincoln Companion*.

To appreciate this phenomenon, we must start with his remarkable presidency. When he came to office, the federal Union was in the process of dissolution, and there was no agreement about what could or should be done about it. Unlike his predecessor, who had helplessly descried the secession of Southern states, Lincoln took a firm stand. He insisted that secession meant the destruction of the United States government, which the president was sworn to preserve. He further insisted that what was ultimately at stake was the American experiment in self-government, with its fundamental principle of majority rule. At the same time, he made it clear that his goal was not vengeance but reconciliation. Even when the firing on Fort Sumter on April 12, 1861, plunged the nation into civil war, Lincoln insisted that the object of the government's effort was not to punish or to destroy but rather simply to return the insurrectionists and the states they controlled to the national authority.

This policy had broad appeal, but to many in his own party it was inadequate because it took no account of slavery, the ultimate cause of all the difficulty. Lincoln famously replied in 1862: "My paramount object in this struggle is to save the Union, and is not either to save or to destroy slavery." But even as he wrote this he was planning to announce a proclamation emancipating the slaves held by those still in rebellion against the government. Since slavery was expressly guaranteed in the Constitution, the Emancipation Proclamation of January 1, 1863, was promulgated strictly on the grounds of "military necessity," a means to preserve the Union, rather than as an end in itself. But Lincoln eventually came to see these issues from something like the opposite perspective, that saving the Union was the means designed by Providence for destroying slavery. In his Second Inaugural address, he implied that the war had been visited upon the nation, both North and South, for its complicity in the wrong of slavery: "He [God] gives to both north and south this terrible war as the woe due to those by whom the offence came."

As readers of *The Abraham Lincoln Companion* will readily learn, his successful prosecution of the war was only the beginning of Lincoln's fame. He had, in the course of his presidency, earned a reputation for honesty and fair dealing, for compassion and mercy, for wit and humor, and perhaps most impressively, for a lack of vindictiveness — toward his critics and political adversaries, and toward the rebels themselves. After his assassination, these qualities were often magnified as saintly, and their persistence in the public mind laid the basis for an enduring legend. For example, when he had taken office, his lack of formal schooling and his self-education were often cited as liabilities, but after his death they became marks of distinction. Eventually the picture of a self-made man, honest and humane, rising from humble origins to become the savior of his country, became a part of the national identity, symbolic of what it means to be an American.

But there is yet another reason that Abraham Lincoln has remained alive in the imaginations of Americans and of people around the world, namely, the legacy of his words. More than those of any other American, Lincoln's words have continued through the years to resonate with meaning. Not only have they retained the power to evoke intense feelings and to inspire successive generations of Americans, but they have also continued to shape the understanding of American history. Some of Lincoln's most important writings are included in this volume.

Lincoln's four years as president were a relentless nightmare, with tens of thousands of Americans being killed and maimed by other Americans. Without sentimentality or evasion, Lincoln's words put those horrific events into perspective. Significantly, his most memorable expressions are not celebratory but are rather designed to remind his countrymen of their responsibilities and to set forth difficult tasks.

> Fellow-citizens, we cannot escape history. . . . The fiery trial through which we pass, will light us down, in honor or dishonor, to the latest generation. . . . We — even we here — hold the power, and bear the responsibility. In giving freedom to the slave, we assure freedom to the free — honorable alike in what we give, and what we preserve. We shall nobly save, or meanly lose, the last best hope of earth.

> That we here highly resolve that these dead shall not have died in vain — that his nation, under God, shall have a new birth of freedom.

And Lincoln's words continue to be read and to inspire, as well, for the universality of their appeal:

> With malice toward none; with charity for all; with firmness in the right as God gives us to see the right, let us strive on to finish the work we are in.

Douglas L. Wilson
Lincoln Studies Center
Knox College

Preface

Abraham Lincoln, the 16th president of the United States, is widely considered one of the greatest leaders—if not the greatest leader—in our nation's history. He guided the country through the devastating Civil War and brought about the abolition of slavery. Many who have approached Lincoln—whether in person, as a friend or colleague, or from across the decades, as a scholar or admirer—have remarked on a mystique about him. They often find that he was, in the end, essentially unknowable. But they agree that Lincoln was a man of great integrity, honesty, and commitment to America's founding ideals.

Lincoln's appeal remains unprecedented. More places in the United States—23 counties and more than 120 cities and towns—have been named after him than anyone other than George Washington. More books have been written about Lincoln than any other American, and they number in the thousands. Among these were numerous books of tributes to and reminiscences of Lincoln published in the late 19th and early 20th centuries. *The Abraham Lincoln Companion* follows that tradition, but with a difference. In these earlier tribute volumes, the overwhelming majority of voices heard were those of presidents, congressmen, military officers, and other leaders in society. Many of those voices are included in this volume as well, but are mixed with those of African Americans, women, and ordinary citizens whose perspectives did not appear in the earlier books. Taken together, these varied voices provide a much fuller view of Lincoln as an American icon.

Purpose and Scope

The purpose of this volume is to present a portrait of Lincoln from his birth in 1809 to the centennial of his birth in 1909. Lincoln is revealed through the voices of those closest to him personally and professionally, those who met him only once, and those who only "knew" him from afar. Together, these voices attempt to answer these questions: what was Lincoln like, and what made him so great?

The selections in this book were chosen to introduce readers to Abraham Lincoln as he was known and remembered by those around him. They show Lincoln as a serious and extremely conscientious individual who successfully negotiated the unprecedented responsibilities of his presidency. They also reveal other aspects—a man who doted on his family, was fond of animals, loved to tell stories and jokes, and, on occasion, betrayed a charmingly silly side to his personality. Lincoln was also one of the most accessible American presidents. He met with thousands on a one-on-one basis: women seeking pardons or releases from military service for their sons and husbands, citizens wanting to give him their opinions on issues of the day, and the never-ending stream of those asking for appointments to positions in the government. Some of these voices appear in this volume as well.

The Abraham Lincoln Companion is intended for a general audience. It will be useful to students and teachers, as well as interested adults and civic groups.

Organization and Content

The selections in this volume are organized by topic into the following seven sections:

Early Life and Career—This section contains excerpts focusing on Lincoln's childhood, family, friends, education, and jobs as a younger adult.

The 16th President: Great Emancipator and Commander-in-Chief—This section concerns Lincoln as president, including accounts from people who met or worked with him in that capacity and highlighting major events of his presidency.

The Man Behind the Legend—This section sheds light on Lincoln's domestic life, relationships, and personality.

The Death of Lincoln—This section includes descriptions of Lincoln's last day, his assassination, and the aftermath, including eulogies and poetic memorials.

Tributes and Legacy—This section gathers tributes and assessments from a range of prominent Americans from the time of Lincoln's death to just after the turn of the 20th century.

Centennial Celebrations—This section includes speeches and other commemorative texts written for the 100th anniversary of his birth in 1909.

A Selection of Lincoln's Speeches and Writings—This section contains text from some of Lincoln's most important addresses and proclamations.

Each section begins with a brief introduction that describes the type of information covered there, the time period during which the pieces were written, the authors of the various pieces, and the format of those pieces. Within each section, each piece begins with an annotation with information about the writer and his or her relationship to Lincoln and concludes with bibliographic information about the source.

A Note on Spelling and Punctuation

The articles reprinted here appear in their original form, with some archaic spelling and punctuation. Some of the earliest pieces, in particular, contain irregular or inaccurate phrasing, making them somewhat difficult to read. Still, in order to retain the integrity of the documents, each piece has been reprinted in its original form.

Other Features

Cross References

See-also references within the selections guide the reader to related pieces elsewhere in the book.

Chronology

The Chronology lists prominent events in Lincoln's life as well as notable commemorative observances after his death. Cross references in the Chronology link important events in Lincoln's life to relevant documents in the volume.

Bibliography

The Bibliography lists sources used in compiling this volume and suggestions for further reading. It is organized by type of resource: reference, biography, studies of Lincoln's presidency, books on Lincoln's image and legacy, commemorative volumes, young adult titles, journals, and works by Lincoln.

Contact Information for Lincoln Groups

This section lists contact information, including web sites, for associations, educational institutes, landmarks and historic sites, libraries, and museums related to Lincoln.

Author Index
The Author Index lists the authors and speakers whose texts appear in this volume.

Subject Index
The Subject Index includes people, places, and events discussed in the documents in this volume.

Acknowledgments

We are grateful to Douglas L. Wilson of the Lincoln Studies Center at Knox College for contributing his authoritative and insightful foreword to this volume. We would also like to thank the Lincoln Museum, Fort Wayne, Indiana; the Plymouth Historical Museum, Plymouth, Michigan; the Abraham Lincoln Presidential Library, Springfield, Illinois; the Smithsonian Institution, Washington, D.C.; and the Library of Congress, Washington, D.C., for providing photos and illustrations.

Comments and Suggestions

We welcome your comments on *The Abraham Lincoln Companion*. Correspondence should be addressed to:

Editor, *The Abraham Lincoln Companion*
Omnigraphics, Inc.
P.O. Box 31-1640
Detroit, MI 48231-1640
Email: editorial@omnigraphics.com

The Abraham Lincoln Companion

*This daguerreotype, taken in 1846 or 1847, is thought to be the
earliest photographic image of Lincoln.*

Part 1
Early Life and Career

Abraham Lincoln's rise from humble beginnings on the American frontier to national hero have inspired millions of Americans and others around the world. The excerpts in this section concern his childhood, education, friends, acquaintances, and jobs as a young adult, including a stint in the Illinois militia during the Black Hawk War of 1832. Many of the pieces in this section consist of recollections of relatives, friends, and colleagues close to Lincoln up through the 1850s, before he was elected president. After Lincoln's death in 1865, William H. Herndon, his law partner, conducted interviews and correspondence with these people from Lincoln's early life. Some selections have been transcribed from original documents and reflect the fact that spelling and punctuation inconsistencies abound in 19th-century writings.

This section begins with autobiographical pieces by Lincoln and continues with a summary of his life by early biographer Osborn H. Oldroyd, followed by reminiscences from some of his relatives and early friends and acquaintances. These accounts are from interviews and correspondence with Lincoln's stepmother Sarah Bush Johnston Lincoln, stepsister Matilda Moore, cousins Dennis Hanks and John Hanks, neighbor Clarissa Tuft Vannattin, best friend Joshua Speed, and early colleague Leonard Swett. These selections offer unique personal memories of Lincoln as a boy and a young man.

Despite his lack of formal education, Lincoln worked hard to educate himself, not only in order to practice law, but also because he loved literature. Horace Greeley and Hamilton Wright Mabie furnish assessments of his early education and literary talents. A poem written by Lincoln and one of his favorite poems help illustrate his literary sensibility.

In addition to practicing law, Lincoln embarked on a political career during the 1830s. His first elected office was as a state representative in Illinois. Lincoln continued to be elected to this office and served until 1846, when he ran for a seat in, and was elected to, the U.S. House of Representatives, where he served until 1849. Lincoln then moved back to Springfield and resumed his legal practice full time. In 1854 he reentered political life and was again elected to the Illinois House of Representatives. Biographer Ida M. Tarbell describes Lincoln's political ascendance through his debates with Stephen A. Douglas during his Senate campaign of 1858, which brought him to national prominence and his election to the presidency in 1860.

Finally, two sets of excerpts date from Lincoln's presidential campaign and election: correspondence with Grace Bedell, a girl from New York who advised Lincoln to grow a beard, and Lincoln's moving farewell words to his friends in Springfield, Illinois, as he left to take office in Washington, D.C.

1-1
Abraham Lincoln's Autobiographies

Lincoln wrote this autobiographical statement in 1858 at the request of Charles Lanman, who was compiling the Dictionary of the United States Congress (1859):

Born February 12, 1809, in Hardin Co., Kentucky.

Education Defective. Profession a Lawyer. Have been a Captain of Volunteers in Black Hawk War. Postmaster at a very small office. Four times a member of the Illinois Legislature, and was a member of the Lower House of Congress.

Yours, etc.

Lincoln.

Lincoln composed the longer autobiography below on December 20, 1859. Fellow Illinois lawyer and politician Jesse Wilson Fell had asked Lincoln for his autobiography to assist in publicizing his presidential campaign. Lincoln sent it along with the following note: "Herewith is a little sketch, as you requested. There is not much of it, for the reason, I suppose, that there is not much of me."

Fell relayed the piece to a friend in Pennsylvania who arranged for its publication in newspapers around the East, where people knew little or nothing about Lincoln.

I was born February 12, 1809, in Hardin Co., Ky. My parents were born in Virginia, of undistinguished families—second families, perhaps I should say. My mother, who died in my tenth year, was of a family of the name of Hanks, some of whom now reside in Adams Co., and others in Mason Co., Ill. My paternal grandfather, Abraham Lincoln, emigrated from Rockingham Co., Va., to Kentucky, about 1781 or 1782, where, a year or two later, he was killed by Indians, not in battle, but

There was absolutely nothing to excite ambition for education. Of course, when I came of age I did not know much. Still, somehow, I could read, write, and cipher to the rule of three, but that was all. I have not been to school since. The little advance I now have upon this store of education I have picked up from time to time under the pressure of necessity.

by stealth, when he was laboring to open a farm in the forest. His ancestors, who were Quakers, went to Virginia from Berks Co., Pa. An effort to identify them with the New England family of the same name ended in nothing more definite than a similarity of Christian names in both families, such as Enoch, Levi, Mordecai, Solomon, Abraham, and the like.

My father, at the death of his father, was but six years of age, and grew up literally without any education. He removed from Kentucky to what is now Spencer Co., Ind., in my eighth year. We reached our new home about the time the State came into Union. It was a wild region, with many bears and other wild animals still in the woods. There I grew up. There were some schools, so-called, but no qualifications was ever required of a teacher beyond 'readin', writin', and cipherin', to the rule of three. If a straggler, supposed to understand Latin, happened to sojourn in the neighborhood, he was looked upon as a wizard. There was absolutely nothing to excite ambition for education. Of course, when I came of age I did not know much. Still, somehow, I could read, write, and cipher to the rule of three, but that was all. I have not been to school since. The little advance I now have upon this store of education I have picked up from time to time under the pressure of necessity.

I was raised to farm work, at which I continued till I was twenty-two. At twenty-one I came to Illinois, and passed the first year in Macon County. Then I got to New Salem, at that time in Sangamon, now Menard County, where I remained a year as a sort of clerk in a store. Then came the Black Hawk War, and I was elected a captain of volunteers—a success, which gave me more pleasure than any I have had since. I went into campaign, was elected, ran for the Legislature the same year (1832), and was beaten—the only time I have ever been beaten by the people. The next and three succeeding biennial elections I was elected to the Legislature. I was not a candidate afterward. During the legislative period I had studied law, and removed to Springfield to practice it. In 1846 I was elected to the Lower House of Congress. Was not a candidate for re-election. From 1849 to 1854, both inclusive practiced law more assiduously than ever before. Always a Whig in politics, and generally on the Whig electoral ticket, making active canvasses. I was losing interest in politics when the repeal of the Missouri Compromise aroused me again. What I have done since then is pretty well known.

If any personal description of me is thought desirable, it may be said I am in height six feet four inches, nearly; lean in flesh, weighing, on an average, one hundred and eighty pounds; dark complexion, with coarse black hair and gray eyes—no other marks or brands recollected.

Yours very truly,

A. Lincoln.

Sources:

Excerpt 1: Lincoln, Abraham. Autobiographical Statement, 1858. Available online at Abraham Lincoln Papers, Library of Congress. http://memory.loc.gov/ammem/alhtml/malhome.html.

Excerpt 2: Lincoln, Abraham. Autobiographical Statement, December 20, 1859. Available online at Abraham Lincoln Papers, Library of Congress. http://memory.loc.gov/ammem/alhtml/malhome.html.

1-2
Osborn H. Oldroyd's Summary of Lincoln's Life

Osborn H. Oldroyd was a Civil War veteran who was one of the earliest—if not the earliest—serious collectors of Lincoln mementos. In 1927 the U.S. government purchased his collection, which can still be seen at Ford's Theatre National Historic Site. Oldroyd published this brief summary of Lincoln's life in his Words of Lincoln *(1895).*

The sun, which rose on the 12th of February 1809, lighted up a little log cabin on Nolin Creek, Hardin Co., Ky., in which Abraham Lincoln was that day ushered into the world. Although born under the humblest and most unpromising circumstances, he was of honest parentage. In this backwoods hut, surrounded by virgin forests, Abraham's first four years were spent. His parents then moved to a point about six miles from Hodgensville, where he lived until he was seven years of age, when the family again moved, this time to Spencer Co., Ind.

The father first visited the new settlement alone, taking with him his carpenter tools, a few farming implements, and ten barrels of whisky (the latter being the payment received for his little farm) on a flatboat down Salt Creek to the Ohio River. Crossing the river, he left his cargo in care of a friend, and then returned for his family. Packing the bedding and cooking utensils on two horses, the family of four started for their new home. They wended their way through the Kentucky forests to those of Indiana, the mother and daughter (Sarah) taking their turn in riding.

Fourteen years were spent in the Indiana home. It was from this place that Abraham, in company with young [Allen] Gentry, made a trip to New Orleans on a flatboat loaded with country produce. During these years Abraham had less than twelve months of schooling, but acquired a large experience in the rough work of pioneer life. In the autumn of 1818 the mother died, and Abraham experienced the first great sorrow of his life. Mrs. Lincoln had possessed a very limited education, but was noted for intellectual force of character.

The year following the death of Abraham's mother his father returned to Kentucky, and brought a new guardian to the two motherless children. Mrs. Sally [Sarah Bush] Johnston, as Mrs. Lincoln, brought into the family three children of her own, a goodly amount of household furniture, and, what proved a blessing above all others, a kind heart. It was not intended that this should be a permanent home; accordingly, in March, 1830, they packed their effects in wagons, drawn by oxen, bade adieu to their old home, and took up a two weeks' march over untraveled roads, across mountains, swamps, and through dense forests, until they reached a spot on the Sangamon River, ten miles from Decatur, Ill., where they built another primitive home. Abraham had now arrived at manhood, and felt at liberty to go out into the world and battle for himself. He did not leave, however, until he saw his parents comfortably fixed in their new home, which he helped build; he also split enough rails to surround the house and ten acres of ground.

In the fall and winter of 1830, memorable to the early settlers of Illinois as the year of the deep snow, Abraham worked for the farmers who lived in the neighborhood. He made the acquaintance of a man of the name of [Denton] Offutt, who hired him, together with his stepbrother, John D. Johnston, and his uncle [cousin], John Hanks, to take a flatboat loaded with country produce down the Sangamon River to Beardstown, thence down the Illinois and Mississippi Rivers to New Orleans. Abraham and his companions assisted in building the boat, which was finally launched and loaded in the spring of 1831, and their trip successfully made. In going over the dam at Rutledge mill, New Salem, Ill., the boat struck and remained stationary, and a day passed before it was again started on its voyage. During this delay Lincoln made the acquaintance of New Salem and its people.

On his return from New Orleans, after visiting his parents,—who had made another move, to Goose-Nest Prairie, Ill.,— he settled in the little village of New Salem, then in Sangamon, now Menard County. While living in this place, Mr. Lincoln served in the Black Hawk War, in 1832, as captain and private. His employment in the village was varied; he was at times a clerk, county surveyor, postmaster, and partner in the grocery business under the firm name of Lincoln & Berry. He was defeated for the Illinois Legislature in 1832 by Peter Cartwright, the Methodist pioneer preacher. He was elected to the Legislature in 1834, and for three successive terms thereafter.

Mr. Lincoln wielded a great influence among the people of New Salem. They respected him for his uprightness and admired him for his genial and social qualities. He had an earnest sympathy for the unfortunate and those in sorrow. All confided in him, honored and loved him. He had an unfailing fund of anecdote, was a sharp, witty talker, and possessed an accommodating spirit, which led him to exert himself for the entertainment of his friends. During the political canvass of 1834, Mr. Lincoln made the acquaintance of Mr. John T. Stuart of Springfield, Ill. Mr. Stuart saw in the young man that which, if properly developed, could not fail to confer distinction on him. He therefore loaned Lincoln such law books as he needed, the latter often walking from New Salem to Springfield, a distance of twenty miles, to obtain them. It was very fortunate for Mr. Lincoln that he finally became associated with Mr. Stuart in the practice of law. He moved from New Salem to Springfield, and was admitted to the bar in 1837.

On the 4th of November 1842, Mr. Lincoln married Miss Mary Todd of Lexington, Ky., at the residence of Ninian W. Edwards of Springfield, Ill. The fruits of this marriage were four sons; Robert T., born August 1, 1843; Edward Baker, March 10, 1846, died February 1, 1850; William Wallace, December 21, 1850, died at the White House, Washington, February 20, 1862; Thomas ("Tad"), April 4, 1853, died at the Clifton House, Chicago, Ill., July 15, 1871. Mrs. Lincoln died at the house of her sister, Springfield, July 16, 1882.

In 1846 Mr. Lincoln was elected to Congress, as a Whig, his opponent being Peter Cartwright, who had defeated Mr. Lincoln for the Legislature in 1832.

In 1860 Mr. Lincoln came before the country as the chosen candidate of the Republican Party for the Presidency. The campaign was a memorable one, characterized by a novel organization called "Wide Awakes," which had its origin in Hartford, Conn. There were rail fence songs, rail-splitting on wagons in processions, and the building of fences by the torch-light marching clubs.

The most remarkable political canvass witnessed in the country took place between Mr. Lincoln and Stephen A. Douglas in 1858. They were candidates of their respective parties for the United States Senate. Seven joint debates took place in different parts of the State. The Legislature being of Mr. Douglas' political faith, he was elected.

In 1860 Mr. Lincoln came before the country as the chosen candidate of the Republican Party for the Presidency. The campaign was a memorable one, characterized by a novel organization called "Wide Awakes," which had its origin in Hartford, Conn. There were rail fence songs, rail-splitting on wagons in processions, and the building of fences by the torch-light marching clubs.

The triumphant election of Mr. Lincoln took place in November, 1860. On the 11th of February, 1861, he bade farewell to his neighbors, and as the train slowly left the depot his sad face was forever lost to the friends who gathered that morning to bid him God speed. The people along the route flocked at the stations to see him and hear his words. At all points he was greeted as the President of the people, and such he proved to be. Mr. Lincoln reached Washington on the morning of the 23rd of February, and on the 4th of March was inaugurated President. Through four years of terrible war his guiding star was justice and mercy. He was sometimes censured by officers of the army for granting pardons to deserters and others, but he could not resist an appeal for the life of a soldier. He was the friend of the soldiers, and felt and acted toward them like a father. Even workingmen could write him letters of encouragement and receive appreciative words in reply.

When the immortal Proclamation of Emancipation was issued, the whole world applauded, and slavery received its death-blow. The terrible strain of anxiety and responsibility borne by Mr. Lincoln during the war had worn him away to a marked degree, but that God who was with him throughout the struggle permitted him to live, and by his masterly efforts and unceasing vigilance pilot the ship of state back into the haven of peace.

On the 14th of April, 1865, after a day of unusual cheerfulness in those troublous times, and seeking relaxation from his cares, the President, accompanied by his wife and a few intimate friends, went to Ford's Theater, on Tenth Street, N.W. There the foul assassin, J. Wilkes Booth, awaited his coming and at twenty minutes past ten o'clock, just as the third act of "Our American Cousin" was about to commence, fired the shot that took the life of Abraham Lincoln. The bleeding President was carried to a house across the street, No. 516, where he died at twenty-two minutes past seven the next morning. The body was taken to the White House and, after lying in state in the East Room and at the Capitol, left Washington on the 21st of April, stopping at various places en route, and finally arriving at Springfield on the 3rd of May. On the following day the funeral ceremonies took place at Oak Ridge Cemetery, and there the remains of the martyr were laid at rest.

Abraham Lincoln needs no marble shaft to perpetuate his name; his words are the most enduring monument, and will forever live in the hearts of the people.

Source:

Oldroyd, Osborn H. *Words of Lincoln, Including Several Hundred Opinions of His Life and Character by Eminent Persons of This and Other Lands.* Washington, D.C.: O. H. Oldroyd, 1895.

1-3
Stepmother Sarah Bush Johnston Lincoln on His Childhood

Sarah Bush Johnston Lincoln was the president's stepmother. His mother, Nancy Hanks Lincoln, died in 1818. Sarah Bush Johnston became his step-mother when she married Thomas Lincoln on December 2, 1819. According to Lincoln, "she proved a good and kind mother." Mrs. Lincoln offered her reminiscences below in an interview conducted by William H. Herndon, Lincoln's law partner, on September 8, 1865, at her home in Coles County, Illinois.

Friday—Old Mrs Lincolns Home—8 m South of Charleston

Mrs Thomas Lincoln Says— . . .

When we landed in Indiana Mr Lincoln had erected a good log cabin—tolerably Comfortable. . . . Abe was then young—so was his Sister. I dressed Abe & his sister up—looked more human. Abe slept up stairs—went up on pins stuck in the logs—like a ladder—Our bed steds were original creations—none such now—made of poles & Clapboards—Abe was about 9 ys of age when I landed in Indiana—The country was wild—and desolate. Abe was a good boy: he didn't like physical labor—was diligent for Knowledge—wished to Know & if pains & Labor would get it he was sure to get it. He was the best boy I ever saw. He read all the books he could lay his hands on—I can't remember dates nor names—am about 75 ys of age—Abe read the bible some, though not as much as said: he sought more congenial books—suitable for his age. I think newspapers were had in Indiana as Early as 1824 & up to 1830 when we moved to Ills—Abe was a Constant reader of them—I am sure of this for the years of 1827-28-29-30. The name of the Louisville Journal seems to sound like one. Abe read histories, papers—& other books—cant name any one—have forgotten. Abe had no particular religion—didnt think of that question at the time, if he ever did—He never talked about it. He read diligently—studied in the day time—didnt after night much—went to bed Early—got up Early & then read—Eat his breakfast—go to work in the field with the men. Abe read all the books he could lay his hands on—and when he came across a passage that Struck him he would write it down on boards if he had no paper & keep it there till he did get paper—then he would re-write it—look at it repeat it—He had a copy book—a kind of scrap book in which he put down all things and this preserved them. He ciphered on boards when he had no paper or no slate and when the board would get too black he would shave it off with a drawing knife and go on again: When he had paper he put his sums down on it. His copy book is here now or was lately (Here it was shown me by Mr Thos Johnson) Abe, when old folks were at our house, was a silent & attentive observer—never speaking or asking questions till they were gone and then he must understand Every thing—even to the smallest thing—Minutely & Exactly—: he would then repeat it over to himself again & again—sometimes in one form and then in another & when it was fixed in his mind to suit him he became Easy and he never lost that fact or his understanding of it. Sometimes

Lincoln's stepmother, Sarah Bush Johnston Lincoln, in a photograph taken around 1865.

he seemed pestered to give Expression to his ideas and got mad almost at one who couldn't Explain plainly what he wanted to convey. He would hear sermons preached—come home—take the children out—get on a stump or log and almost repeat it word for word— He made other Speeches—Such as interested him and the children. His father had to make him quit sometimes as he quit his own work to speak & made the other children as well as the men quit their work. As a usual thing Mr Lincoln never made Abe quit reading to do anything if he could avoid it. He would do it himself first. Mr. Lincoln could read a little & could scarcely write his name: hence he wanted, as he himself felt the uses & necessities of Education his boy Abraham to learn & he encouraged him to do it in all ways he could—Abe was a poor boy, & I can say what scarcely one woman—a mother—can say in a thousand and it is this—Abe never gave me a cross word or look and never refused in fact, or Even in appearance, to do any thing I requested him. I never gave him a cross word in all my life. He was Kind to Every body and to Every thing and always accommodate others if he could—would do so willingly if he could. His mind & mine—what little I had seemed to run together—move in the same channel—Abe could Easily learn & long remember and when he did learn anything he learned it well and thoroughly. What he thus learned he stowed away in his memory which was Extremely good—What he learned and Stowed away was well defined in his own mind—repeated over & over again & again till it was so defined and fixed firmly & permanently in his Memory. He rose Early—went to bed Early, not reading much after night. Abe was a moderate Eater and I now have no remembrance of his Special dish: he Sat down & ate what was set before him, making no complaint: he seemed Careless about this. I cooked his meals for nearly 15 years—. He always had good health—never was sick—was very careful of his person—was tolerably neat and clean only—Cared nothing for clothes—so that they were clean & neat—fashion cut no figure with him—nor Color—nor Stuff nor material—was Careless about these things. He was more fleshy in Indiana than Ever in Ills—. I saw him Every year or two—He was here—after he was Elected President of the US. (Here the old lady stopped—turned around & cried—wiped her eyes—and proceeded) As Company would Come to our house Abe was a silent listener—wouldn't speak—would sometimes take a book and retire aloft—go to the stable or field or woods—and read—. Abe was always fond of fun—sport—wit & jokes—He was sometimes very witty indeed. He never drank whiskey or other strong drink—was temperate in all things—too much so I thought sometimes—He never told me a lie in his life—never Evaded—never Equivocated never dodged—nor turned a Corner to avoid any chastisement or other responsibility. He never swore or used profane language in my presence nor in others that I now remember of—He duly reverenced old age—loved those best around his own age—played with those under his age—he listened to the aged—argued with his Equals—but played with the children—. He loved animals genery and treated them Kindly: he loved children well very well—. There seemed to be nothing unusual in his love for animals or his own Kind—through he treated Every body & Every thing Kindly—humanely—Abe didnt Care much for crowds of people: he chose his own Company which was always good. He was not very fond of girls as he seemed to me. He sometimes attended Church. He would repeat the sermon over again to the children. The sight of such a thing amused all and did Especially tickle the Children. When Abe was reading My husband took particular Care not to disturb him—would let him read on and on till Abe quit of his own accord. He was dutiful to me always—he loved me truly I think. I had a son John who was raised with Abe Both were good boys, but I must Say—both now being dead that Abe was the best boy I Ever Saw or Ever Expect to see. I wish I had died when my husband died. I did not want Abe to run for Presdt—did not want him Elected—was afraid Somehow or other—felt it in my heart that Something [would] happen him and when he came down to see me after he was Elected Predt I still felt that Something told me that Something would befall Abe and that I should see him no more. Abe & his father are in Heaven I have no doubt, and I want to go there—go where they are—God bless Abm

Source:

Lincoln, Sarah Bush Johnston. Interview with William H. Herndon, September 8, 1865. Herndon-Weik Collection, Manuscript Division, Library of Congress, Washington, D.C. Published in *Herndon's Informants: Letters, Interviews, and Statements about Abraham Lincoln.* Edited by Douglas L. Wilson and Rodney O. Davis, with the assistance of Terry Wilson. Urbana: University of Illinois Press, 1998.

1-4
Stepsister Matilda Johnston Moore on Her Older Stepbrother

Matilda Johnston Moore was Sarah Johnston Lincoln's youngest daughter. Matilda, who was about five years younger than Abraham, became his stepsister when their parents married in 1819. Here she relates some memories of Abraham and the other children in the family in an interview conducted by William H. Herndon, Lincoln's law partner, at her mother's home on September 8, 1865.

I am the youngest Step Sister of A Lincoln—remember coming from Ky—remember Ohio River—My Earliest recollection of Abe is playing—Carrying water about one mile—had a pet cat that would follow him to the spring—went to school about 2 miles or more—Abe was not Energetic Except in one thing—he was active & persistant in learning—read Everything he Could—Ciphered on boards—on the walls—read Robinson Crusoe—the bible—Watts hymns—. When father & Mother would go to Church, they walked about 1fi miles—Sometimes rode—When they were gone—Abe would take down the bible, read a verse—give out a hymn—and we would sing—were good singers. Abe was about 15 years of age—: he would preach & we would do the Crying—sometimes he would join in the Chorus of Tears—One day my bro John Johnston caught a land terrapin—brought it to the place where Abe was preaching—thre it against the tree—crushed the shell and it Suffered much—quivered all over—Abe preached against Cruelty to animals, Contending that an ants life was to it, as sweet as ours to us—Abe read I think Grimshaws History of the U.S—and other books—Cant now remember what—Abe would go out to work in the field—get up on a stump and repeat almost word for word the sermon he had heard the Sunday before—Call the Children and friends around him—His father would come and make him quit—send him to work—Often Abe would make political speeches such as he had heard spoken or seen written &c—. He never forgot anything—was truthful, good to me—good to all—Once when he was going to the field to work I ran—jumped on his back—cut my foot on the axe—we said—"What will we tell Mother as to how this happened: I said I would tell her "I cut my foot on the axe" that will be no lie—said Lincoln, but it won't be all the truth—the whole truth—will it Tilda—Tell the whole truth and risk your Mother Abe seemed to love Every body and Every thing: he loved us all and Especially Mother—My Mother, I think has given Abes character well—I am about 50 years of age—

Source:

Moore, Matilda Johnston. Interview with William H. Herndon, September 8, 1865. Herndon-Weik Collection, Manuscript Division, Library of Congress, Washington, D.C. Published in *Herndon's Informants: Letters, Interviews, and Statements about Abraham Lincoln.* Edited by Douglas L. Wilson and Rodney O. Davis, with the assistance of Terry Wilson. Urbana: University of Illinois Press, 1998.

1-5
Cousin Dennis Hanks on Lincoln's Early Life

Dennis Hanks was the first cousin of Abraham Lincoln's mother, Nancy Hanks
Lincoln, and a cousin of John Hanks (see document 1-6). In 1818 Dennis
moved in with the Lincoln family. He was about nineteen when Abraham was
about nine years old, and the two became close. In an interview in Chicago on
June 13, 1865, with William H. Herndon, Lincoln's law partner, Hanks
offered some remembrances of Lincoln's early life.

Thomas Lincoln—Abrahams was married to Nancy Sparrow about the year 1808 in Hardin County & State of Kentucky. Nancy Sparrow—the child of Henry Sparrow married Thomas Lincoln when she was about 20 years of age: she was born in Mercer Co Ky. Thomas Lincoln was born in Virginia. Thomas Lincoln the father of Abraham owned about 30 acres in Hardin County on a little Creek called Knob Creek which Empties into the Roling Fork. . . . After the marriage of Thomas Lincoln and Nancy Sparrow. . .Abraham was born at that place. The cabin was a double one, with a passage or entry between. About the year 1813 or 14 as the volunteers of the War of 1812 were returning home they came by Lincolns house and he fed and Cared for them by Companies—by strings of them. I was a little boy at that time—Abraham was a little child and Sarah his sister and senior by 2 or 3 years was then likewise living and a little girl. They had no other children—Cause a private matter. It is said in the Biographies that Mr. Lincoln left the State of Ky because and only because Slavery was there. This is untrue. He movd off to better his Condition—to a place where he could buy land for his Children & Thos. At $125 per acre [$1.25]-Slavery did not operate on him. I know too well this whole matter. Mrs. Lincoln-Abrahams mother was 5-8 in high—Spare made—affectionate, the most affectionate I ever saw—never knew her to be out of temper—and thought strange of it.

He [probably meant "she"] seemed to be immovably Cam [calm]: she was keen—shrewd—smart & I do say highly intellectual by nature. Her memory was strong—her [perception?] was quick—her judgement was acute almost. She was Spiritually & ideally inclined—not dull—not material—not heavy in thought—feeling or action. Her hair was dark hair—Eyes bluish green—keen and loving. Her weight was one

Lincoln's cousins Dennis and John Hanks pose in front of the log cabin Lincoln and his father built in Macon County, Illinois, in 1830.

hundred-thirty—. Thomas Lincoln Abrahams father—was 5—10 fi high—very stoutly built and weighed 196 pounds—His hair dark—his Eyes hazel. He was a man of great streght & courage—not one bit of Cowardice about him—He could *[illegible]* fatigue for any length of time—was a man of uncommon Endurance. . .Thomas Lincoln the father of Abraham could beat his son telling a good story— cracking a joke—Mr Thomas Lincoln was a good, clean, social, truthful & honest man, loving like his wife Evry thing & every body. He was a man who took the world Easy—did not possess much Envy. He never thought that gold was God and the same idea runs through the family. One day when Lincolns mother was weaving in a little shed Abe came in and quizzically asked his good mother who was the father of Zebedee's Children: she saw the drift and laughed, saying get out of her you nasty little pup, you: he saw he had got his mother and ran off laughing. About Abs Early Education: and his sisters Education let me say this—Their mother first learned their

Abc's and then Ab's. She learned them this out of Websters old spelling book: it belonged to me & cost in those days c75, it being Covered with Calf skin—or such-like Covering. I taught Abe his first lesson in spelling—reading & writing—. I taught Abe to write with a buzzards quillen which I killed with a rifle & having made a pen—put Abes hand in mind & moving his fingers by my hand to give him the idea of how to write—. We had no geese then—for the Country was a forrest. I tried to kill an Eagle but it was too smart—wanted to learn Abe to write with that. Lincolns mother learned him to read the Bible—study it & the stories in it and all that was morally & affectionate in it, repeating it to Abe & his sister when very young. Lincoln was often & much moved by the stories. This Bible was bought in Philadelphia about 1801—by my Father & Mother & was mine when Abe was taught to read in it. . .I was ten years older than Abraham and knew him intimately and well from the day of his birth to 1830—I was the second man who touched Lincoln after his birth—a custom then in Ky of running to greet the newborn babe. A man by the name of Hazel hellped to teach Abraham his letters Abc—spelling reading & writing &c—. Lincoln went to school about 3. mo—with his sister—all the Education he had in Ky—Parson Elkin a preacher of the old Babtist religion Came to Mr Thomas Lincoln's and frequently preached in that neighborhood.

At about the year 1818 Thomas Lincoln—the father of Abraham had a notion in his head—formed a determination to sell out his place and move to Indiana, then a new State where he could buy land as said before at $125 per [$1.25]. . .Mr. Lincoln as stated before sold his farm for whisky. He cut down trees—made a kind of flat boat out of yellow poplar. He made the boat on the Rolling fork at the mouth of Knob Creek Hardin Co Ky—loaded his household furniture—his tools—whisky and other Effects, including pots—vessels—rifles. & c. &c on the boat. He took no dogs—chickens—cats—geese or other domestic animals. He floated on awhile down the Rolling Fork and upset—and lost the most of the tools &c and some of his Whisky. He went along by himself not taking his family. From the Rolling Fork he ran into the Beach fork and thence into the great Ohio. He landed at Thompsons Ferry at Poseys—house or farm. He stared out from his ferry in search of a place and found one and located it by making blazes—brush heaps &c to make a location, which he afterwards bought at $2.00 per acre. . .When he had Cornered the land—blazed it off—marked the boundaries he proceeded on horse back, with his own food & his horses fodder behind him to Vincennes where he paid the $200 per acre as stated before. Mr. Lincoln never owned the land—more than a kind of preemption right & sold it when he moved to Ills. I fared like him in all these particulars. He then returned to the State of Kentucky from Spencer Co Indiana, then Perry Co—since divided—as Hardin Co Ky was—as Sangamon Co—, From the old homestead in Ky Hardin—now Lareau Co Thomas Lincoln—Nancy father & mother of Sarah & Abe ther two children, & two feather beds—Clothing &c mounted 2 horses and went back to Spencer Co—then Perry Co Indian where said land was located on a little Creek Called pigeon Creek—about north of the Ohio—&across & north of the Ohio—. They had no wagons—no dogs—cats—hogs—cows—chickens or such like domestic animals. Abe was at this time 7 years of age.—Abe read no books in Ky— Abe was a good boy—an affectionate one—and a boy who loved his father & mother dearly & well always minding them well— Sometimes Abe was a little rude. When strangers would ride up along & up to his fathers fence Abe always, through pride & to tease his father, would be sure to ask the stranger the first question, for which his father would sometimes knock him a rod. Abe was then a rude and forward boy Abe when whipped by his father never bawled but dropt a kind of silent unwelcome tear, as evidence of his sensations—or other feelings. The family landed at Thompson's Ferry on the Ohio & on the other side crossed the Ohio, and landed at Poseys Farm on the Indiana side. Hence 17 miles northwest of the ferry. I went myself with them backwards & forwards—to Indiana—& back to Ky & back to Ky & back to Indiana and know the story & all the facts well. We all started from Ky in Septr 1818 & was three or four days to the ferry & one day from the Ferry out to the place of location—Here they stopt—Camped—erected a little two face Camp open in front, serving a monumentary purpose. Lincoln saw a wild turkey near the Camp on the second day after landing and Mrs. Lincoln,—abs good mother loaded the gun—Abe poked the gun through the crack of the camp and accidentally killed one, which he brought to the Camp house. Thomas Lincoln then went to cutting trees for the logs of his house—cutting down the brush and underwood—Indiana then being a wilderness and wholly a timbered Country. I assisted him to do this—to cut timber—hawl logs. &c and helped him erect his log Cabin—& Camp—one story high—just high Enough to stand under—no higher. This took only one day. Abe Could do little jobs—such as Carry water—go to the springs—branches &c, for water which was got by digging holes— this was a temporary affair. This was in 1818. We—Lincolns family, including Sally & Abe & my self slept & lodged in this Cabin all winter & till next Spring. We in the winter & spring cut down brush—

under wood—trees—cleared ground—made a field of about 6. acres on which we raised our crops—. We all hunted pretty much all the time. Especially so when we got tired of work—which was very often I will assure you. We did not have to go more than 4 or 5 hundred yards to kill deer—turkeys & other wild game. We found bee trees all over the forests. . .We had no trouble with the Indians in Indiana, they soon left and westward. In the fall & winter of 1819 & 20 we Commenced to cut the trees—clear out the brush and underwoods & forest for our new grand old log cabin, which we Erected that winter: it was one Story—18 by 20 feet—no passage—on window—no glass in it. The lights were made from the leaf Coming off from the hog's fat. This was good mellow light & lasted well. The house was sufficiently high to make a kind of bedroom over head—a loft. This was approached by a kind of ladder made by boring holes in the logs, forming [illegible] one side of the house and this peg over peg we Climed aloft, the pegs creaking & screeching as we went. Here were the beds—the floor of the loft was clap boards & the beds lay on this. Here I and Abe slept & I was married there to Abes stepsister—Miss Elizabeth Johnston—not Johnson. During this fall Mrs. Lincoln was taken sick. with what is known with the Milk sick: she struggled on day day by day—a good Christian woman and died on the 7th day after she was taken sick. Abe & his sister did some work—little jobs—Errand & light work. There was no physician near than 35 miles—She knew she was going to die & Called up the Children to her dying side and told them to be good & kind to their father—to one an other and to the world, Expressing a hope that they might live as they had been taught by her to love men—love—reverence and worship God. Here in this rude house, of the Milk Sick, died one of the very best women in the whole race, known for kindness—tenderness—charity & love to the world. Mrs Lincoln always taught Abe goodness taught him sweetness & benevolence as well. From this up to 1821—Mr Lincoln lived single, Sarah cooking for us, she then being about 14 years of age. We still Kept up hunting—and farming it Mr

> *In the fall & winter of 1819 & 20 we Commenced to cut the trees—clear out the brush and underwoods & forest for our new grand old log cabin, which we Erected that winter: it was one Story—18 by 20 feet—no passage—on window—no glass in it.*

Lincoln—Ab's father was a Cabinet maker & house joiner &c—: he worked at this trade in the winter at odd times, farming it—in The summer. We always hunted it made no difference what came for we more or less depended on it for a living—nay for life. We had not been long at the log Cabin before We got the usual domestic Animals, Known to Civilization. These were driven out from near the Ohio river or halled in a car pulled by one yoke of oxen. Mrs Lincoln was buried about one fourth of a mile from the log cabin and the babtist Church, the Pastor was [Lamar?]. Abraham learned to write so that we could understand it in 1821—. David Elkin of Hardin C Ky—called Parson Elkin whose name has been mentioned before paid a visit— I do not think Elkin Came at the solicitation & letter writing of Abe, but Came of his own accord or through the solicitation of the Church to which Mrs Lincoln belonged. She being a hard shell Babtist Abe was now 12 years old. Elkin Cam over to Indiana in about one year after the death of Mrs Elkin—and preach a funeral sermon on the death of Mrs Lincoln. Parson Elkin was a good—true—man and the best preacher & finest orator I Ever heard. I have heard his words distinctly & clearly one fourth of a mile. Some little time before this funeral service he Thomas Lincoln went to Kentucky and married Johnson [Johnston] whose maiden name was Bush. When Thomas Lincoln married her she had 3 children—2 daughters—& 1 son. The family Came to Indiana with their Step-father and their own mother. There was now 5 Children in the family—Sarah—& Abe. Lincoln—Elizabeth, John D—& Matilda Johnston. . .Now at this time Abe was getting hungry for book, reading Evry thing he could lay his hands on. The marriage of Thomas Lincoln & the widow Johnson [Johnston] was in 1821—Abraham being now 12 years old. Websters old Spelling Book—The life Henry Clay. Robinson Crusoe—Weems Life of Washington—Esops fables—Bunyan's Pilgrim's progress—. I do not Sy that Lincoln read thse books just then but he did between this time & 1825. He was a Constant and I my Say Stubborn reader, his father having Sometimes to slash him for neglecting his work by reading. Mr Lincoln—A bs father—often Said I had to pull the old sow up to the trough—when speaking of Abes reading & how he got to it, then and now he had to pull her away" From the time of the marriage Thos Lincoln & Mrs Johnson [Johnston], Mrs

> *Now at this time Abe was getting hungry for book, reading Evry thing he could lay his hands on.*

Lincoln proved an Excellent Step mother: When she Came into Indiana Abe & his sister was wild—ragged & dirty. Mrs Lincoln had been raised in Elizabethtown in somewhat a high life: She Soaped—rubbed and washed the Children Clean so that they look pretty neat—well & clean. She sewed and mended their Clothes & the Children onc more looked human as their own good mother left them. Thomas Lincoln and Mrs Lincoln never had any Children, accident & nature stopping things short. From 1820 to 1825. Mr Lincoln and Mrs Lincoln Each worked a head at their own business—Thomas at farming—Cabinet making—& hunting: She at Cooking—washing—sewing—weaving &c. &c—About the year 1825 or 1826, Abe borrowed of Josiah Crawford Ramseys life of Washington—which got spoiled as specified generally in The Presidents life and paid as therein described—: he pulled fodder at 25c per dy to py for it. He worked 3 or 4 dys—. Abe was then growing to be a man and about 15 or 16 ys of age. He was then just the Same boy in Evry particular that he subsequently Exhibited to the world from 1831—to the time of his death—at this Early age he was more humerous than in after life—full of fun—wit—humor and if he Ever got a news story—new book or new fact or idea he never forgot it. He was honest—faithful—loving truth, Speaking it at all times—& never flinching therefrom. Physically he was a stout & powerful boy—fat round—plump & well made as well as proportioned. This Continued to be so up to the time he landed in Salem. Sangamon County. In 1825 or 1826 he then Exhibited a love for Poetry and wrote a piece of humorous Rhyme on his friend Josiah Crawford that made all the neighbors, Crawford included burst their sides with laughter. I had it was lost in the fire. He was humorously funny—witty & good humored in all times. Sarah [Abraham's older sister] married a man [Aaron Grigsby]: she married him in 1822 and died in about 12 mo in childbed. About 1826 & 7 myself and Abe went down to the Ohio & cut Cord wood at 25c per Cord & bought stuff to make Each a shirt. We were proud of this— It must have been about this time that Abe got kicked by a horse in the mill and who did not Speak for several hours and when he did speak—he ended the sentence which he Commenced to the horse as I am well informed & blieve. From this last period 1825-6 & 7 Lincoln was Constantly reading, writing—cipher a little in Pikes Arithmatic. He Excelled any boy I ever saw, putting his opportunities into Conversation. He then Some had or got Barclay's English Dictionary. . . During these years the ports [sports] of Mr Lincoln were hunting—shooting squirrels—jumping—wrestling—playing ball— throwing the mall over head— The story about his Carrying home a drunken man is not true as I think or re cellect. He was good Enough & tender Enough & Kind Enough to have saved Any man from Evil—wrong—difficulties or damnation. Let his claim nothing but what is true— Truth & Justice—& Mankind will make him the great of the world: he needs no fictions to back him. Lincoln sometimes attempted to sing but always failed, but while this is true he was harmony & time—& sound. He loved such music as he knew the words of. He was a tricky man and sometimes when he went to log house raising—Corn shucking & such like things he would say to himself and sometimes to to others—I don't want thes fellows to work any more and instantly he would Commence his pranks— tricks—jokes—stories—and sure Enough all would stop—gather around Abe & listen, sometimes Crying—and sometimes bursting their sides with laughter. He sometimes would mount a stump—chair or box and make speeches—Speech with stories—anecdotes & such like thing: he never failed here. At this time Abe was Somewhat He was now and well as before a kind of forward boy & sometimes forward too when he got stubborn: His nature went an Entire revolution. One thing is true of him—always was up to 1830 when our intimacy ended, because he went to Sangamon & I went to Coles Co.: he was ambitious & determined & when he attempted to Excel by man or boy his whole soul & his Energies were bent on doing it—and he in this generally—almost always accomplished his Ends. From these years 1826—& 7 what has been said of other years is applicable up to 1830—working—chopping—toiling—woman child & man—. The plays & sports were the Same. In 1829 (March) Thomas Lincoln moved from Spencer Co Indiana and landed in Macon Co Ills, ten miles west of Decatur. In that spring & summer the log cabin which I now have on Exhibition at the Sanitary fair in Chicago was Erected. Lincoln helped Cut the logs—so did John Hanks— Abe halled them & I hewed them all in & raised it the next day we raised the Cabin. Abraham & his neighbors had a mall, [railing?] party 1830 and he & they then split the rails to fence the ten acres of land which was done. In the Spring & Summer of 1830 the ten acres of land were broken up with the place—. This was on the north fork of Sangamon River in Macon Co Ills—Lincoln was 20 years of [age] when he left Indiana, not 21—as said in the Books. In the fall of 1830 he went down the Sangamon, he then being 21 years of age with John Hanks in a boat of some kind.

I now have told you all I recollect & think worthy of being told. I hope this will put history right, as I have taken time to reflect & to refresh my memory by Conversations—times of well authenticated date—by records—friends & papers. All of which

I do hereby certify to be true in substance—time & fact-knowing what is said to be true personally, as I was an actor pretty much all my life in the scene—

Your Friend

D. F. Hanks

Source:

Hanks, Dennis. Interview with William H. Herndon, June 13, 1865. Herndon-Weik Collection, Manuscript Division, Library of Congress, Washington, D.C. Published in *Herndon's Informants: Letters, Interviews, and Statements about Abraham Lincoln.* Edited by Douglas L. Wilson and Rodney O. Davis, with the assistance of Terry Wilson. Urbana: University of Illinois Press, 1998.

1-6
John Hanks Reminisces about His Younger Cousin

John Hanks was the first cousin of Abraham Lincoln's mother and a cousin of Dennis Hanks (see document 1-5). Lincoln and Hanks met in 1822 when John first came to live with the Lincoln family. When Abraham was twenty-two years old, the two were hired to maneuver a flatboat laden with goods down the Mississippi River. John described the trip, as well as offered other memories of young Lincoln in an interview conducted by William H. Herndon, Lincoln's law partner, in Chicago, Illinois, on June 13, 1865.

Dear Sir.

You have asked me some questions in your letter dated the ___which I duly received.

My cousin Dennis Hanks has told you all he knew & I could but repeat the same thing to you. What I shall say shall be short. I first became acquainted with "Abe" Lincoln when he was 14 years of age his father—& his family were then living in Indiana—Spencer Co about 17 miles from the Ohio river. I lived with Thos Lincoln four years in Indiana working on the farm My Cousin has said Abraham was farming—grubbing—hoeing—making fences &c.: he went to school but little whilst I was there—say one or two months & his father has offen told me he had not gone to

This painting, Lincoln the Rail Splitter, *was created by J. L. G. Ferris around 1909.*

school one year in all his life. He read the life of Washington—Histories—some poetry,—all he could get & learned the most of it by heart quickly & well & alwys remembering it. He often for amusement for his play fellows—neighbors & friends made quite good stump speeches when between the age of 15 & 20. I went to Indiana in 1823 and left ther after my four years were out and went back to Kentucky & stayed there till 1828—when I moved to Macon Co Ills preseding Thomas Lincoln & his family. Thomas Lincoln moved to Macon Co in 1830. when the little Cabbin was built; it was built in March 1830. This I am sure of. The ground was broken up 1830—the same year—the 10 acre tract has been Spoken of by my Cousin Dennis. I and Abe went down the Sangamon River from Decatur to Springfield in a canoe. The spring we went down the River was the spring after the deep snow. Lincoln went into Sangamon Co in 1831. We went from Springfield—to the mouth of Spring Creek where it Empties into the Sangamon River and there we cut & cared—& hewed timber to frame a flat boat—80 feet long & 18 feet wide. The timbers were floated down to Sangamon town on a raft. The timbers were taken out of the Sangamon River—framed & put together at that place. . .We Camped in a Camp on the Sangamon River—done our own Cooking—mending & washing. Lincoln boarded awhile with Carman. I don't think he ever worked for Kirkpatrick at that time, for he was continually and busily Engaged on the boat. David Offutt was our Employer and it was for him we worked, getting about $16—or $20 pr mo. The boat was loaded, for I saw it loaded with bacon—pork—Corn & live hogs. We proceeded on the 1st of May down the Sangamon River & landed for a short time at New Salem now in Menard Co. Ills. The boat got on the mill dam and was fast. We got a small ferry boat & partly unloaded—got over the dam—reloaded & proceeded down the river—Abe—his step brother—Johnston & myself doing the navigating of the boat—feeding the hogs &c— We got near the mouth of Salt Creek and it was there that the pigs got their Eyes sewed up by Offutts men. Abe did not do this— Abe was fixing. Abe said I Can't sew the Eyes up, He held the head of hogs whilst Offutt did so [sew] up their Eyes— Lincoln did bore a hole in the bottom of one End of the boat, for the water to run out which it did—It did so in this way By putting out Pork—corn & one one of the boat sprang upwards—so that End did not touch water way below the dam—and a foot or two below the boat. When the other End was lightened the heavy End Sank, but did not reach the water or dam— The water in the other End of the boat ran down hill according to him and did not run out at the hold bored by Abe this I saw—After the hogs a new & additional lot were put in the at or near the mouth of Salt Creek where it Empties into the Sangamon River we then proceeded down the Sangamon-got into the Ills—passes Beardstown—Alton St. Louis & c. we landed in New Orleans—in the year 1831. We both Came back to St. Louis from New Orleans together, Johnston being with us from Decatur to New Orleans, and back with us. There can be and is no mistake in these facts or the time when they took place. We walked from St. Louis out to Edwards afoot and there the Roads parted, he taking the Charleston—Coles Co road & I the Decatur Road—both afoot all the way. The next time I saw him he was at Dixon on Rock River—called Dixons ferry in the year 1832-month of May. He was the Capt of a Company from Menard Co—then Sangamon. This was a few days before the Stillman defeat on Sycamore Creek—about 30 miles from Dixons ferry—North east from there—Abe Lincoln footed it from Beardstown in 1832 coming from the Black Hawk war and not as we went down the River to New Orleans. . . . Abe Lincoln did Carry a drunken man home one night to keep him from freezing— but my Cousin did not know this & hence did not state it. The man I think his name was Carter told me Abe did— Abe told me— Abes father told me and all this is good evidence enough. Carter told me Abe was right good & clever to pack him to the fire.

Abrm was after the black Hawk war a Candidate of the legislature—in 1832-34- 36—I saw him some time after this pleading law at Decatur.

John Hanks (x) his mark

Source:

Hanks, John. Interview with William H. Herndon, June 13, 1865. Herndon-Weik Collection, Manuscript Division, Library of Congress, Washington, D.C. Published in *Herndon's Informants: Letters, Interviews, and Statements about Abraham Lincoln.* Edited by Douglas L. Wilson and Rodney O. Davis, with the assistance of Terry Wilson. Urbana: University of Illinois Press, 1998.

1-7
Clarissa Tuft Vannattin Tells How Lincoln Helped Her Sister

Clarissa Tuft, whose married name was Mrs. Norman Vannattin (or Van Nattan), lived near the Lincolns in Springfield, Illinois. In an interview with William H. Herndon in the late 1880s, she related an encounter she and her sister, ages fifteen and thirteen, had with Lincoln around 1855.

[T hey were] sent out in the praire to drive up the Cows. They got the cow & were Coming home with her and as they came into the outskirts of the City they were running & romping as young girls do. The younger sister got on the pavement & was running backwards as fast as she could run. Lincoln's face was towards her back & her back towards Lincoln's face. As she was running with her head toward Lincoln, he going east and she going west her foot caught in the pavement somehow & was about to receive a terrible fall, when Lincoln stretched out his long arms and caught her and saved her from a hard fall on the bricks. Lincoln looked down into the girl's face while he held her in his arms with one of his kind, tender, and sympathetic looks and instantly thereby assured the girl that she was safe in his great arms. The little girl looked up and smiled and thanked Lincoln for what he did. Lincoln put the girl on her feet, saying to her—"Now my little daughter you can say that you have been in Abraham's bosom." The girl laughed most heartily at Lincoln's offhand hit.

Source:

Vannattin, Clarissa Tuft. Interview with William H. Herndon in the late 1880s. Herndon-Weik Collection, Manuscript Division, Library of Congress, Washington, D.C. Published in *Herndon's Informants: Letters, Interviews, and Statements about Abraham Lincoln*. Edited by Douglas L. Wilson and Rodney O. Davis, with the assistance of Terry Wilson. Urbana: University of Illinois Press, 1998.

1-8
Horace Greeley on Lincoln's Education

Horace Greeley (1811-1872) was the well-known and influential editor of the New York Tribune. *Their acquaintance began in 1848 when Lincoln wrote his first letter to Greeley, and they carried on a lively correspondence. In this selection Greeley reflects on Lincoln's lack of formal education.*

Let me pause here to consider the surprise often expressed when a citizen of limited schooling is chosen to fill, or is presented for one of the highest civil trusts. Has that argument any foundation in reason, any justification in history?

Of our country's great men, beginning with Ben Franklin, I estimate that a majority had little if anything more than a common-school education while many had less. Washington, Jefferson, and Madison had rather more; Clay and Jackson somewhat less; Van Buren perhaps a little more; Lincoln decidedly less. How great was his consequent loss? I raise the question; let others decide it. Having seen much of Henry Clay, I confidently assert that not one in ten of those who knew him late in life would have suspected, from aught in his conversation or bearing that his education had been inferior to that of the college graduates by whom he was surrounded. His knowledge was different from theirs; and the same is true of Lincoln's as well. Had the latter lived to be seventy years old, I judge that whatever of hesitation or rawness was observable in his manner would have vanished, and he would have met and mingled with educated gentlemen and statesmen on the same easy footing of equality with Henry Clay in his later prime of life. How far his two flatboat voyages to New Orleans are to be classed as educational exercise above or below a freshman's year in college, I will not say; doubtless some freshmen learn more, others less, than those journeys taught him. Reared under the shadow of the primitive woods, which on every side hemmed in the petty clearings of the generally poor, and rarely energetic or diligent, pioneers of the Southern Indiana wilderness, his first introduction to the outside world from the deck of a "broad-horn" must have been wonderfully interesting and suggestive. To one whose utmost experience of civilization had been a county, consisting of a dozen to twenty houses, mainly log, with a shabby little courthouse, including jail, and a shabbier, ruder little church, that must have been a marvelous spectacle which glowed in his face from the banks of the Ohio and the

Horace Greeley, editor of the New York Tribune, *in 1865.*

lower Mississippi. Though Cairo was then but a desolate swamp, Memphis a wood-landing, and Vicksburg a timbered ridge with a few stores at its base, even these were in striking contrast to the somber monotony of the great woods. The rivers were enlivened by countless swift-speeding steamboats, dispensing smoke by day and flame by night; while New Orleans, though scarcely one fourth the city she now is, was the focus of a vast commerce, and of a civilization which (for America) might be deemed antique. I doubt not that our tall and green young backwoodsman needed only a piece of well-tanned sheepskin suitably (that is, learnedly) inscribed to have rendered those two boat trips memorable as his degrees in capacity to act well his part on that stage which has mankind for its audience.

Source:

Greeley, Horace. *Greeley on Lincoln, with Mr. Greeley's Letters to Charles A. Dana and a Lady Friend; To Which Are Added Reminiscences of Horace Greeley.* Edited by Joel Benton. New York: The Baker & Taylor Co., 1893.

1-9
James C. Ambrose on "Choosing 'Abe' Captain"

Lincoln enlisted in the Illinois militia during the Black Hawk War in 1832. On April 21 he was elected captain of his regiment, an event he remembered in 1859 as "a success, which gave me more pleasure than any I have had since." In the issue of the Menasha (WI) Daily Twin City News *dated July 2, 1882, James C. Ambrose wrote the following document about how Lincoln was elected captain.*

When the Black Hawk war broke out in Illinois about 1832, young Abraham Lincoln was living at New Salem, a little village of the class familiarly known out west as "one horse towns" and located near the capital city of Illinois.

He had just closed his clerkship of a year in a feeble grocery, and was the first to enlist under the call of Governor Reynolds for volunteer forces to go against the Sacs and Foxes, of which Black Hawk was chief.

By treaty these Indians had been removed west of the Mississippi into Iowa; but thinking their old hunting ground the better, they had recrossed the river with their war-paint on, causing some trouble, and a great deal of alarm among the settlers. Such was the origin of the war, and the handful of government troops stationed at Rock Island wanted help. Hence the State call.

Mr. Lincoln was twenty-three years old at that time, nine years older than his adopted state. The country was thinly settled, and a company of ninety men who could be spared from home for military service had to be gathered from a wide district. When full, the company met at the neighboring village of Richland to choose its officers. In those days the militia men were allowed to select their leaders in their own way; and they had a very peculiar mode of expressing their preference for captains. For then, as now, there were almost always two candidates for one office.

They would meet on the green somewhere, and at the appointed hour the competitors would step out from the crowds on the opposite sides of the ground, and each would call on all the "boys" who wanted him for captain to fall in behind him. As the line formed, the man next to the candidate would put his hands on the candidate's shoulder; the third man also in the same manner to the second man; and so on to the end. And then they would march and cheer for their leader like so many wild men, in order to win over the fellows who didn't seem to have a choice, or whose minds were sure to run after the greater noise. When all had taken sides, the man who led the longer line, would be declared captain.

Mr. Lincoln never outgrew the familiar nickname, "Abe," but at that time he could hardly be said to have any other name than "Abe"; in fact he had emerged from clerking in that little corner grocery as "Honest Abe." He was not only liked, but loved, in the rough fashion of the frontier by all who knew him. He was a good hand at gunning, fishing, racing, wrestling and other games; he had a tall and strong figure; and he seemed to have been as often "reminded of a little story" in '32 as in '62. And the few men not won by these qualities were won and held by his great common sense, which restrained him from excesses even in sports, and made him a safe friend.

It is not singular therefore that though a stranger to many of the enlisted men, he should have had his warm friends who at once determined to make him captain.

But Mr. Lincoln hung back with the feeling, he said, that if there was any older and better established citizen whom the "boys" had confidence in, it would be better to make such a one captain. His poverty was even more marked than his modesty; and for his stock in education about that time, he wrote a letter to a friend twenty-seven years later:

> "I did not know much; still, somehow I could read, write, and cipher to the rule of three, but that was all."

That, however, was up to the average education of the community; and having been clerk in a country grocery he was considered an educated man.

In the company Mr. Lincoln had joined, there was a dapper little chap for whom Mr. Lincoln had labored as a farm hand a year before, and whom he had left on account of ill-treatment from him. This man was eager for the captaincy. He put in his days and nights "log-rolling" among his fellow volunteers; said he had already smelt gun-powder in a brush with Indians, thus urging the value of experience; even thought he had a "martial bearing"; and he was very industrious in getting those men to join the company who would probably vote for him to be captain.

Muster-day came, and the recruits met to organize. About them stood several hundred relatives and other friends.

The little candidate was early on hand and busily bidding for votes. He had felt so confident of the office in advance of muster-day, that he had rummaged through several country tailor-shops and got a new suit of the nearest approach to a captain's uniform that their scant stock could finish. So there he was, arrayed in jaunty cap, and a swallow-tailed coat with brass buttons. He even wore fine boots, and moreover, had them blacked—which was almost a crime among a country crowd of that day.

Young Lincoln took not one step to make himself captain; and not one to prevent it. He simply put himself "in the hands of his friends," as the politicians say. He stood and quietly watched the trouble others were borrowing over the matter as if it were an election of officers they had enlisted for, rather than for fighting Indians. But after all, a good deal depends in war, on getting good officers.

As two o'clock drew near, the hour set for making a captain, four or five of young Lincoln's most zealous friends, with a big stalwart fellow at the head, edged along pretty close to him, yet not in a way to excite suspicion of a "conspiracy." Just a little bit before two, without even letting "Abe" himself know exactly "what was up," the big fellow stepped directly behind him, clapped his hands on the shoulders before him, and shouted as only prairie giants can, "Hurrah for Captain Abe Lincoln!" and plunged his really astonished candidate forward into a march.

At the same instant, those in league with him also put hands to the shoulders before them, pushed, and took up the cheer, "Hurrah for Captain Abe Lincoln!" so loudly that there seemed to be several hundred already on their side; and so there were, for the outside crowd was already cheering for "Abe."

This little "ruse" of the Lincoln "boys" proved a complete success. "Abe" had to march, whether or no to the music of their cheers; he was truly "in the hands of his friends" then, and couldn't get away; and it must be said he didn't feel very bad over the situation. The storm of cheers and the sight of tall Abraham (six feet and four inches) at the head of the marching column before the fussy little chap in brass buttons was quite ready, caused a quick stampede even among the boys who intended to vote for the little fellow. One after another they rushed for a place in "Captain Abe's" line as though to be first to fall in was to win a prize.

A few rods away stood that suit of captain's clothes alone, looking smaller than ever, "the starch all taken out of 'em," their occupant confounded, and themselves for sale. "Abe's" old "boss" said he was "astonished," and so he had good reason to be, but everybody could see it without his saying so. His "style" couldn't win among the true and shrewd though unpolished "boys" in coarse garments. They saw right through him.

"Buttons," as he became known from that day, was the last man to fall into "Abe's" line. He said he'd make it unanimous.

But his experience in making "Abe" Captain made himself so sick that he wasn't able to move when the company left for the "front," though he soon grew able to move out of the procession.

Thus was "Father Abraham," so young as twenty-three, chosen captain of a militia company over him whose abused, hired-hand he had been. It is little wonder that in '59, after three elections to the State Legislature and one to Congress, Mr. Lincoln should write of this early event as "a success which gave me more pleasure than any I have had since." The war was soon over with but little field-work for the volunteers; but no private was known to complain that "Abe" wasn't a good captain.

Source:

Ambrose, James C. "Choosing 'Abe' Captain." *Menasha (WI) Daily Twin City News,* July 2, 1882.

1-10
Best Friend Joshua Speed on Lincoln's Early Career

Joshua Speed (1814-1882) was Lincoln's closest friend. They met in 1837 when Lincoln came to Springfield, and Speed provided lodging for Lincoln. In this excerpt, he relates their meeting and describes events in this period of Lincoln's life. This excerpt is taken from a statement given to William H. Herndon in 1882.

In 1834, I was a citizen of Springfield, Sangamon Co, Ill. Mr Lincoln lived in the country, fourteen miles from the town. He was a laborer, and a deputy surveyor, and at the same time a member of the legislature, elected the year previously. In 1835, he was a candidate for reelection. I had not seen him for the first six months of my residence there, but had heard him spoken of as a man of wonderful ability on the stump. He was a long, gawky, ugly, shapeless, man. He had never spoken as far as I know of, at the county seat, during his first candidacy. The second time he was a candidate, he had already made in the legislature, considerable reputation, and on his renomination to the legislature, advertised to meet his opponents, and speak in Springfield, on a given day. I believe, that that was the first public speech, he ever made at the court-house.

He was never ashamed so far as I know, to admit his ignorance upon any subject, or of the meaning of any word no matter how ridiculous it might make him appear. As he was riding into town the evening before the speech he passed the handsomest house in the village which had just been built by Geo. Forquer. Upon it he had placed a lightning rod. The first one in the town or country. Some ten or twelve young men were riding with Lincoln. He asked them what that rod was for. They told him it was to keep off the lightning. "How does it do it?" he asked. None of them could tell. He rode into town, bought a book on the properties of lightning, and before morning he knew all about it. When he was ignorant upon any subject, he addressed himself to the task of being ignorant no longer. On this occasion a large number of citizens came from a distance to hear him speak. He had very able opponents. I stood near him, and heard the speech. I was fresh from Kentucky then, and had heard most of her great orators. It struck me then, as it seems to me now, that I never heard a more effective speaker. All the party weapons of offense, and defense, seemed to be entirely under his control. The large crowd, seemed to be swayed by him as he pleased. He was a whig, and quite a number of candidates were associated with him on the whig ticket; seven I think in number; there were seven democrats opposed to them. The debate was a joint one, and Lincoln was appointed to close it, which he did as I have heretofore described in a most masterly style.

The people commenced leaving the court-house, when Geo. Forquer, a man of much celebrity in the state, rose, and asked the people to hear him. He was not a candidate, but was a man of talents, and of great state notoriety as a speaker. He commenced his speech by turning to Lincoln and saying, "This young man will have to be taken down, and I am truly sorry that the task devolves upon me." He then proceeded in a vein of irony, sarcasm, and wit, to ridicule Lincoln in every way that he could. Lincoln stood, not more than ten feet from him, with folded arms, and an eye flashing fire, and listened attentively to him, without ever interrupting him, Lincoln then took the stand for reply. He was pale and his spirits seemed deeply moved. His opponent was one worthy of his steel. He answered him fully, and completely. The conclusion of his speech I remember even now, so deep an impression did it make on me then. He said, "The gentleman commenced his speech by saying that this young man would have to be taken down, alluding to me; I am not so young in years as I am in the tricks and trades of a politician; but live long, or die young, I would rather die now, than, like the gentleman change my politics, and simultaneous with the change, receive an office worth three thousand dollars per year, and then have to erect a lightning-rod over my house, to protect a guilty conscience from an offended God."

He used the lightning-rod against Forquer as he did everything in after life.

In 1837, after his return to the legislature, Mr Lincoln obtained a license to practice law. He lived fourteen miles in the country, and had ridden into town on a borrowed horse, with no earthly goods but a pair of saddle-bags, two or three law books, and some clothing which he had in the saddle-bags. He took an office and engaged from the only cabinet-maker then in the village, a single bedstead. He came into my store (I was a merchant then), set his saddle-bags on the counter, and asked me "what the furniture for a single bedstead would cost." I took slate and pencil, and made calculation, and found the sum for furniture complete, would amount to seventeen dollars in all. Said he, "It is probably cheap enough; but I want to say that cheap as it is I have not the money to pay. But if you will credit me until Christmas, and my experiment here as a lawyer is a success, I will pay you then. If I fail in that I will probably never be able to pay you at all." The tone of his voice was so melancholy that I felt for him. I looked up at him, and I thought then as I think now, that I never saw so gloomy, and melancholy a face. I said to him, "The contraction of so small a debt, seems to affect you so deeply, I think I can suggest a plan by which you will be able to attain your end, without incurring any debt. I have a very large room, and a very large double-bed in it; which you are perfectly welcome to share with me if you choose." "Where is your room?" asked he. "Upstairs" said I, pointing to the stairs leading from the store to my room. Without saying a word, he took his saddle-bags on his arm, went up stairs, set them down on the floor, came down again, and with a face beaming with pleasure and smiles exclaimed "Well Speed I'm moved." Mr Lincoln was then twenty-seven years old, almost without friends, and with no property except the saddle-bags with clothes mentioned within.

Now for me to have lived to see such a man rise from point to point, and from place to place, filling all the places to which he was called, with honor and distinction, until he reached the presidency, filling the presidential chair in the most trying times that any ruler ever had, seems to me more like fiction than fact. None but a genius like his could have accomplished so much, and none but a government like ours could produce such a man. It gave the young eagle scope for his wing. He tried it and soared to the top!

In 1839 Mr Lincoln, being then a lawyer in full practice, attended all the courts adjacent to Springfield. He was then attending court at Christiansburg, about thirty miles distant. I was there when the court broke up. Quite a number of lawyers were coming from court, to Springfield. We were riding along a country road, two and two together, some distance apart. Lincoln and [John] J. Hardin being behind. (Hardin was afterward made Colonel and was killed at Buena Vista). We were passing through a thicket of wild plum, and crab-apple trees, where we stopped to water our horses. After waiting some time Hardin came up and we asked him where Lincoln was. "Oh," said he, "when I saw him last" (there had been a severe wind storm), "he had caught two little birds in his hand, which the wind had blown from their nest, and he was hunting for the nest." Hardin left him before he found it. He finally found the nest, and placed the birds, to use his own words, "in the home provided for them by their mother." When he came up with the party they laughed at him.

Joshua Speed, Lincoln's closest friend.

Said he, earnestly, "I could not have slept tonight if I had not given those two little birds to their mother."

This was the the flower that bloomed so beautifully in his nature, on his native prairies. He never lost the nobility of his nature, nor the kindness of his heart, by being removed to a higher sphere of action. On the contrary both were increased. The enlarged sphere of his action, developed the natural promptings of his heart.

I enclose these incidents in the early life of Mr Lincoln—I do hope that you may prize them—. . .

Source:

Speed, Joshua. Interview with William H. Herndon, 1882. Speed Papers, Illinois State Historical Library. Published in *Herndon's Informants: Letters, Interviews, and Statements about Abraham Lincoln.* Edited by Douglas L. Wilson and Rodney O. Davis, with the assistance of Terry Wilson. Urbana: University of Illinois Press, 1998.

1-11
Fellow Lawyer and Friend Leonard Swett Recounts Two Versions of Meeting Lincoln

Leonard Swett was a fellow lawyer with Lincoln on the Eighth Judicial Circuit in Illinois during the 1850s. Interestingly, Swett related two very different versions of how he first met Lincoln. The first excerpt, published in 1886 in a book of remembrances of Lincoln, provides one version of their meeting.

In the autumn of 1849, I was sitting with Judge David Davis in a small country hotel in Mt. Pulaski, Illinois, when a tall man, with a circular blue cloak thrown over his shoulders, entered one door of the room, and passing through without speaking, went out another. I was struck by his appearance. It was the first time I had ever seen him, and I said to Judge Davis, when he had gone, "Who is that?" "Why, don't you know him? That is Lincoln." In a few moments he returned, and, for the first time, I shook the hand and made the acquaintance of that man who since then has so wonderfully impressed himself upon the hearts and affections of mankind.

But Swett also told another version of first meeting Lincoln. In an interview with Jesse W. Weik between 1887 and 1889, Swett described a decidedly more colorful first meeting with the future president.

[I shall never forget,] the first time I saw Mr. Lincoln. I had expected to encounter him at Springfield, but he was absent from home, nor did our meeting occur till later. It was at the town of Danville. When I called at the hotel it was after dark, and I was told that he was upstairs in Judge Davis's room. In the region where I had been brought up, the judge of the court was usually a man of more or less gravity so that he could not be approached save with some degree of deference. I was not a little abashed, therefore, after I had climbed the unbanistered stairway, to find myself so near the presence and dignity of Judge Davis in whose room I was told I could find Mr. Lincoln. In response to my timid knock two voices responded almost simultaneously, "Come in." Imagine my surprise when the door opened to find two men undressed, or rather dressed for bed, engaged in a lively battle with pillows, tossing them at each other's heads. One, a low, heavy-set man who leaned against the foot of the bed and puffed like a lizard, answered to the description of Judge Davis. The other was a man of tremendous stature; compared to Davis he looked as if he were eight feet tall. He was encased in a long, indescribable garment, yellow as saffron, which reached to his heels, and from beneath which protruded two of the largest feet I had, up to that time, been in the habit of seeing. This immense shirt, for shirt it must have been, looked as if it had been literally carved out of the original bolt of flannel of which it was made and the pieces joined together without reference to measurement or capacity. The only thing that kept it from slipping off the tall and angular frame it covered was the single button at the throat; and I confess to a succession of shudders when I thought of what might happen should that button by any mischance lose its hold. I cannot describe my sensations as this apparition, with modest announcement, "My name is Lincoln," strode across the room to shake my trembling hand. I will not say he reminded me of Satan, but he was certainly the ungodliest figure I had ever seen.

Sources:

Excerpt 1. Swett, Leonard. A Remembrance of Lincoln, 1886. Published in *Reminiscences of Abraham Lincoln by Distinguished Men of His Time.* Edited by Allen Thorndike Rice. New York: North American Publishing Company, 1886.

Excerpt 2. Swett, Leonard. Interview with Jesse W. Weik between 1887 and 1889. Published in *The Real Lincoln, A Portrait* by Jesse W. Weik. Boston and New York: Houghton Mifflin Company, 1922.

1-12
Hamilton Wright Mabie on Lincoln as a Man of Letters

Writer Hamilton Wright Mabie (1845-1916) wrote the following early assessment of Lincoln's literary influences and talents for a late 19th-century tome, A Library of the World's Best Literature, Ancient and Modern *(1897).*

Born in 1809 and dying in 1865, Mr. Lincoln was the contemporary of every distinguished man of letters in America to the close of the war; but from none of them does he appear to have received literary impulse or guidance. He might have read, if circumstances had been favorable, a large part of the work of Irving, Bryant, Poe, Hawthorne, Emerson, Lowell, Whittier, Holmes, Longfellow, and Thoreau, as it came from the press; but he was entirely unfamiliar with it apparently until late in his career, and it is doubtful if even at that period he knew it well or cared greatly for it. He was singularly isolated by circumstances and by temperament from those influences which usually determine, within certain limits, the quality and character of a man's style.

And Mr. Lincoln had a style,—a distinctive, individual, characteristic form of expression. In his own way he gained an insight into the structure of English, and a freedom and skill in the selection and combination of words, which not only made him the most convincing speaker of his time, but which have secured for his speeches a permanent place in literature. One of those speeches is already known wherever the English language is spoken; it is a classic by virtue not only of its unique con-

ABRAHAM LINCOLN,

REPUBLICAN CANDIDATE FOR PRESIDENT OF THE UNITED STATES.

This poster was created in 1860 for Lincoln's presidential campaign.

densation of the sentiment of a tremendous struggle into the narrow compass of a few brief paragraphs, but by virtue of the instinctive felicity of style which gives to the largest thought the beauty of perfect simplicity. The two Inaugural Addresses are touched by the same deep feeling, the same large vision, the same clear, expressive, and persuasive eloquence; and these qualities are found in a great number of speeches, from Mr. Lincoln's first appearance in public life. In his earliest expressions of his political views there is less range; but there is structural order, clearness, sense of proportion, ease, and simplicity which give classic quality to the later utterances. Few speeches have so little of what is commonly regarded as oratorical quality; few have approached so constantly the standards and character of literature. While a group of men of gift and opportunity in the East were giving American literature its earliest direction, and putting the stamp of a high idealism on its thought and a rare refine-

41

ment of spirit on its form, this lonely, untrained man on the old frontier was slowly working his way through the hardest and rudest conditions to perhaps the foremost place in American history, and forming at the same time a style of singular and persuasive charm.

There is, however, no possible excellence without adequate education, no possible mastery of any art without thorough training. Mr. Lincoln has sometimes been called an accident, and his literary gift an unaccountable play of nature; but few men have ever more definitely and persistently worked out what was in them by clear intelligence than Mr. Lincoln, and no speaker or writer of our time has, according to his opportunities, trained himself more thoroughly in the use of English prose. Of educational opportunity in the scholastic sense, the future orator had only the slightest. He went to school "by littles," and these "littles" put together aggregated less than a year; but he discerned very early the practical uses of knowledge, and set himself to acquire it. This pursuit soon became a passion, and this deep and irresistible yearning did more for him perhaps than richer opportunities would have done. It made him a constant student, and it taught him the value of fragments of time. "He was always at the head of his class," writes one of his schoolmates, "and passed us rapidly in his studies. He lost no time at home, and when he was not at work was at his books. He kept up his studies on Sunday, and carried his books with him to work, so that he might read when he rested from labor." "I induced my husband to permit Abe to read and study at home as well as at school," writes his stepmother. "At first he was not easily reconciled to it, but finally he too seemed willing to encourage him to a certain extent. Abe was a dutiful son to me always, and we took particular care when he was reading not to disturb him,—would let him read on and on until he quit of his own accord."

The books within his reach were few, but they were among the best. First and foremost was that collection of great literature in prose and verse, the Bible: a library of sixty-six volumes, presenting nearly every literary form, and translated at the fortunate moment when the English language had received the recent impress of its greatest masters of the speech of imagination. This literature Mr. Lincoln knew intimately, familiarly, and fruitfully; as Shakespeare knew it in an earlier version, and as Tennyson knew it and was deeply influenced by it in the form in which it entered into and trained Lincoln's imagination. Then there was that wise and very human textbook of the knowledge of character and life, "Aesop's Fables"; that masterpiece of clear presentation, "Robinson Crusoe"; and that classic of pure English, "The Pilgrim's Progress." These four books — in the hands of a meditative boy, who read until the last ember went out on the hearth, began again when the earliest light reached his bed in the loft of the log cabin, who perched himself on a stump, book in hand, at the end of every furrow in the plowing season—contained the elements of a movable university.

To these must be added many volumes borrowed from more fortunate neighbors for he had "read through every book he had heard of in that country, for a circuit of fifty miles." A history of the United States and a copy of Weem's "Life of Washington" laid the foundations of his political education. That he read with his imagination as well as with his eyes is clear from certain words spoken in the Senate Chamber at Trenton in 1861. "May I be pardoned," said Mr. Lincoln, "if on this occasion I mention that way back in my childhood, the earliest days of my being able to read, I got hold of a small book, such a one as few of the members have ever seen,—Weem's 'Life of Washington.' I remember all the accounts there given of the battle-fields and struggles for the liberties of the country; and none fixed themselves upon my imagination so deeply as the struggle here at Trenton, New Jersey. The crossing of the river, the contest with the Hessians, the great hardships endured at that time,—all fixed themselves on my memory more than any single Revolutionary event; and you all know, for you have all been boys, how those early impressions last longer than any others."

> *He fed himself with thought, and he trained himself in expression; but his supreme interest was in the men and women about him, and later, in the great questions which agitate them.*

"When Abe and I returned to the house from work," writes John Hanks, "he would go to the cupboard, snatch a piece of corn bread, sit down, take a book, cock his legs up as high as his head, and read. We grubbed, plowed, weeded, and worked together barefooted in the field. Whenever Abe had a chance in the field while at work, or at the house, he would stop and read." And this habit was kept up until Mr. Lincoln had found both his life work and his individual expression. Later he devoured Shakespeare and Burns; and the poetry of these masters of the dramatic and lyric form, sprung like himself from the common soil, and like him self-trained and directed, furnished a kind of running accompaniment to his work and his play. What he read he not only held tenaciously, but took into his imagination and incorporated into himself. His familiar talk was enriched with frequent and striking illustrations from the Bible and "Aesop's Fables."

This passion for knowledge and for companionship with the great writers would have gone for nothing, so far as the boy's training in expression was concerned, if he had contented himself with acquisition; but he turned everything to account. He was as eager for expression as for the material of expression; more eager to write and to talk than to read. Bits of paper, stray sheets, even boards served his purpose. He was continually transcribing with his own hand thoughts or phrases which had impressed him. Everything within reach bore evidence of his passion for reading, and for writing as well. The flat sides of logs, the surface of the broad wooden shovel, everything in his vicinity which could receive a legible mark, was covered with his figures and letters. He was studying expression quite as intelligently as he was searching for thought. Years afterwards, when asked how he had attained such extraordinary clearness of style, he recalled his early habit of retaining in his memory words or phrases overheard in ordinary conversation or met in books and newspapers, until night, meditating on them until he got at their meaning, and then translating them into his own simpler speech. This habit, kept up for years, was the best possible training for the writing of such English as one finds in the Bible and in "The Pilgrim's Progress." His self-education in the art of expression soon bore fruit in a local reputation both as a talker and a writer. His facility in rhyme and essay-writing was not only greatly admired by his fellows, but awakened great astonishment, because these arts were not taught in the neighboring schools.

In speech too he was already disclosing that command of the primary and universal elements of interest in human intercourse which was to make him, later, one of the most entertaining men of his time. His power of analyzing a subject so as to be able to present it to others with complete clearness was already disclosing itself. No matter how complex a question might be, he did not rest until he had reduced it to its simplest terms. When he had done this he was not only eager to make it clear to others, but to give his presentation freshness, variety, attractiveness. He had, in a word, the literary sense. "When he appeared in company," writes one of his early companions, "the boys would gather and cluster around him to hear him talk. Mr. Lincoln was figurative in his speech, talks, and conversation. He argued much from analogy, and explained things hard for us to understand by stories, maxims, tales, and figures. He would almost always point his lesson or idea by some story that was plain and near to us, that we might instantly see the force and bearing of what he said."

In that phrase lies the secret of the closeness of Mr. Lincoln's words to his theme and to his listeners,—one of the qualities of genuine, original expression. He fed himself with thought, and he trained himself in expression; but his supreme interest was in the men and women about him, and later, in the great questions which agitate them. He was in his early manhood when society was profoundly moved by searching questions which could neither be silenced nor evaded; and his lot was cast in a section where, as a rule, people read little and talked much. Public speech was the chief instrumentality of political education and the most potent means of persuasion; but behind the platform, upon which Mr. Lincoln was to become a commanding figure, were countless private debates carried on at street corners, in hotel rooms, by the country road, in every place where men met even in the most casual way. In these wayside schools Mr. Lincoln practiced the art of putting things until he became a past-master in debate, both formal and informal.

If all these circumstances, habits, and conditions are studied in their entirety, it will be seen that Mr. Lincoln's style, so far as its formal qualities are concerned, is in no sense accidental or even surprising. He was all his early life in the way of doing precisely what he did in his later life with a skill which had become instinct. He was educated, in a very unusual way, to speak for his time and to his time with perfect sincerity and simplicity; to feel the moral bearing of the questions which were before the country; to discern the principles involved; and to so apply the principles to the questions as to clarify and illuminate them. There is little difficulty in accounting for the lucidity, simplicity, flexibility, and compass of Mr. Lincoln's style; it is not until we turn to its temperamental and spiritual qualities, to the soul of it, that we find ourselves perplexed and baffled.

But Mr. Lincoln's possession of certain rare qualities is in no way more surprising than their possession by Shakespeare, Burns, and Whitman. We are constantly tempted to look for the sources of a man's power in his educational opportunities instead of in his temperament and inheritance. The springs of genius are purified and directed in their flow by the processes of training, but they are fed from deeper sources. The man of obscure ancestry and rude surroundings is often in closer touch with nature, and with those universal experiences which are the very stuff of literature, than the man who is born on the upper reaches of social position and opportunity. Mr. Lincoln's ancestry for at least two generations were pioneers and frontiersmen, who knew hardship and privation, and were immersed in that great wave of energy and life which fertilized and humanized the central West. They were in touch with those original experiences out of which the higher evolution of civilization slowly rises; they knew the soil and the sky at first hand; they wrested a meager subsistence out of the stubborn earth by constant toil; they shared to the full the vicissitudes and weariness of humanity at its elemental tasks.

It was to this nearness to the heart of a new country, perhaps, that Mr. Lincoln owed his intimate knowledge of his people and his deep and beautiful sympathy with them. There was nothing sinuous or secondary in his processes of thought: they were broad, simple, and homely in the old sense of the word. He had rare gifts, but he was rooted deep in the soil of the life about him, and so completely in touch with it that he divined its secrets and used its speech. This vital sympathy gave his nature a beautiful gentleness, and suffused his thought with a tenderness born of deep compassion and love. He carried the sorrows of his country as truly as he bore its burdens; and when he came to speak on the second immortal day at Gettysburg, he condensed into few sentences the innermost meaning of the struggle and the victory in the life of the nation. It was this deep heart of pity and love in him which carried him far beyond the reaches of statesmanship or oratory, and gave his words that finality of expression which marks the noblest art.

> *He had rare gifts, but he was rooted deep in the soil of the life about him, and so completely in touch with it that he divined its secrets and used its speech.*

That there was a deep vein of poetry in Mr. Lincoln's nature is clear to one who reads the story of his early life; and this innate idealism, set in surroundings so harsh and rude, had something to do with his melancholy. The sadness which was mixed with his whole life, was, however, largely due to his temperament; in which the final tragedy seemed always to be predicted. In that temperament too is hidden the secret of the rare quality of nature and mind which suffused his public speech and turned so much of it into literature. There was humor in it, there was deep human sympathy, there was clear mastery of words for the use to which he put them; but there was something deeper and more pervasive,—there was the quality of his temperament; and temperament is a large part of genius. The inner forces of his nature played through his thought; and when great occasions touched him to the quick, his whole nature shaped his speech and gave it clear intelligence, deep feeling, and that beauty which is distilled out of the depths of the sorrows and hopes of the world. He was as unlike Burke and Webster, those masters of the eloquence of statesmanship, as Burns was unlike Milton and Tennyson. Like Burns, he held the key of the life of his people; and through him, as through Burns, that life found a voice, vibrating, pathetic and persuasive.

Source:

Mabie, Hamilton Wright. "Abraham Lincoln." In *A Library of the World's Best Literature, Ancient and Modern,* edited by Charles Dudley Warner. Vol. 23. New York: The International Society, 1897.

1-13
"Oh, Why Should the Spirit of Mortal Be Proud?"
by William Knox

Scottish poet William Knox (1789-1825) wrote one of Lincoln's favorite poems, "Oh, Why Should the Spirit of Mortal Be Proud?" One of Lincoln's friends in Illinois, the physician Jason Duncan, showed him the poem during the 1830s. Having committed the poem to memory, Lincoln recited it often.

Oh, Why Should the Spirit of Mortal Be Proud?

Oh! why should the spirit of mortal be proud?
Like a swift fleeting meteor, a fast-flying cloud,
A flash of the lightning, a break of the wave,
Man passeth from life to his rest in the grave.

The leaves of the oak and the willow shall fade,
Be scattered around and together be laid;
And the young and the old, and the low and the high,
Shall moulder to dust and together shall lie.

The infant a mother attended and loved;
The mother that infant's affection who proved;
The husband that mother and infant who blessed,
Each, all, are away to their dwellings of rest.

The maid on whose cheek, on whose brow, in whose eye,
Shone beauty and pleasure,— her triumphs are by;
And the memory of those who loved her and praised,
Are alike from the minds of the living erased.

The hand of the king that the scepter hath borne;
The brow of the priest that the mitre hath worn;
The eye of the sage and the heart of the brave,
Are hidden and lost in the depth of the grave.

The peasant whose lot was to sow and to reap;
The herdsman, who climbed with his goats up the steep;
The beggar, who wandered in search of his bread,
Have faded away like the grass that we tread.

The saint who enjoyed the communion of heaven.
The sinner who dared to remain unforgiven,
The wise and the foolish, the guilty and just,
Have quietly mingled their bones in the dust.

So the multitude goes, like the flower or the weed
That withers away to let others succeed;
So the multitude comes, even those we behold,
To repeat every tale that has often been told.

For we are the same our fathers have been;
We see the same sights our fathers have seen,—
We drink the same stream and view the same sun,
And run the same course our fathers have run.

The thoughts we are thinking our fathers would think;
From the death we are shrinking our fathers would shrink;
To the life we are clinging they also would cling;
But it speeds for us all, like a bird on the wing.

They loved, but the story we cannot unfold;
They scorned, but the heart of the haughty is cold;
They grieved, but no wail from their slumbers will come;
They joyed, but the tongue of their gladness is dumb.

They died, aye! they died: we things that are now,
That walk on the turf that lies over their brow,
Who make in their dwelling a transient abode,
Meet the things that they met on their pilgrimage road.

Yea! hope and despondency, pleasure and pain,
We mingle together in sunshine and rain;
And the smiles and the tears, the song and the dirge,
Still follow each other, like surge upon surge.

'Tis the wink of an eye, 'tis the draught of a breath,
From the blossom of health to the paleness of death,
From the gilded saloon to the bier and the shroud,—
Oh, why should the spirit of mortal be proud?

Source:

Knox, William. *Oh, Why Should the Spirit of Mortal Be Proud?* Boston: Lee and Shepard, 1883.

1-14
"My Child-hood Home I See Again" by Abraham Lincoln

Lincoln wrote this poem between 1844 and 1846, inspired by a trip in autumn 1844 to Spencer County, Indiana, where he spent some of his early childhood. As he wrote to a friend, Andrew Johnston, "I went into the neighborhood of that State in which I was raised, where my mother and only sister were buried, and from which I had been absent about fifteen years. That part of the country is, within itself, as unpoetical as any spot of the earth; but still, seeing it and its objects and inhabitants aroused feelings in me which were certainly poetry; though whether my expression of those feelings is poetry is quite another question."

My Child-hood Home I See Again

My child-hood home I see again,
And gladden with the view;
And still as mem'ries crowd my brain,
There's sadness in it too—

O memory! thou mid-way world
'Twixt Earth and Paradise;
Where things decayed, and loved ones
    lost
In dreamy shadows rise—

And freed from all that's gross or vile,
Seem hallowed, pure, and bright,
Like scenes in some enchanted isle,
All bathed in liquid light—

As distant mountains please the eye,
When twilight chases day—
As bugle-tones, that, passing by,
In distance die away—

As leaving some grand water-fall
We ling'ring list it's roar,
So memory will hallow all
We've known, but know no more—

Now twenty years have passed away,
Since here I bid farewell
To woods, and fields, and scenes of play
And school-mates loved so well—

Where many were, how few remain
Of old familiar things!
But seeing these to mind again
The lost and absent brings—

The friends I left that parting day—
How changed as time has sped!
Young child hood grown, strong
    manhood grey,
And half of all are dead—

I hear the lone survivors tell
How nought from death could save,
Till every sound appears a knell
And every spot a grave—

I range the fields with pensive tread,
I pace the hollow rooms;
And feel (companion of the dead)
I'm living in the tombs—

A here's an object more of dread,
Than ought the grave contains—
A human-form, with reason fled
While wretched life remains—

Poor Matthew! Once of genius bright,—
A fortune-favored child—
Now locked for age, in mental night,
A haggard mad-man wild—

Poor Matthew! I have ne'er forgot
When first with maddened will,
Yourself you maimed, your father
          fought,
And mother strove to kill;

And terror spread, and neighbours ran,
Your dang'rous strength to bind;
And soon a howling crazy man,
Your limbs were fast confined—

How then you writhed and shrieked
          aloud,
Your bones and sinnews bared;
And fiendish on the gaping crowd,
With burning eye-balls glared—

And begged, and swore, and wept, and
          prayed,
With maniac laughter joined—
How fearful are the signs displayed,
By pangs that kill the mind!

And when at length, tho, dreer and long,
Time soothed your fiercer woes—
How plantively your mournful song,
Upon the still night rose—

I've heard it oft, as if I dreamed,
Far-distant, sweet, and lone;
The funeral dirge, it ever seemed
Of reason dead and gone—

To drink it's strains I've stole away,
All silently and still,
Ere yet the rising god of day
Had streaked the Eastern hill—

Air held his breath, the trees all still
Seemed sorr'wing angels round:
Their swelling tears in dew-drops fell
Upon the list'ning ground—

But this is past, and nought remains
That raised you o'er the brute—
Your mad'ning shrieks and soothing
          strains
Are like forever mute—

Now fare thee well: more thou the
          cause
Than subject now of woe.
All mental pangs, by time's kind laws,
Hast lost the power to know—

51

And now away to seek some scene
Less painful than the last—
With less of horror mingled in
The present and the past—

The very spot where grew the bread,
That formed my bones, I see
How strange, old field, on thee to tread
And feel I'm part of thee!

Source:

Lincoln, Abraham. "My Child-hood Home I See Again." Abraham Lincoln Papers at the Library of Congress. Transcribed and annotated by the Lincoln Studies Center, Knox College, Galesburg, Illinois. Available online at http://memory.loc.gov/ammem/alhtml/malhome.html.

1-15
Correspondence between Joshua Speed and Lincoln about Their Marriages

As best friends and bachelors, Lincoln and Joshua Speed counseled each other in their efforts to find wives and settle down. Speed was married first, to Fanny Henning in February 1842, and wrote Lincoln about how happy he was. On February 25, Lincoln responded to Speed's report in the following letter.

Yours of the 16th instant, announcing that Miss Fanny and you are 'no more twain, but one flesh,' reached me this morning. I have no way of telling you how much happiness I wish you both, though I believe you both can conceive it. I feel somewhat jealous of both of you now: you will be so exclusively concerned for one another, that I shall be forgotten entirely. My acquaintance with Miss Fanny (I call her this, lest you should think I am speaking of your mother) was too short for me to reasonably hope to long be remembered by her; and still I am sure I shall not

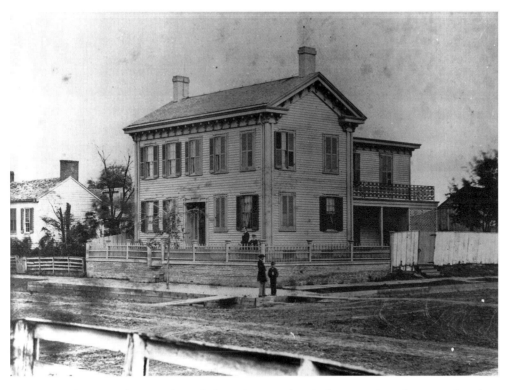

In 1860 the Lincolns purchased their first and only house. This photograph taken the same year shows Lincoln and his young son Willie on the porch.

forget her soon. Try if you cannot remind her of that debt she owes me—and be sure you do not interfere to prevent her paying it.

I regret to learn that you have resolved not to return to Illinois. I shall be very lonesome without you. How miserably things seem to be arranged in this world! If we have no friends, we have no pleasure; and if we have them, we are sure to lose them, and be doubly pained by the loss. I did hope she and you would make your home here; but I own I have no right to insist. You owe obligations to her ten thousand times more sacred than you can owe to others, and in that light let them be respected and observed. It is natural that she should desire to remain with her relatives and friends. As to friends, however, she could not need them anywhere: she would have them in abundance here.

Give my kind regards to Mr. Williamson and his family, particularly Miss Elizabeth; also to your mother, brother and sisters. Ask little Eliza Davis if she will ride to town with me if I come there again. And, finally, give Fanny a double reciprocation of all the love she sent me. Write me often, and believe me

> Yours forever,
> LINCOLN.

Encouraged by Speed's success, Lincoln married his fiancee Mary Todd, a daughter of Robert S. Todd of Lexington, Kentucky, on November 4, 1842. On May 18, 1843, Lincoln wrote the following to Speed.

We are not keeping house, but boarding at the Globe Tavern, which is very well kept now by a widow lady of the name of Beck. Our room (the same that Dr. Wallace occupied there) and boarding only costs us four dollars a week. . . . I most heartily wish you and your Fanny would not fail to come. Just let us know the time, and we will have a room provided for you at our house, and all be merry together for a while.

Sources:

Excerpt 1: Lincoln, Abraham. Letter to Joshua F. Speed, Springfield, February 25, 1842. In *Complete Works of Abraham Lincoln*. Vol. 1. Edited by John G. Nicolay and John Hay. Lincoln Memorial University, 1894.

Excerpt 2: Lincoln, Abraham. Letter to Joshua F. Speed, Springfield, May 18, 1843. In *Complete Works of Abraham Lincoln*. Vol. 1. Edited by John G. Nicolay and John Hay. Lincoln Memorial University, 1894.

1-16
Ida M. Tarbell on Lincoln's Rise in National Stature

Ida Minerva Tarbell (1857-1944) was a journalist who wrote the first popular biography of Lincoln, published in 1900. She was too young to have known him, but she vividly remembered her parents' sadness and the draping of their doors with black crepe on the day he died. In this excerpt from her biography, Tarbell describes the Lincoln-Douglas debates of 1858 and Lincoln's subsequent national reputation.

In June [1858], the State convention, meeting in Springfield to nominate its candidate for Senator, declared that Abraham Lincoln was its first and only choice as the successor of Stephen A. Douglas. The press was jubilant. "Unanimity is a weak word," wrote the editor of the Bloomington "Pantograph," "to express the universal and intense feeling of the convention. *Lincoln!* LINCOLN!! LINCOLN!!! was the cry everywhere, whenever the senatorship was alluded to. Delegates from Chicago and from Cairo, from the Wabash and the Illinois, from the north, the center, and the south, were alike fierce with enthusiasm, whenever that loved name was breathed. . . .

On the evening of the day of his nomination, Lincoln addressed his constituents. The first paragraph of his speech gave the key to the campaign he proposed. "A house divided against itself cannot stand. I believe this government cannot endure permanently half slave and half free. I do not expect the house to fall—but I do expect it will cease to be divided. It will become all one thing or all the other." . . .

The speech was severely criticized by Lincoln's friends. It was too radical. It was sectional. He heard the complaints unmoved. "If I had to draw a pen across my record," he said, one day, "and erase my whole life from sight, and I had one poor gift of choice left as to what I should save from the wreck, I should choose that speech and leave it to the world unerased."

The speech was, in fact, one of great political adroitness. It forced Douglas to do exactly what he did not want to do in Illinois; explain his own record during the past four years; explain the true meaning of the Kansas-Nebraska bill; discuss the Dred Scott decision; say whether or not he thought slavery so good a thing that the

Writer and early Lincoln biographer Ida M. Tarbell, in a photo taken sometime between 1890 and 1910.

country could afford to extend it instead of confining it where it would be in course of gradual extinction. Douglas wanted the Republicans of Illinois to follow Greeley's advice: "Forgive the past." He wanted to make the most among them of his really noble revolt against the attempt of his party to fasten an unjust constitution on Kansas. Lincoln would not allow him to bask for an instant in the sun of that revolt. He crowded him step by step through his party's record, and compelled him to face what he called the "profound central truth" of the Republican Party, "slavery is wrong and ought to be dealt with as wrong." . . .

Then Lincoln resolved to force Douglas to meet his arguments, and challenged him to a series of joint debates. Douglas was not pleased. . . . Publicly, however, he carried off the prospect confidently, even jauntily. "Mr. Lincoln," he said patronizingly, "is a kind, amiable, intelligent gentleman." . . .

If one will take a map of Illinois and locate the points of the Lincoln and Douglas debates held between August 21 and October 15, 1858, he will see that the whole State was traversed in the contest. The first took place in Ottawa, about seventy-five miles southwest of Chicago, on August 21, the second at Freeport, near the Wisconsin boundary, on August 27. The third was in the extreme southern part of the State, at Jonesboro, on September 15. Three days later the contestants met one hundred and fifty miles northeast of Jonesboro, at Charleston. The fifth, sixth, and seventh debates were held in the western part of the State; at Galesburg, October 7; Quincy, October 13; and Alton, October 15. . . .

On arrival at the towns where the joint debates were held, Douglas was always met by a brass band and a salute of thirty-two guns (the Union was composed of thirty-two States in 1858), and was escorted to the hotel in the finest equipage to be had.

Lincoln's supporters took delight in showing their contempt of Douglas's elegance by affecting a Republican simplicity, often carrying their candidate through the streets on a high and unadorned hayrack drawn by farm horses. . . .

When the crowd was massed at the place of the debate, the scene was one of the greatest hubbub and confusion. On the corners of the squares, and scattered around the outskirts of the crowd, were fakirs of every description, selling painkillers and ague cures, watermelons and lemonade; jugglers and beggars plied their trades, and the brass bands of all the four corners within twenty-five miles tooted and pounded at "Hail Columbia, Happy Land," or "Columbia, the Gem of the Ocean." . . .

It was in the second debate, at Freeport, that Lincoln made the boldest stroke of the contest. Soon after the Ottawa debate, in discussing his plan for the next encounter, with a number of his political friends,—Washburne, Cook, Judd, and others,—he told them he proposed to ask Douglas four questions, which he read. One and all cried halt at the second question. Under no condition, they said, must he put it. If it were put, Douglas would answer it in such a way as to win the senatorship. The morning of the debate, while on the way to Freeport, Lincoln read the same questions to Mr. Joseph Medill. "I do not like this second question, Mr. Lincoln," said Mr. Medill. The two men argued to their journey's end, but Lincoln was still unconvinced. Even after he reached Freeport several Republican leaders came to him pleading, "Do not ask that question." He was obdurate; and he went on the platform with a higher head, a haughtier step than his friends had noted in him before. Lincoln was going to ruin himself, the committee said despondently; one would think he did not want the senatorship.

The mooted question ran in Lincoln's notes: "Can the people of a United States territory in any lawful way, against the wish of any citizen of the United States, exclude slavery from its limits prior to the information of a State Constitution?" Lincoln had seen the irreconcilableness of Douglas's own measure of popular sovereignty, which declared that the people of a territory should be left to regulate their domestic concerns in their own way subject only to the Constitution, and the decision of the Supreme court in the Dred Scott case that slaves, being property, could not under the Constitution be excluded from a territory. He knew that if Douglas said no to this question, his Illinois constituents would never return him to the Senate. He believed that if he said yes, the people of the South would never vote for him for President of the United States. He was willing himself to lose the senatorship in order to defeat

Douglas for the Presidency in 1860. "I am after larger game; the battle of 1860 is worth a hundred of this," he said confidently.

The question was put, and Douglas answered it with rare artfulness. "It matters not," he cried, "what way the Supreme Court may hereafter decide as to the abstract question whether slavery may or may not go into a territory under the Constitution; the people have lawful means to introduce it or exclude it as they please, for the reason that slavery cannot exist a day or an hour anywhere unless it is supported by local police regulations. Those police regulations can only be established by the local legislature, and if the people are opposed to slavery, they will elect representatives to that body who will, by unfriendly legislation, effectually prevent the introduction of it into their midst. If, on the contrary, they are for it, their legislature will favor its extension."

His democratic constituents went wild over the clever way in which Douglas had escaped Lincoln's trap. He now practically had his election. The Republicans shook their heads. Lincoln only was serene. He alone knew what he had done. The Freeport debate had no sooner reached the proslavery press than a storm of protest went up. Douglas had betrayed the South. He had repudiated the Supreme Court decision. He had declared that slavery could be kept out of the territories by other legislation than a State Constitution. "The Freeport doctrine, "or "the theory of unfriendly legislation," as it became known, spread month by month, and slowly but surely made Douglas an impossible candidate in the South. The force of the question, was not realized in full by Lincoln's friends, until the Democratic Party met in Charleston, S.C., in 1860, and the Southern delegates refused to support Douglas because of the answer he gave to Lincoln's question in the Freeport debate of 1858.

"Do you recollect the argument we had on the way up to Freeport two years ago over the question I was going to ask Judge Douglas?" Lincoln asked Mr. Joseph Medill, when the latter went to Springfield a few days after the election of 1860.

"Yes," said Medill, "I recollect it very well."

"Don't you think I was right now?"

"We were both right. The question hurt Douglas for Presidency, but it lost you the senatorship."

"Yes, and I have won the place he was playing for." . . .

By his debates with [Stephen] Douglas and the speeches in Ohio, Kansas, New York and New England, Lincoln had become a national figure in the minds of all the political leaders of the country, and of the thinking men of the North. Never in the history of the United States had a man become prominent in a more logical and intelligent way. At the beginning of the struggle against the repeal of the Missouri Compromise in 1854, Abraham Lincoln was scarcely known outside of his own State. Even most of the men whom he had met in his brief term in Congress had forgotten him. Yet in four years he had become one of the central figures of his party; and now, by worsting the greatest orator and politician of his time, he had drawn the eyes of the nation to him.

This lithograph of a clean-shaven Lincoln was created in 1860.

It had been a long road he had traveled to make himself a national figure. Twenty-eight years before he had deliberately entered politics. He had been beaten, but had persisted; he had succeeded and failed; he had abandoned the struggle and returned to his profession. His outraged sense of justice had driven him back, and for six years he traveled up and down Illinois trying to prove to men that slavery extension was wrong. It was by no one speech, by no one argument that he had wrought. Every day his ceaseless study and pondering gave him new matter, and every speech he made was fresh. He could not repeat an old speech, he said, because the subject enlarged and widened so in his mind as he went on that it was "easier to make a new one than an old one." He had never yielded in his campaign to tricks of oratory—never played on emotions. He had been so strong in his convictions of the right of his case that his speeches had been arguments pure and simple. Their elegance was that of a demonstration in Euclid. They persuaded because they proved. He had never for a moment counted personal ambition before the cause. To insure an ardent opponent of the Kansas-Nebraska bill in the United States Senate, he had at one time given up his chance for the senatorship. To show the fallacy of Douglas's argument, he had asked a question which his party pleaded with him to pass by, assuring him that it would lose him the election. In every step of the six years he had been disinterested, calm, unyielding, and courageous. He knew he was right, and could afford to wait. "The result is not doubtful," he told his friends. "We shall not fail—if we stand firm. We shall not fail. Wise counsel may accelerate or mistakes delay it; but, sooner or later, the victory is sure to come."

The country, amazed at the rare moral and intellectual character of Lincoln, began to ask questions about him, and then his history came out; a pioneer home, little schooling, few books, hard labor at all the many trades of the frontier-man, a profession mastered o'nights by the light of a friendly cooper's fire, an early entry into politics and law—and then twenty-five years of incessant poverty and struggle.

The homely story gave a touch of mystery to the figure, which loomed so large. Men felt a sudden reverence for a mind and heart developed to these noble proportions in so unfriendly a habitat. They turned instinctively to one so familiar with strife for help in solving the desperate problem with which the nation had grappled. And thus it was that, at fifty years of age, Lincoln became a national figure.

Source:

Tarbell, Ida M. "Chapter XVIII: The Lincoln-Douglas Debates." *The Life of Abraham Lincoln.* Vol. 1. New York: Doubleday & McClure Company, 1900.

1-17
Correspondence between Grace Bedell and Lincoln about His Beard

Grace Bedell (1848-1936) was an eleven-year-old girl who wrote a letter to Lincoln when he was running for president in 1860 and suggested he grow a beard. Her letter is reprinted below.

Westfield, Chatauque Co N Y
Oct 18, 1860

Hon A B Lincoln
Dear Sir

My father has just home from the fair and brought home your picture and Mr. Hamlin's. I am a little girl only eleven years old, but want you should be President of the United States very much so I hope you wont think me very bold to write to such a great man as you are. Have you any little girls about as large as I am if so give them my love and tell her to write to me if you cannot answer this letter. I have got 4 brother's and part of them will vote for you any way and if you will let your whiskers grow I will try and get the rest of them to vote for you you would look a great deal better for your face is so thin. All the ladies like whiskers and they would tease their husband's to vote for you and then you would be President. My father is a going to vote for you and if I was a man I would vote for you to but I will try and get every one to vote for you that I can. I think that rail fence around your picture makes it look very pretty. I have got a little baby sister she is nine weeks old and is just as cunning as can be. When you direct your letter direct to Grace Bedell Westfield Chatauque County New York

I must not write any more answer this letter right off Good bye

Grace Bedell.

ABRAHAM LINCOLN.

SIXTEENTH PRESIDENT OF THE UNITED STATES

ASSASSINATED APRIL 14TH 1865.

Currier and Ives created this lithograph of Lincoln.

Lincoln's reply cast some doubt on whether he would follow her advice.

Springfield, Oct 19th, 1860.

Miss Grace Bedell,
My Dear Little Miss:

Your very agreeable letter of the 15th is received—I regret the necessity of saying that I have no daughter—I have three sons—one seventeen, one nine, and one seven. They, with their mother, constitute my whole family. As to the whiskers, as I have never worn any, do you not think that people would call it a piece of silly affectation, if I were to begin wearing them now?

I am, your fine friend
And sincere well-wisher
A. Lincoln

Years later, on December 14, 1866, Bedell wrote to William H. Herndon and recounted her meeting with President-elect Lincoln on his way to Washington, D.C.:

Hon. L. R. Herndon:

Hearing that you were preparing for press the Life of the noblest of men, and that you wished all unpublished letters of his composing sent to you, I concluded that I would ask if a letter which he once wrote me would prove acceptable. I do not know that it would answer your purpose of I would send a copy of it now. however, I will tell you its subject and you shall judge. Before Mr Lincoln's election in 1860, I, then a child of eleven years, was presented with his lithograph. Admiring him with my whole heart I though, still, that his appearance would be much improved should he cultivate his whiskers. Childish thoughts must have utterance, so I proposed the idea to him, expressing, as well as I was able, the esteem in which he was held among honest men. A few days after I received an answer to my communication. A kind and friendly letter which is still in my possession. It appears that I was not forgotten, for, after his election to the presidency, while on his journey to Washington, the train stopped at Westfield, Chautauque Co, at which place I then resided. Mr Lincoln said, "I have a correspondent in this place, a little girl, her name is Grace Bedell, and I would like to see her. "I was conveyed to him, he stepped from the cars extending his hand and saying, "You see I have let these whiskers grow for you, Grace." Kissed me shook me cordially by the hand and, was gone. Afterward I was frequently assured of his remembrance. If this letter would be of any service in completing your book, I should be pleased to send you a copy. Asking pardon for consuming so much of your valuable time.

I remain

Grace G. Bedell

Sources:

Excerpt 1: Bedell, Grace. Letter to Abraham Lincoln, October 18, 1860. Available online at Abraham Lincoln Papers, Library of Congress. http://memory.loc.gov/ammem/alhtml/malhome.html.

Excerpt 2: Lincoln, Abraham. Letter to Grace Bedell, October 19, 1860. Herndon-Weik Collection, Manuscript Division, Library of Congress, Washington, D.C. Published in *Herndon's Informants: Letters, Interviews, and Statements about Abraham Lincoln.* Edited by Douglas L. Wilson and Rodney O. Davis, with the assistance of Terry Wilson. Urbana: University of Illinois Press, 1998.

Excerpt 3: Bedell, Grace G. Letter to William H. Herndon, December 14, 1866. Herndon-Weik Collection, Manuscript Division, Library of Congress, Washington, D.C. Published in *Herndon's Informants: Letters, Interviews, and Statements about Abraham Lincoln.* Edited by Douglas L. Wilson and Rodney O. Davis, with the assistance of Terry Wilson. Urbana: University of Illinois Press, 1998.

1-18
Lincoln's Farewell to the Citizens of Springfield

President-elect Abraham Lincoln stood in a railroad car and gave this touching farewell speech to fellow townspeople of Springfield, Illinois, assembled to see him off on February 11, 1861. He had lived in the town since 1837 and was beginning a 12-day journey to Washington, D.C., to be sworn in as president of the United States. This is a transcription of the handwritten notes.

My friends.

No one, not in my situation, can appreciate my feeling of sadness, at this parting—To this place, and the kindness of these people, I owe every thing— Here I have been a quarter of a century, and have passed from a young to an old man. Here my children have been born, and one is buried. I now ~~leave not~~ leave, not knowing when, or whether ever, I may return, with a task before me greater than that which rested upon Washington. Without the assistance of that Divine Being, [~~whom?~~] who ever attended him, I cannot succeed. With that assistance I cannot fail. Trusting in Him, who can go with me, and remain with you and be everywhere for good, let us confidently hope that all will yet be well— To His care [~~H~~] commending you, as I hope in your prayers you will commend me, I bid you an affectionate farewell.

Source:

Lincoln, Abraham. Farewell Speech Given in Springfield, Illinois, February 11, 1861. Abraham Lincoln Papers at the Library of Congress. Transcribed and Annotated by the Lincoln Studies Center, Knox College, Galesburg, Illinois. Available online at http://memory.loc.gov/ammem /alhtml/malhome.html.

Part 2
The 16th President: Great Emancipator and Commander-in-Chief

Lincoln was elected president in November 1860, charged with leading a nation on the brink of civil war. By the time he was inaugurated in March 1861, several southern states had seceded from the Union, and the war's first shot was little over a month away. The excerpts in this section touch on major events of Lincoln's presidency—the Civil War, the emancipation of slaves, the Gettysburg Address, and his second inaugural—as well as offer vignettes of his day-to-day life as president.

This section includes essays, reminiscences, letters, speeches, poems, and newspaper reports focusing on Lincoln as president, commander-in-chief, and emancipator. Most of these accounts are from people who met or worked with him. This section begins with an essay by writer James Russell Lowell which describes the personal qualities Lincoln brought to the Executive Office.

Lincoln was generous with his time for citizens and he maintained a quite liberal open-door policy at the White House. Excerpts from memoirs by Nathaniel Hawthorne and Sojourner Truth illustrate the authors' impressions of meeting Lincoln. Harriet Beecher Stowe, who also met the president, shares her insights on his leadership style.

Lincoln issued the Emancipation Proclamation on January 1, 1863, which freed slaves in areas controlled by the Confederacy. Several pieces focus on this historic proclamation. An excerpt of a memoir by Thomas T. Eckert, head of the War Department's telegraph office, tells how Lincoln worked on drafts of the preliminary Emancipation Proclamation there during the summer of 1862. Artist Francis B. Carpenter painted Lincoln presenting his cabinet members with the Emancipation Proclamation, and a segment from his book describes the scene. "The Emancipation Group," a poem by John Greenleaf Whittier, is a lyrical companion to Carpenter's painting. Speech excerpts by Frederick Douglass and James Abram Garfield pay tribute to the proclamation, while letters between Lincoln and the Pennsylvania Anti-

Slavery Society and Chicago Sanitary Commission give a flavor of the public's interest in both the preliminary proclamation of September 22, 1862, and the official Emancipation Proclamation.

Lincoln was reelected president in 1864. Mary Todd Lincoln's dressmaker Elizabeth Keckley, a regular presence in the White House, fondly recalls the scene of his second inaugural speech and shares a poignant anecdote concerning Frederick Douglass on that day.

Several pieces concern Lincoln's qualities as commander-in-chief during the Civil War. Evidence of his compassionate and merciful nature can be found in selections by James Shrigley, James Speed, and Joshua Speed. Lincoln appointed Shrigley hospital chaplain over the objections of some that Shrigley believed in the salvation of the rebels. The Speed brothers describe incidents in which they witnessed Lincoln grant discharges to soldiers and release imprisoned draft resistors. Over the latter half of 1862, in the wake of Lincoln's call for more soldiers, a song titled "We are coming Father Abraham" became popular, particularly among Union troops; the lyrics are reprinted in this section. Remembrances by E. W. Andrews and Jacob Hoke give two eyewitness perspectives of Lincoln at the dedication of the national cemetery at Gettysburg. Poet Bayard Taylor commemorated that episode with "The Gettysburg Ode," a portion of which is reprinted in this section.

Finally, a group of excerpts relate Lincoln's visit to Richmond, Virginia, the capital of the Confederacy, after Jefferson Davis evacuated the government from that city. One is by Lincoln's bodyguard William H. Crook, who accompanied the President on this trip and described it in his memoir. Two newspaper accounts—one by a *New York Times* reporter, another by *Boston Journal* correspondent Charles Carleton Coffin—describe Richmond, its war-weary residents and newly freed slaves, as Lincoln walks to Davis's abandoned mansion.

2-1
James Russell Lowell on Lincoln as President

James Russell Lowell (1819-1891) was an American poet and essayist and a supporter of Lincoln. In the following excerpt, Lowell furnishes an assessment of Lincoln's character as president, detailing his many strengths.

Never did a President enter upon office with less means at his command, outside his own strength of heart and steadiness of understanding, for inspiring in the people, and so winning it for himself, than Mr. Lincoln. All that was known to him was that he was a good stump-speaker, nominated for his availability—that is, because he had no history—and chosen by a party with whose more extreme opinions he was not in sympathy. It might well be feared that a man past fifty, against whom the ingenuity of hostile partisans could rake up no accusation, must be lacking in manliness of character, in decision of principle, in strength of will; that a man who was at best only the representative of a party, and who yet did not fairly represent even that, would fail of political, much more of popular, support. And certainly no one ever entered upon office with so few resources of power in the past, and so many materials of weakness in the present, as Mr. Lincoln. Even in that half of the Union, which acknowledged him as President, there was a large, and at that time dangerous minority, that hardly admitted his claim to the office, and even in the party that elected him there was also a large minority that suspected him of being secretly a communicant with the church of Laodicea. All that he did was sure to be virulently attacked as ultra by one side; all that he left undone, to be stigmatized as proof of luke-warmness and backsliding by the other. Meanwhile he was to carry on a truly colossal war by means of both; he was to disengage the country from diplomatic entanglements of unprecedented peril undisturbed by help or the hindrance of either, and to win from the crowning dangers of his administration in the confidence of the people, the means of his safety and their own. He has contrived to do it, and perhaps none of our Presidents since Washington has stood so firm in the confidence of the people as he does after three years of stormy administration.

Mr. Lincoln's policy was a tentative one, and rightly so. He laid down no programme, which must compel him to be either inconsistent or unwise, no cast-iron theorem to which circumstances must be fitted as they rose, or else be useless to his ends. He seemed to have chosen Mazarin's motto, *Le temps et moi.* The *moi*, to be sure, was not very prominent at first; but it has grown more and more so, till the world is beginning to be persuaded that it stands for a character of marked individuality and capacity for affairs. Time was his prime minister, and, we began to think, at one period, his general-in-chief also. At first he was so slow that he tired out all those who see no evidence of progress but in blowing up the engine; then he was so fast, that he took the breath away from those who think there is no getting on safely while there is a spark of fire under the boilers. God is the only being who has time enough; but a prudent man, who knows how to seize occasion, can commonly make a shift to find as much as he needs. Mr. Lincoln, as it seems to us in reviewing his career, though we have sometimes in our impatience thought otherwise, has always waited, as a wise man should, till the right moment brought up all his reserves. *Semper nocuit differre paratis,* is a sound axiom, but the really efficacious man will also be sure to know when he is not ready, and be firm against all persuasion and reproach till he is.

One would be apt to think, from some of the criticism made on Mr. Lincoln's course by those who mainly agree with him in principle; that the chief object of a statesman should be rather to proclaim his adhesion to certain doctrines, than to achieve their triumph by quietly accomplishing his ends. In our opinion, there is no more of an unsafe politician than a conscientiously rigid doctrinaire, nothing more sure to end in disaster than a theoretic scheme of policy that admits of no pliability for contingencies. True, there is a popular image of an impossible He, in whose plastic hands the submissive destinies of mankind become as wax, and to whose commanding necessity the toughest facts yield with the graceful pliancy of fiction; but in real life we commonly find that the men who control circumstances, as it is called, are those who have learned to allow for the influence of their eddies, and have the nerve to turn them to account at the happy instant. Mr. Lincoln's perilous task has been to carry a rather shaky raft through the rapids, making fast the unrulier logs as he could snatch opportunity, and the country is to be congratulated that he did not think it was his duty to run straight at all hazards, but cautiously to assure himself with his setting pole where the main current was, and keep steadily to that. He is still in wild water, but we have faith that his skill and sureness of eye will bring him out right at last. . . .

People of more sensitive organizations may be shocked, but we are glad that in this our true war of independence, which is to free us forever from the Old World, we

As Lincoln traveled to Washington, D.C., for his presidential inauguration, he made several stops along the way. This photograph was taken as he spoke to a crowd on February 22, 1861, in Philadelphia, Pennsylvania.

have had at the head of our affairs a man whom America made as God made Adam, out of the very earth, unancestried, unprivileged, unknown, to show us how much statecraft await the call of opportunity in simple manhood when it believed in the justice of God and the worth of man. Conventionalities are all very well in their proper place, but they shrivel at the touch of nature like stubble in the fire. The genius that sways a nation by its arbitrary wills seems less august to us than that which multiplies and reinforces it self in the instincts and convictions of an entire people. Autocracy may have something in it more melodramatic than this, but falls far short of it in human value and interest.

Experience would have bred in us a rooted distrust of improvised statesmanship, even if we did not believe politics to be a science, which, if it cannot always command men of special aptitude and great powers, at least demands the long and steady application of the best powers of such men as it can command to master even its first principles. It is curious that in a country, which boasts of its intelligence, the theory should be so generally held that the most complicated of human contrivances, and one which every day becomes more complicated, can be worked at sight by any man able to talk for an hour or two without stopping to think.

Mr. Lincoln is sometimes claimed as an example of a ready-made ruler. But no case could well be less in point; for, besides that he was a man of such fair-mindedness as is always the raw material of wisdom, he had in his profession a training precisely the opposite of that to which a partisan is subjected. His experience as a lawyer compelled him not only to see that there is a principle underlying every phenomenon in human affairs, but that there are always two sides to every question, both of which must be fully understood in order to understand either, and that it is of greater advantage to an advocate to appreciate the strength than the weakness of his antagonist's position. Nothing is more remarkable than the unerring tact with which, in his debate with Mr. Douglas, he went straight to the reason of the question; nor have we ever had a more striking lesson in political tactics than the fact, that, opposed to a man exceptionally adroit in using popular prejudice and bigotry to his purpose, exceptionally unscrupulous in appealing to those baser motives that turn a meeting of citizens into a mob of barbarians, he should yet have won his case before a jury of the people. Mr. Lincoln was as far as possible from an impromptu politician. His wisdom was made up of a knowledge of things as well as of men; his sagacity resulted from a clear perception and honest acknowledgment of difficulties, which enabled him to see that the only durable triumph of political opinion is based, not on any abstract right, but upon so much of justice, the highest attainable at any given moment in human affairs, as may be had in the balance of mutual concession. Doubtless he had an ideal, but it was the ideal of a practical statesman—to aim at the best, and to take the next best, if he is lucky enough to get even that. His slow, but singularly masculine intelligence taught him that precedent is only another name for embodied experience, and that it counts for even more in the guidance of communities of men than in that of the individual life. He was not a man who held it good public economy to pull down on the mere chance of rebuilding better. Mr. Lincoln's faith in God was qualified by a very well founded distrust of the wisdom of man. Perhaps it was his want of self-confidence that more than anything else won him the unlimited confidence of the people, for they felt that there would be no need of retreat from any position he had deliberately taken. The cautious, but steady, advance of his policy during the war was like that of a Roman army. He left behind him a firm road on which public confidence could follow; he took America with him where he went; what he gained he occupied, and his advanced posts became colonies. The very homeliness of his genius was its distinction. His kingship was conspicuous by its workday homespun. Never was a ruler so absolute as he, nor so little conscious of it; for he was the incarnate common sense of people. With all that tenderness of nature whose sweet sadness touched whoever saw him with something of its own pathos, there was no trace of sentimentalism in his speech or action. He seems to have had but one rule of conduct, always that of practical and successful politics, to let himself be guided by events, when they were sure to bring him out where he wished to go, though by what seemed to unpractical minds, which let go the possible to grasp at the desirable, a longer road. . . .

No higher compliment was ever paid to a nation than the simple confidence, the fireside plainness, with which Mr. Lincoln always addresses himself to the reason of the American people. This was, indeed, a true democrat, who grounded himself on the assumption that a democracy can think. "Come, let us reason together about this matter," has been the tone of all his addresses to the people; and accordingly we have never had a chief magistrate who so won to himself the love and at the same time the judgment of his countrymen. To us, that simple confidence of his in the right-mindedness of his fellowmen is very touching, and its success is as strong an argument as we have ever seen in favor of the theory that men can govern themselves. He never appeals to any vulgar sentiment, he never alludes to the humbleness of his origin; it probably never occurred to him, indeed that there was anything higher to start from than manhood; and he put himself on a level with those he addressed, not by going down to them, but only by taking it for granted that they had brains and would come up to a common ground of reason. In an article lately printed in "The Nation," Mr. Bayard Taylor mentions the striking fact, that in the foulest dens of the Five Points he found the portrait of Lincoln. The wretched population that makes its hive there threw all its votes and more against him, and yet paid this instinctive tribute to the sweet humanity of his nature. Their ignorance sold its vote and took its money, but all that was left of manhood in them recognized its saint and martyr.

Mr. Lincoln is not in the habit of saying, "This is my opinion, or my theory," but, "This is the conclusion to which, in my judgment, the time has come, and to which,

73

accordingly the sooner we come the better for us." His policy has been the policy of public opinion based on adequate discussion and on a timely recognition of the influence of passing events in shaping the features of events to come.

One secret of Mr. Lincoln's remarkable success in captivating the popular mind is undoubtedly an unconsciousness of self which enables him though under the necessity of constantly using the capital I, to do it without any suggestion of egotism. There is no single vowel, which men's mouths can pronounce with such difference of effect. That which one shall hide away, as it were, behind the substance of his discourse, or, if he bring it to the front, shall use merely to give an agreeable accent of individuality to what he says, another shall make an offensive challenge to the self-satisfaction of all his hearers, and an unwarranted intrusion upon each man's sense of personal importance, irritating every pore of his vanity, like a dry northeast wind, to a goose-flesh of opposition and hostility. Mr. Lincoln has never studied Quintillion; but he has, in the earnest simplicity and unaffected Americanism of his own character, one art of oratory worth all the rest. He forgets himself so entirely in his object as to give his I the sympathetic and persuasive effect of We and with the great body of his countrymen. Homely, dispassionate, showing all the rough-edged process of his thought as it goes along, yet arriving at his conclusion with an honest kind of every-day logic, he is so eminently our representative man, that, when he speaks, it seems as if the people were listening to their own thinking out aloud. The dignity of his thought owes nothing to any ceremonial garb of words, but to the manly movement that comes of settled purpose and an energy of reason that knows not what rhetoric means. There has been nothing of Cleon, still less of Strepsiades striving to underbid him in demagoguism, to be found in the public utterances of Mr. Lincoln. He has always addressed the intelligence of men, never their prejudice, their passion, or their ignorance. . . .

On the day of his death, this simple Western attorney, who according to one party was a vulgar joker, and whom the doctrinaires among his own supporters accused of wanting every element of statesmanship, was the most absolute ruler in Christendom, and this solely by the hold his good-humored sagacity had laid on the hearts and understandings of his countrymen. Nor was this all, for it appeared that he had drawn the great majority, not only of his fellow citizens, but of mankind, also, to his side. So strong and persuasive is honest manliness without a single quality of romance or unreal sentiment to help it! A civilian during times of the most captivating military achievement, awkward, with no skill in the lower technicalities of manners, he left behind him a fame beyond that of any conqueror, the memory of a grace higher than that of outward person, and of gentlemanliness deeper than mere breeding. Never before that startled April morning did such multitudes of men shed tears for the death of one they had never seen, as if with him a friendly presence had been taken away from their lives, leaving them colder and darker. Never was funeral panegyric so eloquent as the silent look of sympathy, which strangers exchanged when they met on that day. Their common manhood had lost a kinsman.

Source:

Lowell, James Russell. *My Study Windows.* Boston: Houghton, Mifflin & Company, 1871.

2-2
Nathaniel Hawthorne on Meeting Lincoln

Nathaniel Hawthorne (1804-1864) was an American novelist and short-story writer who met Lincoln at the White House in March 1862. He wrote an article about his trip to Washington for the Atlantic Monthly *that detailed his deep respect for Lincoln. But the magazine omitted part of the article that described Lincoln's appearance. In 1883 writer and critic George Parsons Lathrop edited a collection of Hawthorne's work and restored the passages in the excerpt below.*

Of course, there was one other personage, in the class of statesmen, whom I should have been truly mortified to leave Washington without seeing; since (temporarily, at least, and by force of circumstances) he was the man of men. But a private grief had built up a barrier about him, impeding the customary free intercourse of Americans with their chief magistrate; so that I might have come away without a glimpse of his very remarkable physiognomy, save for a semi-official opportunity of which I was glad to take advantage. The fact is, we were invited to annex ourselves, as supernumeraries, to a deputation that was about to wait upon the President, from a Massachusetts whip-factory, with a present of a splendid whip.

Our immediate party consisted of four or five (including Major Ben Perley Poore, with his notebook and pencil), but we were joined by several other persons, who seemed to have been lounging about the precincts of the White House, under the spacious porch, or within the hall, and who swarmed in with us to take the chances of a presentation. Nine o'clock had been appointed as the time for receiving the deputation, and we were punctual to the moment; but not so the President, who sent us word that he was eating his breakfast, and would come as soon as he could. His appetite, we were glad to think, must have been a pretty fair one; for we waited about half an hour in one of the antechambers, and then were ushered into a reception-room, in one corner of which sat the Secretaries of War and of the Treasury, expecting, like ourselves, the termination of the Presidential breakfast. During this interval, there were several new additions to our group, one or two of whom were in a working-garb, so that we formed a very miscellaneous collection of people, mostly unknown to each other, and without any common sponsor, but all with an equal right to look our head-servant in the face.

> *By and by there was a little stir on the staircase and in the passage-way, and in lounged a tall, loose-jointed figure, of an exaggerated Yankee port and demeanor, whom (as being about the homeliest man I ever saw, yet by no means repulsive or disagreeable) it was impossible not to recognize as Uncle Abe.*

By and by there was a little stir on the staircase and in the passage-way, and in lounged a tall, loose-jointed figure, of an exaggerated Yankee port and demeanor, whom (as being about the homeliest man I ever saw, yet by no means repulsive or disagreeable) it was impossible not to recognize as Uncle Abe.

Unquestionably, Western man though he be, and Kentuckian by birth, President Lincoln is the essential representative of all Yankees, and the veritable specimen, physically, of what the world seems determined to regard as our characteristic qualities. It is the strangest and yet the fittest thing in the jumble of human vicissitudes, that he, out of so many millions, unlooked for, unselected by any intelligible process that could be based upon his genuine qualities, unknown to those who chose him, and unsuspected of what endowments may adapt him for his tremendous responsibility, should have found the way open for him to fling his lank personality into the chair of state,—where, I presume, it was his first impulse to throw his legs on the council-table, and tell the Cabinet Ministers a story. There is no describing his lengthy awkwardness, nor the uncouthness of his movement; and yet it seemed as if I had been in the habit of seeing him daily, and had shaken hands with him a thousand times in some village street; so true was he to the aspect of the pattern American, though with a certain extravagance which, possibly, I exaggerated still further by the delighted eagerness with which I took it in. If put to guess his calling and livelihood, I should have taken him for a country schoolmaster as soon as anything else. He was dressed in a rusty black frock-coat and pantaloons, unbrushed, and worn so faithfully that the suit had adapted itself to the curves and angularities of his figure, and had grown to be an outer skin of the man. He had shabby slippers on his feet. His hair was black, still unmixed with gray, stiff, somewhat bushy, and had apparently been acquainted with neither brush nor comb that morning, after the disarrangement of the pillow; and as to a night-cap, Uncle Abe probably knows nothing of such effeminacies. His complexion is dark and sallow, betokening, I fear, an insalubrious atmosphere around the White House; he has thick black eyebrows and an impending brow; his nose is large, and the lines about his mouth are very strongly defined.

The whole physiognomy is as coarse a one as you would meet anywhere in the length and breadth of the States; but, withal, it is redeemed, illuminated, softened, and brightened by a kindly though serious look out of his eyes, and an expression of homely sagacity, that seems weighted with rich results of village experience. A great deal of native sense; no bookish cultivation, no refinement; honest at heart, and thoroughly so, and yet, in some sort, sly—at least, endowed with a sort of tact and wisdom that are akin to craft, and would impel him, I think, to take an antagonist in flank, rather than to make a bull-run at him right in front. But, on the whole, I like this sallow, queer, sagacious visage, with the homely human sympathies that warmed it; and, for my small share in the matter, would as lief have Uncle Abe for a ruler as any man whom it would have been practicable to put in his place.

Immediately on his entrance the President accosted our member of Congress, who had us in charge, and, with a comical twist of his face, made some jocular remark about the length of his breakfast. He then greeted us all round, not waiting for an introduction, but shaking and squeezing everybody's hand with the utmost cordiality, whether the individual's name was announced to him or not. His manner towards us was wholly without pretence, but yet had a kind of natural dignity, quite sufficient to keep the forwardest of us from clapping him on the shoulder and asking him for a story. A mutual acquaintance being established, our leader took the whip out of its case, and began to read the address of presentation. The whip was an excessively long one, its handle wrought in ivory (by some artist in the Massachusetts State Prison, I believe), and ornamented with a medallion of the President, and other equally beautiful devices; and along its whole length there was a succession of golden bands and ferrules. The address was shorter than the whip, but equally well made, consisting chiefly of an explanatory description of these artistic designs, and closing with a hint that the gift was a suggestive and emblematic one, and that the President would recognize the use to which such an instrument should be put.

This suggestion gave Uncle Abe rather a delicate task in his reply, because, slight as the matter seemed, it apparently called for some declaration, or intimation, or faint foreshadowing of policy in reference to the conduct of the war, and the final treatment of the Rebels. But the President's Yankee aptness and not-to-be-caughtness stood him in good stead, and he jerked or wiggled himself out of the dilemma with an uncouth dexterity that was entirely in character; although, without his gesticulation of eye and mouth,—and especially the flourish of the whip, with which he imagined himself touching up a pair of fat horses,—I doubt whether his words would be worth recording, even if I could remember them. The gist of the reply was, that he accepted the whip as an emblem of peace, not punishment; and, this great affair over, we retired out of his presence in high good humor, only regretting that we could not have seen the President sit down and fold up his legs (which is said to be a most extraordinary spectacle), or have heard him tell one of those delectable stories for which he is so celebrated. A good many of them are afloat upon the common talk of Washington, and are certainly the aptest, pithiest, and funniest little things imaginable; though, to be sure, they smack of the frontier freedom, and would not always bear repeating in a drawing-room, or on the immaculate page of the Atlantic.

Good Heavens! what liberties have I been taking with one of the potentates of the earth, and the man on whose conduct more important consequences depend than on that of any other historical personage of the century! But with whom is an American citizen entitled to take a liberty, if not with his own chief magistrate? However, lest the above allusions to President Lincoln's little peculiarities (already well known to the country and to the world) should be misinterpreted, I deem it proper to say a word or two, in regard to him, of unfeigned respect and measurable confidence. He is evidently a man of keen faculties, and, what is still more to the purpose, of powerful character. As to his integrity, the people have that intuition of it which is never deceived. Before he actually entered upon his great office, and for a considerable time afterwards, there is no reason to suppose that he adequately estimated the gigantic task about to be imposed on him, or, at least, had any distinct idea how it was to be managed; and I presume there may have been more than one veteran politician who proposed to himself to take the power out of President Lincoln's hands into his own, leaving our honest friend only the public responsibility for the good or ill success of the career. The extremely imperfect development of his statesmanly qualities, at that period, may have justified such designs. But the President is teachable by events, and has now spent a year in a very arduous course of education; he has a flexible mind, capable of much expansion, and convertible towards far loftier studies and activities than those of his early life; and if he came to Washington a backwoods humorist, he has already transformed himself into as good a statesman (to speak moderately) as his prime-minister. . . .

Source:

Hawthorne, Nathaniel. "Chiefly About War Matters." *Atlantic Monthly*, July 1862. Reprinted in *Tales, Sketches, and Other Papers*. Vol. 12. *The Complete Works of Nathaniel Hawthorne.* Edited by George Parsons Lathrop. Boston: Houghton Mifflin Company, 1883.

2-3
"We are coming Father Abraham, or, Three hundred thousand more: inscribed to our volunteers" by James Sloan Gibbons

James Sloan Gibbons (1810-1892) was a poet and the author of "We Are Coming, Father Abraham." On July 1, 1862, Lincoln issued a call for 300,000 more volunteers to fight in the Union Army. Less than three weeks later, on July 16, the New York Evening Post *published the poem by Gibbons. "We Are Coming, Father Abraham" was set to music by various composers and rapidly became a favorite song among the soldiers.*

We are coming Father Abraham, or,
Three hundred thousand more: inscribed to our volunteers

We are coming Father Abraham, three hundred thousand more,
From Mississippi's winding stream & from New England's shore;
We leave our ploughs & workshops, our wives and children dear,
With heart's too full for utterance, with but a silent tear;
We dare not look behind us, but steadfastly before
We are coming, Father Abraham, three hundred thousand more!

Chorus:

We are coming, coming, coming, We are coming, coming, coming,
We are coming, Father Abraham, three hundred thousand more.

If you look across the hill tops that now meet the northern sky,
Long moving lines of rising dust your vision may descry;
And now the wind, an instant tears the cloudy veil aside,
And floats aloft our spangled flag in glory and in pride;
And bayonets in the sunlight gleam, and bands brave music pour
We are coming, Father Abraham, three hundred thousand more!

If you look all up our valley's, where the growing harvests shine,
You may see our sturdy farmer-boys fast forming into line;

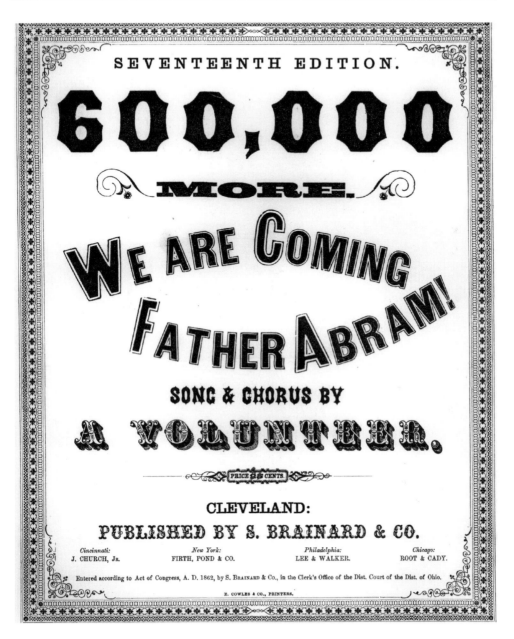

In July 1862 Lincoln called for 300,000 additional troops to fight the Civil War, and James Sloan Gibbons wrote a poem that became a popular song: "We are coming Father Abraham, or, Three hundred thousand more." As this sheet music cover illustrates, a variation of the song asserted that twice as many soldiers would enlist.

And children at their mother's knees are pulling at the weeds,
And learning how to reap and sow, against their country's needs;
And a farewell group stands weeping at ev'ry cottage door
We are coming, Father Abraham, three hundred thousand more!

You have call'd us, and we're coming, by Richmond's bloody tide,
To lay us down for freedom's sake, our brother's bones beside;
Or from foul treason's savage grasp to wrench the murd'rous blade,
And in the face of foreign foes its fragments to parade.
Six hundred thousand loyal men and true have gone before
We are coming, Father Abraham, three hundred thousand more!

Source:

Gibbons, James Sloan. "We are coming Father Abraham, or, Three hundred thousand more: inscribed to our volunteers." *New York Evening Post*, July 16, 1862. Sheet music available online at the Alfred Whital Stern Collection of Lincolniana, Library of Congress. http://memory.loc.gov/ammem/scsmhtml/scsmhome.html.

2-4
James Shrigley Recalls Lincoln Appointing Him Hospital Chaplain

Reverend James Shrigley was nominated by Lincoln to be a hospital chaplain to minister to wounded soldiers. Some members of the Y.M.C.A protested to Lincoln about this nomination. In the excerpt below, Shrigley recalls this episode.

My first visit with Mr. Lincoln was a few days before he issued his Emancipation Proclamation, when I was introduced by the Hon. John Covode. The President was walking his room, apparently under great excitement, and spoke to Mr. Covode in nearly the following words, which made a deep impression on my mind: "I have studied that matter well; my mind is made up—it *must be done.* I am driven to it. There is to me no other way out of our troubles. But although my duty is plain, it is in some respects *painful*, and I trust the people will understand that I act not in anger, but in expectation of a greater good." These few words revealed to me some of the noble attributes of his nature. "I do it not in anger, but in expectation of a greater good." Nothing but the honest sense of duty could have induced him to issue that proclamation, and this he desired the people to know, that his motives might not be misunderstood. No man was ever more free from the spirit of revenge or more conscientious in the discharge of his duties. President Lincoln was also remarkably tolerant. He was the friend of all, and never, to my knowledge, gave the influence of his great name to encourage sectarianism in any of its names or forms; he had "charity for all and malice toward none."

The following is in proof. Immediately after the earliest battles of the war most of the sick and wounded were brought to the Philadelphia hospitals for treatment, and I was in daily receipt of letters from my denominational friends soliciting me to visit husbands or brothers who were among the sick and wounded. As much of my time was thus occupied, and at considerable expense, it was suggested by the Hon. Henry D. Moore that application be made for the position of hospital chaplain, and it was on the recommendation of Mr. Moore and Governor Curtin that the President made the nomination. Soon as it was announced in the papers that my name had been sent to the Senate for confirmation a self-constituted committee of "Young Christians" (?) consulted with a few others, as bigoted as themselves, and volunteered their services to visit Washington and try to induce the President to withdraw the name. It so happened that when these gentlemen called on the President Mr. Covode was present and made known the interview to a reporter, and it thus became public. It was in substance as follows:

The Interview

"We have called, Mr. President, to confer with you in regard to the appointment of Mr. Shrigley, of Philadelphia, as hospital chaplain."

The President responded: "Oh, yes, gentlemen; I have sent his name to the Senate, and he will no doubt be confirmed at an early day."

One of the young men replied: "We have not come to ask for the appointment, but to solicit you to withdraw the nomination."

"Ah," said Lincoln, "that alters the case; but on what ground do you wish the nomination withdrawn?"

The answer was, "Mr. Shrigley is not sound in his theological opinions."

The President inquired: "On what question is the gentleman unsound?"

Response.—"He does not believe in endless punishment; not only so, sir, but he believes that even the rebels themselves will finally be saved."

"Is that so?" inquired the President.

The members of the committee both responded, "Yes," Yes."

"Well, gentlemen, if that be so, and there is any way under heaven whereby the rebels can be saved, then, for God's sake and their sakes, let the man be appointed."

And he *was appointed*, and served until the war closed.

Source:

Shrigley, James. Published in *The Lincoln Memorial: Album-Immortelles*. Edited by Osborn H. Oldroyd. Springfield, IL: Lincoln Publishing Company, 1890.

2-5
Thomas T. Eckert Remembers Lincoln at the War Department

Major Thomas T. Eckert (1825-1910) was head of the telegraph office at the War Department. He knew Lincoln from the president's frequent visits to the office for news of the Civil War. Lincoln invited Eckert to be in the presidential party to attend the theater on April 14, 1865, but Eckert did not go. In the excerpt below, Eckert recounts Lincoln's work on a document in the telegraph office during the summer of 1862 amid an occasional interruption. He claims this document was an early draft of the Emancipation Proclamation (see document 7-6).

As you know, the President came to the office every day and invariably sat at my desk while there. Upon his arrival early one morning in June, 1862, shortly after McClellan's "Seven Days' Fight," he asked me for some paper, as he wanted to write something special. I procured some foolscap and handed it to him. He then sat down and began to write. I do not recall whether the sheets were loose or had been made into a pad. There must have been at least a quire. He would look out of the window a while and then put his pen to paper, but he did not write much at once. He would study between times and when he had made up his mind he would put down a line or two, and then sit quiet for a few minutes. After a time he would resume his writing, only to stop again at intervals to make some remark to me or to one of the cipher-operators as a fresh despatch from the front was handed to him.

Once his eye was arrested by the sight of a large spider-web stretched from the lintel of the portico to the side of the outer window-sill. This spider-web was an institution of the cipher-room and harbored a large colony of exceptionally big ones. We frequently watched their antics, and Assistant Secretary Watson dubbed them "Major Eckert's lieutenants." Lincoln commented on the web, and I told him that my lieutenants would soon report and pay their respects to the President. Not long after a big spider appeared at the crossroads and tapped several times on the strands, where-upon five or six others came out from different directions. Then what seemed to be a great confab took place, after which they separated, each on a different strand of the web. Lincoln was much interested in the performance and thereafter, while working at his desk, would often watch for the appearance of his visitors.

On the first day Lincoln did not cover one sheet of his special writing paper (nor indeed on any subsequent day). When ready to leave, he asked me to take charge of what he had written and not allow any one to see it. I told him I would do this with pleasure and would not read it myself. "Well," he said, "I should be glad to know that no one will see it, although there is no objection to your looking at it; but please keep it locked up until I call for it to-morrow." I said his wishes would be strictly complied with.

When he came to the office on the following day he asked for the papers, and I unlocked my desk and handed them to him and he again sat down to write. This he did nearly every day for several weeks, always handing me what he had written when ready to leave the office each day. Sometimes he would not write more than a line or two, and once I observed that he had put question-marks on the margin of what he had written. He would read over each day all the matter he had previously written and revise it, studying carefully each sentence.

On one occasion he took the papers away with him, but he brought them back a day or two later. I became much interested in the matter and was impressed with the idea that he was engaged upon something of great importance, but did not know what it was until he had finished the document and then for the first time he told me that he had been writing an order giving freedom to the slaves in the South, for the purpose of hastening the end of the war. He said he had been able to work at my desk more quietly and command his thoughts better than at the White House, where he was frequently interrupted. I still have in my possession the ink-stand which he used at that time and which, as you know, stood on my desk until after Lee's surrender. The pen he used was a small barrel-pen made by Gillott—such as were supplied to the cipher-operators.

Source:

Eckert, Thomas T. "The First Draft of the Emancipation Proclamation." In *Lincoln in the Telegraph Office: Recollections of the United States Military Telegraph Corps during the Civil War* by David Homer Bates. New York: Century Co., 1907.

2-6
The Pennsylvania Anti-Slavery Society Congratulates Lincoln on Emancipation

Lincoln received this missive from the Pennsylvania Anti-Slavery Society after issuing the preliminary Emancipation Proclamation on September 22, 1862. It contains both a congratulatory letter and a proclamation from the society.

Anti-Slavery Office
Philada Sept. 27th 1862

To Abraham Lincoln
President of the United States

Honored Sir:

It is made my duty to convey to you the enclosed resolutions; a duty which I perform with unfeigned pleasure.

The joy which your great proclamation imparts is not of a kind that shows itself in noisy demonstration, nor is its extent and depth to be judged of by outward appearance. The virtuous, the reflecting, the intelligently patriotic, the people in whom inheres the nation's life, the people who make—not those who speculate in, public opinion, these are they who, as one man, hail your edict with delight and bless and thank God that he put it in your heart to issue it.

Without trespassing on your time and attention with further words I beg to subscribe myself, with sentiments of the sincerest respect,

Your obedient servant
J.M. McKim
Corresponding sec'y
Penna Anti-Slavery Society

The Pennsylvania Anti-Slavery Society also drafted a proclamation, including the following resolutions:

"Resolved, that we hail, with inexpressible satisfaction, the Proclamation of Liberty just uttered by the President of the United States, and that without qualifying our joy by regrets that it had not appeared earlier, or that it is not more immediate and unconditional in its operation—we tender to him our sincerest thanks, and invoke upon his head Heaven's best blessings.

Resolved, that regarding Slavery, as the sole cause of the War and the direst curse of the Country, and not doubting that the effect of the Proclamation will be to put an early, and in the more Southern States, a fixed period to its existence, we cannot but regard the act as one of wise humanity, of enlightened patriotism, and prudent Statesmanship.

Ordered that the Corresponding Secretary be requested to forward to the President a copy of these Resolutions at his earliest Convenience."

> A. Kimber
> Secretary pro. Tem
> Philada. Sept. 27, 1862.

Source:

Pennsylvania Anti-Slavery Society. Letter and Proclamation, September 27, 1862. Available online at Abraham Lincoln Papers, Library of Congress. http://memory.loc.gov/ammem/alhtml/malhome.html.

2-7
Frederick Douglass Recalls Emancipation Day

*Frederick Douglass (1817-1895) was an abolitionist leader and former
slave. He was acquainted with Lincoln and met with him on both official
and social occasions. Douglass spoke at the unveiling of the Freedmen's
Monument, also called the Emancipation Group, in Washington, D.C., on
April 14, 1876 (for a photo of the monument, see page 308). He congratu-
lates the African Americans who worked to commission the monument,
honors Lincoln, and remembers the issuance of the Emancipation Proclamation (see document 7-6).*

... We stand to-day at the national centre to perform something like a national act—an act which is to go into history; and we are here where every
pulsation of the national heart can be heard, felt, and reciprocated. A thousand wires,
fed with thought and winged with lightning, put us in instantaneous communication with the loyal and true men all over this country.

Few facts could better illustrate the vast and wonderful change which has taken place
in our condition as a people than the fact of our assembling here for the purpose we
have to-day. Harmless, beautiful, proper, and praiseworthy as this demonstration is, I
cannot forget that no such demonstration would have been tolerated here twenty
years ago. The spirit of slavery and barbarism, which still lingers to blight and destroy
in some dark and distant parts of our country, would have made our assembling here
the signal and excuse for opening upon us all the flood-gates of wrath and violence.
That we are here in peace to-day is a compliment and a credit to American civilization, and a prophecy of still greater national enlightenment and progress in the future.
I refer to the past not in malice, for this is no day for malice but simply to place more
distinctly in front the gratifying and glorious change which has come both to our
white fellow-citizens and ourselves, and to congratulate all upon the contrast between
now and then; the new dispensation of freedom with its thousand blessings to both
races, and the old dispensation of slavery with its ten thousand evils to both races—
white and black. In view, then, of the past, the present, and the future, with the long
and dark history of our bondage behind us, and with liberty, progress, and enlightenment before us, I again congratulate you upon this auspicious day and hour.

"The Union Christmas Dinner," a cartoon by Thomas Nast,
appeared in Harper's Weekly *on December 31, 1864, one day short of a*
year after Lincoln issued the Emancipation Proclamation.
It illustrates the president's desire for national reconciliation.

Friends and fellow-citizens, the story of our presence here is soon and easily told. We are here in the District of Columbia, here in the city of Washington, the most luminous point of American territory; a city recently transformed and made beautiful in its body and in its spirit; we are here in the place where the ablest and best men of the country are sent to devise the policy, enact the laws, and shape the destiny of the Republic; we are here, with the stately pillars and majestic dome of the Capitol of the nation looking down upon us; we are here, with the broad earth freshly adorned with the foliage and flowers of spring for our church, and all races, colors, and conditions of men for our congregation—in a word, we are here to express, as best we may, by appropriate forms and ceremonies, our grateful sense of the vast, high, and pre-eminent services rendered to ourselves, to our race, to our country, and to the whole world by Abraham Lincoln.

The sentiment that brings us here to-day is one of the noblest that can stir and thrill the human heart. It has crowned and made glorious the high places of all civilized nations with the grandest and most enduring works of art, designed to illustrate the characters and perpetuate the memories of great public men. It is the sentiment which from year to year adorns with fragrant and beautiful flowers the graves of our loyal, brave, and patriotic soldiers who fell in defence of the Union and liberty. It is the sentiment of gratitude and appreciation, which often, in presence of many who hear me, has filled yonder heights of Arlington with the eloquence of eulogy and the sublime enthusiasm of poetry and song; a sentiment which can never die while the Republic lives.

For the first time in the history of our people, and in the history of the whole American people, we join in this high worship, and march conspicuously in the line of this time-honored custom. First things are always interesting, and this is one of our first things. It is the first time that, in this form and manner, we have sought to do honor to an American great man, however deserving and illustrious. I commend the fact to notice; let it be told in every part of the Republic; let men of all parties and opinions hear it; let those who despise us, not less than those who respect us, know that now and here, in the spirit of liberty, loyalty, and gratitude, let it be known everywhere, and by everybody who takes an interest in human progress and in the amelioration of the condition of mankind, that, in the presence and with the approval of the members of the American House of Representatives, reflecting the general sentiment of the country; that in the presence of that august body, the American Senate, representing the highest intelligence and the calmest judgment of the country; in presence of the Supreme Court and Chief-Justice of the United States, with the members of his wise and patriotic Cabinet, we, the colored people, newly emancipated and rejoicing in our blood-brought freedom, near the close of the first century in the life of this Republic, have now and here unveiled, set apart, and dedicated a monument of enduring granite and bronze, in every line, feature, and figure of which the men of this generation may read, and those of after-coming generations may read, something of the exalted character and great works of Abraham Lincoln, the first martyr President of the United States. . .

Fellow-citizens, ours is no new-born zeal and devotion—merely a thing of this moment. The name of Abraham Lincoln was near and dear to our hearts in the darkest and most perilous hours of the Republic. We were no more ashamed of him when shrouded in clouds of darkness, of doubt, and defeat than when we saw him crowned with victory, honor, and glory. Our faith in him was often taxed and strained to the uttermost, but it never failed. When he tarried long in the mountain; when he strangely told us that we were the cause of the war; when he still more strangely told us to leave the land in which we were born; when he refused to employ our arms in defence of the Union; when, after accepting our services as colored soldiers, refused to retaliate our murder and torture as colored prisoners; when he told us he would save the Union if he could with slavery; when he revoked the Proclamation of Emancipation of General Fremont; when he refused to remove the popular commander of the Army of the Potomac, in the days of its inaction and defeat, who was more zealous in his efforts to protect slavery than to suppress rebellion; when we saw all this, and more, we were at times grieved, stunned, and greatly bewildered; but our hearts believed while they ached and bled. Nor was this, even at the time, a blind and unreasoning superstition. Despite the mist and haze that surrounded him; despite the tumult, the hurry, and confusion of the hour, we were able to take a comprehensive view of Abraham Lincoln, and to make reasonable allowance for the circumstances of his position. We saw him, measured him, and estimated him; not by stray utterances to injudicious and tedious degradations, who often tried his patience; not by isolated facts torn from their connection; not by any partial and imperfect glimpses, caught at inopportune moments; but by a broad survey, in the light of the stern logic of great events, and in view of that divinity which shapes our ends, rough hew them how we will, we came to the conclusion that the hour and the man of our redemption had somehow met in the person of Abraham Lincoln. It mattered little to us what language he might employ on special occasions; it mattered little to us, when we fully knew him, whether he was swift or slow in his movements; it was enough for us that Abraham Lincoln was at the head of a great movement, and was in living and earnest sympathy with that movement, which, in the nature of things, must go on until slavery should be utterly and forever abolished in the United States.

When, therefore, it shall be asked what we have to do with the memory of Abraham Lincoln, or what Abraham Lincoln had to do with us, the answer is ready, full, and complete. Though he loved Caesar less than Rome, though the Union was more to him than our freedom or our future, under his wise and beneficent rule we saw ourselves gradually lifted from the depths of slavery to the heights of liberty and manhood; under his wise and beneficent rule, and by measures approved and vigorously pressed by him, we saw that the handwriting of ages, in the form of prejudice and proscription, was rapidly fading away from the face of our whole country; under his rule, and in due time, about as soon after all as the country could tolerate the strange spectacle, we saw our brave sons and brothers laying off the rags of bondage, and being clothed all over in the blue uniforms of the soldiers of the United States; under his rule we saw two hundred thousand of our dark and dusky people responding to the call of Abraham Lincoln, and with muskets on their shoulders, and eagles on their buttons, timing their high foot-steps to liberty and union under the national flag; under his rule we saw the independence of the black republic of Hayti, the special object of slaveholding aversion and horror, fully recognized, and her minister, a colored gentleman, duly received here in the city of Washington; under his rule we saw the internal slave-trade, which so long disgraced the nation, abolished, and slavery abolished in the District of Columbia; under his rule we saw for the first time the law enforced against the foreign slave-trade, and the first slave-trader hanged like any other pirate or murderer; under his rule, assisted by the greatest captain of our age, and his inspiration, we saw the Confederate States, based upon the idea that our race must be slaves, and slaves forever, battered to pieces and scattered to the four winds; under his rule, and in the fullness of time, we saw Abraham Lincoln, after giving the slave-holders three months' grace in which to save their hateful slave system, penning the immortal paper, which, though special in its language, was general in its principles and effect, making slavery forever impossible in the United States. Though we waited long, we saw all this and more.

Can any colored man, or any white man friendly to the freedom of all men, ever forget the night which followed the first day of January, 1863, when the world was to see if Abraham Lincoln would prove to be as good as his word? I shall never forget that memorable night, when in a distant city I waited and watched at a public meeting, with three thousand others not less anxious than myself, for the word of deliverance which we have heard read to-day. Nor shall I ever forget the outburst of joy and thanksgiving that rent the air when the lightning brought to us the emancipation proclamation. In that happy hour we forgot all the delay, and forgot all tardiness, forgot that the President had bribed the rebels to lay down their arms by a promise to withhold the bolt which would smite the slave-system with destruction; and we were thenceforward willing to allow the President all the latitude of time, phraseology, and every honorable device that statesmanship might require for the achievement of a great and beneficent measure of liberty and progress.

Fellow-citizens, there is little necessity on this occasion to speak at length and critically of this great and good man, and of his high mission in the world. That ground has been fully occupied and completely covered both here and elsewhere. The whole field of fact and fancy has been gleaned and garnered. Any man can say thing that are true of Abraham Lincoln, but no man can say anything that is new of Abraham Lincoln. His personal traits and public acts are better known to the American people than are those of any other man of his age. He was a mystery to no man who saw him and heard him. Though high in position, the humblest could approach him and feel at home in his presence. Though deep, he was transparent; though strong, he was gentle; though decided and pronounced in his convictions, he was tolerant towards those who differed from him, and patient under reproaches. Even those who only knew him through his public utterances obtained a tolerably clear idea of his character and his personality. The image of the man went out with his words, and those who read them, knew him.

> *His personal traits and public acts are better known to the American people than are those of any other man of his age. He was a mystery to no man who saw him and heard him. Though high in position, the humblest could approach him and feel at home in his presence.*

I have said that President Lincoln was a white man, and shared the prejudices common to his countrymen towards the colored race. Looking back to his times and to the condition of his country, we are compelled to admit that this unfriendly feeling on his part may be safely set down as one element of his wonderful success in organizing the loyal American people for the tremendous conflict before them, and bringing them safely through that conflict. His great mission was to accomplish two things: first, to save his country from dismemberment and ruin, and second, to free the country from the great crime of slavery. To do one without the other, or both, he must have the earnest sympathy and the powerful co-operation of his loyal fellow-countrymen. Without this primary and essential condition to success his efforts must have been vain and utterly fruitless. Had he put the abolition of slavery before the salvation of the Union, he would have inevitably driven from him a powerful class of the American people and rendered resistance to rebellion impossible. Viewed from the genuine abolition round, Mr. Lincoln seemed tardy, cold, dull, and indifferent; but measuring him by the sentiment of his country, a sentiment he was bound as a statesman to consult, he was swift, zealous, radical, and determined.

Though Mr. Lincoln shared the prejudices of his white fellow-countrymen against the Negro, it is hardly necessary to say that in his heart of hearts he loathed and hated slavery. The man who could say, "Fondly do we hope, fervently do we pray, that this mighty scourge of war shall soon pass away, yet if God wills it continue till all the wealth piled by two hundred years of bondage shall have been wasted, and each drop of blood drawn by the lash shall have been paid for by one drawn by the sword, the judgments of the Lord are true and righteous altogether," gives all the needed proof of his feeling on the subject of slavery. He was willing, while the South was loyal, that it should have its pound of flesh, because he thought that it was so nominated in the bond; but farther than this no earthly power could make him go.

Fellow-citizens, whatever else in this world may be partial, unjust, and uncertain, time, time! is impartial, just, and certain in its action. In the realm of mind, as well as in the realm of matter, it is a great worker, and often works wonders. The honest and comprehensive statesman, clearly discerning the needs of his country, and earnestly endeavoring to do his whole duty, though covered and blistered with reproaches, may safely leave his course to the silent judgment of time. Few great public men have ever been the victims of fiercer denunciation than Abraham Lincoln was during his administration. He was often wounded in the house of his friends. Reproaches came thick and fast upon him from within and from without, and from opposite quarters. He was assailed by Abolitionists; he was assailed by slaveholders; he was assailed by the men who were for peace at any price; he was assailed by those who were for a more vigorous prosecution of the war; he was assailed for not making the war an abolition war; and he was most bitterly assailed for making the war an abolition war.

But now behold the change: the judgment of the present hour, that taking him for all in all, measuring the tremendous magnitude of the work before him, considering the necessary means to ends, and surveying the end from the beginning, infinite wisdom has seldom sent any man into the world better fitted for his mission than Abraham Lincoln. His birth, his training, and his natural endowments, both mental and physical, were strongly in his favor. Born and reared among the lowly, a stranger to wealth and luxury, compelled to grapple single handed with the flintiest hardships of life, from tender youth to sturdy manhood, he grew strong in the manly and heroic qualities demanded by the great mission to which he was called by the votes of his countrymen. The hard condition of his early life, which would have depressed and broken down weaker men, only gave greater life, vigor, and buoyancy to the heroic spirit of Abraham Lincoln. He was ready for any kind and any quality of work. What other young men dreaded in the shape of toil, he took hold of with the utmost cheerfulness.

> A spade, a rake, a hoe,
> A pick-axe, or a bill;
> A hook to reap, a scythe to mow,
> A flail, or what you will.

All day long he could split heavy rails in the woods, and half the night long he could study his English Grammar by the uncertain flare and glare of the light made by a pine-knot. He was at home on the land with his axe, with his maul, with gluts, and his wedges; and he was equally at home on water, with his oars, with his poles, with his planks, and with his boat-hooks. And whether in his flat-boat on the Mississippi river, or at the fireside of his frontier cabin, he was a man of work. A son of toil himself, he was linked in brotherly sympathy with the sons of toil in every loyal part of the Republic. This very fact gave him tremendous power with the American people, and materially contributed not only to selecting him to the Presidency, but in sustaining his administration of the Government.

Upon his inauguration as President of the United States, an office, even where assumed under the most favorable conditions, fitted to tax and strain the largest abilities, Abraham Lincoln was met by a tremendous crisis. He was called upon not merely to administer the Government, but to decide, in the face of terrible odds, the fate of the Republic.

A formidable rebellion rose in his path before him; the Union was already practically dissolved; his country was torn and rent asunder at the centre. Hostile armies were already organized against the Republic, armed with the munitions of war which the Republic had provided for its own defence. The tremendous question for him to decide was whether his country should survive the crisis and flourish, or be dismembered and perish. His predecessor in office had already decided the question in favor of national dismemberment, by denying to it the right of self-defence and self-preservation—a right which belongs to the meanest insect.

Happily for the country, happily for you and me, the judgment of James Buchanan, the patrician, was not the judgment of Abraham Lincoln, the plebian. He brought his strong common sense, sharpened in the school of adversity, to bear upon the question. He did not hesitate, did not doubt, he did not falter; but at once resolved that at whatever peril, at whatever cost, the union of the States should be preserved. A patriot himself, his faith was strong and unwavering in the patriotism of his countrymen. Timid men said before Mr. Lincoln's inauguration, that we had seen the last President of the United States. A voice in influential quarters said, "Let the Union slide." Some said that a Union maintained by the sword was worthless. Others said a rebellion of 8,000,000 cannot be suppressed; but in the midst of all this tumult and timidity, and against all this, Abraham Lincoln was clear in his duty, and had an oath in heaven. He calmly and bravely heard the voice of doubt and fear all around him; but he had an oath in heaven, and there was not power enough on the earth to make this honest boatman, back-woodsman, and broad-handed splitter of rails evade or violate that sacred oath. He had not been schooled in the ethics of slavery; his plain life had favored his love of truth. He had not been taught that treason and perjury were the proof of honor and honesty. His moral training was against his saying one thing when he meant another. The trust which Abraham Lincoln had in himself and in the people was surprising and grand, but it was also enlightened and well founded. He knew the American people better than they knew themselves, and his truth was based upon this knowledge.

> *He did not hesitate, did not doubt, he did not falter; but at once resolved that at whatever peril, at whatever cost, the union of the States should be preserved. A patriot himself, his faith was strong and unwavering in the patriotism of his countrymen.*

Fellow-citizens, the fourteenth day of April, 1865, of which this is the eleventh anniversary, is now and will ever remain a memorable day in the annals of this Republic. It was on the evening of this day, while a fierce and sanguinary rebellion was in the last stages of its desolating power; while its armies were broken and scattered before the invincible armies of Grant and Sherman; while a great nation, torn and rent by war, was already beginning to raise to the skies loud anthems of joy at the dawn of peace, it was startled, amazed, and overwhelmed by the crowning crime of slavery—the assassination of Abraham Lincoln. It was a new crime, a pure act of malice. No purpose of the rebellion was to be served by it. It was the simple gratification of a hell-black spirit of revenge. But it has done good after all. It has filled the country with a deeper abhorrence of slavery and a deeper love for the great liberator.

Had Abraham Lincoln died from any of the numerous ills to which flesh is heir; had he reached that good old age of which his vigorous constitution and his temperate habits gave promise; had he been permitted to see the end of his great work; had the solemn curtain of death come down but gradually—we should still have been smitten with a heavy grief, and treasured his name lovingly. But dying as he did die, by the red hand of violence, killed, assassinated, taken off without warning, not because of personal hate—for no man who knew Abraham Lincoln could hate him—but because of his fidelity to union and liberty, he is doubly dear to us, and his memory will be precious forever.

Fellow-citizens, I end, as I began, with congratulations. We have done a good work for our race to-day. In doing honor to the memory of our friend and liberator, we have been doing highest honors to ourselves and those who come after us; we have been fastening ourselves to a name and fame imperishable and immortal; we have also been defending ourselves from a blighting scandal. When not it shall be said that the colored man is soulless, that he has no appreciation of benefits or benefactors; when the foul reproach of ingratitude is hurled at us, and it is attempted to scourge us beyond the range of human brotherhood, we may calmly point to the monument we have this day erected to the memory of Abraham Lincoln.

Source:

Douglass, Frederick. *Oration by Frederick Douglass Delivered on the Occasion of the Unveiling of the Freedmen's Monument in Memory of Abraham Lincoln in Lincoln Park, Washington, D.C., April 14, 1876.* Washington, D.C.: Gibson Brothers, 1876.

2-8
Correspondence between President Lincoln and the Chicago Sanitary Commission

Mrs. D. P. (Mary) Livermore (1820-1905) was a volunteer for the Chicago branch of the U.S. Sanitary Commission, which provided care packages to Union soldiers in the field and cared for the wounded. She met Lincoln on several occasions while performing her duties. As the head organizer of the fund-raising fair described in her letter below, Livermore asked Lincoln to donate the original Emancipation Proclamation (see document 7-6). Lincoln did provide the document, which sold for $3,000. In 1871 it was destroyed in the Chicago fire. The excerpts below include Livermore's initial request to Lincoln, his response, and Livermore's reply of thanks.

Chicago Sanitary Commission
Branch of U.S. Sanitary Commission
Rooms No. 66 Madison Street
Chicago, Oct. 11th, 1863.

Abraham Lincoln, Pres. U.S.A.,

Dear Sir:

The patriotic women of the Northwestern States will hold a grand fair in Chicago on the last week of Oct., and the first of Nov., to raise funds for the Sanitary Commission of the Northwest whose head quarters are in Chicago. The Commission labors especially for the sick and wounded soldiers of the South western States, of whose bravery, and persistent endurance, we are all justly proud. I enclose you circulars, which will explain to you our entire plan, and show you the magnitude of the enterprise, by which we confidently hope to realize from $25,000 to $50,000.

The greatest enthusiasm prevails in reference to this Fair, which is now only two weeks distant. There are very few towns in Northern Illinois, Wisconsin, Michigan, and Iowa that are not laboring for it. Artists are painting pictures for it, manufactur-

*Lincoln spent much of his time at the Anderson cottage on the grounds
of the Soldiers' Home just outside Washington, D.C. The Soldiers' Home
was established in 1851 as a residence for retired and disabled soldiers.
Lincoln often visited soldiers in the hospitals near the grounds.*

ers are making elegant specimens of their handiwork for the occasion, tradesmen are
donating the choicest of their wares, while women are surpassing their ordinary ingenuity and taste in devising beautiful articles for sale, or decorations for the walls of
the four spacious halls we are to occupy.

The Executive Committee have been urgently requested to solicit from Mrs. Lincoln and yourself some donation to this great Fair—not so much for the value of the gift, as for the éclat which this circumstance would give to the Fair. It has been suggested to us from various quarters that the most acceptable donations you could possibly make, would be the original manuscript of the proclamation of emancipation, and I have been instructed to ask for this, if it is at all consistent with what is proper, for you to donate it. There would be great competition among buyers to obtain possession of it, and to say nothing of the interest that would attach to such a gift, it would prove pecuniarily [sic] of great value. We should take pains to have such an arrangement made as would place the document permanently in either the State or the Chicago Historical Society.

There would seem great appropriateness in this gift to Chicago or Illinois, for the benefit of our Western Soldiers, coming as it would from a Western President. We hope it may be possible for you to donate it to us.

But, if it be not possible, then allow us to ask for some other simple gift, from Mrs. Lincoln and yourself—sufficient to show that your are cognizant of our efforts and are interested in them. Our Fair opens on Tuesday, Oct. 27th, in little more than two weeks.

Yours very respectfully,
Mrs. D. P. Livermore

Lincoln sent the following response, along with the Proclamation.

Executive Mansion
Washington, Oct. 26. 1863

Ladies having in charge of the North Western Fair
For the Sanitary Commission
Chicago, Illinois

According to the request made in your behalf, the original draft of the Emancipation proclamation is herewith enclosed. The formal words at the top, and the conclusion, except the signature, you perceive, are not in my hand-writing. They were written at the State Department by whom I know not. The printed parts was cut from a copy of the preliminary proclamation, and pasted on merely to save writing.

I had some desire to retain the paper; but if it shall contribute to the relief or comfort of the soldiers that will be better.

Your obt. Servt.
A. Lincoln

The members of the Chicago Sanitary Commission replied with this thank-you letter.

Chicago Sanitary Commission
Chicago, Nov. 11th 1863–

President Lincoln

Sir

We profoundly thank you for your gift to our North Western Fair of the original draft of the "Proclamation of Emancipation." It came to us in the midst of a wonderful outpouring of loyalty & liberality from the great throbbing hearts of the North West, nay, almost of the Nation; for all seemed ready to respond and give. Your proclamation is the star of hope, the rainbow of promise, that has risen above the din and carnage of this unholy rebellion, and will fill the brightest page in the history of our struggle for national existence; while it has become the anchor of hope, the rainbow of promise, to the oppressed of every land, at home and abroad. In the midst of so many varied and valuable donations, it has been reserved to you, Abraham Lincoln, the People's President, to bestow the most noble and valuable gift, for the sick and suffering soldiers. The treasure shall be carefully guarded & skilfully managed, so as to produce a revenue that shall make your heart glad, and soothe the woes of hundreds in hospitals. May God bless you, and preserve you, to rule over us another term in peace, with the same ability, uprightness and wisdom which He has given you to guide us through the storms of war at home, and threatening dangers from abroad.

With profound respect & gratitude

> Mrs. A. H. Hoge
> Mrs. D. P. Livermore

Lady Managers of the N. Western Fair

Source:

Livermore, Mrs. D. P., Abraham Lincoln, and Mrs. A. H. Hoge. Correspondence dated October 11, 1863 - November 11, 1863. Available online at Abraham Lincoln Papers, Library of Congress. http://memory.loc.gov/ammem/alhtml/malhome.html.

2-9
Francis B. Carpenter on Painting *The First Reading of the Emancipation Proclamation*

Francis B. Carpenter (1830-1900) was a nineteenth-century American artist. Lincoln allowed him to spend six months in 1864 in the White House working on his famous painting, The First Reading of the Emancipation Proclamation. *In the excerpt below, Carpenter recalls meeting the president, obtaining his permission to work in the White House, and discussing the plan of the painting with Lincoln. Carpenter's reminiscence includes Lincoln's description of that fateful Cabinet meeting.*

To paint a picture which should commemorate this new epoch in the history of Liberty, was a dream which took form and shape in my mind towards the close of the year 1863, —the year mad memorable in its dawn by the issue of the final decree. With little experience to adapt me for the execution of such a work, there had

Francis B. Carpenter between 1850 and 1860.

nevertheless come to me at times glowing conceptions of the true purpose and character of Art, and an intense desire to do something expressive of appreciation of the great issues involved in the war. . . .

In seeking a point of unity or action for the picture, I was impressed with the conviction that important modifications followed the reading of the Proclamation at the suggestion of the Secretary of State, and I determined upon such an incident as the moment of time to be represented. I was subsequently surprised and gratified when Mr. Lincoln himself, reciting the history of the Proclamation to me, dwelt particularly upon the fact that not only was the time of its issue decided by Secretary Seward's advice, but that one of the most important words in the document was added through his strenuous representations.

The central thought of the picture once decided upon and embodied, the rest naturally followed; one after another the seven figures surrounding the President dropped into their places. Those supposed to have held the purpose of the Proclamation as their long conviction, were placed prominently in the foreground in attitudes which indicated their support of the measure; the others were represented in varying moods of discussion or silent deliberation. . . .

From the threshold of the "crimson" parlor as I passed, I had a glimpse of the gaunt figure of Mr. Lincoln in the distance, haggard-looking, dressed in black, relieved only by the prescribed white gloves; standing, it seemed to me, solitary and alone, though surrounded by the crowd, bending low now and then in the process of handshaking, and responding half abstractedly to the well-meant greetings of the miscellaneous assemblage. Never shall I forget the electric thrill which went through my whole being at this instant. I seemed to see lines radiating from every part of the globe, converging to focus at the point where that plain, awkward-looking man stood, and to hear in spirit a million prayers, "as the sound of many waters," ascending in his behalf. Mingled with supplication, I could discern a clear symphony of triumph and blessing, swelling with an ever-increasing volume. It was the voice of those who had been bondmen and bondwomen, and the grand diapason swept up from the coming ages.

It was soon my privilege, in the regular succession, to take that honored hand. Accompanying the act, my name and profession were announced to him in a low tone by one of the assistant private secretaries, who stood by his side. Retaining my hand, he looked at my inquiringly for an instant, and said, "Oh yes; I know; this is the painter." Then straightening himself to his full height, with a twinkle of the eye, he added, playfully, "Do you think, Mr. C——, that you can make a handsome picture of *me*?" emphasizing strongly the last word. Somewhat confused at this point-blank shot, uttered in a tone so loud as to attract the attention of those in immediate proximity, I made a random reply, and took the occasion to ask if I could see him in his study at the close of the reception. To this he responded in the peculiar vernacular of the West, "I reckon," resuming meanwhile the mechanical and traditional exercise of the hand which no President has ever yet been able to avoid, and which, severe as is the ordeal, is likely to attach to the position, so long as the Republic endures.

VII.

The appointed hour found me at the well-remembered door of the official chamber,—that door watched daily, with so many conflicting emotions of hope and fear, by the anxious throng regularly gathered there. The President had preceded me, and was already deep in Acts of Congress, with which the writing-desk was strewed, awaiting his signature. He received me pleasantly, giving me a seat near his own armchair; and after having read Mr. Lovejoy's note, he took off his spectacles, and said, "Well, Mr. C——, we will turn you loose in here, and try to give you a good chance to work out your idea." Then, without paying much attention to the enthusiastic expression of my ambitious desire and purpose, he proceeded to give me a detailed account of the history and issue of the great proclamation.

"It had got to be," said he, "midsummer, 1862. Things had gone on from bad to worse, until I felt that we had reached the end of our rope on the plan of operations we had been pursuing; that we had about played our last card, and must change our tactics, or lose the game! I now determined upon the adoption of the emancipation policy; and, with consultation with, or the knowledge of the Cabinet, I prepared the original draft of the proclamation, and, after much anxious thought, called a Cabinet meeting upon the subject. This was the last of July, or the first part of the month of August, 1862." (The exact date he did not remember.) "This Cabinet meeting took place, I think, upon a Saturday. All were present, excepting Mr. Blair, the Postmaster-General, who was absent at the opening of the discussion, but came in subsequently. I said to the Cabinet that I had resolved upon this step, and had not called them together to ask their advice, but to lay the subject-matter of a proclamation before them; suggestions as to which would be in order, after they had heard it read. "Mr. Lovejoy," said he, "was in error when he informed you that it excited no comment, excepting on the part of Secretary Seward. Various suggestions were offered. Secretary Chase wished the language stronger in reference to the arming of the blacks. Mr. Blair, after he came in, deprecated the policy, on the ground that it would cost the Administration the fall elections. Nothing, however, was offered that I had not already fully anticipated and settled in my own mind, until Secretary Seward spoke. He said in substance: 'Mr. President, I approve of the proclamation, but I question the expediency of its issue at this juncture. The depression of the public mind, consequent upon our repeated reverses, is so great that I fear the effect of so important a step. It may be viewed as the last measure of an exhausted government, a cry for help; the government stretching forth its hands to Ethiopia, instead of Ethiopia stretching forth her hands to the government.' His idea, said the President, "was that it would be considered our last *shriek*, on the retreat." (This was his *precise* expression.) "'Now,' continued Mr. Seward, 'while I approve the measure, I suggest, sir, that you postpone its issue, until you can give it to the country supported by military success, instead of issuing it, as would be the case now, upon the greatest disasters of the war!'" Mr. Lincoln continued: "The wisdom of the view of the Secretary of State struck me with very great force. It was an aspect of the case that, in all my thought upon the subject, I had entirely overlooked. The result was that I put the draft of the proclamation aside, as you do your sketch for a picture, waiting for a victory. From time to time I added or changed a line, touching it up here and there, anxiously watching the progress of events. Well, the next news we had was of Pope's disaster, at Bull Run. Things looked darker than ever. Finally, came the week of the battle of Antietam. I determined to wait no longer. The news came, I think, on Wednesday, that the advantage was on our side. I was then staying at the Soldiers' Home, (three miles out of Washington.) Here I finished writing the second draft of the preliminary proclamation; came up on Saturday; called the Cabinet together to hear it, and it was published the following Monday."

At the final meeting of September 20th, another interesting incident occurred in connection with Secretary Seward. The President had written the important part of the proclamation in these words: —

"That, on the first day of January, in the year of our Lord one thousand eight hundred and sixty-three, all persons held as slaves within any State or designated part of a State, the people whereof shall then be in rebellion against the United States, shall be then, thenceforward, and forever FREE; and the Executive Government of the United States, including the military and naval authority thereof, will *recognize* the freedom of such persons, and will do no act or acts to repress such persons, or any of them, in any efforts they may make for their actual freedom." "When I finished reading this paragraph," resumed Mr. Lincoln, "Mr. Seward stopped me, and said, 'I think, Mr. President, that you should insert after the word "*recognize*," in that sentence, the words "*and maintain.*"' I replied that I had already fully considered the import of that expression in this connection, but I had not introduced it, because it was not my way to promise what I was not entirely *sure* that I could perform, and I was not prepared to say that I thought we were exactly able to 'maintain' this."

"But," said he, "Seward insisted that we ought to take this ground; and the words finally went in!"

"It is a somewhat remarkable fact," he subsequently remarked, "that there were just one hundred days between the dates of the two proclamations issued upon the 22nd of September and the 1st of January. I had not made the calculation at the time."

Having concluded this interesting statement, the President then proceeded to show me the various positions occupied by himself and the different members of the Cabinet, on the occasion of the first meeting. "As nearly as I remember," said he, "I sat near the head of the table; the Secretary of the Treasury and the Secretary of War were here, at my right hand; the others were grouped at the left."

At this point, I exhibited to him a pencil sketch of the composition as I had conceived it, with no knowledge of the facts or details. The leading idea of this I found, as I have stated on a previous page, to be entirely consistent with the account I had just heard. I saw, however, that I should have to reverse the picture, placing the President at the other end of the table, to make it accord with his description. I had resolved to discard all appliances and tricks of picture-making, and endeavor, as faith-

This 1866 print reproduces Francis B. Carpenter's painting The First Reading of the Emancipation Proclamation, *created in 1864. It depicts the cabinet meeting at which Lincoln first presented a draft of the preliminary emancipation proclamation on July 22, 1862. From left to right: Edwin M. Stanton, Secretary of War; Salmon P. Chase, Secretary of the Treasury; Lincoln; Gideon Welles, Secretary of the Navy; Caleb B. Smith, Secretary of the Interior; William H. Seward, Secretary of State (seated); Montgomery Blair, Postmaster-General; and Edward Bates, Attorney General.*

fully as possible, to represent the scene as it actually transpired; room, furniture, accessories, all were to be painted from the actualities. It was a scene second only in historical importance and interest to that of the Declaration of Independence; and I felt assured, that, if honestly and earnestly painted, it need borrow no interest from imaginary curtain or column, gorgeous furniture or allegorical statue. Assenting heartily to what is called the "realistic" school of art, when applied to the illustration of historical events, I felt in this case, that I had no more right to depart from the facts, that has the historian in his record. . .

When, at length, the conception as thus described was sketched upon the large canvas, and Mr. Lincoln came in to see it, his gratifying remark, often subsequently repeated, was, "It is as good as it can be made. . ."

X.

"We will turn you in loose here," proved an "open sesame" to me during the subsequent months of my occupation at the White House. My access to the official chamber was made nearly as free as that of the private secretaries, unless special business was being transacted. Sometimes a stranger, approaching the President with a low tone, would turn an inquiring eye toward the place where I sat, absorbed frequently in a pencil sketch of some object in the room. This would be met by the hearty tones of Mr. Lincoln,—I can hear them yet ringing in my ears,—"Oh, you need not mind him; he is but a painter." There was a satisfaction to me, differing from that of any other experience, in simply sitting with him. Absorbed in his papers, he would become unconscious of my presence, while I intently studied every line and shade of expression in that furrowed face. In repose, it was the saddest face I ever knew. There were days when I could scarcely look into it without crying. During the first week of the battles of the Wilderness he scarcely slept at all. Passing through the main hall of the domestic apartment on one of these days, I met him, clad in a long morning wrapper, pacing back and forth a narrow passage leading to one of the windows, his hands behind him, great black rings under his eyes, his head bent forward upon his breast, —altogether such a picture of the effects of sorrow, care, and anxiety as would have melted the hearts of the worst of his adversaries, who so mistakenly applied to him the epithets of tyrant and usurper. . .

Source:

Carpenter, Francis B. *The Inner Life of Abraham Lincoln. Six Months at the White House.* New York: Hurd and Houghton, 1868.

2-10
James Abram Garfield on the Emancipation Proclamation

James Abram Garfield (1831-1881) was a Republican representative from Ohio who later became president; he was assassinated in his first year in office. Garfield addressed Congress on February 12, 1878, at the presentation of Francis B. Carpenter's painting, The First Reading of the Emancipation Proclamation. *The owner of the painting, Elizabeth Thompson, donated it to the nation to be displayed in the Capitol Building. Below is an excerpt from Garfield's speech. (For Carpenter's account of working on the painting, see document 2-9.)*

Let us pause to consider the actors in that scene. In force of character, in thoroughness and breadth of culture, in experience of public affairs, and in national reputation, the Cabinet that sat around that council-board has had no superior, perhaps no equal in our history. Seward, the finished scholar, the consummate orator, the great leader of the Senate, had come to crown his career with those achievements which placed him in the first rank of modern diplomatists. Chase, with a culture and a fame of massive grandeur, stood as the rock and pillar of the public credit, the noble embodiment of the public faith. Stanton was there, a very Titan of strength, the great organizer of victory. Eminent lawyers, men of business, leaders of states and leaders of men, completed the group.

But the man who presided over that council, who inspired and guided its deliberations, was a character so unique that he stood alone, without a model in history or a parallel among men. Born on this day, sixty-nine years ago, to an inheritance of extremest poverty; surrounded by the rude forces of the wilderness; wholly unaided by parents; only one year in any school; never, for a day, master of his own time until he reached his majority; making his way to the profession of the law by the hardest and roughest road;—yet by force of unconquerable will and persistent, patient work, he attained a foremost place in his profession,

> "And, moving up from high to higher,
>   Became on Fortune's crowning slope
>   The pillar of a people's hope,
> The center of a world's desire."

At first, it was the prevailing belief that he would be only the nominal head of his administration,—that its policy would be directed by the eminent statesmen he had called to his council. How erroneous this opinion was may be seen from a single incident.

Among the earliest, most difficult, and most delicate duties of his administration was the adjustment of our relations with Great Britain. Serious complications, even hostilities, were apprehended. On the 21st of May, 1861, the Secretary of State presented to the President his draught of a letter of instructions to Minister Adams, in which the position of the United States and the attitude of Great Britain were set forth with the clearness and force which long experience and great ability had placed at the command of the Secretary. Upon almost every page of that original draught are erasures, additions, and marginal notes in the handwriting of Abraham Lincoln, which exhibit a sagacity, a breadth of wisdom, and a comprehension of the whole subject, impossible to be found except in a man of the very first order. And these modifications of a great state paper were made by a man who but three months before had entered for the first time the wide theatre of Executive action.

From the first, in his own quaint, original way, without ostentation or offense to his associates, he was pilot and commander of his administration. He was one of the few great rulers whose wisdom increased with his power, and whose spirit grew gentler and tenderer as his triumphs were multiplied.

Gifted with an insight and a foresight which the ancients would have called divination, he saw, in the midst of darkness and obscurity, the logic of events, and forecast the result. From the first, in his own quaint, original way, without ostentation or offense to his associates, he was pilot and commander of his administration. He was one of the few great rulers whose wisdom increased with his power, and whose spirit grew gentler and tenderer as his triumphs were multiplied.

This was the man, and these his associates, who look down upon us from the canvas.

The present is not a fitting occasion to examine, with any completeness, the causes that led to the Proclamation of Emancipation; but the peculiar relation of that act to the character of Abraham Lincoln cannot be understood, without considering one remarkable fact in his history. His earlier years were passed in a region remote from the centres of political thought, and without access to the great world of books. But the few books that came within his reach he devoured with the divine hunger of genius. One paper, above all others, led him captive, and filled his spirit with the majesty of its truth and the sublimity of its eloquence. It was the Declaration of American Independence. The author and signers of that instrument became, in his early youth, the heroes of his political worship. I doubt if history affords any example of a life so early, so deeply, and so permanently influenced by a single political truth, as was Abraham Lincoln's by the central doctrine of the Declaration,—the liberty and equality of all men. Long before his fame had become national he said, "That is the electric cord in the Declaration, that links the hearts of patriotic and liberty-loving men together, and that will link such hearts as long as the love of freedom exists in the minds of men throughout the world."

That truth runs, like a thread of gold, through the whole web of his political life. It was the spear-point of his logic in his debates with Douglas. It was the inspiring theme of his remarkable speech at the Cooper Institute, New York, in 1860, which gave him the nomination to the Presidency. It filled him with reverent awe when on his way to the capital to enter the shadows of the terrible conflict then impending, he uttered, in Independence Hall, at Philadelphia, these remarkable words, which were prophecy then but are history now:—

> "I have never had a feeling, politically, that did not spring from the sentiments embodied in the Declaration of Independence. I have often pondered over the dangers which were incurred by the men who assembled here, and framed and adopted that Declaration of Independence. I have pondered over the toils that were endured by the officers and soldiers of the army who achieved that independence. I have often inquired of myself what great principle or idea it was that kept this confederacy so long together. It was not the mere matter of the separation of the Colonies from the mother land, but that sentiment in the Declaration of Independence which gave liberty, not alone to the people of this country, but, I hope, to the world for all future time. It was that which gave promise that, in due time, the weight would be lifted from the shoulders of all men. This is the sentiment embodied in the Declaration of Independence. Now, my friends, can this country be saved

upon that basis? If it can, I will consider myself one of the happiest men in the world if I can help to save it. If it cannot be saved upon that principle, it will be truly awful. But if this country cannot be saved without giving up that principle, I was about to say, I would rather be assassinated on this spot than surrender it."

Deep and strong was his devotion to liberty; yet deeper and stronger still was his devotion to the Union; for he believed that without the Union permanent liberty for either race on this continent would be impossible. And because of this belief, he was reluctant, perhaps more reluctant than most of his associates, to strike slavery with the sword. For many months, the passionate appeals of millions of his associates seemed not to move him. He listened to all the phases of the discussion, and stated, in language clearer and stronger than any opponent had used, the dangers, the difficulties, and the possible futility of the act. In reference to its practical wisdom, Congress, the Cabinet, and the country were divided. Several of his generals had proclaimed the freedom of slaves within the limits of their commands. The President revoked their proclamations. His first Secretary of War had inserted a paragraph in his annual report advocating a similar policy. The President suppressed it.

On the 19th of August, 1862, Horace Greeley published a letter, addressed to the President, entitled "The Prayer of Twenty Millions," in which he said, "On the face of this wide earth, Mr. President, there is not one disinterested, determined, intelligent champion of the Union cause who does not feel that all attempts to put down the rebellion and at the same time uphold its inciting cause are preposterous and futile."

To this the President responded in that ever-memorable reply on August 22, in which he said:—

"If there be those who would not save the Union unless they could at the same time save slavery, I do not agree with them.

"If there be those who would not save the Union unless they could at the same time destroy slavery, I do not agree with them.

"My paramount object is to save the Union, and not either to save or to destroy slavery.

"If I could save the Union without freeing any slave, I would do it. If I could save it by freeing all the slaves, I would do it,—and if I could do it by freeing some and leaving others alone, I would also do that.

113

"What I do about slavery and the colored race, I do because I believe it helps to save the Union; and what I forbear, I forbear because I do not believe it would help to save the Union. I shall do less whenever I shall believe that what I am doing hurts the cause, and I shall do more whenever I believe doing more will help the cause."

Thus, against all importunities on the one hand and remonstrances on the other, he took the mighty question to his own heart, and, during the long months of that terrible battle-summer, wrestled with it alone. But at length he realized the saving truth, that great, unsettled questions have no pity for the repose of nations. On the 22nd of September, he summoned his Cabinet to announce his conclusion. It was my good fortune, on that same day, and a few hours after the meeting, to hear, from the lips of one who participated, the story of the scene. As the chiefs of the Executive Departments came in, one by one, they found the President reading a favorite chapter from a popular humorist. He was lightening the weight of the great burden which rested upon his spirit. He finished the chapter, reading it aloud. And here I quote, from the published Journal of the late Chief Justice, an entry, written immediately after the meeting, and bearing unmistakable evidence that it is almost a literal transcript of Lincoln's words.

"The President then took a graver tone, and said: 'Gentlemen, I have, as you are aware, thought a great deal about the relation of this war to slavery; and you all remember that, several weeks ago, I read to you an order I have prepared upon the subject, which, on account of objections made by some of you, was not issued. Ever since then my mind has been much occupied with this subject, and I have thought all along that the time for acting on it might probably come. I think the time has come now. I wish it was a better time. I wish that we were in a better condition. The action of the army against the rebels has not been quite what I should have best liked. But they have been driven out of Maryland, and Pennsylvania is no longer in danger of invasion. When the rebel army was at Frederick, I determined as soon as it should be driven out of Maryland to issue a proclamation of emancipation, such as I thought most likely to be useful. I said nothing to any one, but I made a promise to myself and (hesitating a little) to my Maker. The rebel army is now driven out, and I am going to fulfill that promise. I have got you together to hear what I have written down. I do not wish your advice about the main matter, for that I have determined for myself. This I say without intending anything but respect for any one of you. But I already know the views of each on this question. They have been heretofore

This photograph of Lincoln, General George B. McClellan (sixth from left), and other soldiers was taken at Antietam, Maryland, on October 3, 1862. It was after the Union victory there on September 17 that Lincoln decided the time was right to issue his preliminary emancipation proclamation.

expressed, and I have considered them as thoroughly and carefully as I can. What I have written is that which my reflections have determined me to say. If there is anything in the expressions I use, or in any minor matter which any one of you thinks had best be changed, I shall be glad to receive your suggestions. One other observation I will make. I know very well that many others might, in this matter as in others, do better than I can; and if I was satisfied that the public confidence was more fully possessed by any one of them than by me, and knew of any constitutional way in which he could be put in my place, he should have it. I would gladly yield it to him. But though I believe I have not so much of the confidence of the people as I had some time since, I do not know that, all things considered, any other person has more; and, however this may be, there is no way in which I can have any other man put where I am. I am here. I must do the best I can and bear the responsibility of taking the course which I feel I ought to take.'

"The President than proceeded to read his Emancipation Proclamation, making remarks on the several parts as he went on, and showing that he had fully considered the subject in all the lights under which it had been presented to him."

The Proclamation was amended in a few matters of detail. It was signed and published that day. The world knows the rest, and will not forget it till "the last syllable of recorded time."

Source:

Garfield, James Abram. "Lincoln and Emancipation: Address Delivered in the Hall of the House of Representatives, February 12, 1878." In *The Works of James Abram Garfield*. Vol. 2. Edited by Burke A. Hinsdale. Boston: James R. Osgood and Company, 1883.

2-11
"The Emancipation Group" by John Greenleaf Whittier

John Greenleaf Whittier (1807-1892) was an American poet and abolitionist. He wrote "The Emancipation Group" as a tribute to Lincoln and his Proclamation; the poem was written for the unveiling of the Freedmen's Memorial Statue in Boston on December 9, 1879.

The Emancipation Group

Amidst thy sacred effigies
 If old renown give place,
O city, Freedom-loved! to his
 Whose hand unchained a race.

Take the worn frame, that rested not
 Save in a martyr's grave,
The care-lined face, that none forgot,
 Bent to the kneeling slave.

Let man be free! The mighty word
 He spake was not his own;
An impulse from the Highest stirred
 These chiseled lips alone.

The cloudy sign, the fiery guide,
 Along his pathway ran,

And Nature, through his voice, denied
 The ownership of man.

We rest in peace where these sad eyes
 Saw peril, strife, and pain;
His was the nation's sacrifice,
 And ours the priceless gain.

O symbol of God's will on earth
 As it is done above!
Bear witness to the cost and worth
 Of justice and of love.

Stand in the place and testify
 To coming ages long,
That truth is stronger than a lie,
 And righteousness than wrong.

Source:

Whittier, John Greenleaf. "The Emancipation Group." *Anti-Slavery Poems: Songs of Labor and Reform.* New York: Houghton, Mifflin & Co., 1888.

2-12
E. W. Andrews Accompanies Lincoln to Gettysburg

E. W. Andrews was a Union army officer who accompanied Lincoln to Gettysburg for the dedication of the Gettysburg National Cemetery on November 19, 1863. In the excerpt below, Andrews recounts his trip with Lincoln and his observations of the ceremony.

The National Cemetery at Gettysburg was dedicated on the 17th [19th] of November, 1863. Shortly before the dedication was to take place the President sent an invitation of my chief, General W. W. Morris, and his staff, to join him at Baltimore and accompany him on his special train to Gettysburg. General Morris was sick at the time, and requested me, as his chief of staff, to represent him on that occasion. The General was suffering from one of the troubles which tried the patience of Job.

On the day appointed, therefore, I presented myself, with two other members of the staff, to President Lincoln, on his arrival at Baltimore, and offered the apology of my chief for his absence.

After cordially greeting us and directing us to make ourselves comfortable, the President, with quizzical expression, turned to Montgomery Blair (then Postmaster General), and said:

"Blair, did you ever know that fright has sometimes proved a sure cure for boils?"

"No, Mr. President. How is that?"

"I'll tell you. Not long ago, when Colonel—, with his cavalry, was at the front, and the Rebs were making things rather lively for us, the colonel was ordered out on a *reconnaissance.* He was troubled at the time with a big boil where it made horseback riding decidedly uncomfortable. He hadn't gone more than two or three miles when he declared he couldn't stand it any longer, and dismounted and ordered the troops forward without him. He had just settled down to enjoy his relief from change of position when he was startled by the rapid reports of pistols and the helter-skelter approach of his troops in full retreat before a yelling rebel force. He forgot everything but the yells, sprang into his saddle, and made capital time over fences and ditches till safe within the lines. The pain from his boil was gone, and the boil too, and the colonel swore that there was no cure for boils so sure as fright from rebel yells, and that the secession had rendered to loyalty *one* valuable service at any rate."

During the ride to Gettysburg, the President placed every one who approached him at his ease, relating numerous stories, some of them laughable, and others of a character that deeply touched the hearts of his listeners.

I remember well his replay to a gentleman who stated that his "only son fell on 'Little Round Top' at Gettysburg, and I am going to look at the spot."

President Lincoln replied:

"You have been called upon to make a terrible sacrifice for the Union, and a visit to that spot, I fear, will open your wounds afresh. But oh! my dear sir, if we had reached the end of such sacrifices, and had nothing left for us to do but to place garlands on the graves of those who have already fallen, we could give thanks even amidst our tears; but when I think of the sacrifices of life yet to be offered and the hearts and homes yet to be made desolate before this dreadful war, so wickedly forced upon us, is over, my heart is like lead within me, and I feel, at times, like hiding in deep darkness."

> *During the ride to Gettysburg, the President placed every one who approached him at his ease, relating numerous stories, some of them laughable, and others of a character that deeply touched the hearts of his listeners.*

At one of the stopping-places of the train, a very beautiful little child, having a bouquet of rose-buds in her hand, was lifted up to an open window of the President's car. With a childish lisp she said: "Flowerth for the President!"

The President stepped to the window, took the rose-buds, bent down and kissed the child, saying:

"You're a sweet little rose-bud yourself. I hope your life will open into perpetual beauty and goodness."

We had taken with us from Fort McHenry the Second United States Artillery band, one of the oldest and finest of the army.

After our arrival at Gettysburg, two gentlemen, who represented themselves as members of the Committee of Arrangements, applied to me for this band to serenade the President and the several Governors of States who had arrived. . .

The ceremonies of the dedication were imposing and most interesting. The great procession, civic and military, the splendid music, the impressive religious exercises, the great oration by Edward Everett (the last public effort of his life), the dedication, of the ground chosen, in an address by President Lincoln, of beauty and pathos never surpassed—all amidst the scenes where thousands but recently had freely offered up their lives for the life of the Republic—made the day one to be remembered as long as our Union shall last.

Around the platform, on which the addresses were delivered, the military were formed in hollow square several ranks deep. Inside of this square, and but a few feet from the platform, I had my position, and thus enjoyed the best opportunities to see and hear.

The oration of Mr. Everett, although, perhaps, not equal in rhetorical beauty and lofty eloquence to some of his previous efforts, was rich in historical instruction and glowing with patriotic sentiment, and was received with great applause.

At length, and in the name of the American Republic, the President came forward formally to dedicate the place, which had drank so freely of the lifeblood of her sons, as their peaceful resting-place till time should be no more, pledging the fidelity and honor and power of the government to its preservation for this sacred purpose while that government should last.

A description of the President's famous address is needless; it has already become a classic; it is impossible to conceive of anything more beautiful and appropriate for the occasion.

But I may say a word of the appearance of the orator.

President Lincoln was so put together physically that, to him, gracefulness of movement was an impossibility. But his awkwardness was lost sight of in the interest which the expression of his face and what he said awakened.

On this occasion he came out before the vast assembly, and stepped slowly to the front of the platform, with his hands clasped before him, his natural sadness of expression deepened, his head bent forward, and his eyes cast to the ground.

Lincoln and his generals, William Tecumseh Sherman, Philip Henry Sheridan, and Ulysses S. Grant, as rendered in this lithograph by Currier & Ives around 1865.

In this attitude he stood for a few seconds, silent, as if communing with his own thoughts; and when he began to speak, and throughout his entire address, his manner indicated no consciousness of the presence of tens of thousands hanging on his lips, but rather of one who, like the prophet of old, was overmastered by some unseen spirit of the scene, and passively gave utterance to the memories, the feelings, the counsels and the prophecies with which he was inspired.

In his whole appearance, as well as in his wonderful utterances, there was such evidence of a wisdom and purity and benevolence and moral grandeur, higher and beyond the reach of ordinary men, that the great assembly listened almost awe-struck as to a voice from the divine oracle. . .

Source:

Andrews, E. W. In *Reminiscences of Abraham Lincoln by Distinguished Men of His Time.* Edited by Allen Thorndike Rice. New York: North American Publishing Company, 1886.

2-13
Jacob Hoke on Lincoln at Gettysburg

Jacob Hoke was a resident of Chambersburg, Pennsylvania, who attended the dedication of Gettysburg National Cemetery on November 19, 1863. The excerpt below includes Hoke's description of Lincoln giving his famous address at the dedication ceremony. (For the Gettysburg Address, see document 7-8.)

The ground thus purchased and set apart for the burial of those who fell at Gettysburg in defense of the Government, was, on November 19th, 1863, solemnly dedicated to this sacred purpose. There were present, beside a vast concourse of people from all parts of the country, the President of the United States, several members of his cabinet, the ministers of France and Italy, the governors of several States, representatives of the army and navy, members of Congress, and many other distinguished persons. A stand or platform was erected for the speakers and invited quests. This stand stood just where the National Monument now stands. The exercises were opened by music by Birgfield's band, after which followed an eloquent and impressive prayer by Rev. Thomas H. Stockton, D. D. . . .

At the conclusion of this prayer, the Marine Band of Washington rendered excellent and appropriate music, after which Hon. Edward Everett delivered an able and elaborate address. Following this address a choir sang the hymn composed specially for the occasion by B. B. French, Esq. . . . The President of the United States, the honored and revered LINCOLN, then, amidst the tremendous applause of the assembled multitude, arose and slowly advanced to the front of the platform and delivered his celebrated dedicatory address, which was as follows:

"Fourscore and seven years ago our fathers brought forth upon this continent a new nation, conceived in Liberty, and dedicated to the proposition that all men are created equal.

"Now we are engaged in a great civil war, testing whether that nation, or any nation so conceived and so dedicated, can long endure. We are met on a great battlefield of that war. We are met to dedicate a portion of it as a final resting place of those who here gave their lives that that nation might live. It is altogether fitting and proper that we should do this.

"But in a larger sense we can not dedicate, we can not consecrate, we can not hallow this ground. The men, living and dead, who struggled here have consecrated it far above our power to add or detract. The world will little note nor long remember what we say here, but it can never forget what they did here. It is for us, the living, rather to be dedicated here to the unfinished work that they have thus so nobly carried on. It is rather for us to be here dedicated to the great task remaining before us—that from these honored dead we take increased devotion to the cause for which they gave the last full measure of devotion—that we highly resolve that the dead shall not have died in vain; that the nation shall, under God, have a new birth of freedom, and that the government of the people, by the people, and for the people, shall not perish from the earth."

The words of the president were uttered in slow and measured tones, and although not heard by the large majority of the people present, the most profound silence was observed during their delivery. When he uttered the closing sentences, which have become immortal, emphasizing each with a significant nod and jerk of his head,—"that the government of the people, by the people, and for the people, shall not perish from the earth,"—it occurred to the writer, who stood within a few feet of him, that those words were destined to an imperishable immortality.

After the president's dedicatory address, a solemn dirge was sung, after which the benediction was pronounced by Rev. H. L. Baugher, D. D.

The admiration of the people for President Lincoln exceeded that ever bestowed upon any other person within my knowledge. It was evidently not so much for him personally, as representatively. He was recognized as the personification of the cause which was enshrined in every patriot's heart, and for which the armies of the Union were contending. To love the Union was to love Abraham Lincoln. To hate and defame him was the acknowledged evidence of disloyalty. The honored head of the Nation, the humble and unpretending man from Illinois, standing upon the ground where one of the greatest battles of modern times occurred, and in which the existence and destiny of the Government were in part decided, modestly received the willing homage of the assembled thousands. The Man—the President—the Government—the yet undecided peril to which it was exposed—the ground we were on—the sleeping thousands all about us, whose blood had been poured out upon that soil that the Nation might live, all conspired to make the occasion one never to be forgotten.

Source:

Hoke, Jacob. *The Great Invasion of 1863; or, General Lee in Pennsylvania.* Dayton, OH: W. J. Shuey, 1887.

2-14
Excerpt from "The Gettysburg Ode" by Bayard Taylor

Writer Bayard Taylor (1825-1878) composed a long poem titled "The Gettysburg Ode" for the dedication of the Soldiers' National Monument at Gettysburg National Cemetery on July 1, 1869. The first section of the poem, concerning Lincoln's Gettysburg Address (see document 7-8), appears below.

The Gettysburg Ode

After the eyes that looked, the lips that spake
Here, from the shadows of impending death,
Those words of solemn breath,
What voice may fitly break
The silence, doubly hallowed, left by him?
We can but bow the head, with eyes grown dim,

And as a Nation's litany, repeat
The phrase his martyrdom hath made complete,
Noble as then, but now more sadly sweet:
"Let us, the Living, rather dedicate
Ourselves to the unfinished work, which they
Thus far advanced so nobly on its way,
And saved the periled State!
Let us, upon this field where they, the brave,
Their last full measure of devotion gave,
Highly resolve they have not died in vain!—
That, under God, the Nation's later birth
Of Freedom, and the people's gain
Of their own Sovereignty, shall never wane
And perish from the circle of the earth!"
From such a perfect text, shall Song aspire
To light her faded fire,
And into wandering music turn
Its virtue, simple, sorrowful, and stern?
His voice all elegies anticipated;
For, whatsoe'er the strain,
We hear that one refrain;
"We consecrate ourselves to them, the Consecrated!"

Source:

Taylor, Bayard. "The Gettysburg Ode." *Home Pastorals, Ballads and Lyrics.* Boston: J. R. Osgood and Co., 1875.

2-15
James Speed Recalls Lincoln Discharging a Mother's Sons from the Army

James Speed (1812-1887) was Lincoln's attorney general and the brother of Joshua Speed, Lincoln's best friend. In an interview with Lincoln's secretary John G. Nicolay, James Speed related the incident below, in which a woman petitioned Lincoln to release her sons from the Union army.

It is extremely difficult (said Mr. S.) to adequately portray in writing the exquisite pathos of Mr. Lincoln's character as manifested in his action from time to time.

There was the incident of granting a discharge to the woman's sons.

"Is that all?" he asked of Edward, the usher, after the usual multitude of daily visitors had entered and presented their requests, petitions or grievances.

"There is one poor woman there yet Mr. President" replied Edward. She has been there for several days, and has been crying and taking on—and hasn't got a chance to come in yet.

"Let her in," said Mr. L.

The woman came in and told her story. It was just after the battle of Gettysburg. She had a husband and two sons in the army, and she was left alone to fight the hard battle of life. At first her husband had regularly sent her a part of his pay and she had managed to live. But gradually he had yielded to the temptations of camp life and no more remittances came. Her boys had become scattered among the various armies, and she was without help. &c. &c. Would not the President discharge one of them that he might come home to her?

While the pathetic recital was going on the President stood before the fire-place, his hands crossed behind his back, and his head bent in earnest thought. When the woman ended and waited a moment for his reply his lips opened and he spoke—not indeed as if he were replying to what she had said, but rather as if he were in abstracted and unconscious self-communion:

"I have two, and you have none."

That was all he said. Then he walked across to his writing table, at which he habitually sat, and taking a blank card, wrote upon it an order for the son's discharge—and upon another paper he wrote out in great detail where she should present it—to what Department, at what office and to what official giving her such direction that she might personally follow the red tape labyrinth.

A few days later, at a similar close of the "general reception" for the day, Edward said "That woman, Mr. President, is here again, and still crying."

"Let her in" said L. "What can the matter be now."

Once more he stood up in the same place before the fire, and for the second time heard her story. The President's card had been like a magic passport to her. It had opened forbidden doors, and softened the sternness of official countenances. By its help she had found headquarters—camp— Regiment, and company. But instead of giving a mother's embrace to a lost son restored, she had arrived only in time to follow him to the grave. The battle at Gettysburg—his wounds—his death at the hospital—the story came in eloquent fragments through her illy-stifled sobs. And now would not the President give her the next one of her boys?

> *The President's card had been like a magic passport to her. It had opened forbidden doors, and softened the sternness of official countenances. By its help she had found headquarters— camp—Regiment, and company.*

Once more Mr. Lincoln responded with sententious curtness as if talking to himself. "I have two and you have none"—a sharp and rather stern compression of his lips marking the struggle between official duty and human sympathy. Then he again walked to his little writing table and took up his pen to write for the second time an order which should give the pleading woman one of her remaining boys. And the woman, as if moved by a filial impulse she could not restrain moved after him and stood by him at the table as he wrote, and with the fond familiarity of a mother placed her hand upon the President's head and smoothed down his wandering and tangled hair. Human grief and human sympathy had overleaped all the barriers of formality, and the ruler of a great nation was truly the servant, friend and protector of the humble woman clothed for the moment with a paramount claim of loyal sacrifice. The order was written and signed, the President rose and thrust it into her hand with the choking ejaculation "There!" and hurried from the room, followed, so long as he could heard, by the thanks and blessing of an overjoyed mother's heart. The spoken words of the scene were few and common-place; but a volume could not describe the deep suppressed emotion or the simple pathetic eloquence of the act.

Source:

Speed, James. In *An Oral History of Abraham Lincoln: John G. Nicolay's Interviews and Essays.* Edited by Michael Burlingame. Carbondale: Southern Illinois University Press, 1996.

2-16
Harriet Beecher Stowe Shares Her Impressions of Lincoln

Harriet Beecher Stowe (1811-1896) was a writer who was best known for her popular anti-slavery novel Uncle Tom's Cabin (1852). *When she met Lincoln in November 1862, he is reported to have quipped, "Is this the little woman who made this great war?" Stowe recorded her impressions of Lincoln in the article excerpted below.*

Lincoln is a strong man, but his strength is of a peculiar kind; it is not aggressive so much as passive, and among passive things, it is like the strength not so much of a stone buttress as of a wire cable. It is strength swaying to every influence, yielding on this side and on that to popular needs, yet tenaciously, inflexibly bound to carry its great end; and probably by no other kind of strength could our national ship have been drawn safely thus far during the tossings and turnings and tempests which beset her way.

Surrounded by all sorts of conflicting claims, by traitors, by half-hearted, timid men, by Border States men, and Free States men, by radical Abolitionists and Conservatives, he has listened to all, weighed the words of all, waited, observed, yielded now here and now there, but in the main kept one inflexible, honest purpose, and drawn that national ship through.

In times of our trouble Abraham Lincoln had had his turn of being the best abused man of our nation. Like Moses leading his Israel through the wilderness, he has seen the day when every man seemed ready to stone him, and yet, with simple, wiry, steady perseverance, he has held on, conscious of honest intentions and looking to God for help. All the nation have felt, in the increasing solemnity of his proclamations and papers, how deep an education was being wrought in his mind by this simple faith in God, the ruler of nations, and this humble willingness to learn the awful lessons of his providence.

Harriet Beecher Stowe
around 1880.

We do not mean to give the impression that Lincoln is a religious man in the sense in which the term is popularly applied. We believe he has never made any such profession, but we see evidence that in passing through this dreadful national crisis he has been forced by the very anguish of the struggle to look upward, where any rational creature must look for support. No man in this agony has suffered more and deeper, albeit with a dry, weary, patient pain, that seemed to some like insensibility. "Whichever way it ends," he said to the writer, "I have the impression that *I* sha'n't last long after it's over." After the dreadful repulse of Fredericksburg, his heavy eyes and worn and weary air told how our reverses wore upon him, and yet there was a never-failing fund of patience at bottom that sometimes rose to the surface in some droll, quaint saying, or story, that forced a laugh even from himself.

There have been times with many, of impetuous impatience, when our national ship seemed to lie water-logged and we have called aloud for a deliverer of another fashion—a brilliant general, a dashing, fearless statesman, a man who could dare and do, and who would stake all on a die, and win or lose by a brilliant *coup de main*. It may comfort our minds that since He who ruleth in the armies of nations set no such man to this work, that perhaps He saw in the man whom He did send some peculiar fitness and aptitudes therefor.

Slow and careful in coming to resolutions, willing to talk with every person who has anything to show on any side of a disputed subject, long in weighing and pondering, attached to constitutional limits and time-honored landmarks, Lincoln certainly was the *safest* leader a nation could have at a time when the *habeas corpus* must be suspended, and all the constitutional and minor rights of citizens be thrown into the hands of their military leader. A reckless, bold, theorizing, dashing man of genius might have wrecked our Constitution and ended us in a splendid military despotism.

Among the many accusations which in hours of ill-luck have been thrown out upon Lincoln, it is remarkable that he has never been called self-seeking, or selfish. When we were troubled and sat in darkness, and looked doubtfully towards the presidential chair, it was never that we doubted the goodwill of our pilot—only the clearness of his eyesight. But Almighty God has granted to him that clearness of vision which he gives to the true-hearted, and enabled him to set his honest foot in that promised land of freedom which is to be the patrimony of all men, black and white—and from henceforth nations shall rise up to call him blessed.

Source:

Stowe, Harriet Beecher. "Abraham Lincoln." *Littell's Living Age*, February 6, 1864.

2-17
Sojourner Truth on Meeting Lincoln

Sojourner Truth (c.1797-1883) was an abolitionist and women's suffrage advocate. She met Lincoln on October 29, 1864. Truth recorded her account of their visit in a letter to a friend, excerpted here.

I t was about 8 o'clock a.m., when I called on the president. Upon entering his reception room we found about a dozen persons in waiting, among them two colored women. I had quite a pleasant time waiting until he was disengaged, and enjoyed his conversation with others; he showed as much kindness and consideration to the colored persons as to the whites—if there was any difference, more. One case was that of a colored woman who was sick and likely to be turned out of her house on account of her inability to pay her rent. The president listened to her with much attention, and spoke to her with kindness and tenderness. He said he had given so much he could give no more, but told her where to go and get the money, and asked Mrs. C———n to assist her, which she did.

This painting depicts Lincoln's meeting with abolitionist Sojourner Truth at the White House on October 29, 1864.

The president was seated at his desk. Mrs. C. said to him, "This is Sojourner Truth, who has come all the way from Michigan to see you." He then arose, gave me his hand, made a bow, and said, "I am pleased to see you."

I said to him, Mr. President, when you first took your seat I feared you would be torn to pieces, for I likened you unto Daniel, who was thrown into the lion's den; and if the lions did not tear you into pieces, I knew that it would be God that had saved you; and I said if he spared me I would see you before the four years expired, and he has done so, and now I am here to see you for myself.

He then congratulated me on my having been spared. Then I said, I appreciate you, for you are the best president who has ever taken the seat. He replied: "I expect you have reference to my having emancipated the slaves in my proclamation. But," said he, mentioning the names of several of his predecessors (and among them emphatically that of Washington), "they were all just as good, and would have done just as I have done if the time had come. If the people over the river [pointing across the Potomac] had behaved themselves, I could not have done what I have; but they did not, which gave me the opportunity to do these things." I then said, I thank God that you were the instrument selected by him and the people to do it. I told him that I had never heard of him before he was talked of for president. He smilingly replied, "I had heard of you many times before that."

He then showed me the Bible presented to him by the colored people of Baltimore, of which you have no doubt seen a description. I have seen it for myself, and it is beautiful beyond description. After I had looked it over, I said to him, This is beautiful indeed; the colored people have given this to the head of the government, and that government once sanctioned laws that would not permit its people to learn enough to enable them to read this book. And for what? Let them answer who can.

I must say, and I am proud to say, that I never was treated by any one with more kindness and cordiality than were shown to me by that great and good man, Abraham Lincoln, by the grace of God president of the United States for four years more. He took my little book, and with the same hand that signed the death-warrant of slavery, he wrote as follows:

"For Aunty Sojourner Truth,
Oct. 29, 1864.

      A. Lincoln."

As I was taking my leave, he arose and took my hand, and said he would be pleased to have me call again. I felt that I was in the presence of a friend, and I now thank God from the bottom of my heart that I always have advocated his cause, and have done it openly and boldly. I shall feel still more in duty bound to do so in time to come. May God assist me.

Source:

Truth, Sojourner. *Narrative of Sojourner Truth; A Bondswoman of Olden Time, With a History of Her Labors and Correspondence Drawn from Her "Book of Life."* Edited by Olive Gilbert. Battle Creek, MI: The Author, 1878.

2-18
Joshua Speed Remembers One of His Last Visits with Lincoln

Joshua Speed (1814-1882) was Lincoln's closest friend. They met in 1837 when Lincoln came to Springfield, and Speed provided lodging for Lincoln. In the excerpt below from a letter to William H. Herndon on January 12, 1866, Speed remembers one of his last visits with Lincoln, which took place around February 23, 1865.

The last interview but one I had with him—was about ten days previous to his last inauguration. . . . Visitors were coming & going to the President with their various complaints and grievances from morning till night with almost as much regularty as the ebb & flow of the tide. He was worn down in health & spirits—On this occasion I was sent for to come & see him—instructions were given that when I came I should be admitted—When I entered his office it was quite full and many more Senators & Members waiting—. . .

In the room when I entered I observed two ladies in humble attire—sitting across the fire place from where the President sat—modestly waiting their turn—One after another came & went, each and all of them bent on their own business— Some satisfied, and others grumbling—The hour had now come to close the door to all visitors. No one was left in the room except myself the two women & the President—

With rather a peevish & fretful air he turned to them and said "Well ladies what can I do for you?"

They both commenced to speak at once From what they said he soon learned that one was the wife and the other Mother of two men imprisoned for resisting the draft in Western Pennsylvania—

Stop said he—dont say any more—Give me your petition—The old lady responded—Mr. Lincoln—weve got no petition—we couldnt write one, and had no money to pay for writing one—I thought it best to come & see you—Oh said he—Dont say any thing more I understand your cases— He rang his bell & ordered one of the

133

Messengirs to tell Genl [Charles A.] Dana [Assistant Secretary of War] to bring him the names of all the men in prison for resisting the draft in Western Pennsylvania—The Genl soon came with the list—He inquired if there was any in the charges or degrees of guilt The General replied that he knew of none.

"Well said he these fellows have suffered long enough and I have thought so for some time and now that mind is on it, I believe I will turn out the *flock*"—So draw up the order General and let me sign it—It was done & the General left the room— Turning then to these women he said "now ladies you can go—"

The young woman ran forward & was about to kneel in thankfulness—Get up he said don't kneel to me—thank God & go.

The old woman came forward with tears in her eyes to say Good bye—goodbye said she Mr. Lincoln—I shall never see you again till we meet in Heaven—

She had the Presidents hand in hers—He instantly took her right hand in both of his and following her to the door & said I am afraid with all my troubles I shall never get there—But if I do I will find you—That you wish me to get there is the best wish you could make for me—good bye—

We were alone—I said to him—Lincoln with my knowledge of your nervous sesibility it is a wonder that such scenes as this dont kill you—I am said he very unwell—my feet & hands are always cold—I suppose I ought to be in bed—

But things of that sort dont hurt me—For to tell you the truth—that scene which you witnessed is the only thing I have done to day which has given me any pleasure—I have in that made two people happy—That old lady was no counterfeit—The Mother spoke out in all the features of her face—It is more than we can often say that in doing right we have made two people happy in one day—

"Speed die when I may I want it said of me by those who know me best to say that I always plucked a thistle and planted a flower where I thought a flower would grow—
. . .

There are some traits of character for which Lincoln was peculiar above all men I have ever known—He never forgot any thing espically any personal kindness—As an instance of this When he was in Ky in 1841 he was moody & hypochondriac—He was staying at the house of my Mother—She observed him and one morning when they were alone presented him with a Bible—Years rolled round & he was President— The old lady sent him word that she wanted his Photograph

He sent it with this sentence

"To my very good friend Mrs Lucy G Speed who gave me an Oxford bible Twenty years ago

      A. Lincoln"

Source:

Speed, Joshua. Letter to William H. Herndon, January 12, 1866. Herndon-Weik Collection, Manuscript Division, Library of Congress, Washington, D.C. Published in *Herndon's Informants: Letters, Interviews, and Statements about Abraham Lincoln.* Edited by Douglas L. Wilson, and Rodney O. Davis with the assistance of Terry Wilson. Urbana: University of Illinois Press, 1998.

2-19
Elizabeth Keckley Remembers Lincoln's Second Inaugural

Elizabeth Keckley (1818?-1907) was Mary Todd Lincoln's dressmaker and confidante. Keckley had regular contact with Lincoln and witnessed much of the day-to-day life in the household during Lincoln's presidency. She recorded her memories in an 1868 book, Behind the Scenes.

In this excerpt, Keckley remembers Lincoln's second inauguration. Before Lincoln was reelected in 1864, she had asked Mary Lincoln if she could have Lincoln's right-hand glove after his inauguration, to "cherish as a precious memento of the second inauguration of the man who has done so much for my race." The First Lady later fulfilled her request. Later in the excerpt, Keckley relates the account she heard from Frederick Douglass of his finally being admitted to the White House to congratulate Lincoln at a reception for his second inaugural in March 1865. (For the Second Inaugural Address, see document 7-9.)

Elizabeth Keckley.

I held Mrs. Lincoln to her promise. That glove is now in my possession, bearing the marks of the thousands of hands that grasped the honest hand of Mr. Lincoln on that eventful night. . . .

With the first early breath of spring, thousands of people gathered in Washington to witness the second inauguration of Abraham Lincoln as President of the United States. It was a stirring day in the National Capital, and one that will never fade from the memory of those who witnessed the imposing ceremonies. The morning was dark and gloomy; clouds hung like a pall in the sky, as if portending some great disaster. But when the President stepped forward to receive the oath of office, the clouds parted, and a ray of sunshine streamed from the heavens to fall upon and gild his face. It is also said that a brilliant star was seen at noon-day. It was the noon-day of life with Mr. Lincoln, and the star, as viewed in the light of subsequent events, was emblematic of a summons from on high. This was Saturday, and on Monday evening I went to the White House to dress Mrs. Lincoln for the first grand levee. While arranging Mrs. L.'s hair, the President came in. It was the first time I had seen him since the inauguration, and I went up to him, proffering my hand with words of congratulation.

He grasped my outstretched hand warmly, and held it while he spoke: "Thank you. Well, Madam Elizabeth"—he always called me Madam Elizabeth—"I don't know whether I should feel thankful or not. The position brings with it many trials. We do not know what we are destined to pass through. But God will be with us all. I put my trust in God." He dropped my hand, and with solemn face walked across the room and took his seat on the sofa. Prior to this I had congratulated Mrs. Lincoln, and she had answered with a sigh, "Thank you, Elizabeth; but now that we have won the position, I almost wish it were otherwise. Poor Mr. Lincoln is looking so broken-hearted, so completely worn out, I fear he will not get through the next four years." Was it a presentiment that made her take such a sad view of the future? News from the front was never more cheering. On every side the Confederates were losing ground, and the lines of blue were advancing in triumph. As I would look out my window almost every day, I could see the artillery going past on its way to the open space of ground, to fire a salute in honor of some new victory. From every point came glorious news of the success of the soldiers that fought for the Union. And yet, in their private chamber, away from the curious eyes of the world, the President and his wife wore sad, anxious faces.

I finished dressing Mrs. Lincoln, and she took the President's arm and went below. It was one of the largest receptions ever held in Washington. Thousands crowded the halls and rooms of the White House, eager to shake Mr. Lincoln by his hand, and receive a gracious smile from his wife. The jam was terrible, and the enthusiasm great. The President's hand was well shaken, and the next day, on visiting Mrs. Lincoln, I received the soiled glove that Mr. Lincoln had worn on his right hand that night.

Many colored people were in Washington, and large numbers had desired to attend the levee, but orders were issued not to admit them. A gentleman, a member of Congress, on his way to the White House, recognized Mr. Frederick Douglass, the eloquent colored orator, on the outskirts of the crowd.

"How do you do, Mr. Douglass? A fearful jam to-night. You are going in, of course?"

"No—that is, no to your last question."

"Not going in to shake the President by the hand! Why, pray?"

"The best reason in the world. Strict orders have been issued not to admit people of color."

"It is a shame, Mr. Douglass, that you should thus be placed under ban. Never mind; wait here, and I will see what can be done."

The gentleman entered the White House, and working his way to the President, asked permission to introduce Mr. Douglass to him.

"Certainly," said Mr. Lincoln. "Bring Mr. Douglass in, by all means. I shall be glad to meet him."

The gentleman returned, and soon Mr. Douglass stood face to face with the President. Mr. Lincoln pressed his hand warmly, saying: "Mr. Douglass, I am glad to meet you. I have long admired your course, and I value your opinions highly."

Mr. Douglass was very proud of the manner in which Mr. Lincoln received him. On leaving the White House he came to a friend's house where a reception was being held, and he related the incident with great pleasure to myself and others.

Source:

Keckley, Elizabeth. *Behind the Scenes; Or, Thirty Years a Slave, and Four Years in the White House.* New York: G. W. Carlton, 1868.

2-20
William H. Crook on Lincoln's Trip to Richmond Near the War's End

> *William H. Crook (1839-1915) was a police officer in Washington, D.C., who became one of Lincoln's bodyguards on January 4, 1865. As a result, Crook had close contact with the president during the last few months of his life. In the excerpts below, taken from Crook's memoir, he recalls two incidents, from April 3 and 4, 1865, during Lincoln's boat trip to Richmond after that city fell to Union troops.*

Just before we started back [for the boat after Lincoln met with General Grant after his victory at Petersburg, Virginia] a little girl came up with a bunch of wild flowers for the President. He thanked the child for them kindly, and we rode away. Soon after we got back to City Point news came of the evacuation of Richmond.

In the midst of the rejoicing some Confederate prisoners were brought aboard transports at the dock near us. The President hung over the rail and watched them. They were in a pitiable condition, ragged and thin; they looked half starved. When they

William H. Crook in later life.

were on board they took out of their knapsacks the last rations that had been issued to them before capture. There was nothing but bread, which looked as if it had been mixed with tar. When they cut it we could see how hard and heavy it was; it was more like cheese than bread.

"Poor fellow!" Mr. Lincoln said. "It's a hard lot. Poor fellows—"

I looked up. His face was pitying and sorrowful. All the happiness had gone. . . .

We did not start back until the next morning, so there was time for several rumors of designs against the President's life to get abroad. But although he saw many visitors, there was no attempt against him. Nothing worse happened than the interview with Mr. Duff Green.

Duff Green was a conspicuous figure at the time. He was a newspaper man, an ardent rebel. He always carried with him a huge staff, as tall as he was himself—and he was a tall man. Admiral Porter published an account of the interview in the New York *Tribune* of January, 1885, which was not altogether accurate. What really happened was this:

As Mr. Green approached him, the President held out his hand. Mr. Green refused to take it, saying, "I did not come to shake hands." Mr. Lincoln then sat down; so did Mr. Green. There were present at the time General Weitzel, Admiral Porter, one or two others, and myself. Mr. Green began to abuse Mr. Lincoln for the part he had taken in the struggle between the North and the south. His last words were,

"I do not know how God and your conscience will let you sleep at night after being guilty of the notorious crime of setting the n——s free."

The President listened to his diatribe without the slightest show of emotion. He said nothing. There was nothing in his face to show that he was angry. When Mr. Green had exhausted himself, he said,

"I would like, sir, to go to my friends."

The President turned to General Weitzel and said, "General, please give Mr. Green a pass to go to his friends." Mr. Green was set ashore, and was seen no more.

Source:

Crook, William H. *Through Five Administrations: Reminiscences of Colonel William H. Crook.* Compiled and edited by Margarita Spalding Gerry. New York: Harper & Brothers, 1910.

2-21
A News Account of Lincoln's Visit to Richmond

A reporter for the New York Times *wrote the following brief account of Lincoln's visit to Richmond, Virginia, after Confederate President Jefferson Davis evacuated the Southern government from the city.*

Visit of President Lincoln to Richmond—his interview with prominent citizens—immense enthusiasm of the colored population—the City perfectly tranquil.

Headquarters, Army of the James
Richmond, Tuesday, April 4, 1865.

The most interesting fact to be recorded to-day is the visit of the President to Richmond.

Mr. Lincoln, accompanied by his young son and Admiral Porter, arrived at the Rocketts at 2 P.M. in the *Malvern*, and proceeded at once to the mansion of Ex-President Davis, now the headquarters of Maj.-Gen. Weitzel.

The arrival of the President soon got noised abroad, and the colored population turned out in great force, and for a time blockaded the quarters of the President, cheering vociferously.

It was to be expected, that a population that three days since were in slavery, should evince a strong desire to look upon the man whose edict had struck forever the manacles from their limbs. A considerable number of the white population cheered the President heartily, and but for the order of the Provost-Marshal, issued yesterday, ordering them to remain within their homes quietly for a few days, without doubt there would have been a large addition to the number present. After a short interval the president held a levee—Gen. Devins introducing all the officers present. The President shook hands with each, and received the hearty congratulations of all.

The Presidential party, attended by Gens. Weitzel, Devins, Shepley, and a brilliant staff of officers, then made a tour round the city—drove rapidly round the capitol—

stopping for a few moments to admire Crawford's magnificent statue of Washington, in the grounds of the capitol, and returned to Gen. Weitzel's headquarters at 5:30.

The President and part left Richmond at 6:30 P.M.

Source:

"From Richmond." *New York Times*, April 8, 1865. Reprinted in *Abraham Lincoln, A Press Portrait: His Life and Times from the Original Newspaper Documents of the Union, the Confederacy, and Europe.* Edited by Herbert Mitgang. Chicago: Quadrangle Books, 1971.

2-22
Charles Carleton Coffin Describes the President's Entry into Richmond

Charles Carleton Coffin was the Civil War correspondent for the Boston Journal. *He signed this piece and others "Carleton." Here, he recounts the street scene in Richmond, Virginia, when President Lincoln visited the city after Confederate President Jefferson Davis evacuated the Southern government.*

I was standing upon the bank of the river, viewing the scene of desolation, when a boat pulled by twelve sailors came up stream. It contained President Lincoln and his son, Admiral Porter, Capt. Penrose of the army, Captain A. H. Adams of the navy, Lieut. W. W. Clemons of the signal corps. Somehow the Negroes on the bank of the river ascertained that the tall man wearing a black hat was President Lincoln. There was a sudden shout. An officer who had just picked up fifty Negroes to do work on the dock, found himself along. They left work, and crowded round the President. As he approached I said to a coloured woman,—

> "There is the man that made you free."
> "What, masssa?"
> "That is President Lincoln."
> "Dat President Linkum?"
> "Yes."

She gazed at him a moment, clapping her hands, and jumped straight up and down, shouting "Glory, glory, glory!" till her voice was lost in the universal cheer.

There was no carriage near, so the President, leading his son, walked three-quarters of a mile up to Gen. Weitzel's headquarters—Jeff Davis's mansion. What a spectacle it was! Such a hurly-burly—such wild, indescribable ecstatic joy I never witnessed. A coloured man acted as guide. Six sailors, wearing their round blue caps and short jackets and bagging pants, with navy carbines, was the advance guard. Then came the President and Admiral Porter, flanked by the officers accompanying him, and the correspondent of the *Journal,* then six more sailors with carbines—twenty of us all told—amid a surging mass of men, women and children, black, white, and yellow, running, shouting, dancing, swinging their caps, bonnets, and handkerchiefs. The soldiers saw him and swelled the crowd, cheering in wild enthusiasm. All could see him, he was so tall, so conspicuous.

One coloured woman, standing in a doorway, as the President passed along the sidewalk, shouted, "Thank you, dear Jesus, for this! Thank you, Jesus!" Another standing by her side was clapping her hands and shouting "Bless de Lord!"

A coloured woman snatched her bonnet from her head whirled it in the air, screaming with all her might, "God bless you, Massa Linkum!"

A few white women looking out from the houses waved their handkerchief. One lady in a large and elegant building looked awhile, and then turned away her head as if it was a disgusting sight.

President Lincoln walked in silence, acknowledging the salutes of officers and soldiers and of the citizens, *black and white!* It was the man of the people among the people. It was the great deliverer, meeting the delivered. Yesterday morning the majority of the thousands who crowded the streets and hindered our advance were slaves. Now they were free, and beheld him who had given them their liberty. Gen. Shepley met the President in the street, and escorted him to Gen. Weitzel's quarters. Major Stevens, hearing that the President was on his way, suddenly summoned a detachment of the Massachusetts 4th Cavalry, and cleared the way.

After a tedious walk, the mansion of Jeff Davis was reached. The immense crowd swept round the corner of the street and packed the space in front. Gen. Weitzel received the President at the door. Cheer upon cheer went up from the excited multitude, two-thirds of whom were coloured. . . .

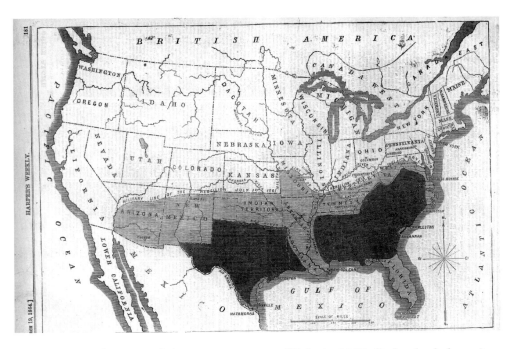

This map shows Confederate territory as of July 1, 1861 (light-shaded area) and in February 1864 (dark-shaded area). It was published in Harper's Weekly *on March 19, 1864.*

The President then took a ride through the city, accompanied by Admiral Porter, Gens. Shepley, Weitzel, and other officers. Such is the simple narrative of this momentous event; but no written page or illuminated canvas can give the reality of the event—the enthusiastic bearing of the people—the blacks and poor whites who have suffered untold horrors during the war, their demonstrations of pleasure, the shouting, dancing, the thanksgivings to God, the mention of the name of Jesus—as if President Lincoln were next to the son of God in their affections—the jubilant cries, the countenances beaming with unspeakable joy, the tossing up of caps, the swinging of arms of a motley crowd—some in rags, some barefoot, some wearing pants of Union blue, and coats of Confederate gray, ragamuffins in dress, through the hardships of war, but yet of stately bearing—men in heart and soul—men from whose limbs the chains fell yesterday morning, men who through many weary years have prayed for deliverance—who have asked sometimes if God were dead—who, when their children were taken from them and sent to the swamps of Carolina and the cane brakes of Louisiana, cried to God for help and cried in vain; who told their sorrows to Jesus and asked for help, but who had no helper—men who have been whipped, scourged, robbed, imprisoned, for no crime. All of these things must be kept in remembrance if we would have the picture complete.

No wonder that President Lincoln who has a child's heart, felt his soul stirred; that the tears almost came to his eyes as he heard from the thanksgivings to God and Jesus, and the blessings uttered for him from thankful hearts. They were true, earnest, and heart-felt expressions of gratitude to God. There were thousands of men in Richmond to-night who would lay down their lives for President Lincoln—their great deliverer, their best friend on earth. He came among them unheralded, without pomp or parade. He walked through the streets as if he were only a private citizen, and not the head of a mighty nation. He came not as a conqueror, not with bitterness in his heart, but with kindness, he came as a friend, to alleviate sorrow and suffering—to rebuild what has been destroyed.

Source:

Carleton [Charles Carleton Coffin]. "The President's Entry into Richmond." Originally printed in the *Boston Journal*. Reprinted in *Littell's Living Age*, April 22, 1865. Also reprinted in *Abraham Lincoln, A Press Portrait: His Life and Times from the Original Newspaper Documents of the Union, the Confederacy, and Europe.* Edited by Herbert Mitgang. Chicago: Quadrangle Books, 1971.

2-23
A Report on the "Ax Incident"

This piece from the New York Independent *relates the famous ax incident during Lincoln's visit to the soldiers' hospital at City Point, Virginia, on April 8, 1865, on his way back to Washington, D.C.*

On the Monday before the assassination, when the President was on his return from Richmond, he stopped at City Point. Calling upon the head surgeon at that place, Mr. Lincoln told him that he wished to visit all the hospitals under his charge, and shake hands with every soldier. The surgeon asked if he knew what he was undertaking, there being five or six thousand soldiers at that place, and it would be quite a tax upon his strength to visit all the wards and shake hands with every soldier. Mr. Lincoln answered with a smile, he "guessed he was equal to the task; at any rate he would try, and go as far as he could; he should never, probably, see the boys again, and he wanted them to know that he appreciated what they had done for their country."

Finding it useless to try to dissuade him, the surgeon began his rounds with the President, who walked from bed to bed, extending his hand to all, saying a few words of sympathy to some, making kind inquiries of others, and welcomed by all with the heartiest cordiality.

As they passed along, they came to a ward in which lay a Rebel who had been wounded and was a prisoner. As the tall figure of the kindly visitor appeared in sight he was recognized by the Rebel soldier, who, raising himself on his elbow in bed, watched Mr. Lincoln as he approached, and extending his hand exclaimed, while tears ran down his cheeks: "Mr. Lincoln, I have long wanted to see you, to ask your forgiveness for ever raising my hand against the old flag." Mr. Lincoln was moved to tears. He heartily shook the hand of the repentant Rebel, and assured him of his good-will, and with a few words of kind advice passed on.

After some hours the tour of the various hospitals was made, and Mr. Lincoln returned with the surgeon to his office. They had scarcely entered, however, when a messenger came saying that one ward had been omitted, and "the boys" wanted to see the President. The surgeon, who was thoroughly tired, and knew Mr. Lincoln must be, tried to dissuade him from going; but the good man said he must go back; he would not knowingly omit one, "the boys" would be disappointed. So he went with the messenger, accompanied by the surgeon, and shook hands with the gratified soldiers, and then returned again to his office.

The surgeon expressed the fear that the President's arm would be lamed with so much handshaking, saying that it certainly must ache. Mr. Lincoln smiled, and saying something about his "strong muscles," stepped out at the open door, took up a very large, heavy axe which lay there by a log of wood, and chopped vigorously for a few moments, sending the chips flying in all directions; and then, pausing, he extended his right arm to its full length, holding the axe horizontally, without it even quivering as he held it. Strong men who looked on—men accustomed to manual labor—could not hold the same axe in that position for a moment. Returning to the office, he took a glass of lemonade, for he would take no stronger beverage; and while he was within, the chips he had chopped were gathered up and safely cared for by a hospital steward, because the were "the chips that Father Abraham chopped." In a few hours more the beloved President was at home in Washington; in a few days more he had passed away and a bereaved nation was in mourning.

Source:

"Correspondence of the *New York Independent.*" *The Inner Life of Abraham Lincoln: Six Months at the White House* by Francis B. Carpenter. New York: Hurd and Houghton, 1868.

Part 3
The Man Behind the Legend

Lincoln was a strong president at a time the nation needed a tough and fair leader. Yet as the pieces in this section demonstrate, his sensitivity, sense of humor, and endearing humility also shone through to those around him. Most of these selections are excerpted from memoirs written by his acquaintances and employees recounting their experiences with the president. They shed light on Lincoln's domestic life and relationships with his family and acquaintances. They also demonstrate his love of Shakespeare and his gift for telling jokes and stories.

The opening pieces in this section consist of reminiscences by people close to Lincoln in the White House, sharing vignettes that offer moving glimpses of his personality. Selections by Elizabeth Keckley, William H. Crook, Noah Brooks, and Francis B. Carpenter describe Lincoln suffering during the Civil War, playing with one son and counseling another, enjoying family pets, and reciting Shakespeare from memory.

Lincoln loved to tell funny stories and had a seemingly endless repertoire. As many of his acquaintances remark, he often related jokes in order to persuade or illuminate a position or situation, evidently adhering to the maxim that one gathers more flies with sugar than with vinegar. Sculptor Leonard Wells Volk recalls humorous encounters with Lincoln while rendering his likeness. Humorist David R. Locke reflects on Lincoln's sense of humor and remembers their meetings, Henry Villard offers a picture of how Lincoln told stories, Albert B. Chandler gives an example of Lincoln's self-deprecating humor, and Henry Clay Whitney shares a joke Lincoln told. In addition to Lincoln's own stories, numerous books are full of poignant and humorous tales people have told about Lincoln. Several such anecdotes, collected by Alexander K. McClure, are also reprinted in this section.

3-1
Elizabeth Keckley Describes Some Domestic Scenes

Elizabeth Keckley (1818?-1907) was Mary Todd Lincoln's dressmaker and confidante. As such, Keckley had regular contact with Lincoln and witnessed much of the day-to-day life in the household during Lincoln's presidency. She recorded her memories in an 1868 book, Behind the Scenes. *In the following excerpt, Keckley recalls an incident in 1863, when the Union was faring poorly in the Civil War:*

These were sad, anxious days to Mr. Lincoln, and those who saw the man in privacy only could tell how much he suffered. One day he came into the room where I was fitting a dress on Mrs. Lincoln. His step was slow and heavy, and his face sad. Like a tired child he threw himself upon a sofa, and shaded his eyes with his hands. He was a complete picture of dejection. Mrs. Lincoln, observing his troubled look, asked:

"Where have you been, father?"

"To the War Department," was the brief, almost sullen answer.

"Any news?"

"Yes, plenty of news, but no good news. It is dark, dark everywhere."

He reached forth one of his long arms, and took a small Bible from a stand near the head of the sofa, opened the pages of the holy book, and soon was absorbed in reading them. A quarter of an hour passed, and on glancing at the sofa the face of the President seemed more cheerful. The dejected look was gone, and the countenance was lighted up with new resolution and hope. The change was so marked that I could not but wonder at it, and wonder led to the desire to know what book of the bible afforded so much comfort to the reader. Making the search for a missing article an excuse, I walked gently around the sofa, and looking into the open book, I discovered that Mr. Lincoln was reading that divine comforter, Job.

In this excerpt, Keckley offers a glimpse into Lincoln's feelings about Confederate General Robert E. Lee at the end of the Civil War, as well as his hopes for his son.

T he very morning of the day on which he was assassinated, his son, Capt. Robert Lincoln, came into the room with a portrait of General Lee in his hand. The President took the picture, laid it on a table before him, scanned the face thoughtfully, and said: "It is a good face; it is the face of a noble, noble, brave man. I am glad that the war is over at last." Looking up at Robert, he continued: "Well, my son, you have returned safely from the front. The war is now closed, and we soon will live in peace with the brave men that have been fighting against us. I trust that the era of good feeling has returned with the war, and that henceforth we shall live in peace. Now listen to me, Robert: you must lay aside your uniform, and return to college. I wish you to read law for three years, and at the end of that time I hope that we will be able to tell whether you will make a lawyer or not." His face was more cheerful than I had seen it for a long while, and he seemed to be in a generous, forgiving mood.

In the excerpt below, Keckley shares a charming memory of Lincoln's affection for the family's pet goats.

M r. Lincoln was fond of pets. He had two goats that knew the sound of his voice, and when he called them they would come bounding to his side. In the warm bright days, he and Tad would sometimes play in the yard with these goats, for an hour at a time. One Saturday afternoon I went to the White House to dress Mrs. Lincoln. I had nearly completed my task when the President came in. It was a bright day, and walking to the window, he looked down into the yard, smiled, and, turning to me, asked:

"Madam Elizabeth, you are fond of pets, are you not?"

"O yes, sir," I answered.

"Well, come here and look at my two goats. I believe they are the kindest and best goats in the world. See how they sniff the clear air, and skip and play in the sunshine.

Whew! what a jump," he exclaimed as one of the goats made a lofty spring. "Madam Elizabeth, did you ever before see such an active goat?" Musing a moment, he continued: "He feeds on my bounty, and jumps with joy. Do you think we could call him a bounty-jumper? But I flatter the bounty-jumper. My goat is far above him. I would rather wear his horns and hairy coat through life, than demean myself to the level of the man who plunders the national treasury in the name of patriotism. The man who enlists into the service for a consideration, and deserts the moment he receives his money but to repeat the play, is bad enough; but the men who manipulate the grand machine and who simply make the bounty-jumper their agent in an outra-

The Lincoln family's dog, Fido.

geous fraud are far worse. They are beneath the worms that crawl in the dark hidden places of earth."

His lips curled with haughty scorn, and a cloud was gathering on his brow. Only a moment the shadow rested on his face. Just then both goats looked up at the window and shook their heads as if to say, "How d'ye do, old friend?"

"See, Madam Elizabeth," exclaimed the President in a tone of enthusiasm, "my pets recognize me. How earnestly they look! There they go again; what jolly fun!" and he laughed outright as the goats bounded swiftly to the other side of the yard.

Source:

Keckley, Elizabeth. *Behind the Scenes; Or, Thirty Years a Slave, and Four Years in the White House.* New York: G.W. Carlton, 1868.

3-2
Noah Brooks and William H. Crook on Lincoln and Tad

Noah Brooks (1830-1903) was a journalist who met Lincoln in 1856. After Lincoln's election, Brooks reported on the president for the Sacramento Daily Union *and became one of his closest acquaintances. In this excerpt, Brooks relates a humorous exchange between Lincoln and his young son Tad on Election Day 1864.*

[O]n the day of his reelection], Lincoln was as bright and cheery as the beautiful November day. He had a new story of Tad's wit and humor; for the lad was very clever. Tad had burst into his father's office, early in the day, with the information that the detachment of Pennsylvania troops, quartered on the White House grounds, on the Potomac front, "were voting for Lincoln and Johnson." The excited lad insisted on his father's going to the window to see this spectacle. Seeing a pet turkey which had been spared from the cook's knife, at Christmas, in answer to Tad's tearful petition, Lincoln said, "What business had the turkey stalking about the polls in that way? Does he vote?"

"No," was the quick reply of the boy, "he's not of age."

William H. Crook (1839-1915) was a police officer in Washington, D.C., who became one of Lincoln's bodyguards on January 4, 1865. Crook was thus in a position to observe various sides of Lincoln. This selection is an excerpt from Crook's memoirs.

Since the death of the older boy, Willie, which almost broke his father's heart, Mr. Lincoln had kept Tad with him almost constantly. When he had a few minutes to spare he would make a child of himself to play with the boy. We all liked to see the President romp up and down the corridors with Tad, playing horse, turn and turn

*This print was based on a photograph of Lincoln
and his son, Tad, taken on February 5, 1865.*

155

about, or blind-man's-buff. Mr. Lincoln was such a sad-looking man usually, it seemed good to have him happy. And he was happy when he was playing with the boy. I am sure the times when he was really resting were when he was galloping around with Tad on his great shoulders.

Sources:

Excerpt 1: Brooks, Noah. "Personal Reminiscences of Lincoln." *Scribner's Monthly Magazine,* February-March 1878.

Excerpt 2: Crook, William H. *Through Five Administrations: Reminiscences of Colonel William H. Crook.* Compiled and edited by Margarita Spalding Gerry. New York: Harper & Brothers, 1910.

3-3
Francis B. Carpenter Describes Lincoln's Love of Shakespeare

Lincoln allowed artist Francis B. Carpenter (1830-1900) to spend six months in the White House working on his famous painting, First Reading of the Emancipation Proclamation. *In the following excerpt, Carpenter describes a sitting for the painting on March 2, 1864, where he was able to observe Lincoln's love of Shakespeare.*

Wednesday, March 2d, I had an unusually long and interesting sitting from the President. . .

resently the conversation turned upon Shakespeare, of whom it is well known Mr. Lincoln was very fond. He once remarked, "It matters not to me whether Shakespeare be well or ill acted; with him the thought suffices." Edwin Booth was playing an engagement at this time at Grover's Theater. He had been announced for the coming evening in his famous part of *Hamlet.* The President had never witnessed his representation of this character, and he proposed being present. The mention of this play, which I afterward learned had at all times a peculiar charm for Mr. Lincoln's mind, waked up a train of thought I was not prepared for. Said he,—and his words have often returned to me with a sad interest since his own assassination,—"There is one passage of the play of "Hamlet" which is very apt to be slurred over by the actor, or omitted altogether, which seems to me the choicest part of the play. It is the soliloquy of the king, after the murder. It always struck me as one of the finest touches of nature in the world."

Then, throwing himself into the very spirit of the scene, he took up the words:—

> "O my offence is rank, it smells to heaven;
> It hath the primal eldest curse upon 't,
> A brother's murder! —Pray can I not,
> Though inclination be as sharp as will;
> My stronger guilt defeats my strong intent;
> And, like a man to double business bound,
> I stand in pause where I shall first begin,
> And both neglect. What if this cursed hand
> Were thicker than itself with brother's blood?
> Is there not rain enough in the sweet heavens
> To wash it white as snow? Whereto serves mercy
> But to confront the visage of offence;
> And what's in prayer but this twofold force—
> To be forestalled ere we come to fall,
> Or pardoned, being down? Then I'll look up;
> My fault is past. But O what form of prayer
> Can serve my turn? Forgive me my foul murder?—
> That cannot be; since I am still possessed
> Of those effects for which I did the murder,—
> My crown, my own ambition, and my queen.
> May one be pardoned and retain the offence?
> In the corrupted currents of this world,
> Offence's gilded hand may shove by justice,
> And oft 't is seen the wicked prize itself
> Buys out the law; but 't is not so *above*.
> There is no shuffling; there the action lies
> In its true nature; and we ourselves compelled,

Event to the teeth and forehead of our faults,
To give in evidence. What then? what rests?
Try what repentance can; what can it not?
Yet what can it when one cannot repent?
O wretched state! O bosom black as death!
O bruised soul that, struggling to be free,
Art more engaged! Help, angels, make assay!
Bow, stubborn knees! And heart with strings of steel,
Be soft as sinews of the new-born babe;
All may be well!"

He repeated this entire passage from memory, with a feeling and appreciation unsurpassed by anything I ever witnessed upon the stage. Remaining in thought for a few moments, he continued:—

"The opening of the play of 'King Richard the Third' seems to me often entirely misapprehended. It is quite common for an actor to come upon the stage, and, in a sophomoric style, to begin with a flourish:—

"'Now is the winter of our discontent
Made glorious summer by this sun of York,
And all the clouds that lowered upon our house,
In the deep bosom of the ocean buried!'

Now," said he, "this is all wrong. Richard, you remember, had been, and was then, plotting the destruction of his brothers, to make room for himself. Outwardly, the most loyal to the newly crowned king, secretly he could scarcely contain his impatience at the obstacles still in the way of his own elevation. He appears upon the stage, just after the crowning of Edward, burning with repressed hate and jealousy. The prologue is the utterance of the most intense bitterness and satire."

Then, unconsciously assuming the character, Mr. Lincoln repeated, also from memory, Richard's soliloquy, rendering it with a degree of force and power that made it seem like a new creation to me. Though familiar with the passage from boyhood, I can truly say that never till that moment had I fully appreciated its spirit. I could not refrain from laying down my palette and brushes, and applauding heartily, upon his conclusion, saying, at the same time, half in earnest, that I was not sure but that he had made a mistake in the choice of a profession, considerably, as may be imagined, to his amusement. . .

Source:

Carpenter, Francis B. *The Inner Life of Abraham Lincoln: Six Months at the White House.* New York: Hurd and Houghton, 1868.

3-4
Leonard Wells Volk on Sculpting Lincoln

Leonard Wells Volk (1828-1895) was a sculptor who created several busts and statues of Lincoln in 1860 and 1861. In the following excerpt, Volk recounted his reminiscences of time spent with the president.

He entered my studio on Sunday morning, remarking that a friend at the hotel (Tremont House) had invited him to attend church, "but," said Mr. Lincoln, "I thought I'd rather come and sit for the bust. The fact is," he continued, "I don't like to hear cut and dried sermons. No—when I hear a man preach, I like to see him act as if he were fighting bees!" And he extended his long arms, at the same time suiting the action to the words. He gave me on this day a sitting of more than four hours, and when it was concluded, went to our family apartment, on the corner of the building across the corridor from the studio, to look at a collection of photographs which I had made in 1855–6–7, in Rome and Florence. While sitting in the rocking-chair, he took my little son on his lap and spoke kindly to him, asking his name, age, etc. I held the photographs up and explained them to him, but I noticed a growing weariness, and his eyelids closed occasionally as if he were sleepy, or were thinking of something besides Grecian and Roman statuary and architecture. Finally he said: "These things must be very interesting to you, Mr. Volk, but the truth is I don't know much of history, and all I do know of it I have learned from lawbooks."

This life-mask of Lincoln's face and hands was created by sculptor Leonard Wells Volk in 1860.

The sittings were continued daily till the Thursday following, and, during their continuance, he would talk almost unceasingly, telling some of the funniest and most laughable of stories, but he talked little of politics or religion during those sittings. He said: "I am bored nearly every time I sit down to a public dining-table by some one pitching into me on politics." Upon one occasion he spoke most enthusiastically of his profound admiration of Henry Clay, saying that he "almost worshiped him."

I remember, also, that he paid a high compliment to the late William A. Richardson, and said: "I regard him as one of the truest men that ever lived; he sticks to Judge Douglas through thick and thin—never deserted him, and never will. I admire such a man! By the way, Mr. Volk, he is now in town, and stopping at the Tremont. May I bring him with me tomorrow to see the bust?" Accordingly, he brought him and two other old friends, ex-Lieut.-Gov. McMurtry, of Illinois, and Ebenezer Peck, all of whom looked a moment at the clay model, saying it was "just like him!" Then they began to tell stories and rehearse reminiscences, one after another. I can imagine I now hear their hearty laughs, just as I can see, as if photographed, the tall figure of Lincoln striding across that stubble-field.

Many people, presumably political aspirants with an eye to future prospects, besieged my door for interviews, but I made it a rule to keep it locked, and I think Mr. Lincoln appreciated the precaution.

The last sitting was given Thursday morning, and I noticed that Mr. Lincoln was in something of a hurry. I had finished the head, but desired to represent his breast and brawny shoulders as nature presented them; so he stripped off his coat, waistcoat, shirt, cravat, and collar, threw them on a chair, pulled his undershirt down a short distance, tying the sleeves behind him, and stood up without a murmur for an hour or so. I then said that I was done, and was a thousand times obliged to him for his promptness and patience, and offered to assist him to redress, but he said: "No, I can do it better alone." I kept at my work without looking toward him, wishing to catch the form as accurately as possible while it was fresh in my memory. Mr. Lincoln left hurriedly, saying he had an engagement, and with a cordial "Good-bye! I will see you again soon," passed out. A few moments after, I recognized his steps rapidly returning. The door opened, and in he came, exclaiming: "Hello, Mr. Volk! I got down to the sidewalk and found I had forgotten to put on my undershirt, and thought it wouldn't do to go through the streets this way." Sure enough, there were the sleeves of that garment dangling below the skirts of his broadcloth frock coat! I went at once to his assistance, and helped to undress and re-dress him all right, and out he went, with a hearty laugh at the absurdity of the thing.

On a Thursday in the month of June [*May*] following, Mr. Lincoln received the nomination on the third ballot for President of the United States. And it happened that on the same day I was on the cars, nearing Springfield. About midday, we reached Bloomington, and there learned of his nomination. At three or four o'clock, we arrived at our destination. The afternoon was lovely—bright and sunny, neither too warm nor too cold; the grass, trees, and the hosts of blooming roses, so profuse in Springfield, appeared to be vying with the ringing bells and waving flags.

As soon as I had brushed off the dust and registered at the old Chenery House, I went straight to Mr. Lincoln's unpretentious little two-story house. He saw me from his door or window coming down the street, and as I entered the gate, he was on the platform in front of the door, and quite alone. His face looked radiant. I exclaimed: "I am the first man from Chicago, I believe, who has the honor of congratulating you on your nomination for President." Then those two great hands took both of mine with a grasp never to be forgotten. And while shaking, I said: "Now that you will doubtless be the next President of the United States, I want to make a statue of you, and shall do my best to do you justice." Said he, "I don't doubt it, for I have come to the conclusion that you are an honest man," and with that greeting I thought my hands were in a fair way of being crushed. I was invited into the parlor, and soon Mrs. Lincoln entered, holding a rose bouquet in her hand, which she presented to me after the introduction; and in return I gave her a cabinet-size bust of her husband, which I had modeled from the large one, and happened to have with me. Before leaving the house, it was arranged that Mr. Lincoln would give Saturday forenoon to obtaining full-length photographs to serve me for the proposed statue. . . .

The last time I saw Mr. Lincoln was in January, 1861, at his house in Springfield. His little parlor was full of friends and politicians. He introduced me to them all, and remarked to me aside that, since he had sat for me for his bust, he had lost forty pounds in weight. This was easily perceptible, for the lines of his jaws were very sharply defined through the short beard which he was allowing to grow. Then he returned to the company, and announced in a general way that I had made a bust of him before his nomination, and that he was then giving daily sittings, at the St. Nicholas Hotel, to another sculptor; that he had sat to him for a week or more, but could not see the likeness, though he might yet bring it out.

"But," continued Mr. Lincoln, "in two or three days after Mr. Volk commenced my bust, there was the animal himself!"

Source:

Volk, Leonard Wells. "The Lincoln Life-Mask and How It Was Made." *Century Magazine*, December 1881.

3-5
"On the Life-Mask of Abraham Lincoln" by Richard Watson Gilder

Richard Watson Gilder (1844-1909) was a poet and editor. He composed the following poem, "On the Life-Mask of Abraham Lincoln," after viewing the life mask created by Leonard Wells Volk (see document 3-4). The poem was published in The Century Illustrated Monthly Magazine *in the issue dated November 1886-April 1887.*

On the Life-Mask of Abraham Lincoln

This bronze doth keep the very form and mold
    Of our great martyr's face. Yes, this is he:
    That brow all wisdom, all benignity;
    That human, humorous mouth; those cheeks that hold
Like some harsh landscape all the summer's gold;
    That spirit fit for sorrow, as the sea
    For storms to beat on; the lone agony
    Those silent, patient lips too well foretold.
Yes, this is he who ruled a world of men
    As might some prophet of the elder day,—
    Brooding above the tempest and the fray
With deep-eyed thought and more than mortal ken.
    A power was his beyond the touch of art
    Or armed strength: It was his mighty heart.

Source:

Gilder, Richard Watson. "On the Life-Mask of Abraham Lincoln." *The Century Illustrated Monthly Magazine*, November 1886-April 1887.

3-6
David R. Locke Recounts Conversations with Lincoln

David R. Locke (1833-1888) was a humorist who wrote satire under the name Petroleum Vesuvius Nasby. Lincoln enjoyed Locke's work, and the two visited several times. In the excerpt below, Locke reminisces about some of those occasions.

To write recollections of Abraham Lincoln is a pleasant task. The greatest man, in some respects, who ever lived, and in all respects the most lovable—a man whose great work gave him the heart of every human being—with a heart—throughout the civilized world. It was an honor to know him, and more than an honor to be approved by him.

The first time I saw the great and good Lincoln (alas! That "great" and "good" cannot be more frequently associated in speaking of public men) was at Quincy, Ill., in October—I think it was—in 1858. It was at the close of the greatest political struggle this country ever witnessed. Stephen A. Douglas was the acknowledged champion of the Democratic Party, a position he had held unquestioned for years. He came into his heritage of leadership at an unfortunate time, just when the scepter was departing from the organization which he had headed, but he was especially unfortunate in being pitted against the most honest statesman in the opposition, a man whose face the Creator had set the assurance of absolute, unselfish integrity—of one whose outward seeming was a true index of the inward man. . .

I found Mr. Lincoln in a room of a hotel, surrounded by admirers, who had made the discovery that one who had previously been considered merely a curious compound of genius and simplicity was a really great man. When Lincoln was put forward as the antagonist of the hitherto invincible Douglas, it was with fear and trembling, with the expectancy of defeat; but this mature David of the new faith had met the Goliath of the old, and had practically slain him. He had swept over the State like a cyclone—not a raging, devastating cyclone, the noise of which equaled its destructive power, but a modest and unassuming force, which was the more powerful because the force could not be seen. It was the cause which won, but in other hands than Lincoln's it might have failed. Therefore, wherever he went crowds of admiring men followed him, all eager to worship at the new shrine around which such glories were gathering.

I succeeded in obtaining an interview with him after the crowd had departed, and I esteem it something to be proud of that he seemed to take a liking to me. He talked to me without reserve. It was many years ago, but I shall never forget it.

He sat in the room with his boots off, to relieve his very large feet from the pain occasioned by continuous standing; or, to put it in his own words: "I like to give my feet a chance to breathe." He had removed his coat and vest, dropped one suspender from his shoulder, taken off his necktie and collar, and thus comfortably attired, or rather unattired, he sat tilted back in one chair with his feet upon another in perfect ease. He seemed to dislike clothing, and in privacy wore as little of it as he could. I remember the picture as though I saw it but yesterday.

Those who accuse Lincoln of frivolity never knew him. I never saw a more thoughtful face, I never saw a more dignified face, I never saw so sad a face. He had humor of which he was totally unconscious, but it was not frivolity. He said wonderfully witty things, but never from a desire to be witty. His wit was entirely illustrative. He used it because, and only because, at times he could say more in this way, and better illustrate the idea with which he was pregnant. He never cared how he made a point so that he made it, and he never told a story for the mere sake of telling a story. When he did it, it was for the purpose

This photograph of Lincoln was taken in 1863 by Alexander Gardner.

of illustrating and making clear a point. He was essentially epigrammatic and parabolic. He was a master of satire, which was at times as blunt as a meat-ax, and at others as keen as a razor; but it was always kindly except when some horrible injustice was its inspiration, and then it was terrible. Weakness he was never ferocious with, but intentional wickedness he never spared.

In this interview the name came up of a recently deceased politician of Illinois, whose undeniable merit was blemished by an overweening vanity. His funeral was very largely attended: "If General—— had known how big a funeral he would have had," said Mr. Lincoln, "he would have died years ago."

But with all the humor in his nature, which was more than humor because it was humor with a purpose (that constituting the difference between humor and wit), his was the saddest face I ever looked upon.

His flow of humor was a sparkling spring gushing out of a rock—the flashing water had a somber background which made it all the brighter. Whenever merriment came over that wonderful countenance it was like a gleam of sunshine upon a cloud—it illuminated, but it did not dissipate. The premonition of fate was on him then; the shadow of the tragic closing of the great destiny in the beyond had already enveloped him.

At the time he said he should carry the State on the popular vote, but that Douglas would, nevertheless, be elected to the Senate, owing to the skillful manner in which the State had been districted in his interest. "You can't overturn a pyramid, but you can undermine it; that's what I have been trying to do.

He undermined the pyramid that the astute Douglas had erected most effectually. It toppled and fell very shortly afterward.

The difference between the two men was illustrated the next day in their opening remarks. Lincoln said (I quote from memory):

"I have had no immediate conference with Judge Douglas, but I am sure that he and I will agree that your entire silence when I speak and he speaks will be most agreeable to us."

Douglas said at the beginning of his speech: "The highest compliment *you can pay* ME is by observing strict silence. *I desire rather to be heard than applauded.*"

The inborn modesty of the one and the boundless vanity of the other could not be better illustrated. Lincoln claimed nothing for himself—Douglas spoke as if applause *must* follow his utterances.

The character of the two men was still better illustrated in their speeches. The self-sufficiency of Douglas in his opening might be pardoned, for he had been fed upon applause till he fancied himself a more than Caesar; but his being a popular idol could not justify the demagogy that saturated the speech itself. Douglas was the demagogue all the way through. There was no trick of presentation that he did not use. He suppressed facts, twisted conclusions, and perverted history. He wriggled and turned and dodged; he appealed to prejudices; in short, it was evident that what he was laboring for was Douglas and nothing else. The cause he professed was lost sight of in the claims of its advocate. Lincoln, on the other hand, kept strictly to the questions at issue, and no one could doubt but that the cause for which he was speaking was the only thing he had at heart; that his personal interests did not weigh a particle. He was the representative of an idea, and in the vastness of the idea its advocate was completely swallowed up.

Lincoln admitted frankly all the weak points in the position of his party in the most open way, and that simple honesty carried conviction with it. His admissions of weakness, where weakness was visible, strengthened his position on points where he was strong. He knew that the people had intelligence enough to strike the average correctly. His great strength was in his trusting the people instead of considering them as babes in arms. He did not profess to know everything. The audience admired Douglas, but they respected his simple-minded opponent.

Nothing so illustrates the fact that events are stronger than men, and that one attacking an evil can never commence using the little end of a club without changing very soon to the butt, that the position of Lincoln at this time. The Republican leaders, and Lincoln as well, were afraid of only one thing, and that was of having imputed to them any desire to abolish slavery. Douglas, in all the debates between himself and Lincoln, attempted to fasten Abolition upon him, and this it was Lincoln's chief desire to avoid. Great as he was, he had not then reached the point of declaring war upon slavery; he could go no farther than to protest against its extension into the territories, and that was pressed in so mild and hesitating a way as to rob it of half its point. Did he foresee that within a few years the irresistible force of events would compel him to demand its extinction, and that his hand would sign the document that killed it? Logic is mightier than man's reason. He did not realize that the reason for preventing its extension was the very best reason for its extinction. Anything that should be restricted should be killed. It took a war to bring about this conclusion. Liberty got its best growth from blood-stained fields.

I met Lincoln again in 1859, in Columbus, Ohio, where he made a speech, which was only a continuation of the Illinois debates of the year before. Douglas had been previously brought there by the Democracy, and Lincoln's speech was, in the main, an answer to Douglas. It is curious to note in this speech that Lincoln denied being in favor of negro suffrage, and took pains to go out of his way to affirm his support of the law of Illinois forbidding the intermarriage of whites and negroes.

I asked him if such a denial was worth while, to which he replied:

"The law means nothing. I shall never marry a negress, but I have no objection to any one else doing so. If a white man wants to marry a negro woman, let him do it— *if the negro woman can stand it.*"

By this time his vision had penetrated the future, and he had got a glimmering of what was to come. In his soul he knew what he should have advocated, but he doubted if the people were ready for the great movement of a few years later. Hence his halting at all the half-way houses.

> *The "Nasby Letters," which I began in 1861, attracted his attention, and he was very much pleased with them. He read them regularly. He kept a pamphlet which contained the first numbers of the series in a drawer in his table, and it was his wont to read them on all occasions to his visitors, no matter who they might be, or what their business was.*

"Slavery," said he, "is doomed, and that within a few years. Even Judge Douglas admits it to be an evil, and an evil can't stand discussion. In discussing it we have taught a great many thousands of people to hate it who had never given it a thought before. What kills the skunk is the publicity it gives itself. What a skunk wants to do is to keep snug under the barn—in the day-time, when men are around with shot-guns."

The discussions with Douglas made him the Republican nominee for the Presidency, and elected him President.

The "Nasby Letters," which I began in 1861, attracted his attention, and he was very much pleased with them. He read them regularly. He kept a pamphlet which contained the first numbers of the series in a drawer in his table, and it was his wont to read them on all occasions to his visitors, no matter who they might be, or what their business was. He seriously offended many of the great men of the Republican Party in this way. Grave and reverend Senators who came charged to the brim with important business—business on which the fate of the nation depended—took it ill that the President should postpone the consideration thereof while he read them a letter from "Saint's Rest, wich is in the state uv Noo Jersey," especially as grave statesmen, as a rule, do not understand humor, or comprehend its meaning or effect. . .

I was in Washington once more in 1864, when the great struggle was nearer its close. My business was to secure a pardon for a young man from Ohio, who had deserted under rather peculiar circumstances. When he enlisted he was under engagement to a young girl, and went to the front very certain of her faithfulness, as a young man should be, and he made a most excellent soldier, feeling that the inevitable "she" at home would be proud of him. It is needless to say that the young girl, being exceptionally pretty, had another lover, whom she had rejected for the young volunteer, and also, it is needless to add, that the stay-at-home rejected hated the accepted soldier with the utmost cordiality. Taking advantage of the absence of the favored lover, the discarded one renewed his suit with great vehemence, and rumors reached the young man at the front that his love had gone over to his enemy, and that he was in danger of losing her entirely. He immediately applied for a furlough, which was refused him, and half mad and reckless of consequences, deserted. He found the information he had received to be partially true, but he came in time. He married the girl, but was immediately arrested as a deserter, tried, found guilty, and sentenced to be shot. I stated the circumstances, giving the young fellow a good character, and the President at once signed a pardon.

"I want to punish the young man—probably in less than a year he will wish I had withheld the pardon. We can't tell, though. I suppose when I was a young man I should have done the same fool thing. . ."

A few months after, the rebellion collapsed, the country rejoiced in the peace that had been so long hoped for but so long delayed, and Abraham Lincoln was the world's hero. A few days later the bullet of a madman ended his career, and a world mourned.

I saw him, or what was mortal of him, on the mournful progress to his last resting-place, in his coffin. The face was the same as in life. Death had not changed the kindly countenance in any line. There was upon it the same sad look that it had worn always, though not so intensely sad as it had been in life. It was as if the spirit had come back to the poor clay, reshaped the wonderfully sweet face, and given it an expression of gladness that he had finally gone "where the wicked cease from troubling, and the weary are at rest." The face had an expression of absolute content, of relief, of throwing off a burden such as few men have been called upon to bear—a burden which few men could have borne. I had seen the same expression on his living face only a few times, when, after a great calamity, he had come to a great victory. It was the look of a worn man suddenly relieved.

Wilkes Booth did Abraham Lincoln the greatest service man could possibly do for him—he gave him peace.

Source:

Locke, David R. In *Reminiscences of Abraham Lincoln by Distinguished Men of His Time*. Edited by Allen Thorndike Rice. New York: North American Publishing Company, 1886.

3-7
Henry Villard Describes Lincoln's Storytelling

Henry Villard (1835-1900) was a journalist who first met Lincoln in 1858 when the latter ran for the U.S. Senate; he later reported on Lincoln's presidential campaign. In his memoirs, Villard recorded the following reminiscence of Lincoln's storytelling.

It was a most interesting study to watch the manner of his intercourse with his callers. As a rule, he showed remarkable tact in dealing with each of them, whether they were rough-looking Sangamon County farmers still addressing him familiarly as "Abe," sleek and pert commercial travelers, staid merchants, sharp politicians, or preachers, lawyers, or other professional men. He showed a very quick and shrewd perception of and adaptation to individual characteristics and peculiarities. He never evaded a proper question, or failed to give a fit answer. He was ever ready for an argument, which always had an original flavor, and, as a rule, he got the better in the discussion. There was, however, one limitation to the freedom of his talks with his visitors. A great many of them naturally tried to draw him out as to his future policy as President regarding the secession movement in the South, but he would not commit himself. The most remarkable and attractive feature of those daily "levees," however, was his constant indulgence of his story-telling propensity. Of course, all the visitors had heard of it and were eager for the privilege of listening to a practical illustration of his pre-eminence in that line. He knew this, and took special delight in meeting their wishes. He never was at a loss for a story or an anecdote to explain a meaning or enforce a point, the aptness of which was always perfect. His supply was apparently inexhaustible, and the stories sounded so real that it was hard to determine whether he repeated what he had heard from others, or had invented [them] himself.

None of his hearers enjoyed the wit—and wit was an unfailing ingredient—of his stories half as much as he did himself. It was a joy indeed to see the effect upon him. A high-pitched laughter lighted up his otherwise melancholy countenance with thorough merriment. His body shook all over with gleeful emotion, and when he felt particularly good over his performance, he followed his habit of drawing up his knees, with his arms around them, up to his very face, as I had seen him do in 1858.

Source:

Villard, Henry. *Memoirs of Henry Villard, Journalist and Financier, 1835-1900.* 2 vols. Boston: Houghton, Mifflin & Co., 1904. Reprinted in *Lincoln as I Knew Him: Gossip, Tributes, and Revelations from His Best Friends and Worst Enemies.* Edited by Harold Holzer. Chapel Hill, NC: Algonquin Books, 1999.

He never was at a loss for a story or an anecdote to explain a meaning or enforce a point, the aptness of which was always perfect. His supply was apparently inexhaustible, and the stories sounded so real that it was hard to determine whether he repeated what he had heard from others, or had invented [them] himself.

3-8
Albert B. Chandler on Lincoln's Hair and Newsboys

Albert B. Chandler (1840-?) was a cipher operator for Major Thomas Eckert, Assistant Secretary of War. As such, Chandler often found himself in Lincoln's company as the president routinely visited the office for news of the war. Chandler relayed the following incident to Harper's Monthly *magazine in 1866.*

The President was sitting by my table . . . one evening, as was his custom almost every evening, reading the dispatches of the afternoon. There was nothing in any of the dispatches of much importance. All was still without, save the peculiar nasal, whining cry of newsboys' song—"Philadelphia In-*qui*-ry!" The President laid down the last slip and his spectacles simultaneously, and caught up the newsboys' cry, repeating, "Philadelphia In-*qui*-ry!" in their very accent and key. After singing about three verses of the laconic song, he said: "Boys, did I ever tell you the joke the Chicago newsboys came on me?" And Albert and [David] Bates and Charley Tinker, the only audience of the President, as with one voice, said, "No," and intimated that they would like to know it. "Well," said Mr. Lincoln, "soon after I was nominated for President at Chicago, I went up one day, and one of the first really distinguished men who waited on me was a pictureman, who politely asked me to favor him with a sitting for my picture. Now at that time there were less photographs of my phiz than at present, and I went straightaway with the artist, who detained me but a moment, and took one of the most really life-like pictures I have ever seen of myself, from the fact that he gave me no *fixing* nor *positions*. But this stiff, ungovernable hair of mine was all sticking every way, very much as it is now, I suppose; and so the operation of his camera was but 'holding the mirror up to nature' [a quote from *Hamlet*]. I departed, and did not think of pictures again until that evening I was gratified and flattered at the cry of newsboys who had gone to vending the pictures: 'Ere's yer last picter of Old Abe! He'll look better when he gets his *hair* combed!'"

Source:

Chandler, Albert B. "The Editor's Drawer." *Harper's Monthly,* February 1866. Reprinted in *Abe Lincoln Laughing: Humorous Anecdotes from Original Sources by and about Abraham Lincoln.* Edited by Paul M. Zall. Knoxville: University of Tennessee Press, 1995.

3-9
Henry Clay Whitney Relates a Lincoln Quip about Weighty Men

Henry Clay Whitney (1831-1905) was an Illinois lawyer who traveled the Eighth Judicial Circuit with Lincoln and later worked on his Senate campaign. In his memoir, Whitney related the following joke.

[A New Jersey congressman] called on the President with two of his constituents, in order to see Lincoln, as they would a show. "Mr. President," said he, "this is Mr. X and Mr. Y., and they are among the weightiest men in Southern New Jersey." After they had gone Lincoln said: "I wonder that end of the state didn't tip up when they got off of it."

Source:

Whitney, Henry Clay. *Life on the Circuit with Lincoln.* Boston: Estes and Lauriat, 1892. Reprinted in *Abe Lincoln Laughing: Humorous Anecdotes from Original Sources by and about Abraham Lincoln.* Edited by Paul M. Zall. Knoxville: University of Tennessee Press, 1995.

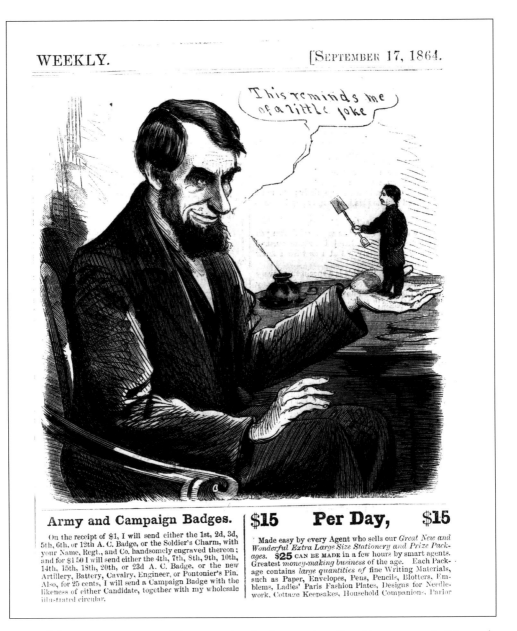

Lincoln's customary storytelling opening is the caption for this cartoon in Harper's Weekly, *September 17, 1864. The artist for the pro-Lincoln publication depicts a tiny George B. McClellan in Lincoln's hand shortly after McClellan announced his intention to run against Lincoln in the upcoming presidential campaign.*

3-10
Alexander K. McClure Shares Popular Anecdotes about Lincoln

Alexander K. McClure (1828-1909) was a Pennsylvania journalist who was acquainted with Lincoln and led his reelection campaign in Pennsylvania. Lincoln's reputation for honesty and compassion inspired many to tell stories illustrating these qualities. This section includes some popular anecdotes told about Lincoln that were collected by McClure and published in 1904. The veracity of these stories is uncertain, but they reflect the mythology Americans created on the basis of Lincoln's character.

Abe Lincoln's Honesty

Lincoln could not rest for an instant under the consciousness that, even unwittingly, he had defrauded anybody. On one occasion, while clerking in Offutt's store, at New Salem, he sold a woman a little bale of goods, amounting, by the reckoning, to $2.20. He received the money, and the woman went away.

On adding the items of the bill again to make himself sure of its correctness, he found that he had taken six and a quarter cents too much.

It was night, and, closing and locking the store, he started out on foot, and a distance to two or three miles, for the house of his defrauded customer, and delivering to her the sum whose possession had so much troubled him, went home satisfied.

On another occasion, just as he was closing the store for the night, a woman entered and asked for a half pound of tea. The tea was weighed out and paid for, and the store was left for the night.

The next morning, Lincoln, when about to begin the duties of the day, discovered a four-ounce weight on the scales. He saw at once that he had made a mistake, and, shutting the store, he took a long walk before breakfast to deliver the remainder of the tea.

These are very humble incidents, but they illustrate the man's perfect conscientiousness—his sensitive honesty—better, perhaps, than they would if they were of greater moment.

The Boy That Hungered for Knowledge

In his eagerness to acquire knowledge, young Lincoln had borrowed of Mr. Crawford, a neighboring farmer, a copy of *Weems' Life of Washington*—the only one known to be in existence in that section of country. Before he had finished reading the book, it had been left, by a not unnatural oversight, in a window. Meantime, a rainstorm came on, and the book was so thoroughly wet as to make it nearly worthless. This mishap caused him much pain; but he went, in all honesty, to Mr. Crawford with the ruined book, explained the calamity that had happened through his neglect, and offered, not having sufficient money, to "work out" the value of the book.

"Well, Abe", said Mr. Crawford, after due deliberation, "as it's you, I won't be hard on you. Just come over and pull fodder for me for two days, and we will call our accounts even."

The offer was readily accepted, and the engagement literally fulfilled. As a boy, no less than since, Abraham Lincoln had an honorable conscientiousness, integrity, industry, and an ardent love of knowledge.

Young Lincoln's Kindness of Heart

An instance of young Lincoln's practical humanity at an early period of his life is recorded, as follows: One evening, while returning from a "raising" in his wide neighborhood, with a number of companions, he discovered a straying horse, with saddle and bridle upon him. The horse was recognized as belonging to a man who was accustomed to excess in drink, and it was suspected at once that the owner was not far off. A short search only was necessary to confirm the suspicions of the young men.

The poor drunkard was found in a perfectly helpless condition, upon the chilly ground. Abraham's companions urged the cowardly policy of leaving him to his fate, but young Lincoln would not hear to the proposition. At his request, the miserable sot was lifted to his shoulders, and he actually carried him eighty rods to the nearest house. Sending word to his father that he should not be back that night, with the reason for his absence, he attended and nursed the man until the morning, and had the pleasure of believing that he had saved his life.

How Lincoln and Judge B——— Swapped Horses

When Abraham Lincoln was a lawyer in Illinois, he and a certain Judge once got to bantering one another about trading horses; and it was agreed that next morning at 9 o'clock they should make a trade, the horses to be unseen up to that hour, and no backing out, under a forfeiture of $25.

At the hour appointed the Judge came up, leading the sorriest-looking specimen of a horse ever seen in those parts. In a few minutes Mr. Lincoln was seen approaching with a wooden sawhorse upon his shoulders. Great were the shouts and the laughter of the crowd, and both were greatly increased when Mr. Lincoln, on surveying the Judge's animal, set down his saw-horse and exclaimed: "Well, Judge, this is the first time I ever got the worst of it in a horse trade."

The Question of Legs

Whenever the people of Lincoln's neighborhood engaged in dispute; whenever a bet was to be decided; when they differed on points of religion or politics; when they wanted to get out of trouble, or desired advice regarding anything on the earth, below it, above it, or under the sea, they went to "Abe."

Two fellows, after a hot dispute lasting some hours, over the problem as to how long a man's legs should be in proportion to the size of his body, stamped into Lincoln's office one day and put the question to him.

Lincoln listened gravely to the arguments advanced by both contestants, spent some time in "reflecting" upon the matter, and then, turning around in his chair and facing the disputants, delivered his opinion with all the gravity of a judge sentencing a fellow-being to death.

"This question has been a source of controversy," he said, slowly and deliberately, "for untold ages, and it is about time it should be definitely decided. It has led to bloodshed in the past, and there is no reason to suppose it will not lead to the same in the future.

"After much thought and consideration, not to mention mental worry and anxiety, it is my opinion, all side issues being swept aside, that a man's lower limbs, in order to preserve harmony of proportion, should be at least long enough to reach from his body to the ground."

A Famous Story—How Lincoln Was Presented with a Knife!

"In the days when I used to be 'on the circuit," said Lincoln, "I was accosted in the cars by a stranger, who said:

"'Excuse me, sir, but I have an article in my possession which belongs to you.'

"'How is that?' I asked, considerably astonished.

"The stranger took a jack-knife from his pocket. 'This knife,' said he, 'was placed in my hands some years ago, with the injunction that I was to keep it until I found a man uglier than myself. I have carried it from that time to this. Allow me now to say, sir, that I think you are fairly entitled to the property.'"

Lincoln's Confab with a Committee on Grant's Whisky

J ust previous to the fall of Vicksburg, a self-constituted committee, solicitous for the morale of our armies, took it upon themselves to visit the President and urge the removal of General Grant.

In some surprise Mr. Lincoln inquired, "For what reason?"

"Why," replied the spokesman, "he drinks too much whisky."

"Ah!" rejoined Mr. Lincoln, dropping his lower lip. "By the way, gentlemen, can either of you tell my where General Grant procures his whisky? Because, if I can find out, I will send every general in the field a barrel of it!"

Slow Horse

O n the occasion when Mr. Lincoln was going to attend a political convention one of his rivals, a liveryman, provided him with a slow horse, hoping that he would not reach his destination in time. Mr. Lincoln got there, however, and when he returned with the horse he said: "You keep this horse for funerals, don't you?" "Oh, no," replied the liveryman. "Well, I'm glad of that, for if you did you'd never get a corpse to the grave in time for the resurrection."

Source:

McClure, Alexander K. *"Abe" Lincoln's Yarns and Stories: A Complete Collection of the Funny and Witty Anecdotes That Made Lincoln Famous as America's Greatest Story Teller.* Chicago: The Educational Company, 1904.

Part 4
The Death of Lincoln

The assassination of Lincoln on April 14, 1865, came as a tremendous shock to the nation. Americans reeled from the news—not only because he was widely beloved, and not only because this was the first time an American president was killed in office, but also because the Civil War had ended with the surrender of Confederate General Robert E. Lee just days before. Americans were still celebrating the war's end when the tragic news came. Even Lincoln's bodyguard, William H. Crook, who recounts Lincoln's last day in the first selection, admits he did not feel as vigilant once they had left Richmond after the fall of that city.

Other essays included here recount those early reactions. Walt Whitman, in a well-known lecture, furnishes a dramatic account of the scene of the assassination at Ford's Theatre. Elizabeth Keckley remembers her efforts that night to go comfort the First Lady, her employer. Secretary of War Edwin M. Stanton and Assistant Secretary of the Treasury Maunsell B. Field rushed to Lincoln's side after he had been taken to a house near the theatre. Their first-hand accounts of that night are included as well. In addition, Caroline Richards, Lucretia Mott, and Jane Addams offer their perspectives on the immediate impact of the tragedy.

Lincoln was eulogized across the nation. One of the first such events was a funeral service conducted at the White House on April 19. Lincoln's body was then placed on a funeral train, which left Washington, D.C., on April 21 and traveled to several cities before bringing Lincoln's body to rest at Oak Ridge Cemetery in Springfield, Illinois. At many stops across the nation, memorial services were held for the fallen leader. Excerpts follow from eulogies given by Ralph Waldo Emerson in Concord, New Hampshire, on April 19; Henry Ward Beecher in Brooklyn, New York, Seth Sweetser in Worcester, Massachusetts, and Phillips Brooks in Philadelphia, Pennsylvania, all on April 23; Matthew Simpson, who conducted the burial service in Springfield on May 4; and Charles Sumner in Boston, Massachusetts, on June 1.

After Lincoln's death, many poetic tributes were written in his honor. William Cullen Bryant, James Russell Lowell, and Walt Whitman wrote several memorial poems after Lincoln's death, all reprinted in this section.

4-1
William H. Crook Remembers Lincoln's Last Day

William H. Crook (1839-1915) was a police officer in Washington, D.C., who became one of Lincoln's bodyguards on January 4, 1865. In the excerpt below, Crook recounts the time he spent with Lincoln on the day of the assassination.

During the next three days—as, in fact, since the fall of Richmond—Washington was a little delirious. Everybody was celebrating. . . . Every day there was a stream of callers who came to congratulate the President, to tell how loyal they had been, and how they had always been sure he would be victorious. . . . Those about the President lost somewhat of the feeling, usually present, that his life was not safe. It did not seem possible that, now that the war was over and the government . . . had been so magnanimous in its treatment of General Lee, after President Lincoln had offered himself a target for Southern bullets in the streets of Richmond and had come out unscathed, there could be danger. For my part, I had drawn a full breath of relief after we got out of Richmond, and had forgotten to be anxious since.

Because of the general joyousness, I was surprised when, late on the afternoon of the 14th, I accompanied Mr. Lincoln on a hurried visit to the War Department, I found that the President was more depressed than I had ever seen him and his step unusually slow. Afterward Mrs. Lincoln told me that when he drove with her to the Soldiers' Home earlier in the afternoon he had been extremely cheerful, even bouyant. She said that he had talked of the calm future that was in store for them, of the ease which they had never known, when, his term over, they would go back to their home in Illinois. He longed, a little wistfully, for that time to come, with its promise of peace. The depression I noticed may have been due to one of the sudden changes in mood to which I have been told the President was subject. I had heard of the transitions from almost wild spirits to abject melancholy which marked him. I had never seen anything of the sort, and had concluded that all this must have belonged to his earlier days. In the time when I knew him his mood, when there was no outside sorrow to disturb him, was one of settled calm. I wondered at him that day and felt uneasy.

In crossing over to the War Department we passed some drunken men. Possibly their violence suggested the thought to the President. After we had passed them, Mr. Lincoln said to me,

"Crook, do you know, I believe there are men who want to take my life?" Then, after a pause, he said, half to himself, "And I have no doubt they will do it."

The conviction with which he spoke dismayed me. I wanted to protest, but his tone had been so calm and sure that I found myself saying, instead, "Why do you think so, Mr. President?"

"Other men have been assassinated," was his reply, still in that manner of stating something to himself.

All I could say was, "I hope you are mistaken, Mr. President."

We walked a few paces in silence. Then he said, in a more ordinary tone:

"I have perfect confidence in those who are around me—in every one of you men. I know no one could do it and escape alive. But if it is to be done, it is impossible to prevent it."

By this time we were at the War Department, and he went in to his conference with Secretary Stanton. It was shorter than usual that evening. Mr. Lincoln had been belated. When Mrs. Lincoln and he came home from their drive he had found friends awaiting him. He had slipped away from dinner, and there were more people waiting to talk to him when he got back. He came out of the Secretary's office in a short time. Then I saw that every trace of depression, or perhaps I should say intense seriousness, which had surprised me before had vanished. He talked to me as usual. He said that Mrs. Lincoln and he, with a party, were going to the theatre to see *Our American Cousin.*

"It has been advertised that we will be there," he said, "and I cannot disappoint the people. Otherwise I would not go. I do not want to go."

I remember particularly that he said this, because it surprised me. The President's love for the theatre was well known. He went often when it was announced that he would be there; but more often he would slip away, alone or with Tad, get into the theatre, unobserved if he could, watch the play from the back of the house for a short time, and then go back to his work. Mr. Buckingham, the doorkeeper of Ford's Theatre, used to say that he went in just to "take a laugh." So it seemed unusual to hear him say he did not want to go. When we had reached the White House and he had climbed the steps he turned and stood there a moment before he went in. Then he said,

The last photograph of Lincoln, taken on April 10, 1865,
four days before he was assassinated.

"Good-bye, Crook."

It startled me. As far as I remember he had never said anything but "Good-night, Crook," before. Of course, it is possible that I may be mistaken. In looking back, every word that he said has significance. But I remember distinctly the shock of surprise and the impression, at the time, that he had never said it before.

By this time I felt queer and sad. I hated to leave him. But he had gone in, so I turned away and started on my way home. . . .

More and more persons who have heard that I was with Mr. Lincoln come to me asking,

"What was he like?"

These last years, when, at a Lincoln birthday celebration or some other memorial gathering, they ask for a few words from the man who used to be Abraham Lincoln's guard, the younger people look at me as if I were some strange spectacle—a man who lived by Lincoln's side. It has made me feel as if the time had come when I ought to tell the world the little that I know about him. Soon there will be nothing of him but the things that have been written.

Yet, when I try to say what sort of a man he seemed to me, I fail. I have no words. All I can do is to give little snatches of reminiscences—I cannot picture the man. I can say:

He is the only man I ever knew the foundation of whose spirit was love. That love made him suffer. I saw him look at the ragged, hungry prisoners at City Point, I saw him ride over the battle-fields at Petersburg, the man with the hole in his forehead and the man with both arms shot away lying, accusing, before his eyes. I saw him enter into Richmond, walking between lanes of silent men and women who had lost their battle. I remember his face . . . . And yet my memory of him is not of an unhappy man. I hear so much to-day about the President's melancholy. It is true no man could suffer more. But he was very easily amused. I have never seen a man who enjoyed more anything pleasant or funny that came his way. I think the balance between pain and pleasure was fairly struck, and in the last months when I knew him he was in love with life because he found it possible to do so much. . . . I never saw evidence of faltering. I do not believe anyone ever did. From the moment he, who was all pity, pledged himself to war, he kept straight on.

I can follow Secretary John Hay and say, He was the greatest man I have ever known—or shall ever know.

That ought to be enough to say, and yet—nothing so merely of words seems to express him. Something that he did tells so much more.

I remember one afternoon, not long before the President was shot, we were on our way to the War Department, when we passed a ragged, dirty man in army clothes lounging just outside the White House enclosure. He had evidently been waiting to see the President, for he jumped up and went toward him with his story. He had been wounded, was just out of the hospital—he looked forlorn enough. There was something he wanted the President to do; he had papers with him. Mr. Lincoln was in a hurry, but he put out his hands for the papers. Then he sat down on the curbstone, the man beside him, and examined them. When he had satisfied himself about the matter, he smiled at the anxious fellow reassuringly and told him to come back the next day; then he would arrange the matter for him. A thing like that says more than any man could express.

Source:

Crook, William H. "A New Phase of the Assassination." In *Through Five Administrations: Reminiscences of Colonel William H. Crook.* Compiled and edited by Margarita Spalding Gerry. New York: Harper & Brothers, 1910.

4-2
Walt Whitman Describes the Scene of the Assassination

Walt Whitman (1819-1892) is well known for his poems about Lincoln, but he also wrote a popular lecture about Lincoln's death, excerpted below. He delivered this lecture in New York City on April 14, 1879, and also in Philadelphia in 1880 and in Boston in 1881.

The day (April 14, 1865) seems to have been a pleasant one throughout the whole land—the moral atmosphere pleasant, too—the long storm, so dark, so fratricidal, full of blood and doubt and gloom, over and ended at last by the sunrise of such an absolute National victory, and utter breaking down of secessionism—we almost doubted our senses! Lee had capitulated beneath the apple tree at Appomattox. The other armies, the flanges of the revolt, swiftly followed.

And could it really be, then? Out of all the affairs of this world of woe and passion, of failure and disorder and dismay, was there really come the confirmed, unerring sign of peace, like a shaft of pure light—of rightful rule—of God?

But I must not dwell on accessories. The deed hastens. The popular afternoon paper, the little Evening Star, had scattered all over its third page, divided among the advertisements in a sensational manner in a hundred different places: "The President and his lady will be at the theatre this evening." Lincoln was fond of the theatre. I have myself seen him there several times. I remember thinking how funny it was that he, in some respects the leading actor in the greatest and stormiest drama known to real history's stage through centuries, should sit there an be so completely interested in those human jack-straws, moving about with their silly little gestures, foreign spirit, and flatulent text.

So the day, as I say, was propitious. Early herbage, early flowers, were out. I remembered where I was stopping at the time, the season being advanced there were many lilacs in full bloom. By one of those caprices that enter and give tinge to events without being at all a part of them, I find myself always reminded of the great tragedy of that day by the sight and odor of these blossoms. It never fails.

On this occasion the theatre was crowded, many ladies in rich and gay costumes, officers in their uniforms, many well-known citizens, young folks, the usual clusters of gas-lights, the usual magnetism of so many people, cheerful, with perfumes, music of violins and flutes—and over all, and saturating, that vast, vague wonder, Victory, the Nation's victory, the triumph of the Union, filling the air, the thought, the sense, with exhilaration more than all perfumes.

The President came betimes and, with his wife, witnessed the play, from the large stage boxes of the second tier, two thrown into one, and profusely draped with the National flag. The acts and scenes of the piece—one of those singularly witless compositions which have at least the merit of giving entire relief to an audience engaged in mental action or business excitements and cares during the day, as it makes not the slightest call on either the moral, emotional, esthetic or spiritual nature—a piece ("Our American Cousin") in which, among other characters so called, a Yankee, certainly such a one as was never seen, or at least ever seen in North America, is introduced in England, with a varied fol-de-rol of talk, plot, scenery, and such phantasmagoria as goes to make up a modern popular drama—had progressed through perhaps a couple of its acts, when in the midst of this comedy, or tragedy, or non-such, or whatever it is to be called, and to offset it, or finish it out, as if in Nature's and the Great Muse's mockery of these poor mimics, come interpolated that scene, not really or exactly to be described at all (for on the many hundreds who were there it seems to this hour to have left little but a passing blur, a dream, a blotch)—and yet partially to be described as I now proceed to give it:

On this occasion the theatre was crowded, many ladies in rich and gay costumes, officers in their uniforms, many well-known citizens, young folks, the usual clusters of gas-lights, the usual magnetism of so many people, cheerful, with perfumes, music of violins and flutes—and over all, and saturating, that vast, vague wonder, Victory, the Nation's victory, the triumph of the Union, filling the air, the thought, the sense, with exhilaration more than all perfumes.

There is a scene in the play representing the modern parlor, in which two unprecedented English ladies are informed by the unprecedented and impossible Yankee that he is not a man of fortune, and therefore undesirable for marriage catching purposes;

after which, the comments being finished, the dramatic trio make exit, leaving the stage clear for a moment. There was a pause, a hush, as it were. At this period came the murder of Abraham Lincoln. Great as that was, with all its manifold train circling around it, and stretching into the future for many a century, in the politics, history, art, etc., of the New World, in point of fact, the main thing, the actual murder, transpired with the quiet and simplicity of any commonest occurrence—the bursting of a bud or pod in the growth of vegetation, of instance.

Through the general hum following the stage pause, with the change of positions, etc., came the muffled sound of a pistol shot, which not one-hundredth part of the audience heard at the same time—and yet a moment's hush—somehow, surely a vague, startled thrill—and then, through the ornamented, draperied, starred, and striped space way of the President's box, a sudden figure, a man, raises himself with hands and feet, stands a moment on the railing, leaps below to the stage (a distance of perhaps 14 or 15 feet), falls out of position, catching his boot heel in the copious drapery (the American flag), falls on one knee, quickly recovers himself, rises as if nothing had happened (he really sprains his ankle, but unfelt then)—and the figure, Booth the murderer, dressed in plain black broadcloth, bare-headed, with a full head of glossy, raven hair, and his eyes, like some mad animal's flashing with light and resolution, yet with a certain strange calmness, holds aloft in one hand a large knife—walks along not much back of the foot-lights—turns fully towards the audience his face of statuesque beauty, lit by those basilisk eyes, flashing with desperation, perhaps insanity—launches out in a firm and steady voice the words *Sic Semper Tyrannis*—and then walks with neither slow nor very rapid pace diagonally across to the back of the stage, and disappears. (Had not all this terrible scene—making the mimic ones preposterous—had it not all been rehearsed, in blank, by Booth, beforehand?)

A moment's hush, incredulous—a scream—the cry of murder—Mrs. Lincoln leaning out of the box, with ashy cheeks and lips, with involuntary cry, pointing to the retreating figure, "He has killed the President." And still a moment's strange, incredulous suspense—and then the deluge!—then that mixture of horror, noises, uncertainty—(the sound, somewhere back, of a horse's hoofs clattering with speed) the people burst through chairs and railings, and break them up—that noise adds to the queerness of the scene—there is extricable confusion and terror—women faint—quite feeble persons fall, and are trampled on—many cries of agony are heard—the broad stage suddenly fills to suffocation with a dense and motley

Lincoln was sitting in this private box at Ford's Theatre when he was shot.

crowd, like some horrible carnival—the audience rush generally upon it—at least the strong men do—the actors and actresses are there in their play costumes and painted faces, with moral fright showing through the rouge—some trembling, some in tears, the screams and calls, confused talk—redoubled, trebled—two or three manage to pass up water from the stage to the President's box—others try to clamber up—etc., etc.

191

In the midst of all this the soldiers of the President's Guard, with others, suddenly drawn to the scene burst in—some 200 altogether—they storm the house, through all the tiers, especially the upper ones—inflamed with fury, literally charging the audience with fixed bayonets, muskets and pistols, shouting "Clear out! Clear out! … Such the wild scene, or a suggestion of it, rather inside the playhouse that night.

Outside, too, in the atmosphere of shock and craze, crowds of people filled with frenzy, ready to seize any outlet for it, came near committing murder several times on innocent individuals. One such case was especially exciting. The infuriated crowd, through some chance, got started against one man, either for words he uttered, or perhaps without any cause at all, and were proceeding at once to hang him on a neighboring lamp-post, when he was rescued by a few heroic policemen, who placed him in their midst and fought their way slowly and amid great peril toward the station house. It was a fitting episode of the whole affair. The crowd rushing and eddying to and fro, the night, the yells, the pale faces, many frightened people trying in vain to extricate themselves, the attacked man, not yet freed from the jaws of death, looking like a corpse, the silent, resolute half dozen policemen, with no weapons but their little clubs, yet stern and steady through all those eddying swarms—made indeed a fitting side scene to the grand tragedy of the murder. They gained the station house with the protected man, whom they placed in security for the night and discharged in the morning.

And in the midst of that night pandemonium of senseless hate, infuriated soldiers, the audience and the crowd—the stage, and all its actors and actresses, its paint pots, spangles and gaslight—the life blood from those veins, the best and sweetest of the land, drips slowly down….

Thus ended the attempted secession of these States; thus the four years' war. But the main things come subtly and invisibly afterward, perhaps long afterward—neither military, political, nor (great as those are) historical. I say, certain secondary and indirect results, out of the tragedy of this death, are, in my opinion, greatest. Not the event of the murder itself. Not that Mr. Lincoln strings the principal points and personages of the period, like beads, upon the single string of his career. Not that his idiosyncrasy, in its sudden appearance and disappearance, stamps this Republic with a stamp more mark'd and enduring than any yet given by any one man—(more even than Washington's)—but, join'd with these, immeasurable value and meaning of that whole tragedy lies, to me, in senses finally dearest to a nation (and here all our own)—the imaginative and artistic senses—the literary and dramatic ones. Not in any common or low meaning of those terms, but a meaning precious to the race, and to every age. A long and varied series of contradictory events arrives at last at its highest poetic, single, central, pictorial denouement. The whole involved, baffling, multiform whirl of the secession period comes to a head, and is gather'd in one brief flash of lightning-illumination—one simple, fierce deed. Its sharp culmination, and as it were solution, of so many bloody and angry problems, illustrates those climax-moments on the stage of universal Time, where the historic Muse at one entrance, and the tragic Muse at the other, suddenly ringing down the curtain, close an immense act in the long drama of creative thought, and give it radiation, tableau, stranger than fiction. Fit radiation—fit close! How the imagination—how the student loves these things! America, too, is to have them. For not in all great deaths, nor far or near—not Caesar in the Roman senate house, nor Napoleon passing away in the wild night-storm at St. Helena—not Paleologus, falling, desperately fighting, piled over dozens deep with Grecian corpses—not calm old Socrates, drinking the hemlock—outvies that terminus of the secession war, in one man's life, here in our midst, in our time—that seal of the emancipation of three million slaves—that parturition and delivery of our at last really free Republic, born again, henceforth to commence its career of genuine homogeneous Union, compact, consistent with itself.

Source:

Whitman, Walt. Lecture delivered in New York City, April 14, 1879. *Prose Works*. Vol. 2. Philadelphia: David McKay, 1892.

4-3
Edwin M. Stanton Gives a First-Hand Account of Lincoln's Assassination

Edwin M. Stanton (1814-1869) became Lincoln's Secretary of War in 1862. They had first met in 1855 as fellow lawyers working on a legal case. Stanton was at Lincoln's bedside when he died and shared this first-hand account. Afterwards, he is reported to have said, "Now he belongs to the ages."

President Lincoln Shot by an Assassin.
The Deed Done at Ford's Theatre Last Night.
The Act of a Desperate Rebel.
The President Still Alive at Last Accounts.
No Hopes Entertained of His Recovery.
Attempted Assassination of Secretary Seward.
Details of the Dreadful Tragedy.

War Department,
Washington, April 15—1:30 A.M.

Maj.-Gen. Dix:

This evening, at about 9:30 P.M., at Ford's Theatre, the President, while sitting in his private box with Mrs. Lincoln, Mrs. Harris, and Major Rathburn, was shot by an assassin, who suddenly entered the box and approached behind the President.

The assassin then leaped upon the stage, brandishing a large dagger or knife, and made his escape in the rear of the theatre.

The pistol ball entered the back of the President's head and penetrated nearly through his head. The wound is mortal. The President has been insensible ever since it was inflicted, and is now dying.

About the same hour an assassin, whether the same or not, entered Mr. Seward's apartments, and under the pretence of having a prescription, was shown to the Secretary's sick chamber. The assassin immediately rushed to the bed, and inflicted two or three stabs in the throat and two on the face. It is hoped the wounds may not be mortal. My apprehension is that they will prove fatal.

The nurse alarmed Mr. Frederick Seward, who was in an adjoining room, and hastened to the door of his father's room, when he met the assassin, who inflicted upon him one or more dangerous wounds. The recovery of Frederick Seward is doubtful.

It is not probable that the President will live throughout the night. . . .

All the members of the Cabinet except Mr. Seward, are now in attendance upon the President.

I have seen Mr. Seward, but he and Frederick were both unconscious.

Edwin M. Stanton,
Secretary of War

Source:

Stanton, Edwin M. "President Lincoln Shot by an Assassin." *New York Times*, April 15, 1865.

4-4
Maunsell B. Field Describes the Night of Lincoln's Death

Maunsell B. Field (1822-1875) was the assistant to the Secretary of the Treasury during President Lincoln's administration. On the night of Lincoln's assassination, he was staying in a nearby hotel. On hearing the news, he hurried to the site and was admitted to the house where the president had been taken. Field's account of that night follows.

On Friday evening, April 14, 1865, I was reading the evening paper in the reading room of Willard's Hotel at about 10 1/2 o'clock, when I was startled by the report that an attempt had been made a few minutes before to assassinate the President at Ford's Theatre. At first I could hardly credit it, but in a few minutes the statement was confirmed by a number of people who came in separately, all telling

After he was shot, Lincoln was carried to this house (center), which belonged to William Petersen. Lincoln died there on the morning of April 15, 1865.

the same story. About fifteen minutes previously I had parted with Mr. Meller, of the Treasury Department, and he had retired to his room. Immediately on receiving this intelligence I notified him of it, and we together proceeded to the scene of the alleged assassination. We found not only considerable crowds on the streets leading to the theatre, but a very large one in front of the theatre, and of the house directly opposite, where the President had been carried after the attempt upon his life. With some difficulty I obtained ingress to the house. I was at once informed by Miss Harris, daughter of Senator Harris, that the President was dying, which statement was confirmed by three or four other persons whom I met in the hall: but I was desired not to communicate his condition to Mrs. Lincoln, who was in the front parlor. I went into this parlor, where I found Mrs. Lincoln, no other lady being present, except Miss Harris, as already mentioned. She at once recognized me, and begged me to run for Dr. Stone, or some other medical man. She was not weeping, but appeared hysterical, and exclaimed in rapid succession, over and over again: "Oh! Why didn't he kill me? Why didn't he kill me?" I was starting from the house to go for Dr. Stone, when I met at the door, Major Eckert, of the War Department, who informed me he was going to Stone's house, Stone having already been sent for, but not having yet arrived. I then determined to go for Dr. Hall, whose precise residence I did not know. Upon inquiring of the crowd, I was told it was over Frank Taylor's bookstore, on the avenue. This proved to be a mistake, and I was compelled to return to his actual residence on the avenue, above Ninth-Street. I found the doctor at home and dressed, and he at once consented to accompany me. Arrived in the neighborhood of the house, I had great difficulty in passing the guard, and only succeeded at last in having the doctor introduced, admission being refused to myself. I returned to Willard's, it now being about 2 o'clock in the morning, and remained there until between 3 and 4 o'clock, when I again went to the house were the President was lying, in company with Mr. Andrews, late Surveyor of the port of New York. I obtained ingress this time without any difficulty, and was enabled to take Mr. Andrews in with me. I proceeded at once to the room in which the President was lying, which was a bedroom in an extension, on the first or parlor floor of the house. The room is small, and is ornamented with prints—a very familiar one of Landseer's, a white horse, being prominent directly over the bed. The bed was a double one, and I found the President lying diagonally across it, with his head at the outside. The pillows were saturated with blood, and there was considerable blood on the floor immediately under him. There was a patchwork coverlet thrown over the President, which was only so far removed, from time to time, as to enable the physicians in attendance to feel the arteries of the neck or the heart, and he appeared to have been divested of all clothing. His eyes were closed and injected with blood, both the lids and the portions surrounding the eyes being as black as if they had been bruised by violence. He was breathing regularly, but with effort, and did not seem to be struggling or suffering.

The persons present in the room were the Secretary of War, the Secretary of the Navy, the Postmaster-General, the Attorney-General, the Secretary of the Treasury, (who, however, remained only till about 5 o'clock), the Secretary of the Interior, the Assistant-Secretary of the Interior, myself, Gen. Auger, Gen. Haleck, Gen. Meigs, and, during the last moments, Capt. Robert Lincoln and Maj. John Hay. On the foot of the bed sat Dr. Stone; above him, and directly opposite the President's face, an army surgeon, to me a stranger; another army surgeon was standing, frequently holding the pulse, and another gentleman, not in uniform, but whom I understood to be also an army surgeon, stood a good deal of the time leaning over the head-board of the bed.

For several hours the breathing above described continued regularly, and apparently without pain or consciousness. But about 7 o'clock a change occurred, and the breathing which had been continuous, was interrupted at intervals. These intervals became more frequent and of longer duration, and the breathing more feeble. Several times the interval was so long that we thought him dead, and the surgeon applied his finger to the pulse, evidently to ascertain if such was the fact. But it was not till 22 minutes past 7 o'clock in the morning that the flame flickered out. There was no apparent suffering, no convulsive action, no rattling of the throat, none of the ordinary premonitory symptoms of death. Death in this case was a mere cessation of breathing.

The fact had not been ascertained one minute when Dr. Gurley offered up a prayer. The few persons in the room were all profoundly affected. The President's eyes after death were not, particularly the right one, entirely closed. I closed them myself with my fingers, and one of the surgeons brought pennies and placed them on the eyes, and subsequently substituted for them half dollars. In a very short time the jaw commenced slightly falling, although the body was still warm. I called attention to this, and had it immediately tied up with a pocket handkerchief. The expression immediately after death was purely negative, but in fifteen minutes there came over the mouth, the nostrils, and the chin, a smile that seemed almost an effort of life. I had never seen upon the President's face an expression more genial and pleasing. The body grew cold very gradually, and I left the room before it had entirely stiffened. Curtains had been previously drawn down by the Secretary of War.

Immediately after the decease, a meeting was held by the members of the Cabinet present, in the back parlor, adjacent to the room in which the President died, to which meeting I, of course, was not admitted. About fifteen minutes before the decease, Mrs. Lincoln came into the room, and threw herself upon her dying husband's body. She was allowed to remain there only a few minutes, when she was removed in a sobbing condition, in which, indeed, she had been during all the time she was present.

After completing his prayer in the chamber of death, Dr. Gurley went into the front parlor, where Mrs. Lincoln was, with Mrs. and Miss Kinney and her son Robert, Gen. Todd of Dacotah, (a cousin of hers,) and Gen. Farnsworth, of Illinois. Here another prayer was offered up, during which I remained in the hall. The prayer was continually interrupted by Mrs. Lincoln's sobs. Soon after its conclusion, I went into the parlor and found her in a chair, supported by her son Robert. Presently her carriage came up, and she was removed to it. She was in a state of tolerable composure at that time, until she reached the door, when, glancing at the theatre opposite, she repeated three or four times: "That dreadful house!—That dreadful house!"

Before I myself left, a guard had been stationed at the door of the room in which the remains of the late President were lying. Mrs. Lincoln had been communicated with, to ascertain whether she desired the body to be embalmed or not, and the Secretary of War had issued various orders, necessary in consequence of what had occurred.

I left the house about 8:30 o'clock in the morning, and shortly after met Mr. Chief-Justice Chase, on his way there. He was extremely agitated, as, indeed, I myself had been all through the night. I afterward learned that, at the Cabinet meeting referred to, the Secretary of the Treasury and the Attorney-General were appointed a committee to wait on the Vice-President, which they did, and he was sworn into office early in the morning by the Chief-Justice.

Source:

Field, Maunsell B. "Last Moments of the President." *New York Times*, April 17, 1865.

4-5
Elizabeth Keckley on Hearing of His Death

Elizabeth Keckley (1818?-1907) was Mary Todd Lincoln's dressmaker and confidante. She had regular contact with President Lincoln and witnessed much of the day-to-day life in the household during his years in office. In the following excerpt, Keckley recalls hearing of Lincoln's death and comforting the First Lady.

Scarcely had the fireworks ceased to play, and the lights been taken down from the windows, when the lightning flashed the most appalling news over the magnetic wires. "The President has been murdered!" spoke the swift-winged messenger, and the loud huzza died upon the lips. A nation suddenly paused in the midst of festivity, and stood paralyzed in horror—transfixed with awe.

Oh, memorable day! Oh, memorable night! Never before was joy so violently contrasted with sorrow.

At 11 o'clock at night I was awakened by an old friend and neighbor, Miss M. Brown, with the startling intelligence that the entire Cabinet had been assassinated,

A wanted poster offered a $100,000 reward for the capture of John H. Surratt, John Wilkes Booth, and David E. Herold (some names misspelled on poster). Booth, who shot the President, was killed when resisting capture on April 26. Surratt and Herold were caught and tried for conspiracy to murder. Herold was found guilty and hanged; Surratt's case resulted in a hung jury.

and Mr. Lincoln shot, but not mortally wounded. When I heard the words I felt as if the blood had been frozen in my veins, and that my lungs must collapse for the want of air. Mr. Lincoln shot! the Cabinet assassinated! What could it mean? The streets were alive with wondering, awe-stricken people. Rumors flew thick and fast, and the wildest reports came with every new arrival. The words were repeated with blanched cheeks and quivering lips. I waked Mr. and Mrs. Lewis, and told them that the President was shot, and that I must go to the White House. I could not remain in a state of uncertainty. I felt that the house would not hold me. They tried to quiet me, but gentle words could not calm the wild tempest. They quickly dressed themselves, and we sallied out into the street to drift with the excited throng. We walked rapidly towards the White House, and on our way passed the residence of Secretary Seward, which was surrounded by armed soldiers, keeping back all intruders with the point of the bayonet. We hurried on, and as we approached the White House, saw that it too was surrounded with soldiers. Every entrance was strongly guarded, and no one was permitted to pass. The guard at the gate told us that Mr. Lincoln had not been brought home, but refused to give any other information. More excited than ever, we wandered down the street. Grief and anxiety were making me weak, and as we joined the outskirts of a large crowd, I began to feel as meek and humble as a penitent child. A gray-haired old man was passing. I caught a glimpse of his face, and it seemed so full of kindness and sorrow that I gently touched his arm, and imploringly asked:

"Will you please, sir, to tell me whether Mr. Lincoln is dead or not?"

"Not dead," he replied, "but dying." God help us!" and with a heavy step he passed on.

"Not dead, but dying! then indeed God help us!"

We learned that the President was mortally wounded—that he had been shot down in his box at the theatre, and that he was not expected to live till morning; when we returned home with heavy hearts. I could not sleep. I wanted to go to Mrs. Lincoln, as I pictured her wild with grief; but then I did not know where to find her, and I must wait till morning. Never did the hours drag so slowly. Every moment seemed an age, and I could do nothing but walk about and hold my arms in mental agony.

Morning came at last, and a sad morning was it. The flags that floated so gayly yesterday now were draped in black, and hung in silent folds at half-mast. The President was dead, and a nation was mourning for him. Every house was draped in black, and every face wore a solemn look. People spoke in subdued tones, and glided whisperingly, wonderingly, silently about the streets.

About eleven o'clock on Saturday morning a carriage drove up to the door, and a messenger asked for "Elizabeth Keckley."

"Who wants her?" I asked.

"I come from Mrs. Lincoln. If you are Mrs. Keckley, come with me immediately to the White House."

I hastily put on my shawl and bonnet, and was driven at a rapid rate to the White House. Everything about the building was sad and solemn. I was quickly shown to Mrs. Lincoln's room, and on entering, saw Mrs. L. tossing uneasily about upon a bed. The room was darkened, and the only person in it besides the widow of the President was Mrs. Secretary Welles, who had spent the night with her. Bowing to Mrs. Welles, I went to the bedside.

"Why did you not come to me last night, Elizabeth—I sent for you?" Mrs. Lincoln asked in a low whisper.

"I did try to come to you, but I could not find you," I answered, as I laid my hand upon her hot brow.

I afterwards learned, that when she had partially recovered from the first shock of the terrible tragedy in the theatre, Mrs. Welles asked:

"Is there no one, Mrs. Lincoln, that you desire to have with you in this terrible affliction?"

"Yes, send for Elizabeth Keckley. I want her just as soon as she can be brought here."

Three messengers, it appears, were successively despatched for me, but all of them mistook the number and failed to find me.

Shortly after entering the room on Saturday morning, Mrs. Welles excused herself, as she said she must go to her own family, and I was left alone with Mrs. Lincoln.

She was nearly exhausted with grief, and when she became a little quiet, I asked and received permission to go into the Guests' Room, where the body of the President lay in state. When I crossed the threshold of the room, I could not help recalling the day on which I had seen little Willie lying in his coffin where the body of his father now lay. I remembered how the President had wept over the pale beautiful face of his gifted boy, and now the President himself was dead. The last time I saw him he spoke kindly to me, but alas! the lips would never move again. The light had faded from his eyes, and when the light went out the soul went with it. What a noble soul was his—noble in all the noble attributes of God! Never did I enter the solemn chamber of death with such palpitating heart and trembling footsteps as I entered it that day. No common mortal had died. The Moses of my people had fallen in the hour of his triumph. Famed had woven her choicest chaplet for his brow. Though the brow was cold and pale in death, the chaplet should not fade, for God had studded it with the glory of the eternal stars.

When I entered the room, the members of the Cabinet and many distinguished officers of the Cabinet were grouped around the body of their fallen chief. They made room for me, and, approaching the body, I lifted the white cloth from the white face of the man that I had worshipped as an idol—looked upon as a demi-god. Notwithstanding the violence of the death of the President, there was something beautiful as well as grandly solemn in the expression of the placid face. There lurked the sweetness and gentleness of childhood, and the stately grandeur of god-like intellect. I gazed long at the face, and turned away with tears in my eyes and a choking sensation in my throat. Ah! never was man so widely mourned before. The whole world bowed their heads in grief when Abraham Lincoln died. . .

In packing, Mrs Lincoln gave away everything intimately connected with the President, as she said that she could not bear to be reminded of the past. The articles were given to those who were regarded as the warmest of Mr. Lincoln's admirers. All of the presents passed through my hands. The dress that Mrs. Lincoln wore on the night of the assassination was given to Mrs. Slade, the wife of an old and faithful messenger. The cloak, stained with the President's blood, was given to me, as also was the bonnet worn on the same memorable night. Afterwards I received the comb and brush that Mr. Lincoln used during his residence at the White House. With this same comb and brush I had often combed his head. When almost ready to go down to a reception, he would turn to me with a quizzical look: "Well, Madam Elizabeth, will you brush my bristles down to-night?"

"Yes, Mr. Lincoln."

Then he would take his seat in an easy-chair, and sit quietly while I arranged his hair. As may well be imagined, I was only too glad to accept this comb and brush from the hands of Mrs. Lincoln. The cloak, bonnet, comb, and brush, the glove worn at the first reception after the second inaugural, and Mr. Lincoln's over-shoes, also given to me, I have since donated for the benefit of Wilberforce University, a colored college near Xenia, Ohio, destroyed by fire on the night that the President was murdered.

Source:

Keckley, Elizabeth. "Chapter XI. The Assassination of President Lincoln." *Behind the Scenes; Or, Thirty Years a Slave, and Four Years in the White House.* New York: G. W. Carlton, 1868.

4-6
"The Sorrow of the People" from the *Chicago Tribune*

Immediately following Lincoln's assassination, newspapers around the country were filled with reports on the assassination and statements of mourning. This article from the Chicago Tribune *expresses the sudden grief many Americans experienced upon learning of Lincoln's death.*

The intelligence of the cruel assassination of our great and good President fell upon every loyal family in the United States with a force as crushing as the news would be of the murder of the head of the household. The people were stunned—stupefied—incredulous. It was too shocking for immediate belief. Even now it seems more like a frightful dream than a reality. Abraham Lincoln was looked up to as the father of his people. His loss is felt as the loss of a father, and the nation mourns its sudden bereavement with tears of sorrow and anguish. The news of his assassination will shock the civilized world. His name was a household word, a synonym of all that was good and just, around millions of hearthstones, in countries beyond the seas as well as in his own. His death will cause mankind to execrate the slaveholders' accursed rebellion. Abraham Lincoln, among the oppressed and down-trodden of all lands, had become the embodiment of human freedom, the loving friend of the poor and lowly, the defender of constitutional liberty and the rights of men. His memory will be imperishable in the hearts of the people to the last syllable of recorded time.

Source:

"The Sorrow of the People." *Chicago Tribune*, April 17, 1865.

4-7
Americans Recall Where They Were: Caroline Richards, Lucretia Mott, and Jane Addams

For many Americans, the moment they learned of Lincoln's death was a pivotal event they would remember forever. Caroline Richards was a thirteen-year-old girl residing in Canandaigua, New York, when Lincoln was assassinated. She recorded local reaction in her diary, which is excerpted below.

April 15.—The news came this morning that our dear president, Abraham Lincoln, was assassinated yesterday, on the day appointed for thanksgiving for Union victories. I have felt sick over it all day and so has every one that I have seen. All seem to feel as though they had lost a personal friend, and tears flow plenteously. How soon has sorrow followed upon the heels of joy! One week ago tonight we were celebrating our victories with loud acclamations of mirth and good cheer. Now everyone is silent and sad and the earth and heavens seem clothed in sack-cloth. The bells have been tolling this afternoon. The flags are all at half mast, draped with mourning, and on every store and dwelling-house some sign of the nation's loss is visible. Just after breakfast this morning, I looked out of the window and saw a group of men listening to the reading of the morning paper, and I feared from their silent, motionless interest that something dreadful had happened, but I was not prepared to hear of the cowardly murder of our President. And William H. Seward, too, I suppose cannot survive his wounds. Oh, how horrible it is! I went down town shortly after I heard the news, and it was wonderful to see the effect of the intelligence upon everybody, small or great, rich or poor. Every one was talking low, with sad and anxious looks. But we know that God still reigns and will do what is best for us all. Perhaps we're "putting our trust too much in princes," forgetting the Great Ruler, who alone can create or destroy, and therefore He has taken from us the arm of flesh that we may lean more confidingly and entirely upon Him. I trust that the men who committed these foul deeds will soon be brought to justice.

Lucretia Mott (1793-1880) was a women's suffrage leader and abolitionist. She described the reaction to Lincoln's assassination in Philadelphia, Pennsylvania, in a letter to her sister, Martha Coffin Wright.

Roadside,
4th mo.
17th, 1865.

My Dear Sister,—A beautiful day! When a great calamity has befallen the nation, we want the sun to be darkened, and the moon not give her light; but "how everything goes on," as Maria said after her dear little Charley died, "just as though such an awful event had not occurred." Was there ever such universal sorrow? The "mirth" of the day before so suddenly "turned into heaviness." Men crying in the streets! As we opened our paper, the overwhelming news stunned us, and we could hardly attend to our dear invalid [their dying daughter Elizabeth], and when the fatal result was known here by hearing the bells toll, she burst into tears.

Such a display of mourning, as now in the city, was never before. All business is suspended. . . .

With affectionate remembrances to one and all of your house hold,

I am thine most tenderly, L. Mott

Jane Addams (1860-1935) was a young child when Lincoln was assassinated. Her father John, an Illinois state senator and businessman, corresponded with the president. Lincoln addressed him as "My dear Double-D'ed Addams." Addams grew up to become a prominent social reformer, famous for her institution of Hull-House, a "settlement house" providing lodging and assistance to poor people. In the excerpts here, Addams recalls the presence and influence of Lincoln in her life.

The funeral service at the White House was held on April 19, 1865.
This illustration of the scene appeared in Harper's Weekly, *May 6, 1865.*

I suppose all the children who were born about the time of the Civil War have recollections quite unlike those of the children who are living now. Although I was but four and a half years old when Lincoln died, I distinctly remember the day when I found on our two white gateposts American flags companioned with black. I tumbled down on the harsh gravel walk in my eager rush into the house to inquire what they were "there for." To my amazement I found my father in tears, something that I had never seen before, having assumed, as all children do, that grown-up people never cried. The two flags, my father's tears, and his impressive statement that the greatest man in the world had died, constituted my initiation, my baptism, as it were, into the thrilling and solemn interests of a world lying quite outside the two white gateposts. . .

My childish admiration for Lincoln is closely associated with a visit made to the war eagle, Old Abe, who, as we children well knew, lived in the state capitol of Wisconsin, only sixty-five miles north of our house, really no farther than an eagle could easily fly! He had been carried by the Eight Wisconsin Regiment through the entire war, and now dwelt an honored pensioner in the state building itself.

Many times, standing in the north end of our orchard, which was only twelve miles from that mysterious line which divided Illinois from Wisconsin, we anxiously scanned the deep sky, hoping to see Old Abe fly southward right over our apple trees, for it was clearly possible that he might at any moment escape from his keeper, who, although he had been a soldier and a sentinel, would have to sleep sometimes. We gazed with thrilled interest at one speck after another in the flawless sky, but although Old Abe never came to see us, a much more incredible thing happened, for we were at last taken to see him.

We started one golden summer's day, two happy children in the family carriage, with my father and mother and an older sister to whom, because she was just home from boarding school, we confidently appealed whenever we needed information. We were driven northward hour after hour, past harvest fields in which the stubble glinted from bronze to gold and the heavy-headed grain rested luxuriously in rounded shocks, until we reached that beautiful region of hills and lakes which surrounds the capital city of Wisconsin.

But although Old Abe, sitting sedately upon his high perch, was sufficiently like an uplifted ensign to remind us of a Roman eagle, and although his veteran keeper, clad in an old army coat, was ready to answer all our questions and to tell us of the thirty-six battles and skirmishes which Old Abe had passed unscathed, the crowning moment of the impressive journey came to me later, illustrating once more that children are as quick to catch the meaning of a symbol as they are unaccountably slow to understand the real world about them.

The entire journey to the veteran war eagle had itself symbolized that search for the heroic and perfect which so persistently haunts the young; and as I stood under the great white dome of Old Abe's stately home, for one brief moment the search was rewarded. I dimly caught a hint of what men have tried to say in their world-old effort to imprison a space in so divine a line that it shall hold only yearning devotion and high-hearted hopes. Certainly the utmost rim of my first dome was filled with the tumultuous impression of soldiers marching to death for freedom's sake, of pioneers streaming westward to establish self-government in yet another sovereign state. Only the great dome of St. Peter's itself has ever clutched my heart as did that modest curve which had sequestered from infinitude, in a place small enough for my child's mind, the courage and endurance which I could not comprehend so long as it was lost in the "void of unresponsible space" under the vaulting sky itself. But through all my vivid sensations there persisted the image of the eagle in the corridor below and Lincoln himself as an epitome of all that was great and good. I dimly caught the notion of the martyred President as the standard bearer to the conscience of his countrymen, as the eagle had been the ensign of courage to the soldiers of the Wisconsin regiment. . .

My father always spoke of the martyred President as Mr. Lincoln, and I never heard the great name without a thrill. I remember the day—it must have been one of comparative leisure, perhaps a Sunday—when at my request my father took out of his desk a thin packet marked "Mr. Lincoln's Letters," the shortest one of which bore unmistakable traces of that remarkable personality. These letters began, "My dear Double-D'ed Addams," and to the inquiry as to how the person thus addressed was about to vote on a certain measure then before the legislature, was added the assurance that he knew that this Addams "would vote according to his conscience," but he begged to know in which direction the same conscience "was pointing." As my father folded up the bits of paper I fairly held my breath in my desire that he should go on with the reminiscence of this wonderful man, whom he had known in his comparable obscurity, or better still, that he should be moved to tell some of the exciting incidents of the Lincoln-Douglas debates. There were at least two pictures of Lincoln that always hung in my father's room, and one in our old-fashioned upstairs parlor, of Lincoln with little Tad. For one or all of these reasons I always tend to associate Lincoln with the tenderest thoughts of my father. . .

There were at least two pictures of Lincoln that always hung in my father's room, and one in our old-fashioned upstairs parlor, of Lincoln with little Tad. For one or all of these reasons I always tend to associate Lincoln with the tenderest thoughts of my father. . .

Of the many old friends of my father who kindly came to look up his daughter in the first days of Hull-House, I recall none with more pleasure than Lyman Trumbull, whom we used to point out to the members of the Young Citizens' Club as the man who had for days held in his keeping the Proclamation of Emancipation until his friend President Lincoln was ready to issue it. I remember the talk he gave at Hull-House on one of our early celebrations of Lincoln's birthday, his assertion that Lincoln was no cheap popular hero, that the "common people" would have to make an effort if they would understand his greatness, as Lincoln painstakingly made a long effort to understand the greatness of the people. There was something in the admiration of Lincoln's contemporaries, or at least of those men who had known him personally, which was quite unlike even the best of the devotion and reverent understanding which has developed since. In the first place, they had so large a fund of common experience; they too had pioneered in a western country, and had urged the development of canals and railroads in order that the raw prairie crops might be transported to market; they too had realized that if this last tremendous experiment in self-government failed here, it would be the disappointment of the centuries and that upon their ability to organize self-government in state, county, and town depended the verdict of history. These men also knew, as Lincoln himself did, that if this tremendous experiment was to come to fruition, it must be brought about by the people themselves; that there was no other capital fund upon which to draw. . .

Is it not Abraham Lincoln who has cleared the title to our democracy? He made plain, once for all, that democratic government, associated as it is with all the mistakes and shortcomings of the common people, still remains the most valuable contribution America has made to the moral life of the world.

Sources:

Excerpt 1: Richards, Caroline. Diary entry, April 15, 1865. *Village Life in America, 1852-1872.* New York: Henry Holt and Company, 1913.

Excerpt 2: Mott, Lucretia. Letter to Martha Coffin Wright, April 17, 1865. *James and Lucretia Mott: Life and Letters.* Edited by Anna Davis Hallowell. Boston: Houghton, Mifflin, 1884.

Excerpt 3: Addams, Jane. "Influence of Lincoln." *Twenty Years at Hull-House.* New York: Macmillan Co., 1910.

4-8
"The Death of Lincoln" by William Cullen Bryant

Poet William Cullen Bryant (1794-1878) met Lincoln when he introduced the young politician from Illinois at Cooper Union (for the speech Lincoln delivered there, see document 7-3). Cullen wrote this poem after Lincoln's death in 1865.

The Death of Lincoln

O, slow to smite and swift to spare,
Gentle and merciful and just!
Who, in the fear of God, didst bear
The sword of power—a nation's trust.
In sorrow by thy bier we stand,
Amid the awe that hushes all,
And speak the anguish of a land
That shook with horror at thy fall.
Thy task is done—the bonds are free;
We bear thee to an honored grave,
Whose noblest monument shall be
The broken fetters of the slave.
Pure was thy life; its bloody close
Hath placed thee with the sons of light,
Among the noble host of those
Who perished in the cause of right.

Source:

Bryant, William Cullen. "The Death of Lincoln." *The Poetical Works of William Cullen Bryant, Roslyn Edition: With Chronologies of Bryant's Life and Poems and a Bibliography of His Writings By Henry C. Sturges, and a Memoir of His Life By Richard Henry Stoddard.* New York: D. Appleton and Company, 1903.

4-9
Eulogy by Ralph Waldo Emerson, April 19, 1865

Ralph Waldo Emerson (1803-1882) was a poet, philosopher, and acquaintance of Lincoln. He met the president in 1862, when he accompanied his friend, Secretary of State William H. Seward, on a visit to the White House. Emerson delivered the eulogy below on April 19, 1865, at the Unitarian Church in Concord, Massachusetts.

We meet under the gloom of a calamity which darkens down over the minds of good men in all civil society, as the fearful tidings travel over sea, over land, from country to country, like the shadow of an uncalculated eclipse over the planet. Old as history is, and manifold as are its tragedies, I doubt if any death has caused so much pain to mankind as this has caused, or will cause, on its announcement; and this, not so much because nations are by modern arts brought so closely together, as because of the mysterious hopes and fears which, in the present day, are connected with the name and institutions of America.

In this country, on Saturday, every one was struck dumb, and saw at first only deep below deep, as he meditated on the ghastly blow. And perhaps, at this hour, when the coffin which contains the dust of the President sets forward on its long march through mourning States, on its way to his home in Illinois, we might well be silent, and suffer the awful voices of the time to thunder to us. Yes, but that first despair was brief: the man was not so to be mourned. He was the most active and hopeful of men; and his work had not perished: but acclamations of praise for the task he had accomplished burst out into a song of triumph, which even tears for his death cannot keep down.

The President stood before us as a man of the people. He was thoroughly American, had never crossed the sea, had never been spoiled by English insularity or French dissipation; a quiet native, aboriginal man, as an acorn from the oak; no aping of foreigners, no frivolous accomplishments, Kentuckian born, working on a farm, a flatboat-man, a captain in the Black Hawk war, a country lawyer, a representative in the rural legislature of Illinois;—on such modest foundations the broad structure of his fame was laid. How slowly, and yet by happily prepared steps, he came to his place. All of us remember,—it is only a history of five or six years,—the surprise and the disappointment of the country at his first nomination by the convention at Chicago. Mr. Seward, then in the culmination of his good fame, was the favorite of the Eastern States. And when the new and comparatively unknown name of Lincoln was announced (notwithstanding the report of the acclamations of that Convention), we heard the result coldly and sadly. It seemed too rash, on a purely local reputation, to build so grave a trust in such anxious times; and men naturally talked of the chances in politics as incalculable. But it turned out not to be chance. The profound good opinion which the people of Illinois and of the West had conceived of him, and which they had imparted to their colleagues that they also might justify themselves to their constituents at home, was not rash, though they did not begin to know the riches of his worth.

A plain man of the people, an extraordinary fortune attended him. He offered no shining qualities at the first encounter; he did not offend by superiority. He had a face and manner which disarmed suspicion, which inspired confidence, which confirmed good-will. He was a man without vices. He had a strong sense of duty, which it was very easy for him to obey. Then, he had what farmers call a long head; was excellent in working out the sum for himself; in arguing his case and convincing you fairly and firmly. Then, it turned out that he was a great worker; had prodigious faculty of performance; worked easily. A good worker is so rare; everybody has some disabling quality. In a host of young men that start together and promise so many brilliant leaders for the next age, each fails on trial; one by bad health, one by conceit, or by love of pleasure, or lethargy, or an ugly temper,—each has some disqualifying fault that throws him out of the career. But this man was sound to the core, cheerful, persistent, all right for labor, and liked nothing so well.

Then, he had a vast good-nature, which made him tolerant and accessible to all; fair-minded, leaning to the claim of the petitioner; affable, and not sensible to the affliction which the innumerable visits paid to him when President would have brought to any one else. And how this good-nature became a noble humanity, in many a tragic case which the events of the war brought to him, every one will remember; and with what increasing tenderness he dealt when a whole race was thrown on his compassion. The poor negro said of him, on an impressive occasion, "Massa Linkum am eberywhere."

Then his broad good-humor, running easily into jocular talk, in which he delighted and in which he excelled, was a rich gift to this wise man. It enabled him to keep his

Ralph Waldo Emerson.

secret; to meet every kind of man and every rank in society; to take off the edge of the severest decisions; to mask his own purpose and sound his companion; and to catch with true instinct the temper of every company he addressed. And, more than all, it is to a man of severe labor, in anxious and exhausting crises, the natural restorative, good as sleep, and is the protection of the overdriven brain against rancor and insanity.

He is the author of a multitude of good sayings, so disguised as pleasantries that it is certain they had no reputation at first but as jests; and only later, by the very acceptance and adoption they find in the mouths of millions, turn out to be the wisdom of the hour. I am sure if this man had ruled in a period of less facility of printing, he would have become mythological in a very few years, like Aesop or Pilpay, or one of the Seven Wise Masters, by his fables and proverbs. But the weight and penetration of many passages in his letters, messages and speeches, hidden now by the very closeness of their application to the moment, are destined hereafter to wide fame. What pregnant definitions; what unerring common sense; what foresight; and, on great occasion, what lofty, and more than national, what humane tone! His brief speech at Gettysburg will not easily be surpassed by words on any recorded occasion. This, and one other American speech, that of John Brown to the court that tried him, and a part of Kossuth's speech at Birmingham, can only be compared with each other, and with no fourth.

His occupying the chair of State was a triumph of the good-sense of mankind, and of the public conscience. This middle-class country had got a middle-class President, at last. Yes, in manners and sympathies, but not in powers, for his powers were superior. This man grew according to the need. His mind mastered the problem of the day; and, as the problem grew, so did his comprehension of it. Rarely was man so fitted to the event. In the midst of fears and jealousies, in the Babel of counsels and parties, this man wrought incessantly with all his might and all his honesty, laboring to find what the people wanted, and how to obtain that. It cannot be said there is any exaggeration of his worth. If ever a man was fairly tested, he was. There was no lack of resistance, nor of slander, nor of ridicule. The times have allowed no state secrets; the nation has been in such ferment, such multitudes had to be trusted, that no secret could be kept. Every door was ajar, and we know all that befell.

Then, what an occasion was the whirlwind of the war. Here was place for no holiday magistrate, no fair-weather sailor; the new pilot was hurried to the helm in a tornado. In four years,—four years of battle-days,—his endurance, his fertility of resources, his magnanimity, were sorely tried and never found wanting. There, by his courage, his justice, his even temper, his fertile counsel, his humanity, he stood a heroic figure in the centre of a heroic epoch. He is the true history of the American people in his time. Step by step he walked before them; slow with their slowness, quickening his march by theirs, the true representative of this continent; an entirely public man; father of his country, the pulse of twenty millions throbbing in his heart, the thought of their minds articulated by his tongue.

Adam Smith remarks that the axe, which in Houbraken's portraits of British kings and worthies is engraved under those who have suffered at the block, adds a certain lofty charm to the picture. And who does not see, even in this tragedy so recent, how fast the terror and ruin of the massacre are already burning into glory around the victim? Far happier this fate than to have lived to be wished away; to have watched the decay of his own faculties; to have seen,—perhaps even he,—the proverbial ingratitude of statesmen; to have seen mean men preferred. Had he not lived long enough to keep the greatest promise that ever man made to his fellow-men,—the practicable abolition of slavery? He had seen Tennessee, Missouri and Maryland emancipate their slaves. He had seen Savannah, Charleston and Richmond surrendered; had seen the main army of the rebellion lay down its arms. He had conquered the public opinion of Canada, England and France. Only Washington can compare with him in fortune.

And what if it should turn out, in the unfolding of the web, that he had reached the term; that this heroic deliverer could no longer serve us; that the rebellion had

215

touched its natural conclusion, and what remained to be done required new and uncommitted hands,—a new spirit born out of the ashes of the war; and that Heaven, wishing to show the world a completed benefactor, shall make him serve his country even more by his death than by his life? Nations, like kings, are not good by facility and complaisance. "The kindness of kings consists in justice and strength." Easy good-nature has been the dangerous foible of the Republic, and it was necessary that its enemies should outrage it, and drive us to unwonted firmness, to secure the salvation of this country in the next ages.

The ancients believed in a serene and beautiful Genius which ruled in the affairs of nations; which, with a slow but stern justice, carried forward the fortunes of certain chosen houses, weeding out single offenders or offending families, and securing at last the firm prosperity of the favorites of Heaven. It was too narrow a view of the Eternal Nemesis. There is a serene Providence which rules the fate of nations, which makes little account of time, little of one generation or race, makes no account of disasters, conquers alike by what is called defeat or by what is called victory, thrusts aside enemy and obstruction, crushes everything immoral as inhuman, and obtains the ultimate triumph of the best race by the sacrifice of everything which resists the moral laws of the world. It makes its own instruments, creates the man for the time, trains him in poverty, inspires his genius, and arms him for his task. It has given every race its own talent, and ordains that only that race which combines perfectly with the virtues of all shall endure.

Source:

Emerson, Ralph Waldo. "Abraham Lincoln: Remarks at the Funeral Services Held in Concord, April 19, 1865." *Emerson's Complete Works.* Vol. 11, *Miscellanies.* Boston: Houghton, Mifflin and Company; Cambridge, MA: The Riverside Press, 1885.

4-10
Eulogy by Henry Ward Beecher, April 23, 1865

Pastor Henry Ward Beecher (1813-1887) was acquainted with Lincoln, who had attended Beecher's Plymouth Church in Brooklyn, New York, when visiting nearby to present his speech at Cooper Institute in 1860 (see document 7-3). On Easter Sunday, April 23, 1865, Beecher gave a eulogy for the late president, which is excerpted below.

Again a great leader of the people has passed through toil, sorrow, battle and war, and come near to the promised land of peace, into which he might not pass over. Who shall recount our martyr's sufferings for this people? Since the November of 1860, his horizon has been black with storms. By day and night, he trod a way of danger and darkness. On his shoulders rested a government dearer to him than his own life. At its integrity millions of men were striking at home. Upon this government foreign eyes lowered. It stood like a lone island in a sea full of storms; and every tide and wave seemed eager to devour it. Upon thousands of hearts great sorrows and anxieties have rested, but not on one such, and in such measure, as upon that simple, truthful noble soul, our faithful and sainted Lincoln. Never rising to the enthusiasm of more impassioned natures in hours of hope, and never sinking with the mercurial in hours of defeat to the depths of despondency, he held on with immovable patience and fortitude, putting caution against hope, that it might not be premature, and hope against caution, that it might not yield to dread and danger. He wrestled ceaselessly, through four black and dreadful purgatorial years, wherein God was cleansing the sin of his people as by fire.

At last, the watcher beheld the gray dawn for the country. The mountains began to give forth their forms from out the darkness; and the East came rushing toward us with arms full of joy for all our sorrows. Then it was for him to be glad exceedingly, that had sorrowed immeasurably. Peace could bring to no other heart such joy, such rest, such honor, such trust, such gratitude. But he looked upon it as Moses looked upon the promised land. Then the wail of a nation proclaimed that he had gone from among us. Not thine the sorrow, but ours, sainted soul. Thou hast indeed entered the promised land, while we are yet on the march. To us remains the rocking of the deep, the storm upon the land, days of duty and nights of watching; but thou art sphered high above all darkness and fear, beyond all sorrow and weariness. Rest, oh weary heart! Rejoice exceedingly, thou that hast enough suffered! Thou hast beheld Him who invisibly led thee in this great wilderness. Thou standest among the elect. Around thee are the royal men that have ennobled human life in every age. Kingly art thou, with glory on thy brow as a diadem. And joy is upon thee for ever more. Over all this land, over all the little cloud of years that now from thine infinite horizon moves back as a speck, thou art lifted up as high as the star is above the clouds that hide us, but never reach it. In the goodly company of Mount Zion thou shalt find that rest which thou hast sorrowing sought in vain; and thy name, an ever-lasting name in heaven, shall flourish in fragrance and beauty as long as men shall last upon the earth, or hearts remain, to revere truth, fidelity and goodness.

Never did two such orbs of experience meet in one hemisphere, as the joy and the sorrow of the same week in this land. The joy was as sudden as if no man had expected it, and as entrancing as if it had fallen a sphere from heaven. It rose up over sobriety, and swept business from its moorings, and ran down through the land in irresistible course. Men embraced each other in brotherhood that were strangers in the flesh. They sang, or prayed, or, deeper yet, many could only think thanksgiving and weep gladness. That peace was sure; that government was firmer than ever; that the land was cleansed of plague; that the ages were opening to our footsteps, and we were to begin a march of blessings; that blood was staunched, and scowling enmities were sinking like storms beneath the horizon; that dear fatherland, nothing lost, much gained, was to rise up in unexampled honor among the nations of the earth—these thoughts, and that undistinguishable throng of fancies, and hopes, and desires, and yearnings, that filled the soul with tremblings like the heated air of mid-summer days—all these kindled up such a surge of joy as no words may describe.

In one hour, joy lay without a pulse, without a gleam, or breath. A sorrow came that swept through the land as huge storms sweep through the forest and field, rolling thunder along the sky, disheveling the flowers, daunting every singer in thicket or forest, and pouring blackness and darkness across the land and up the mountains. Did ever so many hearts, in so brief a time, touch two such boundless feelings? It was the uttermost of joy; it was the uttermost of sorrow—noon and midnight, without a space between.

The blow brought not a sharp pang. It was so terrible that at first it stunned sensibility. Citizens were like men awakened at midnight by an earthquake, and bewildered to find everything that they were accustomed to trust wavering and falling. The very earth was no longer solid. The first feeling was the least. Men waited to get straight to feel. They wandered in the streets as if groping after some impending dread, or undeveloped sorrow, or some one to tell them what ailed them. They met each other as if each would ask the other, "Am I awake, or do I dream?" There was a piteous helplessness. Strong men bowed down and wept. Other and common griefs belonged to some one in chief: this belonged to all. It was each and every man's. Every virtuous household in the land felt as if its first-born were gone. Men were bereaved, and walked for days as if a corpse lay unburied in their dwellings. There was nothing else to think of. They could speak of nothing but that; and yet, of that they could speak only falteringly. All business was laid aside. Pleasure forgot to smile. The city for nearly a week ceased to roar. The great Leviathan lay down, and was still. Even avarice stood still, and greed was strangely moved to generous sympathy and universal sorrow. Rear to his name monuments, found charitable institutions, and write his name above their lintels; but no monument will ever equal the universal, spontaneous, and sublime sorrow that in a moment swept down lines and parties, and covered up animosities, and in an hour brought a divided people into unity of grief and indivisible fellowship of anguish. . . .

This nation has dissolved—but in tears only. It stands four-square, more solid, to-day, than any pyramid in Egypt. This people are neither wasted, nor daunted, nor disordered. Men hate slavery and love liberty with stronger hate and love to-day than ever before. The Government is not weakened, it is made stronger. How naturally and easily were the ranks closed! Another stepped forward, in the hour that the one fell, to take his place and his mantle; and I avow my belief that he will be found a man true to every instinct of liberty; true to the whole trust that is reposed in him; vigilant of the Constitution; careful of the laws; wise for liberty, in that he himself, through his life, has known what it was to suffer from the stings of slavery, and to prize liberty from bitter personal experiences. [Applause.]

Where could the head of government in any monarchy be smitten down by the hand of an assassin, and the funds not quiver or fall one-half of one per cent? After a long period of national disturbance, after four years of drastic war, after tremendous drafts on the resources of the country, in the height and top of our burdens, the heart of this people is such that now, when the head of government is stricken down, the public funds do not waver, but stand as the granite ribs in our mountains.

219

Republicans institutions have been vindicated in this experience as they never were before; and the whole history of the last four years, rounded up by this cruel stroke, seems, in the providence of God, to have been clothed, now, with an illustration, with a sympathy, with an aptness, and with a significance, such as we never could have expected nor imagined. God, I think, has said, by the voice of this event, to all nations of the earth, "Republican liberty, based upon true Christianity, is firm as the foundation of the globe." [Applause.]

Even he who now sleeps has, by this event, been clothed with new influence. Dead, he speaks to men who now willingly hear what before they refused to listen to. Now his simple and weighty words will be gathered like those of Washington, and your children, and your children's children, shall be taught to ponder the simplicity and deep wisdom of utterances which, in their time, passed, in party heat, as idle words. Men will receive a new impulse of patriotism for his sake, and will guard with zeal the whole country which he loved so well. I swear you, on the altar of his memory, to be more faithful to the country for which he has perished. [Applause.] They will, as they follow his hearse, swear a new hatred to that slavery against which he warred, and which, in vanquishing him, has made him a martyr and a conqueror. I swear you, by the memory of this martyr, to hate slavery with an unappeasable hatred. [Applause.] They will admire and imitate the firmness of this man, his inflexible conscience for the right; and yet his gentleness, as tender as a woman's, his moderation of spirit, which, not all the heat of party could inflame, nor all the jars and disturbances of this country shake out of its place. I swear you to an emulation of his justice, his moderation, and his mercy.

> *God, I think, has said, by the voice of this event, to all nations of the earth, "Republican liberty, based upon true Christianity, is firm as the foundation of the globe."*

You I can comfort; but how can I speak to that twilight million to whom his name was as the name of an angel of God? There will be wailing in places, which no minister shall be able to reach. When, in hovel and in cot, in wood and in wilderness, in the field throughout the South, the dusky children, who looked upon him as that Moses whom God sent before them to lead them out of the land of bondage, learn that he has fallen, who shall comfort them? O, thou Shepherd of Israel, that didst comfort thy people of old, to thy care we commit the helpless, the long-wronged, and grieved.

And now the martyr is moving in triumphal march, mightier than when alive. The nation rises up at every stage of his coming. Cities and states are his pall-bearers, and the cannon beats the hours with solemn progression. Dead, *dead*, DEAD, he yet speaketh! Is Washington dead? Is Hampden dead? Is David dead? Is any man that was ever fit to live dead? Disenthralled of flesh, and risen in the unobstructed sphere where passion never comes, he begins his illimitable work. His life now is grafted upon the infinite, and will be fruitful as no earthly life can be. Pass on, thou that hast overcome! Your sorrows, oh people, are his peace! Your bells, and bands, and muffled drums, sound triumph in his ear. Wail and weep here; God made it echo joy and triumph there. Pass on!

Four years ago, oh, Illinois, we took from your midst an untried man, and from among the people. We return him to you a mighty conqueror. Not thine any more, but the nation's; not ours, but the world's. Give him place, oh, ye prairies! In the midst of this great continent his dust shall rest, a sacred treasure to myriads who shall pilgrim to that shrine to kindle anew their zeal and patriotism. Ye winds that move over the mighty places of the West, chant his requiem! Ye people, behold a martyr whose blood, as so many articulate words, pleads for fidelity, for law, for liberty!

Source:

Beecher, Henry Ward. "Sermon II. Rev. Henry Ward Beecher." *Our Martyr President, Abraham Lincoln: Voices from the Pulpit of New York and Brooklyn.* New York: Tibbals and Whiting, 1865.

4-11
Eulogy by Phillips Brooks, April 23, 1865

Phillips Brooks (1835-1893) was an Episcopal pastor. He delivered Lincoln's eulogy, excerpted below, on April 23, 1865, in Philadelphia, Pennsylvania.

While I speak to you to-day, the body of the President who ruled this people is lying honored and loved, in our City. It is impossible with that sacred presence in our midst for me to stand and speak of ordinary topics which occupy the pulpit. I must speak of him to-day; and I therefore undertake to do what I had intended to do at some future time, to invite you to study with me the character of Abraham Lincoln, the impulses of his life, and the causes of his death. I know how hard it is to do it rightly, how impossible it is to do it worthily. But I shall speak with confidence because I speak to those who love him, and whose ready love will fill out the deficiencies in a picture which my words will weakly try to draw. . . .

We take it for granted first of all, that there is an essential connection between Mr. Lincoln's character and his violent and bloody death. It is no accident, no arbitrary decree of Providence. He lived as he did, and he died as he did, because he was what he was. The more we see of events the less we come to believe in any fate or destiny except the destiny of character. It will be our duty, then, to see what there was in the character of our great President that created the history of his life and at last produced the catastrophe of his cruel death. After the first trembling horror, the first outburst of indignant sorrow has grown calm, these are the questions which we are bound to ask and answer.

It is not necessary for me even to sketch the biography of Mr. Lincoln. He was born in Kentucky, fifty-six years ago, when Kentucky was a pioneer State. He lived, as boy and man, the hard and needy life of a backwoodsman, a farmer, a river boatman, and, finally, by his own efforts at self-education, of an active, respected, influential citizen in the half organized and manifold interests of a new and energetic community. From his boyhood up he lived in direct and vigorous contact with men and things, not as in older states and easier conditions with words and theories; and both his moral convictions and his intellectual opinions gathered from that contact a supreme degree of that character by which men knew him—that character which is the most distinctive possession of the best American nature—that almost indescribable quality which we call in general clearness or truth, and which appears in the physical structure as health, in the moral constitution as honesty, in the mental structure as sagacity, and in the region of active life as practicalness. This one character, with many sides all shaped by the same essential force and testifying to the same inner influences, was what was powerful in him and decreed for him the life he was to live and the death he was to die. We must take no smaller view than this of what he was. . . .

It is the great boon of such characters as Mr. Lincoln's, that they reunite what God has joined together and man has put asunder. In him was vindicated the greatness of real goodness and the goodness of real greatness. The twain were one flesh. Not one of all the multitudes who stood and looked up to him for direction with such a loving and implicit trust can tell you to-day whether the wise judgments that he gave came most from a strong head or a sound heart. If you ask them, they are puzzled. There are men as good as he, but they do bad things. There are men as intelligent as he, but they do foolish things. In him goodness and intelligence combined and made their best result of wisdom. For perfect truth consists not merely in the right constituents of character, but in their right and intimate conjunction. This union of the mental and moral into a life of admirable simplicity is what we most admire in children, but in them it is unsettled and unpractical. But when it is preserved into a manhood, deepened into reliability and maturity, it is that glorified childlikeness, that high and reverend simplicity which shames and baffles the most accomplished astuteness, and is chosen by God to fill his purposes when he needs a ruler for his people of faithful and true heart, such as he had who was our President.

Another evident quality of such character as this, will be its freshness or newness, so to speak. Its freshness, or readiness—call it what you will—its ability to take up new duties and do them in a new way will result of necessity from its truth and clearness. The simple natures and forces will always be the most pliant ones. Water bends and shapes itself to any channel. Air folds and adapts itself to each new figure. They are the simplest and the most infinitely active things in nature. So this nature, in very virtue of its simplicity, must be also free, always fitting itself to each new need. It will always start from the most fundamental and eternal conditions, and work in the straightest even although they may be the newest ways to the present prescribed purpose. In one word it must be broad and independent and radical. So that freedom and radicalness in the character of Abraham Lincoln were not separate qualities, but the necessary results of his simplicity and childlikeness and truth.

223

Here then we have some conception of the man. Out of this character came the life which we admire and the death which we lament to-day. He was called in that character to that life and death. It was just the nature, as you see, which a new nation such as ours ought to produce. All the conditions of his birth, his youth, his manhood, which made him what he was, were not irregular and exceptional, but were the normal conditions of a new and simple country. His pioneer home in Indiana, was a type of the pioneer land in which he lived. If ever there was a man who was a part of the time and country he lived in this was he. The same simple respect for labor won in the school of work and incorporated into blood and muscle; the same unassuming loyalty to the simple virtues of temperance and industry and integrity; the same sagacious judgment which had learned to be quick-eyed and quick-brained in the constant presence of emergency; the same direct and clear thought about things, social, political and religious, that was in him supremely, was in the people he was sent to rule. Surely, with such a type-man for ruler, there would seem to be but a smooth and even road over which he might lead the people whose character he represented into the new region of national happiness and comfort and usefulness, for which that character had been designed. . . .

The cause that Abraham Lincoln died for shall grow stronger by his death; stronger and sterner. Stronger to set its pillars deep into the structure of our nation's life; sterner to execute the justice of the Lord upon his enemies. Stronger to spread its arms and grasp our whole land into freedom; sterner to sweep the last poor ghost of slavery out of our haunted homes. . . .

So let him lie here in our midst to-day, and let our people go and bend with solemn thoughtfulness and look upon his face and read the lessons of his burial. As he passed here on his journey from his western home and told us what by the help of God he meant to do, so let him pause upon his way back to his western grave and tell us with a silence more eloquent than words how bravely, how truly by the strength of God he did it. God brought him up as he brought David up from the sheepfolds to feed Jacob, his people, and Israel, his inheritance. He came up in earnestness and faith and he goes back in triumph. As he pauses here to-day, and from his cold lips bids us bear witness how he has met the duty that was laid on him, what can we say out of our full hearts but this—"He fed them with a faithful and true heart and ruled them prudently with all his power." The *Shepherd of the People!* that old name that the best rulers ever craved. What ruler ever won it like this dead President of ours? He fed us faithfully and truly. He fed us with counsel when we were in doubt, with inspiration

The funeral procession in New York City, April 25, 1865.

when we sometimes faltered, with caution when we would be rash, with calm, clear, trustful cheerfulness through many an hour when our hearts were dark. He fed hungry souls all over the country with sympathy and consolation. He spread before the whole land feasts of great duty and devotion and patriotism on which the land grew strong. He fed us with solemn, solid truths. He taught us the sacredness of government, the wickedness of treason. He made our souls glad and vigorous with the love of Liberty that was in his. He showed us how to love truth and yet be charitable—how to hate wrong and all oppression, and yet not treasure one personal injury or insult. He fed *all* his people from the highest to the lowest, from the most privileged down to the most enslaved. Best of all, he fed us with a reverent and genuine religion.

225

He spread before us the love and fear of God just in that shape in which we need them most, and out of his faithful service of a higher Master who of us has not taken and eaten and grown strong. "He fed them with a faithful and true heart." Yes, till the last. For at the last, behold him standing with hand reached out to feed the South with Mercy and the North with Charity, and the whole land with Peace, when the Lord who had sent him called him and his work was done.

He stood once on the battle-field of our own State, and said of the brave men who had saved it words as noble as any countryman of ours ever spoke. Let us stand in the country he has saved, and which is to be his grave and monument, and say of Abraham Lincoln what he said of the soldiers who had died at Gettysburg. He stood there with their graves before him, and these are the words he said: "We cannot dedicate, we cannot consecrate, we cannot hallow this ground. The brave men who struggled here have consecrated it far beyond our power to add or detract. The world will little note nor long remember what we say here, but it can never forget what they did here. It is for us the living rather to be dedicated to the unfinished work which they who fought here have thus far so nobly advanced. It is rather for us to be here dedicated to the great task remaining before us, that from these honored dead we take increased devotion to that cause for which they gave the last full measure of devotion; that we here highly resolve that these dead shall not have died in vain; that this nation, under God shall have a new birth of freedom, and that Government of the people, by the people and for the people shall not perish from the earth."

May God make us worthy of the memory of ABRAHAM LINCOLN.

Source:

Brooks, Phillips. *The Life and Death of Abraham Lincoln: A Sermon Preached at the Church of the Holy Trinity, Philadelphia, Sunday Morning, April 23, 1865.* Philadelphia: Henry B. Ashmead, 1865.

4-12
Eulogy by Seth Sweetser, April 23, 1865

Seth Sweetser (1807-1878), was pastor of the Central Congregational Church in Worcester, Massachusetts. He delivered a eulogy there for Lincoln on April 23, 1865, which included these lines.

He ascended the mount where he could see the fair fields and the smiling vineyards of the promise land. But, like the great leader of Israel, he was not permitted to come to the possession.

Source:

Sweetser, Seth. In *Lincoln's Birthday: A Comprehensive View of Lincoln as Given in the Most Noteworthy Essays, Orations and Poems, in Fiction and in Lincoln's Own Writings.* Edited by Robert Haven Schauffler. New York: Dodd, Mead and Company, 1909.

4-13
Eulogy by Matthew Simpson, May 4, 1865

After the funeral train brought Lincoln to Springfield, Illinois, Methodist Bishop Matthew Simpson (1811-1884) led his burial service there on May 4, 1865. The following excerpt comes from Simpson's sermon.

Near the capital of this large and growing State of Illinois, in the midst of this beautiful grove, and at the open mouth of the vault which has just received the remains of our fallen chieftain, we gather to pay a tribute of respect and to drop the tears of sorrow around the ashes of the mighty dead. A little more than four years ago he left his plain and quiet home in yonder city, receiving the parting words of the concourse of friends who, in the midst of the dropping of the gentle shower, gathered around him. He spoke of the pain of parting from the place where he had lived for a quarter of a century, where his children had been born, and his home had been rendered pleasant by friendly associations, and, as he left, he made an earnest request, in the hearing of some who are present at this hour, that, as he was about to enter upon responsibilities which he believed to be greater than any which had fallen upon any man since the days of Washington, the people would offer up prayers that God would aid and sustain him in the work which they had given him to do. His company left your quiet city, but, as it went, snares were in waiting for the Chief Magistrate. Scarcely did he escape the dangers of the way or the hands of the assassin, as he neared Washington; and I believe he escaped only through the vigilance of officers and the prayers of his people, so that the blow was suspended for more than four years, which was at last permitted, through the providence of God, to fall.

How different the occasion which witnessed his departure from that which witnessed his return. Doubtless you expected to take him by the hand, and to feel the warm grasp which you had felt in other days, and to see the tall form walking among you which you had delighted to honor in years past. But he was never permitted to come until he came with lips mute and silent, the frame encoffined, and a weeping nation following as his mourners. Such a scene as his return to you was never witnessed. Among the events of history there have been great processions of mourners. There was one for the patriarch Jacob, which went up from Egypt, and the Egyptians wondered at the evidences of reverence and filial affection which came from the hearts of the Israelites. There was mourning when Moses fell upon the heights of Pisgah and was hid from human view. There have been mournings in the kingdoms of the earth when kings and princes have fallen, but never was there, in the history of man, such mourning as that which has accompanied this funeral procession, and has gathered around the mortal remains of him who was our loved one, and who now sleeps among us. If we glance at the procession which followed him, we see how the nation stood aghast. Tears filled the eyes of manly, sunburnt faces. Strong men, as they clasped the hands of their friends, were unable to find vent for their grief in words. Women and little children caught up the tidings as they ran through the land, and were melted into tears. The nation stood still. Men left their plows in the fields and asked what the end should be. The hum of manufactories ceased, and the sound of the hammer was not heard. Busy merchants closed their doors, and in the exchange gold passed no more from hand to hand. Though three weeks have elapsed, the nation has scarcely breathed easily yet. A mournful silence is abroad upon the land; nor is this mourning confined to any class or to any district of country. Men of all political parties, and of all religious creeds, have united in paying this mournful tribute. The archbishop of the Roman Catholic Church in New York and a Protestant minister walked side by side in the sad procession, and a Jewish rabbi performed a part of the solemn services.

Here are gathered around his tomb the representatives of the army and navy, senators, judges, governors, and officers of all the branches of the Government. Here, too, are members of civic processions, with men and women from the humblest as well as the highest occupations. Here and there, too, are tears, as sincere and warm as any that drop, which come from the eyes of those whose kindred and whose race have been freed from their chains by him whom they mourn as their deliverer. More persons have gazed on the face of the departed than ever looked upon the face of any other departed man. More races have looked on the procession for 1,600 miles or more—by night and by day—by sunlight, dawn, twilight, and by torchlight, than ever before watched the progress of a procession.

We ask why this wonderful mourning—this great procession? I answer, first, a part of the interest has arisen from the times in which we live, and in which he that had fallen was a principal actor. It is a principle of our nature that feelings, once excited, turn readily from the object by which they are excited, to some other object which may for the time being take possession of the mind. Another principle is, the deepest affections of our hearts gather around some human form in which are incarnated the living thoughts and ideas of the passing age. If we look then at the times, we see an age of excitement. For four years the popular heart has been stirred to its inmost depth. War had come upon us, dividing families, separating nearest and dearest friends—a war, the extent and magnitude of which no one could estimate—a war in which the blood of brethren was shed by a brother's hand. A call for soldiers was made by this voice now hushed, and all over the land, from hill and mountain, from plain and valley, there sprang up thousands of bold hearts, ready to go forth and save our national Union. This feeling of excitement was transferred next into a feeling of deep grief because of the dangers in which our country was placed. Many said, "Is it possible to save our nation?" Some in our country, and nearly all the leading men in other countries, declared it to be impossible to maintain the Union; and many an honest and patriotic heart was deeply pained with apprehensions of common ruin; and many, in grief and almost in despair, anxiously inquired, What shall the end of these things be? In addition to this wives had given their husbands, mothers their sons, the pride and joy of their hearts. They saw them put on the uniform, they saw them take the martial step, and they tried to hide their deep feeling of sadness. Many

*On May 4, 1865, this hearse carried Lincoln's body to
Oak Ridge Cemetery in Springfield, Illinois.*

dear ones slept upon the battle-field never to return again, and there was mourning in every mansion and in every cabin in our broad land. Then came a feeling of deeper sadness as the story came of prisoners tortured to death or starved through the mandates of those who are called the representatives of the chivalry, and who claimed to be the honorable ones of the earth; and as we read the stories of frames attenuated and reduced to mere skeletons, our grief turned partly into horror and partly into a cry for vengeance.

Then this feeling was changed to one of joy. There came signs of the end of this rebellion. We followed the career of our glorious generals. We saw our army, under the command of the brave officer who is guiding this procession, climb up the heights of Lookout Mountain and drive the rebels from their strongholds. Another brave general swept through Georgia, South and North Carolina, and drove the combined armies of the rebels before him, while the honored Lieutenant-General held Lee and his hosts in a death-grasp.

Then the tidings came that Richmond was evacuated, and that Lee had surrendered. The bells rang merrily all over the land. The booming of cannon was heard; illuminations and torch-light processions manifested the general joy, and families were looking for the speedy return of their loved ones from the field of battle. Just in the midst of this wildest joy, in one hour—nay; in one moment—the tidings thrilled throughout the land that Abraham Lincoln, the best of Presidents, had perished by the hands of an assassin; and then all the feelings which had been gathering for four years, in forms of excitement, grief, horror, and joy, turned into one wail of woe—a sadness inexpressible—an anguish unutterable. But it is not the times merely which caused this mourning. The mode of his death must be taken into the account. Had he died on a bed of illness, with kind friends around him; had the sweat of death been wiped from his brow by gentle hands, while he was yet conscious; could he have had power to speak words of affection to his stricken widow, or words of counsel to us like those which we heard in his parting inaugural at Washington, which shall now be immortal—how it would have softened or assuaged something of the grief. There might, at least, have been preparation for the event. But no moment of warning was given to him or to us. He was stricken down, too, when his hopes for the end of the rebellion were bright, and prospects of a joyous life were before him. There was a cabinet meeting that day, said to have been the most cheerful and happy of any held since the beginning of the rebellion. After this meeting he talked with his friends, and spoke of the four years of tempest, of the storms being over, and of the four years of pleasure and joy awaiting him, as the weight of care and anxiety would be taken from his mind, and could have happy days with his family again. In the midst of these anticipations he left his house never to return alive. The evening was Good Friday, the saddest day in the whole calendar for the Christian Church-henceforth in this country to made sadder, if possible, by the memory of our nation's loss; and so filled with grief was every Christian heart that even all the joyous thought of Easter Sunday failed to remove the crushing sorrow under which the true worshiper bowed in the house of God.

But the great cause of this mourning is to be found in the man himself. Mr. Lincoln was no ordinary man. . . .

231

If you ask me on what mental characteristic his greatness rested, I answer, on a quick and ready perception of facts; on a memory unusually tenacious and retentive; and on a logical turn of mind, which followed sternly and unwaveringly every link in the chain of thought on every subject which he was called to investigate. I think there have been minds more broad in their character, more comprehensive in their scope, but I doubt if ever there has been a man who could follow step by step, with more logical power, the points which he desired to illustrate. He gained this power by the close study of geometry, and by a determination to perceive the truth in all its relations and simplicity, and, when found, to utter it.

It is said of him in childhood, when he had any difficulty in listening to a conversation to ascertain what people meant, if he retired to rest he could not sleep till he tried to understand the precise points intended, and, when understood, to frame language to convey it in a clearer manner to others. Who then has read his messages fails to perceive the directness and the simplicity of his style? And this very trait, which was scoffed at and decried by opponents, is now recognized as one of the strong points of that mighty mind which has so powerfully influenced the destiny of this nation, and which shall, for ages to come, influence the destiny of humanity.

It was not, however, chiefly by his mental faculties that he gained such control over mankind. His moral power gave him pre-eminence. The convictions of men that Abraham Lincoln was an honest man led them to yield to his guidance. As has been said of Cobden, whom he greatly resembled, he made all men feel a sense of himself—a recognition of individuality—a self-relying power. They saw in him a man whom they believed would do what is right, regardless of all consequences. It was this moral feeling which gave him the greatest hold on the people, and made his utterances almost oracular. When the nation was angered by the perfidy of foreign nations in allowing privateers to be fitted out, he uttered the significant expression, "One war at a time," and it stilled the national heart. When his own friends were divided as to what steps should be taken as to slavery, that simple utterance, "I will save the Union, if I can, with slavery; if not, slavery must perish, for the Union must be preserved," became the rallying word. Men felt the struggle was for the Union, and all other questions must be subsidiary.

But, after all, by the acts of a man shall his fame be perpetuated. What are his acts? Much praise is due to the men who aided him. He called able counselors around him—some of whom have displayed the highest order of talent, united with the purest and most devoted patriotism. He summoned able generals into the field—men who have borne the sword as bravely as ever any human arm has borne it. He had the aid of prayerful and thoughtful men everywhere. But, under his own guiding hands, wise counsels were combined and great movements conducted. . . .

There are moments which involve in themselves eternities. There are instants which seem to contain germs which shall develop and bloom forever. Such a moment came in the tide of time to our land, when a question must be settled which affected all the earth. The contest was for human freedom, not for this republic merely; not for the Union simply, but to decide whether the people, as a people, in their entire majesty, were destined to be the government, or whether they were to be subject to tyrants or aristocrats, or to class-rule of any kind. This is the great question for which we have been fighting, and its decision is at hand, and the result of the contest will affect the ages to come. If successful, republics will spread in spite of monarchs, all over this earth. (Exclamations of "Amen." "Thank God.") . . .

But the great act of the mighty chieftan, on which his fame shall rest long after his frame shall molder away, is that of giving freedom to a race. We have all been taught to revere sacred characters. Among them Moses stands pre-eminently high. He received the law from God, and his name is honored among the hosts of heaven. Was not his greatest act the delivering of three millions of his kindred out of bondage? Yet we may assert that Abraham Lincoln, by his proclamation, liberated more enslaved people than ever Moses set free, and those not of his kindred or his race. Such a power, or such an opportunity, God has seldom given to man. When other events shall have been forgotten; when this world shall have become a network of republics; when every throne shall be swept from the face of the earth; when literature shall enlighten all minds; when the claims of humanity shall be recognized everywhere, this act shall still be conspicuous on the pages of history. We are thankful that God gave to Abraham Lincoln the decision and wisdom and grace to issue that proclamation, which stands high above all other papers which have been penned by uninspired men. (Applause.)

Abraham Lincoln was a good man. He was known as an honest, temperate, forgiving man; a just man; a man of noble heart in every way. As to his religious experience, I cannot speak definitely, because I was not privileged to know much of his private sentiments. My acquaintance with him did not give me the opportunity to hear him speak on those topics. This I know, however, he read the Bible frequently;

loved it for its great truths and its profound teachings; and he tried to be guided by its precepts. He believed in Christ the Saviors of sinners; and I think he was sincere in trying to bring his life into harmony with the principles of revealed religion. Certainly if there ever was a man who illustrated some of the principles of pure religion, that man was our departed President. Look over all his speeches, listen to his utterances. He never spoke unkindly of any man. Even the rebels received no word of anger from him, and his last day illustrated in a remarkable manner his forgiving disposition. A dispatch was received that afternoon that Thompson and Tucker were trying to make their escape through Maine, and it was proposed to arrest them. Mr. Lincoln, however, preferred rather to let them quietly escape. He was seeking to save the very men who had been plotting his destruction. This morning we read a proclamation offering $25,000 for the arrest of these men as aiders and abettors of his assassination; so that, in his expiring acts, he was saying, "Father, forgive them, they know not what they do."

> *Certainly if there ever was a man who illustrated some of the principles of pure religion, that man was our departed President. Look over all his speeches, listen to his utterances. He never spoke unkindly of any man.*

As a ruler, I doubt if any President has ever shown such trust in God, or in public documents so frequently referred to Divine aid. Often did he remark to friends and to delegations that his hope for our success rested in his conviction that God would bless our efforts, because we were trying to do right. To the address of a large religious body he replied, "Thanks be unto God, who, in our national trials, giveth us the churches." To a minister who said he hoped the Lord was on our side, he replied that it gave him no concern whether the Lord was on our side or not, for, he added, " I know the Lord is always on the side of the right," and with deep feeling added, "But God is my witness that it is my constant anxiety and prayer that both myself and this nation should be on the Lord's side."

In his domestic life he was exceedingly kind and affectionate. He was a devoted husband and father. During his presidential term, he lost his second son, Willie. To an officer of the army he said, not long since, "Do you ever find yourself talking with the dead?" and added, "Since Willie's death I catch myself every day involuntarily talking with him, as if he were with me." On his widow, who is unable to be here, I need only invoke the blessing of Almighty God that she may be comforted and sustained. For his son, who has witnessed the exercises of this hour, all I can desire is that the mantle of his father may fall upon him. (Exclamations of "Amen.")

Let us pause a moment in the lesson of the hour before we part. This man, though he fell by an assassin, still fell under the permissive hand of God. He had some wise purpose in allowing him so to fall. What more could he have desired of life for himself? Were not his honors full? There was no office to which he could aspire. The popular heart clung around him as around no other man. The nations of the world had learned to honor our chief magistrate. If rumors of a desired alliance with England be true, Napoleon trembled when he heard of the fall of Richmond, and asked what nation would join him to protect him against our Government under the guidance of such a man. His fame was full, his work was done, and he sealed his glory by becoming the nation's great martyr for liberty.

He appears to have had a strange presentiment, early in political life, that some day he would be President. You see it indicated in 1839. Of the slave power he said, "Broken by it I too may be; bow to it I never will. The probability that we may fail in the struggle ought not to deter us from the support of a cause which we deem to be just. It shall not deter me. If ever I feel the soul within me elevate and expand to those dimensions not wholly unworthy of its Almighty architect, it is when I contemplate the cause of my country, deserted by all the world besides, and I standing up boldly and alone and hurling defiance at her victorious oppressors. Here without contemplating consequences, before high Heaven and in the face of the world, I swear eternal fidelity to the just cause, as I deem it, of the land of my life, my liberty, and my love." And yet, secretly, he said to more than one, "I never shall live out the four years of my term. When the rebellion is crushed my work is done." So it was. He lived to see the last battle fought, and dictate a despatch from the home of Jefferson Davis; lived till the power of the rebellion was broken; and then, having done the work for which God had sent him, angels, I trust, were sent to shield him from one moment of pain or suffering, and to bear him from this world to the high and glorious realm where the patriot and the good shall live forever.

His career teaches young men that every position of eminence is open before the diligent and the worthy. To the active men of the country, his example is an incentive to trust in God and do right.

Lincoln's tomb at Oak Ridge Cemetery in Springfield, Illinois.

Standing, as we do to-day, by his coffin and his sepulchre, let us resolve to carry forward the policy which he so nobly began. Let us do right to all men. To the ambitious there is this fearful lesson: Of the four candidates for Presidential honors in 1860, two of them—Douglas and Lincoln—once competitors, but now sleeping patriots, rest from their labors; Bell perished in poverty and misery, as a traitor might perish; and Breckinridge is a frightened fugitive, with the brand of traitor on his brow. Let us vow, in the sight of Heaven, to eradicate every vestige of human slavery; to give every human being his true position before God and man; to crush every form of rebellion, and to stand by the flag which God has given us. How joyful that it floated over parts of every State before Mr. Lincoln's career was ended. How singular that, to the fact of the assassin's heels being caught in the folds of the flag, we are probably indebted for his capture. The flag and the traitor must ever be enemies.

Traitors will probably suffer by the change of rulers, for one of sterner mould, and who himself has deeply suffered from the rebellion, now wields the sword of justice.

Our country, too, is stronger for the trial. A republic was declared by monarchists too weak to endure a civil war; yet we have crushed the most gigantic rebellion in history, and have grown in strength and population every year of the struggle. We have passed through the ordeal of a popular election while swords and bayonets were in the field, and have come out unharmed. And now, in an hour of excitement, with a large majority having preferred another man for President, when the bullet of the assassin has laid our President prostrate, has there been a mutiny? Has any rival proffered his claims? Out of an army of near a million, no officer or soldier uttered one note of dissent, and, in an hour or two after Mr. Lincoln's death, another leader under constitutional forms, occupied his chair, and the government moved forward without one single jar. The world will learn that republics are the strongest governments on earth. . . .

Chieftain! Farewell!! The nation mourns thee. Mothers shall teach thy name to their lisping children. The youth of our land shall emulate thy virtues. Statesmen shall study thy record and learn lessons of wisdom. Mute though thy lips be, yet they still speak. Hushed is thy voice, but its echoes of liberty are ringing through the world, and the sons of bondage listen with joy. Prisoned thou art in death, and yet thou art marching abroad, and chains and manacles are bursting at thy touch. Thou didst fall not for thyself. The assassin had no hate for thee. Our hearts were aimed at, our national life was sought. We crown thee as our martyr—and humanity enthrones thee as her triumphant son. Hero, Martyr, Friend, FAREWELL!

Source:

Simpson, Matthew. "Oration at the Burial at Springfield." In *Our Martyr President, Abraham Lincoln: Voices from the Pulpit of New York and Brooklyn.* New York: Tibbals and Whiting, 1865.

4-14
Eulogy by Charles Sumner, June 1, 1865

Charles Sumner (1811-1874) was a senator from Massachusetts who met president-elect Lincoln shortly after he arrived in Washington in 1861. Though they disagreed at times on various policies, Sumner and Lincoln liked and admired one another. Sumner was at Lincoln's side when he died and comforted his son Robert. On June 1, 1865, he delivered a eulogy, excerpted below, in Boston.

Abraham Lincoln was born, and, until he became President, always lived in a part of the country which at the period of the Declaration of Independence was a savage wilderness. Strange but happy Providence, that a voice from that savage wilderness, now fertile in men, was inspired to uphold the pledges and promises of the Declaration! The Unity of the Republic on the indestructible foundation of Liberty and Equality was vindicated by the citizen of a community, which had no existence when the Republic was formed. . . .

Another cabin was built in primitive rudeness, and the future President spilt the rails for the fence to enclose the lot. These rails have become classical in our history, and the name of rail-splitter has been more than the degree of a college. Not that the splitter of rails is especially meritorious, but because the people are proud to trace aspiring talent to humble beginnings, and because they found in this tribute a new opportunity of vindicating the dignity of free labor.

Source:

Sumner, Charles. *The Promises of the Declaration of Independence. Eulogy on Abraham Lincoln, Delivered before the Municipal Authorities of the City of Boston, June 1, 1865.* Boston: Ticknor & Fields, 1865.

4-15
From "Ode Recited at the Harvard Commemoration" by James Russell Lowell

James Russell Lowell (1819-1891) was an essayist, poet, editor, and also a pro-fessor at Harvard University from 1855 to 1876. He composed "Ode Recited at the Harvard Commemoration" for the university's memorial service, held on July 21, 1865, for students and alumni who had lost their lives in the Civil War. This excerpt from the long poem honors Lincoln.

Ode Recited at the Harvard Commemoration

Life may be given in many ways,
And loyalty to Truth be sealed
As bravely in the closet as the field,
So generous is Fate;
But then to stand beside her,
When craven churls deride her,
To front a lie in arms and not to yield,—
This shows, methinks, God's plan
And measure of a stalwart man,

Limbed like the old heroic breeds,
Who stands self-poised on manhood's solid earth,
Not forced to frame excuses for his birth,
Fed from within with all the strength he needs.

Such was he, our Martyr Chief,
Whom late the Nation he had led,
With ashes on her head,
Wept with the passion of an angry grief:
Forgive me, if from present things I turn
To speak what in my heart will beat and burn,
And hang my wreath on his world-honored urn.
Nature, they say, doth dote,
And cannot make a man

Save on some worn-out plan,
Repeating us by rote:
For him her Old-World mould aside she threw,
And, choosing sweet clay from the breast
Of the unexhausted West,
With stuff untainted shaped a hero new,
Wise, steadfast in the strength of God, and true.
How beautiful to see
Once more a shepherd of mankind indeed,
Who loved his charge, but never loved to lead;
One whose meek flock the people joyed to be,
Not lured by any cheat of birth,
But by his clear-grained human worth,
And brave old wisdom of sincerity!
They knew that outward grace is dust;
They could not choose but trust
In that sure-footed mind's unfaltering skill,
And supple-tempered will
That bent like perfect steel to spring again and thrust.
His was no lonely mountain-peak of mind,
Thrusting to thin air o'er our cloudy bars,
A seamark now, now lost in vapors blind,
Broad prairie rather, genial, level-lined,
Fruitful and friendly for all human kind,
Yet also nigh to heaven and loved of loftiest stars.
Nothing of Europe here,
Or, then, of Europe fronting mornward still,
Ere any names of Serf and Peer
Could Nature's equal scheme deface;
Here was a type of the true elder race,
And one of Plutarch's men talked with us face to face.
I praise him not; it were too late;
And some innative weakness there must be
In him who condescends to victory
Such as the Present gives, and cannot wait,
Safe in himself as in a fate.

So always firmly he:
He knew to bide his time,
And can his fame abide,
Still patient in his simple faith sublime,
Till the wise years decide.
Great captains, with their guns and drums,
Disturb our judgment for the hour,
But at last silence comes;
These are all gone, and, standing like a tower,
Our children shall behold his fame,
The kindly-earnest, brave, foreseeing man,
Sagacious, patient, dreading praise, not blame,
New birth of our new soil, the first American.

Source:

Lowell, James Russell. "Ode Recited at the Harvard Commemoration." In *The Harvard Classics*. Edited by Charles W. Eliot. Vol. 42: *English Poetry III: From Tennyson to Whitman*. New York: P.F. Collier & Son, 1909-14.

4-16
Poems by Walt Whitman

Poet Walt Whitman (1819-1892) wrote some of the finest and best-known poems about Lincoln. The poet and the president never met, but Whitman worked in military hospitals in Washington, D.C., and occasionally saw Lincoln. After Lincoln's death, Whitman wrote the three poems below and published them in Sequel to Drum-Taps *(1865-66): "O Captain! My Captain!" "Hush'd be the Camps To-day," and "Where Lilacs Last in the Door-yard Bloom'd."*

Walt Whitman.

O Captain! My Captain!

O Captain! my Captain! our fearful trip is done;
The ship has weather'd every rack, the prize we sought is won;
The port is near, the bell I hear, the people all exulting,
While follow eyes the steady keel, the vessel grim and daring:
    But O heart! heart! heart!
      O the bleeding drops of red,
        Where on the deck my Captain lies,
          Fallen cold and dead.

O Captain! my Captain! rise up and hear the bells:
Rise up—for you the flag is flung—for you the bugle trills;
For you bouquets and ribbon'd wreaths—for you the shores a-crowding;
For you they call, the swaying mass, their eager faces turning;
    Hear Captain! dear father!
      This arm beneath your head;
        It is some dream that on the deck,
          You've fallen cold and dead.

My Captain does not answer, his lips are pale and still;
My father does not feel my arm, he has no pulse nor will;
The ship is anchor'd safe and sound, its voyage closed and done;
From fearful trip, the victor ship, comes in with object won;
    Exult, O shores, and ring, O bells!
      But I, with mournful tread,
        Walk the deck my Captain lies,
          Fallen cold and dead.

Hush'd be the Camps To-day

Hush'd be the camps to-day;
And, soldiers, let us drape our war-worn weapons;
And each with musing soul retire, to celebrate,
Our dear commander's death.

No more for him life's stormy conflicts;
Nor victory, nor defeat—no more time's dark events,
Charging like ceaseless clouds across the sky.

But sing, poet, in our name;
Sing of the love we bore him—because you, dweller in camps, know it truly.

As they invault the coffin there;
Sing—as they close the doors of earth upon him—one verse,
For the heavy hearts of soldiers.

When Lilacs Last in the' Door-yard Bloom'd

I

When lilacs last in the door-yard bloom'd,
And the great star early droop'd in the western sky in the night,
I mourn'd—and yet shall mourn with ever-returning spring.

O ever-returning spring! trinity sure to me you bring;
Lilac blooming perennial, and drooping star in the west,
And thought of him I love.

II

O powerful, western, fallen star!
O shades of night! O moody, tearful night!
O great star disappear'd! O the black murk that hides the star!
O cruel hands that hold me powerless! O helpless soul of me!
O harsh surrounding cloud, that will not free my soul!

III

In the door-yard fronting an old farm-house, near the white-wash'd palings,
Stands the lilac bush, tall-growing, with heart-shaped leaves of rich green,
With many a pointed blossom, rising, delicate, with the perfume strong I love,

With every leaf a miracle . . . and from this bush in the door-yard,
With delicate-color'd blossoms, and heart-shaped leaves of rich green,
A sprig, with its flower, I break.

IV

In the swamp, in secluded recesses,
A shy and hidden bird is warbling a song.

Solitary, the thrush,
The hermit, withdrawn to himself, avoiding the settlements,
Sings by himself a song.

Song of the bleeding throat!
Death's outlet song of life—(for well, dear brother, I know
If thou wast not gifted to sing, thou would'st surely die.)

V

Over the breast of the spring, the land, amid cities,
Amid lanes, and through old woods,
(where lately the violets peep'd from the ground, spotting the gray debris;)
Amid the grass in the fields each side of the lanes—passing the endless grass;
Passing the yellow-spear'd wheat,
every grain from its shroud in the dark-brown fields uprising;
Passing the apple-tree blows of white and pink in the orchards;
Carrying a corpse to where it shall rest in the grave,
Night and day journeys a coffin.

VI

Coffin that passes through lanes and streets,
Through day and night, with the great cloud darkening the land,
With the pomp of the inloop'd flags, with the cities draped in black,
With the show of the States themselves, as of crape-veil'd women, standing,
With processions long and winding, and the flambeaus of the night,
With the countless torches lit—with the silent sea of faces,

and the unbared heads,
With the waiting depot, the arriving coffin, and the sombre faces,
With dirges through the night,
with the thousand voices rising strong and solemn;
With all the mournful voices of the dirges, pour'd around the coffin,
The dim-lit churches and the shuddering organs—Where amid these you journey,
With the tolling, tolling bells' perpetual clang;
Here! coffin that slowly passes,
I give you my sprig of lilac.

VII

(Nor for you, for one, alone;
Blossoms and branches green to coffins all I bring:
For fresh as the morning—thus would I carol a song for you,

O sane and sacred death.

All over bouquets of roses,
O death! I cover you over with roses and early lilies;
But mostly and now the lilac that blooms the first,
Copious, I break, I break the sprigs from the bushes;
With loaded arms I come, pouring for you,
For you, and the coffins all of you, O death.)

VIII

O western orb, sailing the heaven!
Now I know what you must have meant, as a month since we walk'd,
As we walk'd up and down in the dark blue so mystic,
As we walk'd in silence the transparent shadowy night,
As I saw you had something to tell, as you bent to me night after night,
As you droop'd from the sky low down, as if to my side,
(while the other stars all look'd on;)
As we wander'd together the solemn night, (for something,
I know not what, kept me from sleep;)
As the night advanced, and I saw on the rim of the west, ere you went,

245

how full you were of woe;
As I stood on the rising ground in the breeze, in the cold transparent night,
As I watch'd where you pass'd and was lost in the netherward black of the night,
As my soul, in its trouble, dissatisfied, sank, as where you, sad orb,
Concluded, dropt in the night, and was gone.

IX

Sing on, there in the swamp!
O singer bashful and tender! I hear your notes—I hear your call;
I hear—I come presently—I understand you;
But a moment I linger—for the lustrous star has detain'd me;
The star, my departing comrade, holds and detains me.

X

O how shall I warble myself for the dead one there I loved?
And how shall I deck my song for the large sweet soul that has gone?
And what shall my perfume be, for the grave of him I love?

Sea-winds, blown from east and west,
Blown from the eastern sea, and blown from the western sea,
till there on the prairies meeting:
These, and with these, and the breath of my chant,
I perfume the grave of him I love.

XI

O what shall I hang on the chamber walls?
And what shall the pictures be that I hang on the walls,
To adorn the burial-house of him I love?

Pictures of growing spring, and farms, and homes,
With the Fourth-month eve at sundown, and the gray smoke lucid and bright,
With floods of the yellow gold of the gorgeous,
indolent, sinking sun, burning, expanding the air;
With the fresh sweet herbage under foot, and the pale green leaves of the trees prolific;
In the distance the flowing glaze, the breast of the river,

with a wind-dapple here and there;
With ranging hills on the banks, with many a line against the sky, and shadows;
And the city at hand, with dwellings so dense, and stacks of chimneys,
And all the scenes of life, and the workshops, and the workmen homeward returning.

XII

Lo! body and soul! this land!
Mighty Manhattan, with spires, and the sparkling and hurrying tides, and the ships;
The varied and ample land—the South and the North in the light—Ohio's shores,
  and flashing Missouri,
And ever the far-spreading prairies, cover'd with grass and corn.

Lo! the most excellent sun, so calm and haughty;
The violet and purple morn, with just-felt breezes;
The gentle, soft-born, measureless light;
The miracle, spreading, bathing all—the fulfill'd noon;
The coming eve, delicious—the welcome night, and the stars,
Over my cities shining all, enveloping man and land.

XIII

Sing on! sing on, you gray-brown bird!
Sing from the swamps, the recesses—pour your chant from the bushes;
Limitless out of the dusk, out of the cedars and pines.

Sing on, dearest brother—warble your reedy song;
Loud human song, with voice of uttermost woe.

O liquid, and free, and tender!
O wild and loose to my soul! O wondrous singer!
You only I hear . . . yet the star holds me, (but will soon depart;)
Yet the lilac, with mastering odor, holds me.

XIV

Now while I sat in the day, and look'd forth,

In the close of the day, with its light, and the fields of spring, and the farmer
    preparing his crops,
In the large unconscious scenery of my land, with its lakes and forests,
In the heavenly aerial beauty, (after the perturb'd winds, and the storms;)
Under the arching heavens of the afternoon swift passing, and the voices of children
    and women,
The many-moving sea-tides,—and I saw the ships how they sail'd,
And the summer approaching with richness, and the fields all busy with labor,
And the infinite separate houses, how they all went on, each with its meals and
    minutia of daily usages;
And the streets, how their throbbings throbb'd, and the cities pent—lo! then and
    there,
Falling upon them all, and among them all, enveloping me with the rest,
Appear'd the cloud, appear'd the long black trail;
And I knew Death, its thought, and the sacred knowledge of death.

XV

Then with the knowledge of death as walking one side of me,
And the thought of death close-walking the other side of me,
And I in the middle, as with companions, and as holding the hands of companions,
I fled forth to the hiding receiving night, that talks not,
Down to the shores of the water, the path by the swamp in the dimness,
To the solemn shadowy cedars, and ghostly pines so still.
And the singer so shy to the rest receiv'd me;
The gray-brown bird I know, receiv'd us comrades three;
And he sang what seem'd the carol of death, and a verse for him I love.
From deep secluded recesses,
From the fragrant cedars, and the ghostly pines so still,
Came the carol of the bird.
And the charm of the carol rapt me,
As I held, as if by their hands, my comrades in the night;
And the voice of my spirit tallied the song of the bird.

DEATH CAROL.

XVI

Come, lovely and soothing Death,
Undulate round the world, serenely arriving, arriving,
In the day, in the night, to all, to each,
Sooner or later, delicate Death.

Prais'd be the fathomless universe,
For life and joy, and for objects and knowledge curious;
And for love, sweet love—But praise! praise! praise!
For the sure-enwinding arms of cool-enfolding Death.

Dark Mother, always gliding near, with soft feet,
Have none chanted for thee a chant of fullest welcome?
Then I chant it for thee—I glorify thee above all;
I bring thee a song that when thou must indeed come, come unfalteringly.

Approach, strong Deliveress!
When it is so—when thou hast taken them, I joyously sing the dead,
Lost in the loving, floating ocean of thee,
Laved in the flood of thy bliss, O Death.

From me to thee glad serenades,
Dances for thee I propose, saluting thee—adornments and feastings for thee;
And the sights of the open landscape, and the high-spread sky, are fitting,
And life and the fields, and the huge and thoughtful night.

The night, in silence, under many a star;
The ocean shore, and the husky whispering wave, whose voice I know;
And the soul turning to thee, O vast and well-veil'd Death,
And the body gratefully nestling close to thee.

Over the tree-tops I float thee a song!
Over the rising and sinking waves—over the myriad fields, and the prairies wide;
Over the dense-pack'd cities all, and the teeming wharves and ways,
I float this carol with joy, with joy to thee, O Death!

XVII

To the tally of my soul,
Loud and strong kept up the gray-brown bird,
With pure, deliberate notes, spreading, filling the night.

Loud in the pines and cedars dim,
Clear in the freshness moist, and the swamp-perfume;
And I with my comrades there in the night.

While my sight that was bound in my eyes unclosed,
As to long panoramas of visions.

XVIII

I saw askant the armies;
And I saw, as in noiseless dreams, hundreds of battle-flags;
Borne through the smoke of the battles, and pierc'd with missiles, I saw them,
And carried hither and yon through the smoke, and torn and bloody;
And at last but a few shreds left on the staffs, (and all in silence,)
And the staffs all splinter'd and broken.

I saw battle-corpses, myriads of them,
And the white skeletons of young men—I saw them;
I saw the debris and debris of all the dead soldiers of the war;
But I saw they were not as was thought;
They themselves were fully at rest—they suffer'd not;
The living remain'd and suffer'd—the mother suffer'd,
And the wife and the child, and the musing comrade suffer'd,
And the armies that remain'd suffer'd.

XIX

Passing the visions, passing the night;
Passing, unloosing the hold of my comrades' hands;
Passing the song of the hermit bird, and the tallying song of my soul,
(Victorious song, death's outlet song, yet varying, ever-altering song,
As low and wailing, yet clear the notes, rising and falling, flooding the night,

Sadly sinking and fainting, as warning and warning, and yet again bursting with joy,
Covering the earth, and filling the spread of the heaven,
As powerful psalm in the night I heard from recesses,)
Passing, I leave thee, lilac with heart-shaped leaves;
I leave thee there in the door-yard, blooming, returning with spring,
I cease from my song for thee;
From my gaze on thee in the west, fronting the west, communing with thee,
O comrade lustrous, with silver face in the night.

XX

Yet each I keep, and all, retrievements out of the night;
The song, the wondrous chant of the gray-brown bird,
And the tallying chant, the echo arous'd in my soul,
With the lustrous and drooping star, with the countenance full of woe,
With the lilac tall, and its blossoms of mastering odor;
With the holders holding my hand, nearing the call of the bird,
Comrades mine, and I in the midst,
and their memory ever I keep—for the dead I loved so well;
For the sweetest, wisest soul of all my days and lands . . . and this for his dear sake;
Lilac and star and bird, twined with the chant of my soul,
There in the fragrant pines, and the cedars dusk and dim.

Source:

Whitman, Walt. *Leaves of Grass*. Philadelphia: David McKay, 1900.

Part 5
Tributes and Legacy

Lincoln's force of personality and his remarkable accomplishments—notably, saving the Union and abolishing slavery—have inspired many thousands of spoken and printed words attesting to his role as a beloved icon in American history. This section gathers just a few of those tributes to Lincoln and assessments of his legacy. They speak of his integrity, kindness, intelligence, and strength; his love for his fellow creatures and his highly developed conscience and sense of justice—all of which were set in yet higher relief by the events of his presidency. They also speak of his roots on the frontier and his self-education.

This section opens with pieces authored by those closest to Lincoln, beginning with his widow, Mary Todd Lincoln, and continuing with his friends, colleagues, and acquaintances, including William H. Herndon, Horace Greeley, Shelby M. Cullom, Schuyler Colfax, Frederick Douglass, Ulysses S. Grant, and William Tecumseh Sherman. These pieces are followed by tributes from a wide range of admirers, including Walt Whitman, Robert G. Ingersoll, Lyman Abbott, Rose Terry Cooke, Edwin Markham, James Weldon Johnson, Paul Laurence Dunbar, Jonathan P. Dolliver, Mark Twain, Frederic Harrison, Rutherford B. Hayes, William McKinley, and Theodore Roosevelt. The selections include remembrances, speeches, and brief memorials as well as poetic tributes written from the time of his death to just after the turn of the 20th century.

5-1
Remembrance by Mary Todd Lincoln

Mary Todd (1818-1882) married Abraham Lincoln on November 4, 1842. She was at his side at Ford's Theatre at the time of his assassination. She offered the following remembrances in an interview with William H. Herndon in September 1866.

My husband intended when he was through with his Presdt time to take me & family to Europe—didn't in late days dream of death—was cheery—funny—in high Spirits. He intended to return and go to California—over the Rocy Mountains and see the prospect of the Soldiers &c digging out gold to pay national debt.

He & [Charles] Sumner were like boys during his last days—down on the River after Richmond was taken—they acted like boys—were so glad the war was over. Mr L. wanted to live in Spgfd and be buried there up to 1865—Changed his notion where to live—never settled on any place particularly—moving & traveling—

Mr L was the kindest—most tender and loving husband & father in the world—He gave us all unbounded liberty—Said to me always when I asked him for any thing—You know what you want—go and get it. He never asked me if it was necessary. He was very very indulgent to his children—chided or praised for it he always said "It is my pleasure that my children are free—happy and unrestrained by paternal tyranny. Love is the chain whereby to lock a child to its parent. . ."

I often Said that "God would not let any harm Come of my husband"—we had passed through 5 long—terrible—bloody years unscathed that I thought so—so did Mr L; he was happy over that idea. He was cheerful—almost joyous as he got gradually to see the End of the war.

I used to read News Paper charges—news paper attacks on him—He said—"Don't do that, for I have enough to bear—yet I care nothing for them. If I am right I'll live and if I'm wrong I'll die any how—So let them pass unnoticed." I would playfully say—That's the way to learn—read both sides—

Mr Lincolns maxim and philosophy was —"What is to be will be and no cares of ours can arrest the decree."

Mary Todd Lincoln in 1846 or 1847.

I could tell when Mr. Lincoln had decided any thing: he was cheerful at first—then he pressed—or compressed his lips tightly—firmly When these thing showed themselves to me I fashioned myself and So all others had to do sooner or later—and the world found it out.

When we first went to Washington Many thought Mr. L weak. But he rose grandly with the circumstances and men soon learned that he was above them all. I never saw a man's mind develop so finely: his manners got quite polished.

He used to say to me when I talked to him about [Salmon P.] Chase & those who did him Evil— Do good to those who hate you and turn their ill will to friendship—Sometimes in Washington, being worn down he spoke crabbing to men—harshly so—Yet is seemed the People understood his Condition & forgave him—. . .

Mr Linc[oln] had a Kind of Poetry in his Nature: he was [a terribly] firm man when he set his foot down—none of us—no man not woman Could rule him after he had made up his mind. I told him about [William H.] Sewards intention to rule him—: he said—"I shall rule myself—shall obey my own Conscience and follow God in it." Mr Lincoln had no hope & no faith in the usual acceptation of those words: he never joined a Church: he was a religious man always, as I think: he first thought—to say think—about this subject was when Willie died—never before. He felt religious More than Ever about the time he went to Gettysburg: he was not a technical Christian: he read the bible a good deal about 1864. . .

Source:

Lincoln, Mary Todd. Interview with William H. Herndon, September 1866. Herndon-Weik Collection, Manuscript Division, Library of Congress, Washington, D.C. Published in *Herndon's Informants:*

Letters, Interviews, and Statements about Abraham Lincoln. Edited by Douglas L. Wilson and Rodney O. Davis, with the assistance of Terry Wilson. Urbana: University of Illinois Press, 1998.

5-2
William H. Herndon Gives His Impressions of Lincoln's Character

> *William H. Herndon (1818-1891) became Lincoln's junior law partner in 1844. They practiced together until Lincoln was elected president; Lincoln left the firm in Herndon's hands, expecting to resume the practice when his term ended. After Lincoln's death, Herndon embarked on a massive effort to obtain remembrances from people who had known Lincoln, particularly during his earlier years. The result was a biography originally published in 1889. In the excerpts below, Herndon relates his impressions of Lincoln's character.*

The true peculiarity of Mr. Lincoln has not been seen by his various biographers; or, if seen, they have failed woefully to give it that prominence which it deserves. It is said that Newton saw an apple fall to the ground from a tree, and beheld the law of the universe in that fall; Shakespeare saw human nature in the laugh of a man; Professor Owen saw the animal in its claw; and Spencer saw the evolution of the universe in the growth of a seed. Nature was suggestive to all these men. Mr. Lincoln no less saw philosophy in a story, and a schoolmaster in a joke. No man, no men saw nature, fact, thing, or man from his standpoint. His was a new and original position, which was always suggesting, hinting something to him. Nature, insinuations, hints and suggestions were new, fresh, original and odd to him. The world, fact, man, principle, all had their powers of suggestion to his susceptible soul. They continually put him in mind of something. He was odd, fresh, new, original, and peculiar, for this reason, that he was a new, odd, and original creation and fact. He had keen susceptibilities to the hints and suggestions of nature, which always put him in mind of something known or unknown. Hence his power and tenacity of what is called association of ideas must have been great. His memory was tenacious and strong. His susceptibility to all suggestions and hints enabled him at will to call up readily the associated and classified fact and idea.

As an evidence of this, especially peculiar to Mr. Lincoln, let me ask one question. Were Mr. Lincoln's expression and language odd and original, standing out peculiar from those of all other men? What does this imply? Oddity and originality of vision as well as expression; and what is expression in words and human language, but a telling of what we see, defining the idea arising from and created by vision and view in us? Words and language are but the counterparts of the idea—the other half of the idea; they are but the stinging, hot, heavy, leaden bullets that drop from the mold; and what are they in a rifle with powder stuffed behind them and fire applied, but an embodied force pursuing their object? So are words an embodied power feeling for comprehension in other minds. Mr. Lincoln was often perplexed to give expression to his ideas: first, because he was not master of the English language: and secondly, because there were no words in it containing the coloring, shape, exactness, power, and gravity of his ideas. He was frequently at a loss for a word, and hence was compelled to resort to stories, maxims, and jokes to embody his idea, that it might be comprehended. So true was this peculiar mental vision of his, that though mankind has been gathering, arranging, and classifying facts for thousands of years, Lincoln's peculiar stand-point could give him no advantage of other men's labor. Hence he tore up to the deep foundations all arrangements of facts, and coined and arranged new plans to govern himself. He was compelled, from his peculiar mental organization, to do this. His labor was great, continuous, patient and all enduring.

The truth about this whole matter is that Mr. Lincoln read less and thought more than any man in his sphere in America. No man can put his finger on any great book written in the last or present century that he read. When young he read the Bible, and when of age he read Shakespeare. This latter book was scarcely ever out of his mind. Mr. Lincoln is acknowledged to have been a great man, but the question is, what made him great? I repeat, that he read less and thought more than any man of his standing in America, if not in the world. He possessed originality and power of thought in an eminent degree. He was cautious, cool, concentrated, with continuity of reflection; was patient and enduring. These are some of the grounds of his wonderful success.

Not only was nature, man, fact and principle suggestive to Mr. Lincoln, not only had he accurate and exact perceptions, but he was causative, i.e., his mind ran back behind all facts, things and principles to their origin, history and first cause, to that point where forces act at once as effect and cause. He would stop and stand in the street and analyze a machine. He would whittle things to a point, and then count the numberless inclined planes, and their pitch, making the point. Mastering and defining this, he would then cut that point back, and get a broad transverse section of his pine stick, and peel and define that. Clocks, omnibuses and language, paddle wheels and idioms, never escaped his observation and analysis. Before he could form any idea of anything, before he would express his opinion on any subject, he must know it in origin and history, in substance and quality, in magnitude and gravity. He must know his subject inside and outside, upside and downside. He searched his own mind and nature thoroughly, as I have often heard him say. He must analyze a sensation, an idea, and words, and run them back to their origin, history, purpose and destiny. He was most emphatically a remorseless analyzer of facts things and principles. When all these processes had been well and thoroughly gone through, he could form an opinion and express it, but no sooner. He had no faith. "Say so", he had no respect for, coming though they might from tradition, power or authority.

All things, facts and principles had to run through his crucible and be tested by the fires of his analytic mind; and hence, when he did speak, his utterances rang out gold-like, quick, keen and current upon the counters of the understanding. He reasoned logically, through analogy and comparison. All opponents dreaded him in his originality of idea, condensation, definition and force of expression, and woe be to the man who hugged to his bosom a secret error if Mr. Lincoln got on the chase of it. I say, woe to him! Time could hide the error in no nook or corner of space in which he would not detect and expose it.

The great predominating elements of Mr. Lincoln's peculiar character, were: First, his great capacity and power of reason; secondly, his excellent understanding; thirdly, an exalted idea of the sense of right and equity; and, fourthly, his intense veneration of what was true and good. His reason ruled despotically all other faculties and qualities of his mind. His conscience and heart were ruled by it. His conscience was ruled by one faculty—reason. His heart was ruled by two faculties—reason and conscience. I know it is generally believed that Mr. Lincoln's heart, his love and kindness, his tenderness and benevolence, were his ruling qualities; but this opinion is erroneous in every particular. First, as to his reason. He dwelt in the mind, not in the conscience, and not in the heart. He lived and breathed and acted from his reason—the throne of logic and the home of principle, the realm of Deity in man. It is from this point that Mr. Lincoln must be viewed. His views were correct and original. He was cautious not to be deceived; he was patient and enduring. He had concentration and great continuity of thought; he had a profound analytic power; his visions were clear, and he was emphatically the master of statement. His pursuit of the truth was indefatigable, terrible. He reasoned from his well-chosen principles with such clearness, force, and compactness, that the tallest intellects in the land bowed to him with respect. He was the strongest man I ever saw, looking at him from the standpoint of his reason—the throne of his logic. He came down from that height with an irresistible and crushing force. His printed speeches will prove this; but his speeches before courts, especially before the Supreme Courts of the State and Nation, would demonstrate it: unfortunately, none of them have been preserved. Here he demanded time to think and prepare. The office of reason is to determine the truth. Truth is the power of reason—the child of reason. He loved and idolized truth for its own sake. It was reason's food.

Conscience, the second great quality and force of Mr. Lincoln's character, is that faculty which loves the just: its office is justice; right and equity are its correlatives. It decides upon all acts of all people at all times. Mr. Lincoln had a deep, broad, living conscience. His great reason told him what was true, good and bad, right, wrong, just or unjust, and his conscience echoed back its decision; and it was from this point that he acted and spoke and wove his character and fame among us. His conscience ruled his heart; he was always just before he was gracious. This was his motto, his glory: and this is as it should be. It cannot be truthfully said of any mortal man that he was always just. Mr. Lincoln was not always just; but his great general life was. It follows that if Mr. Lincoln had great reason and great conscience, he was an honest man. His great and general life was honest, and he was justly and rightfully entitled to the application, "Honest Abe". Honesty was his great polar star.

Mr. Lincoln had also a good understanding; that is, the faculty that understands and comprehends the exact state of things, their near and remote relations. The understanding does not necessarily inquire for the reason of things. I must here repeat that Mr. Lincoln was an odd and original man; he lived by himself and out of himself. He

This print by H. B. Hall, titled Diogenes His Lantern Needs No More, An Honest Man Is Found! The Search Is O'er, *was published in 1865. Diogenes was an ancient Greek philosopher who, as legend had it, roamed the streets with a lantern seeking an honest man.*

could absorb. He was a very sensitive man, unobtrusive and gentlemanly, and often hid himself in the common mass of men, in order to prevent the discovery of his individuality. He had no insulting egotism, and no pompous pride, no haughtiness, and no aristocracy. He was not indifferent, however, to approbation and public opinion. He was not an upstart, and had no insolence. He was a meek, quiet, unobtrusive gentleman…. Read Mr. Lincoln's speeches, letters, messages and proclamations, read his whole record in his actual life, and you cannot fail to perceive that he had good understanding. He understood and fully comprehended himself, and what he did and why he did it, better than most living men.

T here are contradictory opinions in reference to Mr. Lincoln's heart and humanity. One opinion is that he was cold and obdurate, and the other opinion is that he was warm and affectionate. I have shown you that Mr. Lincoln first lived and breathed upon the world from his head and conscience. I have attempted to show you that he lived and breathed upon the world through the tender side of his heart, subject at all times and places to the logic of his reason, and to his exalted sense of right and equity; namely, his conscience. He always held his conscience subject to his head; he held his heart always subject to his head and conscience. His heart was the lowest organ, the weakest of the three. Some men would reverse this order, and declare that his heart was his ruling organ; that always manifested itself with love, regardless of truth and justice, right and equity. The question still is, was Mr. Lincoln a cold, heartless man, or a warm, affectionate man? Can a man be a warm-hearted man who is all head and conscience, or nearly so? What, in the first place, do we mean by a warm-hearted man? Is it one who goes out of himself and reaches for others spontaneously because of a deep love of humanity, apart from equity and truth, and does what it does for love's sake? If so, Mr. Lincoln was a cold man. Or, do we mean that when a human being, man or child, approached him in behalf of a matter of right, and that the prayer of such a one was granted, that this is an evidence of his love? The African was enslaved, his rights were violated, and a principle was violated in them. Rights imply obligations as well as duties. Mr. Lincoln was President; he was in a position that made it his duty, through his sense of right, his love of principle, his constitutional obligations imposed upon him by oath of office, to strike the blow against slavery. But did he do it for love? He himself has answered the question: "I would not free the slaves if I could preserve the Union without it." I use this argument against his too enthusiastic friends. If you mean that this is love for love's sake, then Mr. Lincoln was a warm-hearted man—not otherwise. To use a general expression, his general life was cold. He had, however, a strong latent capacity to love; but the object must first come as principles, second as right, and third as lovely. He loved abstract humanity when it was oppressed. This was an abstract love, not concrete in the individual, as said by some. He rarely used the term love, yet was he tender and gentle. He gave the keynote to his own character when he said, "with malice toward none, with charity for all," he did what he did. He had no intense loves, and hence no hates and no malice. He had a broad charity for imperfect man, and let us imitate his great life in this.

"But was not Mr. Lincoln a man of great humanity?" asks a friend at my elbow, a little angrily; to which I reply, "Has not that question been answered already?" Let us suppose that it has not. We must understand each other. What doe you mean by humanity? Do you mean that he had much of human nature in him? If so, I will grant that he was a man of humanity. Do you mean if the above definition is unsatisfactory, that Mr. Lincoln was tender and kind? Then I agree with you. But if you mean to say that he so loved a man that he would sacrifice truth and right for him, for love's sake, then he was not a man of humanity. Do you mean to say that he so loved man, for love's sake, that his heart led him out of himself, and compelled him to go in search of the objects of his love, for their sake? He never, to my knowledge, manifested this side of his character. Such is the law of human nature, that it cannot be all head, all conscience, and all heart at one and the same time in one and the same person. Our Maker made it so, and where God through reason blazed the path, walk therein boldly. Mr. Lincoln's glory and power lay in the just combination of head, conscience, and heart, and it is here that his fame must rest, or not at all.

Not only were Mr. Lincoln's perceptions good; not only was nature suggestive to him; not only was he original and strong; not only had he great reason, good understanding; not only did he love the true and good—the eternal right; not only was he tender and kind—but in due proportion and in legitimate subordination, had he a glorious combination of them all. Through his perceptions—the suggestiveness of nature, his originality and strength; through his magnificent reason, his understanding, his conscience, his tenderness and kindness, his heart, rather than love—he approximated as nearly as most human beings in this imperfect state to an embodiment of the great moral principle, "Do unto others as ye would they should do unto you."

Source:

Herndon, William H. "The Character of Lincoln." In *Lincoln's Birthday: A Comprehensive View of Lincoln as Given in the Most Noteworthy Essays, Orations and Poems, in Fiction and in Lincoln's Own Writings.* Edited by Robert Haven Schauffler. New York: Dodd, Mead and Company, 1909.

5-3
Horace Greeley on Lincoln's Leadership

> *Horace Greeley (1811-1872) was the editor of the influential* New York Tribune. *He was acquainted with Lincoln as an occasional correspondent. In this excerpt, Greeley remembers his last meeting with Lincoln and reflects on his leadership.*

When I last saw him, some five or six weeks before his death, his face was haggard with care, and seamed with thought and trouble. It looked care-ploughed, tempest-tossed and weather-beaten, as if he were some tough old mariner, who had for years been beating up against the wind and tide, unable to make his port or find safe anchorage. Judging from that scathed, rugged countenance, I do not believe he could have lived out his second term had no felon hand been lifted against his priceless life.

> The chief moral I deduce from his eventful career asserts
> The might that slumbers in a peasant's arm!

the majestic heritage, the measureless opportunity, and of the humblest American youth. Here was an heir of poverty and insignificance, obscure, untaught, buried throughout his childhood in the frontier forests, with no transcendent, dazzling abilities, such as make their way in any country, under any institutions, but emphatically in intellect, as in station, one of the millions of strivers for a rude livelihood, who, though attaching himself stubbornly to the less popular party, and especially so in the State which he has chosen as his home, did nevertheless become a central figure of the Western Hemisphere, and an object of honor, love, and reverence throughout the civilized world. Had he been a genius, an intellectual prodigy, like Julius Caesar, or Shakespeare, or Mirabeau, or Webster, we might say: "This lesson is not for us—with such faculties any one could achieve and succeed"; but he was not a born king of men, ruling by the resistless might of his natural superiority, but a child of the people, who made himself a great persuader, therefore a leader by dint of firm resolve, and patient effort, and dogged perseverance. He slowly won his way to eminence and renown by ever doing the work that lay next to him—doing it with all his growing might—doing it as well as he could, and learning by his failure, when failure was encountered, how to do it better. Wendell Phillips once coarsely said, "He grew because we watered him"; which was only true in so far as this—he was open to all impressions and influences, and gladly profited by all the teachings of events and circumstances, no matter how adverse or unwelcome. There was probably no year of his life in which he was not a wiser, larger, better man than he had been the year preceding. It was of such a nature—patient, plodding, sometimes groping; but ever towards the light—that Tennyson sings:

> Perplex in faith, but pure in deeds,
>> At last he beat his music out.
> There lives more faith in honest doubt,
>> Believe me, than in half the creeds.

There are those who profess to have been always satisfied with his conduct of the war, deeming it prompt, energetic, vigorous, masterly. I did not, and could not, so regard it. I believe then,—I believe this hour—that a Napoleon I., a Jackson, would have crushed secession out in a single short campaign—almost in a single victory. I believed that an advance to Richmond 100,000 strong might have been made by the end of June, 1861; that would have insured a counter-revolution throughout the South, and a voluntary return of every State, through a dispersion and disavowal of its rebel chiefs, to the councils and the flag of the Union. But such a return would have not merely left slavery intact—it would have established it on firmer foundations than ever before. The momentarily alienated North and South would have fallen on each other's necks, and, amid tears and kisses, have sealed their reunion by ignominiously making the Black the scapegoat of their bygone quarrel, and wreaking

265

on him the spite which they had purposed to expend on each other. But God had higher ends, to which a Bull Run, a Ball's Bluff, a Gaines's Mill, a Groveton, were indispensable: and so they came to pass, and were endured and profited by. The Republic needed to be passed through chastening, purifying fires of adversity and suffering: so these came and did their work and the verdure of a new national life springs greenly, luxuriantly, from their ashes. Other men were helpful to the great renovation, and nobly did their part in it; yet, looking back through the lifting mists of seven eventful, tragic, trying, glorious years, I clearly discern that the one providential leader, the indispensable hero of the great drama—faithfully reflecting even in his hesitations and seeming vacillations the sentiment of the masses—fitted by his very defects and shortcomings for the burden laid upon him, the good to be wrought out through him, was Abraham Lincoln.

Source:

Greeley, Horace. "An Estimate of Abraham Lincoln." *Greeley on Lincoln*. Edited by Joel Benton. New York: Baker & Taylor Co., 1893.

5-4
Tribute by Shelby M. Cullom

> *Shelby M. Cullom (1829-1914) knew Lincoln in Springfield, Illinois. Lincoln encouraged the younger Cullom to study for the legal profession, and the two eventually were fellow lawyers on the circuit. Cullom was later elected to the Illinois legislature, the Illinois governorship, and the U.S. Senate. As senator, he presented the following speech on Lincoln's birthday in 1890, at the yearly banquet of the Republican Club of New York.*

Mr. President and Gentlemen of the Republican Club of the City of New York: I esteem it a great honor to be present on this occasion, and a still greater honor to be called upon to respond to the announcement just made by your president.

How true the utterance of the matchless Shakespeare of the Old World when applied to immortal Lincoln of the New! "The elements were so mixed in him, that

Nature might stand up and say to all the world, 'This is a man'" [a quote from *Julius Caesar*]. His life was gentle, pure, noble, and courageous; and from his early manhood all who knew him were ready to say of him, "This is a man." The name of Lincoln, Mr. President and gentlemen, has been to me as a household word from my earliest recollection. He was the friend of my father in my early boyhood, and I am proud to believe that he was my friend for many years before his death. I knew him somewhat in the sacred circle of his family. I knew him in the ordinary walks of life. I knew him as a practising lawyer at the bar. I knew him at the hustings as a public speaker and debater. I knew him as President of the United States, in that period in our history when men's souls were tried, and when the life of our nation seemed to be suspended by a thread. In the home circle he was gentle, affectionate, and true. In the ordinary walks of life he was plain, simple, and generous; a perfect type, so far as men can be, of all that makes a worthy citizen of a great Republic. At the bar he was conscientious, fair, powerful, and he seldom failed to gain his cause against the most able legal antagonists.

On the platform of debate he had few, if any, equals in this or any other country.

Mr. President, the world has had few such men as Abraham Lincoln. He was of gentle nature, great in heart, in head, and in deed. As a political leader he was actuated in his movements by strong convictions of duty, and had great power in convincing people of the righteousness of his cause. No man could stand in his presence and hear him without feeling sure of the honesty of his purposes and declarations, or of the strength of his arguments in behalf of whatever cause he championed. I have heard him often. I hear several of the famous debates between him and the great [Stephen] Douglas. I heard his great speech in which he uttered, I may say, that immortal declaration, that a house divided against itself cannot stand. It must be all one thing or the other; and I do not believe that an address was ever delivered in this country that produced a more profound and lasting impression upon the minds of the people of the country than this.

As Chief Magistrate of the nation, he was wise and prudent. He lived to witness that foul blot of slavery, which gave the lie to the Declaration of Independence, swept away. He was the savior of the Union and the liberator by his own hand of four millions of slaves.

Great-hearted patriot, and martyr to the cause of union and liberty, how we honor your name and your memory to-night! You fought a good fight. You finished your work. The world is better for your having lived in it, and it will call you blessed as long as the love of liberty shall dwell in the soul of humanity, which will be as long as time shall last upon the earth.

Mr. President, if I may be allowed to say it, Abraham Lincoln was given to the nation by Illinois. It seems to me but yesterday that I felt the warm grasp of his hand, and saw him leave his home at the capital of his state, where I have the honor of residing, to enter upon a larger field of usefulness at the capital of the nation, where he won immortality and died with a martyr's crown of glory upon his brow.

Never was a nobler man born of woman, and never throbbed a purer heart in human breast. The distinguished of the Old World, proud of their claims of long descent, may sneer at his humble birth; but, in my estimation, he was one of the greatest of men.

I do not know, fellow-citizens, but you may think me too partial toward that great man; but I have read his speeches, have seen him in the common walks of life; walked with him, as my friend here said, upon the streets, heard him talked about ever since I was ten years old, and I have deliberately come to the conclusion that no man has ever existed on the American continent superior to Abraham Lincoln.

By his consummate statesmanship he saved the republic from the evils of anarchy, and with self-denying patriotism refused to assume almost regal power when it was within his reach. He educated public opinion until it became ready to endorse what he knew to be right, and what wise statesmanship demanded at his hands.

Fellow-citizens, if you will think of his career as Chief Magistrate of the nation in that period of national peril, you will agree with me that his course and wisdom were such as to lead the people, and teach them as though he taught them not, and then he did what the country was ready to have done.

While Abraham Lincoln had not the advantages of a scholastic education, yet he fully appreciated and understood the beautiful in sentiment and diction, and no man has uttered more elegant language and tender words, touching the hearts of humanity, than he. To me his utterances were both powerful and elegant, and I would rather be the author of that great paper by which he gave freedom to four millions of slaves than be the author of the poems of Homer or the plays of Shakespeare. He was the savior of the Union, but though he did live to see the power of

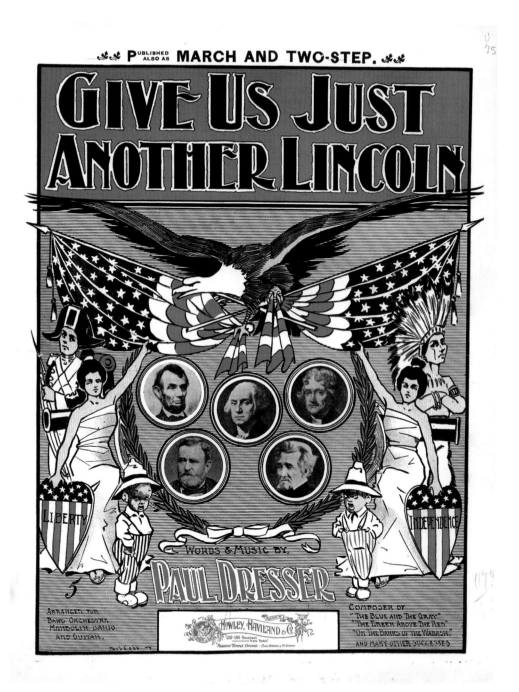

Sheet music for a song composed by Paul Dresser, published in 1900.

the Rebellion broken, he did not live to see the authority of the Union established in all the rebellious States. He was permitted to go up into Mount Nebo and to catch a glimpse of the promised land of the restored Union, but his weary feet were not allowed to cross the border that separated it from the wilderness of Civil War. In the very moment of victory, he was robbed of life by the cruel hand of a traitorous assassin, and his body was brought back amid the lamentations of a whole nation—even his foes giving to his merit the meed of tears—to find its last resting place in the soil of Illinois. As I gazed for the last time upon his face on the solemn occasion, sad and gentle in death as it had been in life, I thanked God that the good that he had done would live after him and give his name in honor to story and to song.

It is said that the story of every human life, if rightly told, may be a useful lesson to those who survive. There are none whose lives teach to Americans or to the world a grander or more profitable lesson than the life of Abraham Lincoln. The study of his life leads to private and public virtue; to correct ideas of our relations to each other; and to moral courage to stand by our convictions.

Lincoln was a child of Providence, raised up in a period of our history when there was need of such a man. A pioneer raised in a cabin, laboring with his hands, acquainted with the woods and fields, he communed with nature in all its beauty and grandeur as it voiced itself to the quiet man of destiny. He was a martyr to the cause of union and liberty, a noble victim to duty.

To repeat the sentiment embodied in the announcement of the President, "The fight must go on," and I am glad to the very bottom of my heart that I have the honor of standing in the presence of a great assembly of intelligent, earnest Republicans, who will join in that sentiment when I say that the fight must go on. "The cause of liberty must not be surrendered at the end of one or even one hundred defeats." Such words uttered by Lincoln, gave evidence of his convictions to duty. "Yes," said he, "I will speak for freedom against slavery so long as the Constitution of our country guarantees free speech; until everywhere in this broad land the sun shall shine, the wind shall blow, and the rain shall fall upon no man who goes forth to unrequited toil."

Mr. President and gentlemen, the fight must go on in favor of liberty and justice to the people of all classes, colors, and conditions in our country until every man in all this broad land shall stand equal before the law, in civil and political rights, equal in fact and equal in law, with no system of intimidation at elections, or fraudulent counting when the polls are closed.

The fight must go on, and no surrender at the end of one or one hundred defeats, until honest elections are secured everywhere in this country.

The fight must go on until merciless monopolists are subordinated, and the interests of the great body of the people are carefully regarded.

The fight must go on until trusts and combinations, prompted by greed and inordinate avarice, shall be broken up.

The fight must go on until the mission of the Republican party, founded by Lincoln and his compeers, shall have been fully accomplished in the destruction of all barriers to perfect equality in the civil and political rights of all the people of the country.

Gentlemen, how glorious the results of the great culminating struggle in which Lincoln was the mighty leader on the side of liberty! Did you ever reflect upon the consequences of a divided Union? Thanks to Lincoln, the great leader; and to that wise statesman, William H. Seward of New York, another great leader of the Republican party; and to my distinguished friend—and I am proud to have him here in your presence to-night—the gallant pathfinder and hero of the late war, General Fremont; and to Grant, that silent man; and to Sherman; and to Sheridan and Thomas; and to Hancock, the gallant leader; and to my dearest friend of latter days, the gallant John A. Logan; and to the great army of patriots whom they and others commanded in the struggle for national life, the dissolution of the Union was not accomplished.

How we are blessed as a nation! No standing army worth the name. No royal dynasty in this country. Fellow-citizens, in a little while every nation on the American continent, I trust, will be in full sympathy with each other, from the frozen regions of the North to the lower peninsula of the South. The people sovereign. No danger from foreign foe. Surrounded by the two oceans, the lakes, and the gulf. What an opportunity to build up the greatest nation the world ever saw!

A career of unprecedented glory awaits the nation. Slavery gone. Secession banished, I trust for all time. No gloomy clouds to obscure the light. "[Let] the mystic chords of memory . . . swell the chorus of the Union, when again touched, as surely they will be, by the better angels of our nature," and let us as citizens study and imitate the life and character of Lincoln, in its devotion to liberty, in the hope that the great principle for which Lincoln lived and died shall preserve this country as the purest and best country on the face of the globe [First Inaugural Address, Mar. 4, 1861].

Source:

Cullom, Shelby M. *Addresses Delivered at the Lincoln Dinners of Republican Club of the City of New York in Response to the Toast: Abraham Lincoln, 1887-1909.* New York: Republican Club of the City of New York, 1909.

5-5
Tribute by Schuyler Colfax

Schuyler Colfax (1823-1885) was a U.S. representative from Indiana and later vice president to President Ulysses S. Grant; he was also a political colleague of Lincoln's.

In his freedom from passion and bitterness; in his acute sense of justice; in his courageous faith in the right, and his inextinguishable hatred of wrong; in his warm and heartfelt sympathy and mercy; in his coolness of judgment; in his unquestioned rectitude of intention—in a word, in his ability to lift himself for his country's sake above all mere partisanship, in all the marked traits of his character combined, he has had no parallel since Washington, and while our republic endures he will live with him in the grateful hearts of his grateful countrymen.

Source:

Colfax, Schuyler. "Tributes to Lincoln." In *Lincoln's Birthday: A Comprehensive View of Lincoln as Given in the Most Noteworthy Essays, Orations and Poems, in Fiction and in Lincoln's Own Writings.* Edited by Robert Haven Schauffler. New York: Dodd, Mead and Company, 1909.

5-6
Tribute by Frederick Douglass

Frederick Douglass (1817-1895) was a former slave and abolitionist leader. He delivered the following speech at the Republican National League's commemoration of Lincoln's 79th birthday. In his moving speech, Douglass recounts a meeting with the president about the status of African-American troops fighting in the Civil War and offers his personal impressions of Lincoln.

I could almost wish to be excused from offering a single remark after the able, eloquent, and comprehensive, and, I might say, faithful, address to which we have just listened [a speech delivered by Senator Shelby M. Cullom of Illinois]. It would, perhaps, have been much better that the meeting should disperse after hearing what we have heard. And yet I am not sure but there is a sort of propriety in my coming to you and saying a few words, at least, in respect to the great and the good man of whom we have heard so much and of whom nothing new can be said.

I think it may be safely affirmed that the moral and mental greatness of no character which has come upon the stage in our day and generation, and in modern times, which has been more generally conceded, or more firmly established, than that great and good man whose birth we have assembled to-day to celebrate. A great cloud of witnesses, which no man can number, composed of all classes and conditions of men, at home and abroad, everywhere, have recognized Abraham Lincoln as one of the greatest and best men ever produced by this country, if not ever produced by the world at large.

I, and those I represent in part, may well enough wish to share with you in your admiration of his character and in the perpetuation of his great memory. You may extol him as a statesman and a patriot: we may, and will, extol him as a man and a philanthropist. You may honor his memory in that he saved your country when the light of its hope was going out, or seemed to be going out, in darkness, certainly in blood; we will cherish his memory in that he struck the galling fetters from four millions of the class to which we belong. You may honor him for the hope, aye, for the possibility, of a united country; we will honor him because he raised us from the depths, from the depths, from the condition of chattelhood to the possibility, the grand possibility of American citizenship. It was once said by Lamartine, one of the most brilliant of all modern French writers, that "William Wilberforce went up to heaven with a million of broken fetters in his arms, as evidence of a life well spent." Four times more than this can we say of Abraham Lincoln. He went up before his Maker with four millions of broken fetters in his arms as evidence of a life well spent. Glorious man! He was a man so broad in his sympathy, so noble in his character, so just in his action, so free from narrow prejudice; he touched the world so completely at all sides that all classes, conditions, all nations, kindreds, tongues, and people could hail him as a countryman, a clansman, a kinsman, a brother beloved, a benefactor.

I knew Abraham Lincoln personally. To have known him as I knew him, to know him as I knew him I regard as one of the grandest privileges experienced by me during a considerable lifetime. I knew him. I would not part with that peep into that noble soul for all the wealth, as Clay once said, that could be bestowed upon the most successful conqueror. It was a new revelation to me, my meeting with that great and good man. I saw him at a time of profound interest; a time when the fate of this Republic appeared to tremble in the balance. Men's hearts were failing them for fear of what was coming upon the land. I came down here from the North—I was not born in the North [Laughter]—but I went North on a mission some fifty years ago. It was not healthy for me to come down here for some twenty-five years after I went North. I came to him early in the year 1863, after the Emancipation Proclamation, of course, and I saw him to great advantage.

It was my first visit to Washington. First things are very important; and this was my first visit to Washington—the first time that I ever looked up and saw the Goddess of American Liberty on the lofty dome of yonder Capitol. My eyes saw something then that thrilled me, for I saw it in the light of the liberty proclaimed by Abraham Lincoln. I saw it in the light of those stars [pointing to the American flag], and it filled me with hope and expectation. It was my first entrance, too, into the White House. No man who has never felt the yoke of American bondage on his neck; no one who has not felt the fetter on his heel can imagine and enter into the tumult of feeling with which I entered the White House. It was a great day for me, a very great day, to enter the Executive Mansion and to approach the President of the United States. I was a little disturbed and a great deal agitated, but there was no real cause for trepidation or for alarm. I was going to see a great man—a *great* man. It is always easier to see a great man than to see a little one. I have noticed that the higher we go up in the gradations of humanity and moral greatness the further we get from prejudices, from narrowness, from everything like pettiness. I found myself without excuse for being alarmed, for being disturbed; for I was in the presence of a great man. Mr. Lincoln was reading when I entered, and I hesitated to approach him until he raised his eyes from the paper he held in his hand. His face and features struck me. They bore the marks of care and toil and solemn responsibility. I think I never saw a face that had so much of the real, I was going to say, saintliness, combined with so much resolution, as I saw in that deeply-ridged forehead of Abraham Lincoln. I went up towards him, and as I came near him I began

Frederick Douglass.

to tell him who I was and what I had been doing, and in his peculiar voice he stopped me. Said he, "I know who you are, Mr. Douglass, and I know what you have been doing; Mr. Seward has told me all about you." This put me at ease; but I had something to say to him. It was not mere courtesy. My mission to him was in regard to the enlistment and the treatment of colored troops. I had assisted in raising two regiments in the State of Massachusetts, and I was then engaged in the same work in the State of Pennsylvania, and I said to him, "I have come, Mr. Lincoln, to say to you three things, and only three things, and one of them is that I may be able to say to the colored soldiers at the North that they will be paid the same wages as the white soldiers.

"Secondly: when they perform brave and honorable deeds in the service of the country, on the battle-field, that you will promote them.

"Thirdly: when they are taken as prisoners and are killed, as the threat has been given that they shall be killed, that we shall retaliate." Those were the three things. I never shall forget how quietly and sympathetically Mr. Lincoln listened to what I had to say. I saw, when I came to the last proposition, the first he received with a smile of approval, the second also, but when it came to the third, that of retaliation, I got a peep into that good man's heart. There came over his face an expression of sadness, deep sadness, and he began to reply to the several propositions that I had made to him. He told me, "Mr. Douglass, you know that it was with great difficulty that I could get the colored soldiers, or get colored men, into the army at all. You know the prejudices existing against them; you know the doubt that was felt in regard to their ability as soldiers, and it was necessary at the first that we should make some discrimination in regard to them; they were on trial." And he argued the point as he only could argue. I never heard a man that could make a statement which should be in itself an overwhelming argument, as Abraham Lincoln could. He argued the question fully, and I was made to see that it was something, whether with wages or without wages, money or without money, it was a grand triumph to get a blue coat on the back of a negro, and the eagle on his button, and the musket on his shoulder. I agreed with him. But he said, "Nevertheless, though we cannot offer them at present the same pay as we pay the white soldiers, that will be done, Mr. Douglass, and you may say to your people that they will eventually be paid," as they were eventually paid, "dollar for dollar, equal with other soldiers."

On the other point of promotion, he was equally willing, but on retaliation he asked, "Where will it stop?" I could see that there was a vista of blood opening to him from which his tender heart shrank. He said, "If I could get hold of the men that murdered your troops, murdered our prisoners of war, I would execute them, but I cannot take men that may not have had anything to do with this murdering of our soldiers and execute them. No, Mr. Douglass, I don't see where it would stop; besides, I understand they are beginning to treat our colored soldiers as prisoners of war."

But this was not all I saw of Mr. Lincoln. After all perhaps I am taking up too much time [cries of go on; go on]. I saw a good deal more of him during the war, and even down to his inauguration, his second inauguration. There, too, I think I caught a glimpse of the soul of this great man, a remarkable glimpse, a deep insight into his mind and his heart. I mean at his second inauguration. I felt at that time there was the spirit of murder here in the District of Columbia (I am glad it is not here now), and I watched his carriage when he was on his way down to the Capitol to be inaugurated, and to deliver his inaugural address. [I had had the pleasure of putting the gown on Chief Justice Chase, who was to administer the oath on that occasion.] I got very near to Mr. Lincoln, for he did not hesitate, you know, to ask me to come even to his table, and ask me to eat with him, and ask me to the Soldiers' Home, dear man! Well, I say, I kept near to the carriage on his way to the Capitol. Pennsylvania avenue was not what it is now. Shepherd has not been along on the avenue. [It was then a sheep without a Shepherd.] I kept close to the carriage nearly up to the hub in mud, for I was afraid every step we took that something would happen to that good and glorious man. Well, when we got to the east portico of the Capitol, there I saw Mr. Lincoln in his true light. He had been abused. Oh, good man are apt to be abused. Men had been denouncing him on the right hand and on the left. Some of them blamed him very much that he hadn't brought the war to a close; another blamed him for not making the war an abolition war, and others blamed him for making it an abolition war, so he was blamed on all sides, and he answered them all in one sentence, and such a sentence I never heard from the lips of any man in his position before. He said: "Fondly do we hope, fervently do we pray, that this mighty scourge of war shall soon pass away; yet if God wills it continue till all the wealth piled up by two hundred years of bondage shall have been wasted, and each drop of blood drawn by the lash shall have been paid for one drawn by the sword, we must still say, as was said three thousand years ago, the judgments of the Lord are true and righteous altogether." Those words rang out over that throng, and they went over the country as never words went before, and they silenced all murmurs. They came down on the land like the summer's thunder shower on the parched ground, and a new life began.

But, my friends, I must not talk longer. I could talk all day about Abraham Lincoln.

Some people have said hard things about Mrs. Lincoln. For my part I take no stock in them. I loved Mrs. Lincoln. I loved her because Abraham Lincoln loved her. That was enough for me. And, besides, I don't take any stock in the stories of those who thought she was not in sympathy with him in his anti-slavery views. She was in sympathy with him. She used to say, when we abolitionists were very impatient with Mr. Lincoln, because he did not move fast enough, "Oh, yes, father is slow." Those words state what existed there. And when Mrs. Lincoln was leaving the White House, for Illinois, she said to her dressmaker [Elizabeth Keckley], who was near by when she was gathering up her things to go away: "Here is Mr. Lincoln's favorite cane [this is the identical cane that I now hold in my hand], and I know of no man who will value it more than Frederick Douglass." And she caused it to be sent to me at Rochester, N.Y., where I then lived; and I am the owner of this cane, you may depend on that; and I mean to hold it and keep in sacred remembrance of Abraham Lincoln, who once leaned upon it.

Source:

Douglass, Frederick. ""Speech of Hon. Frederick Douglass." In *Services Commemorative of the Seventy-Ninth Anniversary of the Birth of Abraham Lincoln by the Republican National League, at the League House, 1401 Massachusetts Avenue, Washington, D.C., February 12, 1888.* Washington, D.C.: Gibson Bros., 1888.

5-7
Tribute by Ulysses S. Grant

Ulysses S. Grant (1822-1885) was president of the United States from 1869 to 1877. Before that, he was a Union Army general who became Lincoln's chief commander of the Civil War in 1864. (See also document 6-6 by his son, Frederick Dent Grant.)

Ulysses S. Grant.

A man of great ability, pure patriotism, unselfish nature, full of forgiveness to his enemies, bearing malice toward none, he proved to be the man above all others for the struggle through which the nation had to pass to place itself among the greatest in the family of nations. His fame will grow brighter as time passes and his great—great work is better understood.

Source:

Grant, Ulysses S. "Tributes to Lincoln." In *Lincoln's Birthday: A Comprehensive View of Lincoln as Given in the Most Noteworthy Essays, Orations and Poems, in Fiction and in Lincoln's Own Writings.* Edited by Robert Haven Schauffler. New York: Dodd, Mead and Company, 1909.

5-8
William Tecumseh Sherman Recalls His Last Meeting with Lincoln

William Tecumseh Sherman (1820-1891) was a Union general who led the Army into the South. In late March 1865, Lincoln traveled on a steamboat to City Point, Virginia. There he had a final conference with Sherman and General Ulysses S. Grant aboard the River Queen. *In the excerpt below, Sherman remembers this last meeting with Lincoln on March 27-28.*

I know, when I left him, that I was more than ever impressed by his kindly nature, his deep and earnest sympathy with the afflictions of the whole people, resulting from the war, and by the march of hostile armies through the South; and that his earnest desire seemed to be to end the war speedily, without more bloodshed or devastation, and to restore all the men of both sections to their homes. In the language of his second inaugural address he seemed to have "charity for all, malice toward none," and, above all, an absolute faith in the courage, manliness, and integrity of the armies in the field. When at rest or listening, his legs and arms seemed to hang almost lifeless, and his face was care-worn and haggard; but the moment he began to talk his face lightened up, his tall form, as it were, unfolded, and he was the very impersonation of good-humor and fellowship. The last words I recall as addressed to me were that he would feel better when I was back at Goldsboro'. We parted at the gang-way of the *River Queen* about noon of March 28th, and I never saw him again. Of all the men I ever met, he seemed to possess more of the elements of greatness, combined with goodness, than any other.

Source:

Sherman, William Tecumseh. "With Charity for All." In *Lincoln's Birthday: A Comprehensive View of Lincoln as Given in the Most Noteworthy Essays, Orations and Poems, in Fiction and in Lincoln's Own Writings.* Edited by Robert Haven Schauffler. New York: Dodd, Mead and Company, 1909.

5-9
Tribute by Walt Whitman

Poet Walt Whitman (1819-1892) was known for his poems about Lincoln (see document 4-16). He also composed the following prose tribute.

Glad am I to give even the most brief and shorn testimony in memory of Abraham Lincoln. Everything I heard about him authentically, and every time I saw him (and it was my fortune through 1862 to '65 to see, or pass a word with, or watch him, personally, perhaps twenty or thirty times), added to and annealed my respect and love at the passing moment. And as I dwell on what I myself heard or saw of the mighty Westerner, and blend it with the history and literature of my age, and conclude it with his death, it seems like some tragic play, superior to all else I know—vaster and fiercer and more convulsionary, for this America of ours, than Eschylus or Shakespeare ever drew for Athens or for England. And then the Moral permeating, underlying all! The lesion that none so remote, none so illiterate—no age, no class —but may directly or indirectly read!

Abraham Lincoln's was really one of those characters, the best of which is the result of long trains of cause and effect—needing a certain spaciousness of time, and perhaps even remoteness, to properly enclose them—having unequaled influence on the shaping of this Republic (and therefore the world) as today, and then far more important in the future. Thus the time has by no means yet come for a thorough measurement of him. Nevertheless, we who live in his era—who have seen him, and heard him, face to face, and in the midst of, or just parting from, the strong and strange events which he and we have had to do with, can in some respects bear valuable, perhaps indispensable testimony concerning him. . . .

How does this man compare with the acknowledged "Father of his country?" Washington was modeled on the best Saxon and Franklin of the age of the Stuarts (rooted in the Elizabethan period)—was essentially a noble Englishman, and just the kind needed for the occasions and the times of 1776-'83. Lincoln, underneath his practicality, was far less European, far more Western, original, essentially non-conventional, and had a certain sort of out-door or prairie stamp. One of the best of the late commentators on Shakespeare (Professor Dowden) makes the height and aggregate of his quality as a poet to be, that he thoroughly blended the ideal with the practical or realistic. If this is so, I should say that what Shakespeare did in poetic expression, Abraham Lincoln essentially did in his personal and official life. I should say the invisible foundations and vertebrae of his character, more than any man's in history, were mystical, abstract, moral and spiritual—while upon all of them was built, and out of all of them radiated, under the control of the average of circumstances, what the vulgar call horse-sense, and a life often bent by temporary but most urgent materialistic and political reasons.

He seems to have been a man of indomitable firmness (even obstinacy) on rare occasions, involving great points; but he was generally very easy, flexible, tolerant, respecting minor matters. I note that even those reports and anecdotes intended to level him down; all leave the tinge of a favorable impression of him. As to his religious nature, it seems to me to have certainly been of the amplest, deepest-rooted kind. . . .

Dear to Democracy, to the very last! And among the paradoxes generated by America not the least curious, was that spectacle of all the kings and queens and emperors of the earth, many from remote distances, sending tributes of condolence and sorrow in memory of one raised through the commonest average of life—a rail-splitter and flatboatman!

Considered from contemporary points of view—who knows what the future may decide?—and from the points of view of current Democracy and The Union (the only thing like passion or infatuation in the man was the passion for the Union of the States), Abraham Lincoln seems to be the grandest figure yet, on all the crowded canvas of the Nineteenth Century.

Source:

Whitman, Walt. *Reminiscences of Abraham Lincoln by Distinguished Men of His Time.* Edited by Allen Thorndike Rice. New York: North American Publishing Company, 1886.

5-10
Robert G. Ingersoll on Lincoln's Legacy

Robert G. Ingersoll (1833-1899) was an Illinois lawyer who served as a colonel in the Union Army and as attorney general of Illinois; he was also a well-known orator. Here, Ingersoll extols Lincoln's many virtues.

S trange mingling of mirth and tears, of the tragic and grotesque, of cap and crown, of Socrates and Rabelais, of Aesop and Marcus Aurelius, of all that is gentle and just, humorous and honest, merciful, wise, laughable, lovable and divine, and all consecrated to the use of man; while through all, and over all, an overwhelming sense of obligation, of chivalric loyalty to truth, and upon all the shadow of the tragic end.

Nearly all the great historic characters are impossible monsters, disproportioned by flattery, or by calumny deformed. We know nothing of their peculiarities, or nothing but their peculiarities. About the roots of these oaks there clings none of the earth of humanity. Washington is now only a steel engraving. About the real man who lived and loved and hated and schemed we know but little. The glass through which we look at him is of such high magnifying power that the features are exceedingly indistinct. Hundreds of people are now engaged in smoothing out the lines of Lincoln's face—forcing all features to the common mold—so that he may be known, not as he really was, but, according to their poor standard, as he should have been.

Lincoln was not a type. He stands alone—no ancestors, no fellows, and no successors. He had the advantage of living in a new country, of social equality, of personal freedom, of seeing in the horizon of his future the perpetual star of hope. He preserved his individuality and his self-respect. He knew and mingled with men of every kind; and, after all, men are the best books. He became acquainted with the ambitions and hopes of the heart, the means used to accomplish ends, the springs of action and the seeds of thought. He was familiar with nature, with actual things, with common facts. He loved and appreciated the poem of the year, the drama of the seasons.

In a new country, a man must possess at least three virtues—honesty, courage and generosity. In cultivated society, cultivation is often more important than soil. A well executed counterfeit passes more readily than a blurred genuine. It is necessary only to observe the unwritten laws of society—to be honest enough to keep out of prison, and generous enough to subscribe in public—where the subscription can be defended as an investment. In a new country, character is essential; in the old, reputation is sufficient. In the new, they find what a man really is; in the old, he generally passes for what he resembles. People separated only by distance are much nearer together than those divided by the walls of caste.

It is no advantage to live in a great city, where poverty degrades and failure brings despair. The fields are lovelier than paved streets, and the great forests than walls of brick. Oaks and elms are more poetic than steeples and chimneys. In the country is the idea of home. There you see the rising and setting sun; you become acquainted with the starts and clouds. The constellations are your friends. You hear the rain on the roof and listen to the rhythmic sighing of the winds. You are thrilled by the resurrection called spring, touched and saddened by autumn, the grace and poetry of death. Every field is a picture, a landscape; every landscape, a poem; every flower, a tender thought; and every forest, a fairyland. In the country you preserve your identity—your personality. There you are an aggregation of atoms, but in the city you are only an atom of an aggregation.

Lincoln never finished his education. To the night of his death he was a pupil, a learner, an inquirer, a seeker after knowledge. You have no idea how many men are spoiled by what is called education. For the most part, colleges are places where pebbles are polished and diamonds are dimmed. If Shakespeare had graduated at Oxford, he might have been a quibbling attorney or a hypocritical parson.

Lincoln was a many-sided man, acquainted with smiles and tears, complex in brain, single in heart, direct as light; and his words, candid as mirrors, gave the perfect image of his thought. He was never afraid to ask—never too dignified to admit that he did not know. No man had keener wit or kinder humor. He was not solemn. Solemnity is a mask worn by ignorance and hypocrisy—it is the preface, prologue, and index to the cunning or the stupid. He was natural in his life and thought—master of the storyteller's art, in illustration apt, in application perfect, liberal in speech, shocking Pharisees and prudes, using any word that wit could disinfect.

He was a logician. Logic is the necessary product of intelligence and sincerity. It cannot be learned. It is the child of a clear head and a good heart. He was candid, and with candor often deceived the deceitful. He had intellect without arrogance, genius

283

without pride, and religion without cant—that is to say, without bigotry and without deceit.

He was an orator—clear, sincere, natural. He did not pretend. He did not say what he thought others thought, but what he thought. If you wish to be sublime you must be natural—you must keep close to the grass. You must sit by the fireside of the heart; above the clouds it is too cold. You must be simple in your speech; too much polish suggests insincerity. The great orator idealizes the real, transfigures the common, makes even the inanimate throb and thrill, fills the gallery of the imagination with statues and pictures perfect in form and color, brings to light the gold hoarded by memory, the miser—shows the glittering coin to the spendthrift, hope—enriches the brain, ennobles the heart, and quickens the conscience. Between his lips, words bud and blossom.

If you wish to know the difference between an orator and an elocutionist—between what is felt and what is said—between what the heart and brain can do together and what the brain can do alone—read Lincoln's wondrous words at Gettysburg, and then the speech of Edward Everett. The oration of Lincoln will never be forgotten. It will live until languages are dead and lips are dust. The speech of Everett will never be read. The elocutionists believe in the virtue of voice, the sublimity of syntax, the majesty of long sentences, and the genius of gesture. The orator loves the real, the simple, and the natural. He places the thought above all. He knows that the greatest ideas should be expressed in the shortest words—that the greatest statues need the least drapery.

Lincoln was an immense personality—firm but not obstinate. Obstinacy is egotism—firmness, heroism. He influenced others without effort, unconsciously; and they submitted to him as men submit to nature, unconsciously. He was severe with himself, and for that reason lenient with others. He appeared to apologize for being kinder than his fellows. He did merciful things as stealthily as other committed crimes. Almost ashamed of tenderness, he said and did the noblest words and deeds with that charming confusion—that awkwardness—that is the perfect grace of modesty. As a noble man, wishing to pay a small debt to a poor neighbor reluctantly offers a hundred-dollar bill and asks for change, fearing that he may be suspected either of making a display of wealth or a pretense of payment, as Lincoln hesitated to show his wealth of goodness, even to the best he knew. A great man, stooping, not wishing to make his fellows feel that they were small or mean.

*This tree in California's Calaveras Big Trees State Park
was named after Lincoln shortly after his death.*

He knew others, because perfectly acquainted with himself. He cared nothing for place, but everything for principle, nothing for money, but everything for independence. Where no principle was involved, easily swayed—willing to go slowly, if in the right direction—sometimes willing to stop, but he would not go back, and he would not go wrong. He was willing to wait. He knew that the event was not waiting, and that fate was not the fool of chance. He knew that slavery had defenders, but no defense, and that they who attack the right must wound themselves. He was neither tyrant nor slave. He neither knelt nor scorned. With him, men were neither great nor small,—they were right or wrong. Through manners, clothes, titles, rags and race he

285

saw the real—that which is. Beyond accident, policy, compromise and war he saw the end. He was patient as Destiny, whose undecipherable hieroglyphs were so deeply graven on his sad and tragic face.

> *But if you wish to know what a man really is, give him power. This is the supreme test. It is the glory of Lincoln that having almost absolute power, he never abused it, except upon the side of mercy.*

Nothing discloses real character like the use of power. It is easy for the weak to be gentle. Most people can bear adversity. But if you wish to know what a man really is, give him power. This is the supreme test. It is the glory of Lincoln that having almost absolute power, he never abused it, except upon the side of mercy.

Wealth could not purchase, power could not awe this divine, this loving man. He knew no fear except the fear of doing wrong. Hating slavery, pitying the master—seeking to conquer, not persons, but prejudices—he was the embodiment of the self-denial, the courage, the hope and the nobility of a nation. He spoke, not to inflame, not to upbraid, but to convince. He raised his hands, not to strike, but in benediction. He longed to pardon. He loved to see the pearls of joy on the cheeks of a wife whose husband he had rescued from death.

Lincoln was the grandest figure of the fiercest civil war. He is the gentlest memory of our world.

Source:

Ingersoll, Robert G. "Reminiscences of Abraham Lincoln." In *Lincoln's Birthday: A Comprehensive View of Lincoln as Given in the Most Noteworthy Essays, Orations and Poems, in Fiction and in Lincoln's Own Writings.* Edited by Robert Haven Schauffler. New York: Dodd, Mead and Company, 1909.

5-11
Tribute by Lyman Abbott

Lyman Abbott (1835-1922) was a Massachusetts clergyman and writer who offered the following assessment of Lincoln.

To comprehend the current of history sympathetically, to appreciate the spirit of the age, prophetically, to know what God, by His providence, is working out in the epoch and the community, and so to work with him as to guide the current and embody in noble deeds the spirit of the age in working out the divine problem,—this is true greatness. The man, who sets his powers, however gigantic, to stemming the current and thwarting the divine purposes, is not truly great.

Abraham Lincoln was made the Chief Executive of a nation whose Constitution was unlike that of any other nation on the face of the globe. We assume that, ordinarily, public sentiment will change so gradually that the nation can always secure a true representative of its purpose in the presidential chair by an election every four years. Mr. Lincoln held the presidential office at a time when public sentiment was revolutionized in less than four years … It was the peculiar genius of Abraham Lincoln, that he was able, by his sympathetic insight, to perceive the change in public sentiment without waiting for it to be formulated in any legislative action; to keep pace with it, to lead and direct it, to quicken laggard spirits, to hold in the too ardent, too impetuous, and too hasty ones, and thus, when he signed the emancipation proclamation, to make his signature, not the act of an individual man, the edict of a military imperator, but the representative act of a great nation. He was the greatest President in American History, because in a time of revolution he grasped the purposes of the American people and embodied them in an act of justice and humanity, which was in the highest sense the act of the American Republic.

Source:

Abbott, Lyman. In *The Lincoln Memorial: Album-Immortelles: Original Life Pictures, with Autographs, from the Hands and Hearts of Eminent Americans and Europeans, Contemporaries of the Great Martyr to Liberty, Abraham Lincoln, Together with Extracts from His Speeches, Letters and Sayings.* Edited by Osborn H. Oldroyd. Springfield, IL: Lincoln Publishing Company, 1890.

5-12
"Abraham Lincoln" by Rose Terry Cooke

Rose Terry Cooke (1827-1892) was an American poet and short-story writer who wrote this tribute to Lincoln.

Abraham Lincoln
"Strangulatus Pro Republica"

Hundreds there have been, loftier than their kind,
Heroes and victors in the world's great wars:
Hundreds, exalted as the eternal stars,
By the great heart, or keen and mighty mind;
There have been sufferers, maimed and halt and blind,
Who bore their woes in such triumphant calm
That God hath crowned them with the martyr's palm;
And there were those who fought through fire to find
Their Master's face, and were by fire refined.
But who like thee, oh Sire! hath ever stood
Steadfast for truth and right, when lies and wrong
Rolled their dark waters, turbulent and strong;
Who bore reviling, baseness, tears and blood
Poured out like water, till thine own was spent,
Then reaped Earth's sole reward—a grave and monument!

Source:

Cooke, Rose Terry. "Abraham Lincoln: 'Strangulatus Pro Republica.'" In *The Lincoln Memorial: Album-Immortelles: Original Life Pictures, with Autographs, from the Hands and Hearts of Eminent Americans and Europeans, Contemporaries of the Great Martyr to Liberty, Abraham Lincoln, Together with Extracts from His Speeches, Letters and Sayings*. Edited by Osborn H. Oldroyd. Springfield, IL: Lincoln Publishing Company, 1890.

5-13
"Lincoln, the Man of the People" by Edwin Markham

Poet Edwin Markham (1852-1940) wrote "Lincoln, the Man of the People," which became one of the most acclaimed poems about Lincoln. Markham penned the poem in 1899 at the request of the Republican Club of New York City for its Lincoln Birthday celebration in 1900.

Lincoln, the Man of the People

When the Norn-Mother saw the Whirlwind Hour,
Greatening and darkening as it hurried on,
She bent the strenuous Heavens and came down
To make a man to meet the mortal need.
She took the tried clay of the common road —
Clay warm yet with the genial heat of Earth,
Dashed through it all a strain of prophecy;
Then mixed a laughter with the serious stuff.
It was a stuff to wear for centuries,
A man that matched the mountains, and compelled
The stars to look our way and honor us.

The color of the ground was in him, the red earth;
The tang and odor of the primal things —
The rectitude and patience of the rocks;
The gladness of the wind that shakes the corn;
The courage of the bird that dares the sea;
The justice of the rain that loves all leaves;
The pity of the snow that hides all scars;
The loving-kindness of the wayside well;
The tolerance and equity of light
That gives as freely to the shrinking weed
As to the great oak flaring to the wind —
To the grave's low hill as to the Matterhorn
That shoulders out the sky.

And so he came.
From prairie cabin up to Capitol,
One fair Ideal led our chieftain on.
Forevermore he burned to do his deed
With the fine stroke and gesture of a king.
He built the rail-pile as he built the State,
Pouring his splendid strength through every blow,
The conscience of him testing every stroke,
To make his deed the measure of a man.

So came the Captain with the mighty heart:
And when the step of Earthquake shook the house,
Wrenching the rafters from their ancient hold,
He held the ridgepole up, and spiked again
The rafters of the Home. He held his place —
Held the long purpose like a growing tree —
Held on through blame and faltered not at praise.
And when he fell in whirlwind, he went down
As when a kingly cedar green with boughs
Goes down with a great shout upon the hills,
And leaves a lonesome place against the sky.

Source:

Markham, Edwin. "Lincoln, the Man of the People." *Lincoln & Other Poems.* New York: McClure, Phillips & Company, 1901.

George Washington is shown welcoming Lincoln into heaven in this 1865 engraving by John Sartain, based on a design by W. H. Hermans.

5-14
"Lift Every Voice and Sing" by James Weldon Johnson

James Weldon Johnson (1871-1938) was a teacher, writer, and civil rights leader. He wrote the lyrics to "Lift Every Voice and Sing" for a celebration of Lincoln's birthday in 1900 held at Stanton School in Jacksonville, Florida. His brother John Rosamond Johnson (1873-1954) composed the music. The song became famous as "The Negro National Anthem."

Lift Every Voice and Sing

Lift every voice and sing
Till earth and heaven ring,
Ring with the harmonies of Liberty;
Let our rejoicing rise
High as the list'ning skies,
Let it resound loud as the rolling sea, —
Sing a song full of the faith that the dark past has taught us
Sing a song full of the hope that the present has brought us;
Facing the rising sun of our new day begun,
Let us march on till victory is won.

Stony the road we trod,
Bitter the chast'ning rod,
Felt in the days when hope unborn had died;
Yet with a steady beat,
Have not our weary feet
Come to the place for which our fathers sighed?
We have come over a way that with tears has been watered
We have come, treading our path thro' the blood of the slaughtered
Out from the gloomy past
Till now we stand at last
Where the white gleam of our bright star is cast.

God of our weary years,
God of our silent tears,

292

Thou who has brought us thus far on the way;
Thou who has by Thy might
Led us into the light,
Keep us forever in the path, we pray.
Lest our feet stray from the places, our God, where we met Thee,
Lest our hearts, drunk with the wine of the world, we forget Thee,
Shadowed beneath Thy hand,
May we forever stand.
True to our God,
True to our native land.

Source:

Johnson, James Weldon, and J. Rosamond Johnson. "Lift Every Voice and Sing." New York: National Association for the Advancement of Colored People, ca. 1920. Available online at University of South Carolina, Department of Rare Books and Special Collections. http://www.sc.edu/library/spcoll/amlit/johnson/johnson2.html.

5-15
"Lincoln" by Paul Laurence Dunbar

Paul Laurence Dunbar (1872-1906) was a poet and the son of escaped slaves. He penned this tribute to Lincoln, which was published in 1903 in his collection Lyrics of Love & Laughter.

Lincoln

Hurt was the Nation with a mighty wound,
And all her ways were filled with clam'rous sound,

Wailed loud the South with unremitting grief,
And wept the North that could not find relief.
Then madness joined its harshest tone to strife:
A minor note swelled in the song of life.

'Till, stirring with the love that filled his breast,
But still, unflinching at the right's behest,
Grave Lincoln came, strong handed, from afar,
The mighty Homer of the lyre of war.
'Twas he who bade the raging tempest cease,
Wrenched from his harp the harmony of peace,
Muted the strings, that made the discord,—Wrong,
And gave his spirit up in thund'rous song.
Oh mighty Master of the mighty lyre,
Earth heard and trembled at thy strains of fire:
Earth learned of thee what Heav'n already knew,
And wrote thee down among her treasured few.

Source:

Dunbar, Paul Laurence. "Lincoln." *Lyrics of Love & Laughter.* New York: Dodd, Mead and Company, 1903.

5-16
Jonathan P. Dolliver on Lincoln's Legacy

Jonathan P. Dolliver (1858-1910) was a senator from Iowa when he offered the following reflections on Lincoln's enduring legacy. Dolliver gave the speech at an annual birthday dinner at the Republican Club of New York City in 1905.

Within less than half a century this man, once despised, once derided, once distrusted and maligned, has been transfigured, in the light of universal history, so that all men and all generations of men may see him and make out if possible the manner of man he was. His life in this world was not long, less than three score years; only ten of them visible above the dead level of affairs. Yet into that brief space events were crowded, so stupendous in their ultimate significance, that we find ourselves laying down the narrative which records them, with a strange feeling coming over us, that may be after all we are not reading about a man at all, but some mysterious personality, in the hands of the higher Powers, with a supernatural commission to help and to bless the human race. Our book shelves were filling up fast with apocryphal literature of the Civil War that if it had not been for the loving labors of the two men, John Hay and John G. Nicolay, who knew him best, and have gathered up the fragments of his life, so that nothing has been lost, we would have had by this time only a blurred and doubtful picture of his retiring and unpretentious character.

Some have told us that he was a great lawyer. He was nothing of the sort. It is true that he grasped without apparent effort the principles of the common law, and his faculties were so normal and complete that he did not need a commentary, nor a copy of the Madison papers, thumb-marked by the doubts and fears of the generations, to make him sure that the men who made the Constitution were building for eternity. But he practiced law without a library, and all who were acquainted with him testify that in a law suit he was of no account, unless he knew the right was on his side. It was against his intellectual and moral grain to accept Lord Bacon's cynical suggestion that there is no way of knowing whether a cause be good or bad till the jury had brought in its verdict.

The familiar judicial circuit around Springfield, where he cracked his jokes about the office stove in country taverns, where he spoke to everybody by his first name and everybody liked to hear him talk, did much for him in every way; but the noble profession, so ably represented about this board, will bear me witness that an attorney who gives his advice away for nothing, who does not have the foresight to ask for a retainer, and usually lacks the business talent to collect his fee, whatever other merits he may have, is not cut out by nature for a lawyer. I have talked with many of the oldtime members of the bar at which he used to practice law, thinking all the while of other things, and from what they say I cannot help believing that the notion even then was slowly forming in his mind, that he held a brief, with Power of Attorney from on High, for the unnumbered millions of his fellow men and was only loitering around the county seats of Illinois until the case came on for trial.

Some tell us that he was a great orator. If that is so, the standards of the schools, ancient and modern, must be thrown away. Perhaps they ought to be; and when they are this curious circuit-rider of the law; who refreshed his companions with wit and argument from the well of English undefiled; this champion of civil liberty, confut-

Thomas Nast created this pictorial tribute to Lincoln's Emancipation Proclamation in 1865.

ing [Stephen] Douglas with a remorseless logic, cast in phrases rich with the homely wisdom of proverbial literature; this advocate of the people, head and shoulders above his brethren, stating their case before the bar of history, in sentences so simple that a child can follow them; surely such a one cannot be left out of the company of the masters who have added something to the conquests of the mother tongue. He was dissatisfied with his modest address at Gettysburg, read awkwardly from poorly written manuscript; and thought Edward Everett's oration was the best he had ever heard, but Mr. Everett himself discerned with a minute for reflection, that the little scrap of crumpled paper which the President held in his unsteady hand that day would be treasured from generation to generation after his own laborious deliverance had been forgotten. The old school of oratory and the new met on that rude platform among the graves under the trees, and congratulated each other. They have not met very often since, for both of them have been pushed aside to make room for the essayists, the declaimers, the statisticians, and other enterprising pedlars of intellectual wares, who have descended like a swarm on all human deliberations.

He has been described as a great statesman. If by that you mean that he was trained in the administrative mechanism of the government, or that he was wiser than his day in the creed of the party in whose fellowship he passed his earlier years, there is little evidence of that at all; the most that can be said is that he clung to the fortunes of the old Whig leadership through evil, as well as good report, and that he stumped the county and afterwards the State; but the speeches which he made, neither he nor anybody else regarded it important to preserve. His platform from the first was brief and to the point. "I am in favor of a national bank. I am in favor of the internal improvement system, and a high protective tariff." But while for half his life he followed Henry Clay, like a lover more than a disciple, yet when that popular hero died and Lincoln was selected to make a memorial address in the old State House, he dismissed the principles of his party creed without a word, and reserved his tribute for the love of liberty and the devotion of the Union which shone even to the end, in that superb career.

To speak of Lincoln as a statesman, whatever adjectives you use, opens no secret of his biography and rather seems to me to belittle the epic grandeur of the drama in which he moved. Of course, he was a statesman; exactly so, Saul of Tarsus, setting out from Damascus, became a famous traveler, and Christopher Columbus, inheriting a taste for the sea, became a mariner of high repute.

There are some who have given a study, more or less profound, to the official records of the rebellion who make of Lincoln an exceptional military genius, skilful in the management of armies and prepared better even than his generals to give direction to their movements. I doubt this very much. He was driven into the war department by the exigency of the times, and if he towered above the ill-fitting uniforms, which made their way, through one influence and another, to positions of brief command during the first campaigns of the Civil War, it is not very high praise after all. One thing, however, he must be given credit for; he perceived the size of the undertaking which he had in hand, and he kept looking until his eyes were weary for the man who could grasp the whole field and get out of the Army what he knew was in it. It broke his heart to see its effort scattered and thrown away by quarrels among its officers, endless in number, and unintelligible for the most part to the outside world. When he passed the command of the Army of the Potomac over to General Hooker, he did it in terms of reprimand and admonition, which read like a father's last warning to a wayward son. He told him that he had wronged

297

his country and done a gross injustice to a brother officer. Recalling Hooker's insubordinate suggestion that the Army and the Government both needed a dictator, he reminded him that "only those generals who gain successes can set up dictators," and added, with a humor as grim as death, "what I now ask of you is military success, and I will risk the dictatorship." If the General did not tear up his commission when he read that letter it was because he was brave enough to bear the severity of the naked truth.

All this time he had his eye upon a man in the West, who had been doing an extensive business down in Tennessee, "a copious worker and fighter, but a very meager writer," as he afterwards described him in a telegram to Burnside. He had watched him with attentive interest, noticing particularly that his plans always squared with the event; that he never regretted to report; and after Vicksburg fell and the tide of invasion had been rolled back from the borders of Maryland and Pennsylvania, he wrote two letters, one to General Meade, calling him to a stern account for not following up his victory, and one to General Grant directing him to report to Washington for duty. The letter to General Meade, now resting peacefully in Nicolay's collection of the writings of Lincoln, all the fires of its wrath long since gone out, was never sent. But General Grant got his. And from that day there were no more military orders from the White House, no exhortations to advance, no dispatches to move upon the enemy's works. He still had his own ideas how the job ought to be done, but he did not even ask the General to tell him his. He left it all to him. And as the plan of the great Captain unfolded, he sent to his headquarters this exultant message:

"I begin to see it. You will succeed. God bless you all.
"A. Lincoln." [to U.S. Grant]

And so these two, each adding something to the other's fame, go down to history together; God's blessing falling like a benediction upon the memory of both.

The whole world now knows his stature. But while he lived hardly anybody was able to take his measure. The foremost statesman of his Cabinet, after pestering him for a month with contradictory pieces of advice, placed before him a memorandum, grotesque in its assumption of superior wisdom, which ended with an accommodating proposal to take the responsibilities of the administration off his hands. After the battle of Bull Run even so incorruptible a patriot as Edwin M. Stanton, known in after years as the organizer of victory, wrote to James Buchanan, then living near the Capital in the quiet of his country seat at Wheatland, these words of mockery and contempt:

> The imbecility of the administration culminated in that catastrophe; and irretrievable misfortune and national disgrace never to be forgotten are to be added to the ruin of peaceful pursuits and national bankruptcy as the result of Lincoln's 'running the machine' for five full months.

From the sanctum of the old Tribune, where for a generation Horace Greeley had dominated the opinions of the people as no American editor has done before or since his day, came a confidential letter, a maudlin mixture of enterprise and despair; a despair which, after seven sleepless nights, had given up the fight; an enterprise which sought for inside information of the inevitable hour of the surrender near at hand. "You are not considered a great man," said Mr. Greeley for the President's eye alone.

Who is this, sitting all night long on a lounge in the public offices of the White House, listening, with the comments of a quaint humor, to privates and officers and scared Congressmen and citizens, who poured across the Long Bridge from the first battlefield of the rebellion to tell their tale of woe to the only man in Washington who had sense enough left to appreciate it, or patience enough left to listen to it? Is it the log cabin student, learning to read and write by the light of the kitchen fire in the woods of Indiana? It is he. Can it be the adventurous voyager of the Mississippi, who gets ideas of lifting vessels over riffles while he worked his frail craft clear of obstructions in the stream; and ideas broad as the free skies, of helping nations out of barbarism as he traced the divine image in the faces of men and women chained together, under the hammer, in the slavemarket at New Orleans? It is he. Can it be the awkward farm hand of the Sangamon who covered his bare feet in the fresh dirt which his plow had turned up to keep them from getting sunburned, while he sat down at the end of the furrow to rest his team and to regale himself with a few more pages of worn volumes borrowed from the neighbors? It is he. Can it be the country lawyer who rode on horseback from county to county, with nothing in his saddlebags except a clean shirt and the code of Illinois to try his cases and to air his views in the cheerful company which always gathered about the court house? It is he. Is it the daring debater, blazing out for a moment with the momentous warning "A house divided against itself cannot stand," then falling back within the defenses of the Constitution, that the cause of liberty, hindered already by the folly of its friends, might not make itself an outlaw in the land? It is he. Is it the weary traveler who begged the prayers of anxious neighbors as he set out for the last time from home, and talked in language sad and mystical of One who could go with him, and remain with them and be everywhere for good? It is he.

> *They said he laughed in a weird way that night on the sofa in the public offices of the White House, and they told funny tales about how he looked, and the comic papers of London and New York portrayed him in brutal pictures of his big hands; hands that were about to be stretched out to save the civilization of the world; and his overgrown feet; feet that for four torn and bleeding years were not too weary in the service of mankind.*

They said he laughed in a weird way that night on the sofa in the public offices of the White House, and they told funny tales about how he looked, and the comic papers of London and New York portrayed him in brutal pictures of his big hands; hands that were about to be stretched out to save the civilization of the world; and his overgrown feet; feet that for four torn and bleeding years were not too weary in the service of mankind. They said that his clothes did not fit him; that he stretched his long legs in ungainly postures; that he was common and uncouth in appearance. Some said that this being a backwoodsman was becoming a rather questionable recommendation for a President of the United States; and they recalled with satisfaction the grace of courtly manners brought home form St. James'. Little did they dream that the rude cabin yonder on the edge of the hill country of Kentucky was about to be transformed by the tender imagination of the people into a mansion more stately than the White House; more royal than all the palaces of the earth; it did not shelter the childhood of a king, but there is one thing in this world more royal than a king—it is a man.

They said he jested and acted unconcernedly as he looked at people through eyes that moved slowly from one to another in the crowd. They did not know him; or they might have seen that he was not looking at the crowd at all; that his immortal spirit was girding for its ordeal. And if he laughed, it may be that he heard cheerful voices from above; for had he not read somewhere that He that sitteth in the heavens sometimes looks down with laughter and derision upon the impotent plans of men to turn aside the everlasting purposes of God?

It took his countrymen the full four years to find Abraham Lincoln out. By the light of the camp fires of victorious armies they learned to see the outline of his gigantic figure, to assess the integrity of his character, to comprehend the majesty of his conscience; and when at last they looked upon his care-worn face as the nation reverently bore his body to the grave, through their tears they saw him exalted above all thrones in the affection of the human race.

We have been accustomed to think of the Civil War as an affair of armies, for we come of a fighting stock and the military instinct in us needs little cultivation or none at all. But it requires no very deep insight into the hidden things of history to see that the real conflict was not between armed forces, was not on battlefields, nor under the walls of besieged cities; and the fact makes Abraham Lincoln greater than all his generals, greater than all his admirals, greater than all the armies and all the navies that responded to his proclamation. He stands apart because he bore the ark of the covenant. He was making not his own fight, not merely the fight of his own country, or of the passing generation. The stars in their courses had enlisted with him; he had a treaty, never submitted to the Senate, which made him the ally of the Lord of Hosts, with infinite reinforcements at his call. The battle he was waging was not in the fallen timber about the old church at Shiloh; nor in the Wilderness of Virginia; he contended not alone with an insurrection of the slave power; he was hand to hand with a rebellion ancient as selfishness and greed which in all centuries has denied the rights of man, made of human governments a pestilent succession of despotisms and turned the history of our race into a dull recital of crimes and failures and misfortunes. Thus he was caught up like Ezekiel, prophet of Israel, and brought to the East gate of the Lord's house; and when he heard it said unto him, "Son of Man, these are the men who devise mischief," he knew what the vision meant; for he understood better than any man who ever lived what this endless struggle of humanity is, and how far the nation of America had fallen away from its duty and its opportunity.

All his life there had dwelt in his recollection a little sentence from an historic document which had been carelessly passed along from one Fourth of July celebration to another, "All men are created equal." To him the words sounded like an answer to a question propounded by the oldest of the Hebrew sages, "If I despise the cause of my man servant, or my maid servant, when he contendeth with me, what shall I do when God riseth up? Did not He that made me make him?"—a strategic question that had to be answered aright before democracy or any other form of civil liberty could make headway in the world [quote from the Book of Job]. All men are created equal. He knew that the hand which wrote that sentence was guided by a wisdom somewhat higher than the front porch of a slave plantation in Virginia; that first principles overshadow time and place; and that when men take their lives in their hands to lay the foundations of free nations, they must speak the truth lest the heavens fall. With a sublime faith, shared within the limits of their light by millions, he believed that sentence. He had tested the depth of it till his plummet touched the foundation of the earth. From his youth that simple saying had been ringing in his ears, "All men are created equal." It was the answer of the Eighteenth Century of Christ, to all the dim millenniums that were before Him; yet he had heard it ridiculed, narrowed down to nothing and explained away. He understood the meaning of the words and came to their defence.

Brushing away the wretched sophistries of partisan expediency, he rescued the handwriting of Thomas Jefferson from obloquy and contempt. "I think," he said, " that the authors of that notable instrument intended to include all men. But they did not intend to declare all men equal in all respects. They did not mean to say that all were equal in color, size, intellect, moral development, or social capacity. They defined, with tolerable distinctness, in what respects they did consider all men created equal—equal, with certain inalienable rights among which are life, liberty and the pursuit of happiness. This they said and this they meant. They did not mean to assert the obvious untruth that all men were then actually enjoying that equality, nor [yet] that they were about to confer it immediately upon them. In fact they had no power to confer such a boon. They meant simply to declare the right, so that the enforcement of it should follow as fast as circumstances would permit. They meant to set up a standard maxim for free society, which should be familiar to all and revered by all; constantly looked to, constantly labored for, and even though never perfectly attained, constantly approximated; thereby constantly spreading and deepening its influence and augmenting the value and happiness of life to all people, of all colors, everywhere." That was the message of Abraham Lincoln to the nations of America. And as if to make it certain, that it was no mere flourish of a joint debate, he turned aside on his triumphal journey to the Capital, just before he took the oath of office, to repeat the sacred precepts of the Declaration in the hall at Philadelphia, where our fathers first spoke them, and to add his pledge to theirs that he would defend them with his life.

Here is the summit, the spiritual height, from which he was able to forecast the doom of all tyrannies, the end of all slaveries, the unconditional surrender of all the strongholds of injustice and avarice and oppression; this is the mountain top from which he sent down these inspiring words of good cheer and hope: "This essentially is a people's contest; on the side of the Union, a struggle to maintain in the world that form and substance of a government, the leading object of which is to elevate the condition of men, to lift artificial weights from shoulders; to clear the [paths] of laudable pursuit for all, and to afford all an unfettered start and a fair chance in the race of life."

Source:

Dolliver, Jonathan P. In *Addresses Delivered at the Lincoln Dinners of the Republican Club of the City of New York in Response to the Toast: Abraham Lincoln, 1887-1909*. New York: Republican Club of the City of New York, 1909.

5-17
Mark Twain on Preserving Lincoln's Birthplace

Mark Twain (1835-1910) was an author, a humorist, and a great admirer of Lincoln. Twain composed the following article for the New York Times *edition dated January 13, 1907. The article refers to efforts to make Lincoln's birthplace a national park.*

There is a natural human instinct that is gratified by the sight of anything hallowed by association with a great man or with great deeds. So many people make pilgrimages to the town whose streets were once trodden by Shakespeare, and Hartford guarded her Charter Oak for centuries because it had once had a hole in it that helped to save the liberties of a Colony. But in most cases the connection between the great man or the great event and the relic we revere is accidental. Shake-

Mark Twain in 1867.

speare might have lived in any other town as well as in Stratford, and Connecticut's charter might have been hidden in a woodchuck hole as well as in the Charter Oak. But it was no accident that planted Lincoln on a Kentucky farm, half way between the lakes and the Gulf. The association there had substance in it. Lincoln belonged just where he was put. If the Union was to be saved, it had to be a man of such an origin that should save it. No wintry New England Brahmin could have done it, or any torrid cotton planter, regarding the distant Yankee as a species of obnoxious foreigner. It needed a man of the border, where civil war meant the grapple of brother and brother and disunion a raw and gaping wound. It needed one who knew slavery not from books only, but as a living thing, knew the good that was mixed with its evil, and knew the evil not merely as it affected the negroes, but in its hardly less baneful influence upon the poor whites. It needed one who knew how human all the parties to the quarrel were, how much alike they were at bottom, who saw them all reflected in himself, and felt their dissensions like the tearing apart of his own soul. When the war came Georgia sent an army in gray and Massachusetts an army in blue, but Kentucky raised armies for both sides. And this man, sprung from Southern poor whites, born on a Kentucky farm and transplanted to an Illinois village, this man, in whose heart knowledge and charity had left no room for malice, was marked by Providence as the one to "bind up the Nation's wounds." His birthplace is worth saving.

Source:

Twain, Mark. "A Lincoln Memorial: A Plea by Mark Twain for the Setting Apart of His Birthplace." *New York Times,* January 13, 1907.

5-18
Tribute by Frederic Harrison

Frederic Harrison (1831-1923) was an English philosopher who admired Lincoln from across the Atlantic. He was a professor at Lincoln's Inn, a 500-year-old British legal association that was named not for the American president but for Henry de Lacy, third Earl of Lincoln, England, who died in 1311. In the excerpt below, Harrison offers his views on his country's relationship with the United States during the Civil War, as well as a tribute to Lincoln.

The great struggle which has forever decided the cause of slavery of man to man, is, beyond all question, the most critical which the world has seen since the great revolutionary outburst. If ever there was a question which was to test political capacity and honesty it was this. A true statesman, here if ever, was bound to forecast truly the issue, and to judge faithfully that cause at stake. We know now, it is beyond dispute, that the cause which won was certain to win in the end, that its reserve force was absolutely without limit, that its triumph was one of the turning points in modern civilization. It was morally certain to succeed, and it did succeed with an overwhelming and mighty success. From first to last both might and right went all one way. The people of England went wholly that way. The official classes went wholly some other way.

One of the great keynotes of England's future is simply this—what will be her relations with the great republic? If the two branches of the Anglo-Saxon race are to form two phases of one political movement, their welfare and that of the world will be signally promoted. If their courses are marred by jealousies or contests, both will be fatally retarded. Real confidence and sympathy extended to that people in the hour of their trial would have forged an eternal bond between us. To discredit and distrust them, then, was to sow deep the seeds of antipathy. Yet, although a union in feeling was of importance so great, although so little would have secured it, the governing classes of England wantonly did all they could to foment a breach.

A great political judgment fell upon a race of men, our own brothers; the inveterate social malady they inherited came to crisis. We watched it gather with exultation and insult. There fell on them the most terrible necessity which can befall men, the necessity of sacrificing the flower of their citizens in civil war, of tearing up their civil and social system by the roots, of transforming the most peaceful type of society into the most military. We magnified and shouted over every disaster; we covered them with insult; we filled the world with ominous forebodings and unjust accusations. There came on them one awful hour when the powers of evil seemed almost too strong; when any but a most heroic race would have sunk under the blows of their traitorous kindred. We chose that moment to give actual succour to their enemy, and stabbed them in the back with a wound which stung their pride even more than it crippled their strength. They displayed the most splendid examples of energy and fortitude which the modern world has seen, with which the defense of Greece against Asia, and of France against Europe, alone can be compared in the whole annals of mankind. They developed almost ideal civic virtues and gifts; generosity, faith, firmness; sympathy the most affecting, resources the most exhaustless, ingenuity the most magical. They brought forth the most beautiful and heroic character that in recent times has ever led a nation, the only blameless type of the statesman since the days of Washington. Under him they created the purest model of government which has yet been seen on the earth—a whole nation throbbing into one great heart and brain, one great heart and brain giving unity and life to a whole nation. The hour of their success came; unchequered in the completeness of its triumph, unsullied by any act of vengeance, hallowed by a great martyrdom.

> *Under him they created the purest model of government which has yet been seen on the earth—a whole nation throbbing into one great heart and brain, one great heart and brain giving unity and life to a whole nation.*

Source:

Harrison, Frederic. "The Crisis and the Hero." In *Lincoln's Birthday: A Comprehensive View of Lincoln as Given in the Most Noteworthy Essays, Orations and Poems, in Fiction and in Lincoln's Own Writings.* Edited by Robert Haven Schauffler. New York: Dodd, Mead and Company, 1909.

5-19
Tribute by Rutherford B. Hayes

Rutherford B. Hayes (1822-1893) was the 19th president of the United States. He met president-elect Lincoln in Indianapolis during his 1861 tour across the country to Washington, D.C.

Now all men begin to see that the plain people, who at last came to love him and to lean upon his wisdom, and trust him absolutely, were altogether right, and that in deed and purpose he was earnestly devoted to the welfare of the whole country, and of all its inhabitants.

Source:

Hayes, Rutherford B. "Tributes." In *Lincoln's Birthday: A Comprehensive View of Lincoln as Given in the Most Noteworthy Essays, Orations and Poems, in Fiction and in Lincoln's Own Writings.* Edited by Robert Haven Schauffler. New York: Dodd, Mead and Company, 1909.

5-20
Tribute by William McKinley

William McKinley (1843-1901) was the 25th president of the United States. He wrote the following tribute to Lincoln and George Washington.

The greatest names in American history are Washington and Lincoln. One is forever associated with the independence of the States and the formation of the Federal Union; the other with universal freedom and the preservation of the Union.

Washington enforced the Declaration of Independence as against England. Lincoln proclaimed the fulfillment not only to a down-trodden race in America, but to all people for all time who may seek the protection of our flag. These illustrious men achieved grander results for mankind within a single century than any other men ever accomplished in all the years since the first flight of time began.

*The **Emancipation Group**, created by sculptor Thomas Ball and also known as the **Freedmen's Monument**, was funded by freed African Americans after the Civil War.*

Washington drew his sword not for a change of rulers upon an established throne, but to establish a new government which should acknowledge no throne but the tribute of the people.

Lincoln accepted war to save the Union, the safeguard of our liberties, and re-established it on indestructible foundations as forever "one and indivisible." To quote his own words: "Now we are contending that this nation under God, shall have a new birth of freedom, and that government of the people, by the people, for the people shall not perish from the earth."

Source:

McKinley, William. "Washington and Lincoln." In *Lincoln's Birthday: A Comprehensive View of Lincoln as Given in the Most Noteworthy Essays, Orations and Poems, in Fiction and in Lincoln's Own Writings.* Edited by Robert Haven Schauffler. New York: Dodd, Mead and Company, 1909.

5-21
Tribute by Theodore Roosevelt

Theodore Roosevelt (1858-1919) was the 26th president of the United States. He offered the following assessment of the contribution of another president he greatly admired.

A braham Lincoln—the spirit incarnate of those who won victory in the Civil War—was the true representative of this people, not only for his own generation, but for all time, because he was a man among men. A man who embodied the qualities of his fellow-men, but who embodied them to the highest and most unusual degree of perfection, who embodied all that there was in the nation of courage, of wisdom, of gentle, patient kindliness, and of common sense.

Source:

Roosevelt, Theodore. "Lincoln." In *Lincoln's Birthday: A Comprehensive View of Lincoln as Given in the Most Noteworthy Essays, Orations and Poems, in Fiction and in Lincoln's Own Writings.* Edited by Robert Haven Schauffler. New York: Dodd, Mead and Company, 1909.

Part 6
Centennial Celebrations

Lincoln was still an important figure even a century after his birth, as shown in these pieces written to celebrate the 100th anniversary of his birth in 1909. Public calls for the observance of this day began as early as 1905, when the *New York Times* published an article titled "The Lincoln Centenary." Local governments and civic organizations began preparations for celebrations soon after. Notable people readied speeches for appearances at banquets and poets composed verse in honor of the occasion. A prominent example of the latter—"The Man of Peace," a tribute written by Canadian-born poet Bliss Carman to commemorate the Lincoln centennial—opens this section.

Many cities hosted special gatherings for the centennial, some of the largest and most elaborate in Lincoln's adopted home state of Illinois. The first seven selections are from speeches delivered at various venues in Illinois. Several observances were held in Chicago, where Lincoln was celebrated in speeches by *Toronto Globe* editor J. A. Macdonald, Rabbi Emil G. Hirsch, Reverend A. J. Carey, Reverend J. W. E. Bowen, and Major-General Frederick Dent Grant, the son of Ulysses S. Grant.

Other areas also hosted commemorations. In Hodgenville, Kentucky, President Theodore Roosevelt laid the cornerstone for the Birthplace Memorial, and Civil War veteran General James Grant Wilson spoke at the gathering. In New York City, Booker T. Washington paid tribute to Lincoln at the Republican Club; Joseph Hodges Choate addressed an audience at Cooper Institute, where Lincoln made a memorable impression nearly 50 years before; and New York Senator Chauncey M. Depew shared his memories of Lincoln at the Seventy-first Regiment Armory. In Bloomington, Indiana, where Lincoln had addressed the Republican Convention in 1856, former Vice President Adlai E. Stevenson spoke at the commemoration.

There was even an international element to the centennial. Several ambassadors from other nations delivered speeches at commemorations honoring Lincoln: French Ambassador Jean Adrian Jusserand in Springfield, Illinois; Japanese Ambassador Kogoro Takahira in Peoria, Illinois; and Brazilian Ambassador Joaquim Nabuco in Washington, D.C. Across the Atlantic Ocean, an observance was held in Manchester,

England, where Major Church Howe related some of his Civil War experiences under Lincoln.

This section concludes with a piece by the poet Carl Sandburg, one of Lincoln's great admirers. Sandburg wrote an editorial published on August 3, 1909, to commemorate the Lincoln penny, issued that year to honor the president. The editorial is believed to be the poet's first published work about Lincoln.

6-1
"The Man of Peace" by Bliss Carman

Poet Bliss Carman (1861-1929) wrote this poem for the 100th anniversary of Lincoln's birth in 1909.

The Man of Peace
(February 12th, 1909)

What winter holiday is this?
In Time's great calendar,
Marked in the rubric of the saints,
And with a soldier's star,
Here stands the name of one who lived
To serve the common weal,
With humor tender as a prayer
And honor firm as steel.

No hundred hundred years can dim
The radiance of his mirth,
That set unselfish laughter free
From all the sons of earth.
Unswerved through stress and scant
    success,
Out of his dreamful youth
He kept an unperverted faith
In the almighty truth.

Born in the fulness of the days,
Up from the teeming soil,
By the world-mother reared and
    schooled
In reverence and toil,
He stands the test of all life's best
Through play, defeat, or strain;

Never a moment was he found
Unlovable nor vain.

Fondly we set apart this day,
And mark this plot of earth
To be forever hallowed ground
In honor of his birth,
Where men may come as to a shrine
And temple of the good,
To be made sweet and strong of heart
In Lincoln's brotherhood.

Here walked God's earth in modesty
The shadow that was man,
A shade of the divine that moved
Through His mysterious plan.
So must we fill the larger mould
Of wisdom, love, and power,
Fearless, compassionate, contained,
And masters of the hour,

As men found faithful to a task
Eternal, pressing, plain,
Accounting manhood more than wealth,
And gladness more than gain;
Distilling happiness from life,
    As vigor from the air,
Not wresting it with ruthless hands,

313

Spoiling our brother's share.

Here shall our children keep alive
The passion for the right,—
The cause of justice in the world,
That was our fathers' fight.
For this the fair-haired stripling rode,
The dauntless veteran died,
For this we keep the ancient code
In stubbornness and pride.

O South, bring all your chivalry;
And West, give all your heart;
And East, your old untarnished dreams
Of progress and of art!
Bid waste and war to be no more,
Bid wanton riot cease;
At your command give Lincoln's land
To Paradise,—to peace.

Source:

Carman, Bliss. "The Man of Peace." *The Rough Rider and Other Poems.* New York: Mitchell Kennerley, 1909.

6-2
Centennial Celebration in Chicago, Illinois—J. A. Macdonald

J. A. Macdonald was the editor of the Toronto Globe. *He delivered a speech at the centennial celebration at the Seventh Regiment Armory in Chicago on the afternoon of February 12, 1909. The following excerpts from his speech offer a Canadian perspective on Lincoln and his legacy.*

Among the men born of American women, there has not arisen a greater than Abraham Lincoln. It is fitting that throughout this Republic, from the capital to the remotest pioneer hamlet, his name should this day be lifted high in loving memory. The honor of that name is the priceless heritage of every State in this great Union, whose integrity he maintained and whose flag he saved from shame.

But if the people of other States raise their voices in this centennial celebration with pride and grateful praise, how much more you—you people of Illinois, whose State gave him that nation; you citizens of Chicago, whose city witnessed his first nomination to the Presidency—how much more should you cherish the name of Lincoln as the honorable birthright of yourselves and your children; and—

> "For many and many an age proclaim
> At civic revel and pomp and game
> With honor, honor, honor to him
> Eternal honor to his name!"

The smoke of war has long since cleared away. Even the darker clouds of ignorance and selfishness and suspicion that blinded the eyes and hardened the hearts of men on both sides, and made not only the Revolution, but the Civil War inevitable, have been shot through with straight white light of reason and charity and truth. The men of the South to-day appreciate the work and venerate the memory of Abraham Lincoln, even as the men of the North are coming to honor the heroism and courage and personal worth of those genuine patriots and noble leaders, Robert E. Lee and "Stonewall" Jackson. We meet as the reconciled members of one great family, all enriched by the memories of each, the heirlooms of one being the treasures of all. We come, all of you the blue, and you, too, of the gray, and we of the red-coat and kilted tartan, heritors of the same history, sharers in the same freedom, sons of the same blood; and in the speech that sways from the Gulf to the Arctic Sea we pay our tribute of honor, and reverence, and love to the memory of that greatest world-citizen this continent has known. For among the men born of American women, there has not arisen a greater than Abraham Lincoln.

It is not for me to tell the story of Abraham Lincoln's life, the incidents of his great career, or the traditions that gather around his name. All of that has been done again and again in every Lincoln renascence that has marked each decade since his day. It is

This memorial ribbon created for the centennial observance features the famous quote from Lincoln's second inaugural address: "With malice toward none, with charity for all."

being done to-day by those who knew him face to face. It is not for me to come from Canada to Illinois to recite Lincoln anecdotes, or to pronounce a Lincoln eulogy. Not as a neighbor, not as an acquaintance, not as a citizen of the same State or of the same nation, may I speak of him as many might speak. To me he stands out, not in the softened light of personal friendship, not even with the glorifying halo of patriotic devotion on his brow. From the long range of another land, from under the shadow of another flag, I see him stand in the great perspective of world-history, not merely the citizen of your State, of the saviour of your Republic, but Lincoln, the world-citizen; Lincoln, the man whose name spells freedom in every land. And for that Lincoln, one of the few immortals of his age and land, I profess the reverence which the nobleness of his character and the heroism of his life must ever command from you of this Republic and from us, too, of the Canadian Dominion. Into our Canadian lives he came as a mighty inspiration, and our childhood's lips were taught to speak his name with that respect we paid our own good and gracious Queen.

I recall as vividly as if it were yesterday the night in that fateful week of April 1865, when into my childhood's home, on a pioneer farm cut out of the primeval forest of Middlesex County, in Upper Canada, the *Toronto Globe* came, bordered in black. Its real story read aloud in the family circle brought pain and grief to Canadian hearts. So it came that my very earliest knowledge of your country and its history was in that tragic martyrdom at Washington, and the very first name outside that backwoods settlement in Canada to be inscribed indelibly on my boyhood's honor roll was the name of your own illustrious Lincoln.

The theme which I choose is this: The Significance of Lincoln. I would have you stand with me for a little, not so close to that life as to lose the sense of its great proportions, but not so far away as to miss the meaning and the majesty of its radiating power. If I express some things with which some may not agree—and that must be so—it is because I am free to voice honest convictions with unreserve in the presence of free and honest men.

I would have you consider the significance of Lincoln, the meaning of his life, and the reach of his influence, in the century to which he belonged, and in this larger century that reaps the harvests which he sowed.

First, consider the significance of Lincoln to democracy in North America. I mean Canada as well as the United States. And by democracy I mean, not any party form or political organization, but, in the words made immortal by Lincoln at Gettysburg, "government of the people, by the people, for the people."

On this continent, democracy is being worked out through republican forms in the United States, and through forms adapted to monarchical institutions in Canada. In both countries it is democracy. The democratic spirit takes little account of mere names and forms. . .

The time had surely come when democracy in the United States must needs justify itself alike to its own children and to the world. It was not enough to point to an academic and speculative declaration that "all men are born free and equal," when, under the Stars and Stripes, three millions of human beings went out to "unrequited toil." It was not enough to talk loftily of "the land of the free," and to echo Jefferson's tirades against monarchy, when, nearly a century after the signing of the Declaration of Independence, the only land on all this continent of North America in which in very truth all men were born free was under monarchial government; and the only flag that gave protection to all classes, without respect of race or color, was the Union Jack. It cost treasure and it cost blood to wipe out that stain, but in wiping it out Lincoln justified American democracy before the nations of the world. . .

Turn now to the Canadian situation. What is the significance of Lincoln for democracy in the Dominion? Was government of the people, by the people, for the people, in Canada served in any significant way by the life he lived and the service he rendered to democracy in the United States?

It is quite true Lincoln knew almost nothing at all about Canada. He never set foot on Canadian soil. He had no direct interest in Canadian problems. But a life so vital as his could not be lived to itself or to the people of his own country alone. Sovereignty stops at the Great Lakes and the international boundary line, but the masterful life overleaps all such limitations. The man is greater than the ruler. In Abraham Lincoln, Canada has had an inheritance that through a half-century has made for the enrichment of public life and the redemption of public service. . .

. . .With what eagerness, therefore, was the rise of Lincoln, the new star on your western horizon, watched by the people of Canada. From the day of his nomination in 1860 until his tragic death, the name of Abraham Lincoln was as highly honored, and his course was as intelligently and as anxiously followed, by the people of the Dominion as by you of the Republic. His success was not only yours; it was ours as well. . .

And Lincoln's work in preserving the Union and determining that there would be but one Republic, even though he may have strained the terms of the Constitution, was approved by the best Canadian opinion. I quote again form the Hon. George Brown. In a speech of unreserved congratulations on Lincoln's Emancipation Proclamation, in Toronto in February, 1863, Mr. Brown said:

> "No man who loves human freedom and desires the elevation of mankind could contemplate without the deepest regret a failure of that great experiment of self-government in the United States. Had Mr. Lincoln consented to the secession of the Southern States, had he admitted that each State could at any moment, and on any plea, take its departure from the Union, he would simply have given his consent to the complete rupture of the federation. The Southern States and the border States would have gone. The Western States might soon have followed. The States on the Pacific would not have been long behind. Where the practice of secession, once commenced, would have ended, would be difficult to say. Petty Republics would have covered the continent; each would have had its standing army and its standing feuds; and we, too, in Canada, were it only in self-defense, must have been compelled to arm. I for one cannot look back on the history of the American Republic without feeling that all this would have been a world-wide misfortune. How can we ever forget that the United States territory has, for nearly a century, been an ever-open asylum

for the poor and persecuted from every land? Millions have fled from suffering and destitution in every corner of Europe to find happy homes and overflowing prosperity in the Republic. Is there a human being could rejoice that all this should be ended?"

That was the view of the soundest and best-informed Canadian public opinion in Lincoln's own day. The years that have intervened have confirmed that opinion. Canadians of to-day rise up and bless the name of Abraham Lincoln, because by him it was determined that the Canadian Dominion, now stretching from ocean to ocean, would have to do on this continent not with two Republics, as seemed inevitable, not with four, as seemed possible, but with one great Nation, along the four thousand miles of international boundary, and holding sovereign sway from the Great Lakes to the Gulf.

For that great fact in our international relationships we in Canada give thanks with you on this Lincoln Centennial day. All that Lincoln did in the cause of human freedom and guarding the sacredness of human rights, he did for us as for you. And his own great life is our inheritance as well as yours. Under his strong hand democracy in the United States survived the utmost strain, and because of that, we in Canada are being heartened in our great task of laying the foundations and erecting the structure of another democracy on the north half of this continent, in which all men shall be born free and equal, and where government of the people, by the people, for the people, shall have another chance. . .

Think for a moment of the world-significance of Lincoln. Think what his life meant for the long, dark struggle of the people of Europe against tyranny and oppression. All down the century they had been coming by thousands from under the despotic systems of the Old World to find freedom and opportunity on this new continent. From France, from Austria, from Prussia, from Italy, from Russia, from Turkey, they came. Some of them were refugees from political tyrants. Some of them sought freedom to worship God. Here they found an open door. They learned the new language of liberty. They sent back to their suffering brethren in Europe great words of cheer from the land of the free. Brave ones among them went back, and, in secret, sowed the seeds of democracy even in the valleys of despotism. Had Lincoln failed, had the Union been destroyed, had the Republic proved unequal to the strain and burden of maintaining free rights for a free people, how the tyrant-monarchs of Europe would have laughed! How the forerunners of European liberty would have been staggered!

319

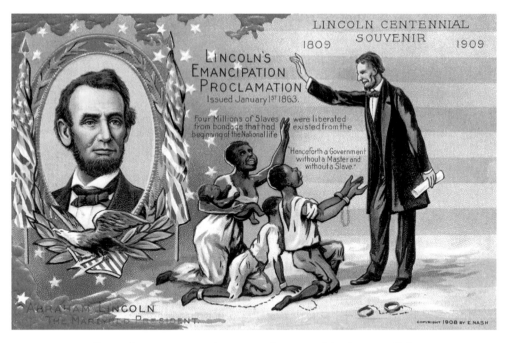

One of many souvenir postcards created in honor of the
100th anniversary of Lincoln's birth.

On the success or the frustration of Lincoln's task the fate of democracy in Europe was trembling in the balance. But Lincoln did not fail. His venture for Union and Liberty triumphed—triumphed gloriously. The reflex of that triumph meant new hope for government of the people, by the people, for the people, in Germany, in Russia, even in Turkey itself. A handful of seed on the tops of the mountains, and lo! The fruit thereof shakes like Lebanon.

And not Europe alone, but Asia as well. In our day the Orient, mysterious, vast, potential, heaves into sight above the skyline. It means something for this Republic this very day that Lincoln stood for the Union, and for supremacy of national integrity over local interests. It means something for world-peace that this Republic presents a united front to the Pacific, behind it a united nation, the Stars and Stripes over every State, and to the North the Union Jack. It means much for the world-brotherhood that this Republic has not only discovered its own power, but is learning its own duty, taking its large share of the great human burden, and playing its part for peace and good-will to the world.

And this—this service to democracy in America, to Anglo-Saxon civilization, to the peace and progress of the world—is what I mean by the Significance of Lincoln...

Who that reads the Lincoln story can miss the sublime significance of his life? Born in obscurity, nurtured in ignorance, he grew to the stature of national heroism. He wrote the decree of Emancipation for his own Republic, changed from war to peace the royal message of the mightiest Empire of the world, and shines to-day a peerless name the world will not let die. Lincoln rather than any other might have stood as the original of Tennyson's master-statesman, for almost as with prophetic vision the great Laureate foresaw the rise of Abraham Lincoln,—

"As some divinely gifted man,
　　Whose life in low estate began,
　　And on a simple village green;

"Who breaks his birth's invidious bar,
　　And grasps the skirts of happy chance,
　　And breasts the blows of circumstance,
　　And grapples with his evil star;

"Who makes by force his merit known,
　　And lives to clutch the golden keys,
　　To mould a mighty State's decrees,
　　And shape the whisper of the throne;

"And, moving up from high to higher,
　　Becomes on Fortune's crowning slope
　　The pillar of a people's hope,
　　The center of a world's desire."

This centennial celebration will have failed of its high purpose if it ends in eulogy of the dead. Our words of praise will vanish into thin air and be forgotten. We ourselves shall turn again to the common ways of men. The tumult and the shouting shall die. And all this acclaim of the mighty dead shall be but a foolish boast unless there comes to us from out the Unseen where they abide the enduring strength and the victorious faith by which they went up to die.

It is but vanity for us to profess honor for the name of Lincoln if we refuse to give ourselves to carry on the work for which he gave his life. That work is not yet done. It cries aloud for strong hands and brave hearts. Slavery, as he knew it, is no more, but the struggle of human rights and social wrongs is not yet ended. The planter autocracy is overthrown, with none to mourn for its defeat, but the sordid and selfish autocracy of wealth and privilege and power is insolent as ever. In the darkness of your terrible streets, they still languish and die, by the sweat of whose faces the privileged and the proud still eat bread. In high place and in low, in this nation and in all nations, there is still the bondage to ignorance and selfishness and sin. Out of the silence there comes back to us this day the voice of him who being dead yet speaketh: "A house divided against itself cannot stand." If indeed we would do honor to the memory of Lincoln, let us hear his great appeal, learn his great language of truth, catch his clear accents of love; and here and now let us, the living, consecrate ourselves to the unfinished work of the dead,—

> It is for us to be here dedicated to the great task remaining before us,— that from these honored dead we take increased devotion to that cause for which they gave the last full measure of devotion,—that we here highly resolve that these dead shall not have died in vain—that this nation, under God, shall have a new birth of freedom, and that government of the people, by the people, for the people, shall not perish from this earth.

Source:

Macdonald, J. A. "The Significance of Lincoln." In *Abraham Lincoln: The Tribute of a Century, 1809-1909; Commemorative of the Lincoln Centenary and Containing the Principal Speeches Made in Connection Therewith.* Edited by Nathan William MacChesney. Chicago: A. C. McClurg & Co., 1910.

6-3
Centennial Celebration in Chicago, Illinois—Emil G. Hirsch

Emil G. Hirsch (1851-1923) was rabbi of Chicago's Sinai congregation and a professor at the University of Chicago. He addressed the audience at the Second Regiment Armory as part of Chicago's centennial celebration. This observance was sponsored by the Illinois National Guard. The following excerpts from his speech juxtapose Lincoln's humble origins and his later distinction.

Great men are like towering mountain peaks. They stand out in bold and sharp loneliness about the lowlands of the many-companied multitude of the undistinguished and the unfamed. And yet they are, for all their grandeur, of one formation with the deeper levels. But they catch the first flash of the morning sun, and the expiring day's regretful good-night kiss is imprinted upon their brow. And when thus the breaking dawn's blush is upon them and the glow of the retreating twilight weaves around them its golden halo, they loom up veritable torches kindled to light the path for the wayfarers in the valleys beneath. Like mountains, their magnitude escapes the beholder from too near a point of observation. While they live they jostle against the throng in the market and the street. Their voice rings out from the platform, indeed, but its peculiar note is not detected because others of lesser quality have aroused the echo as well. And they who in heated debate heard their appeal and argument or touched elbows with them as they hurried to their daily task, cannot but carry from the contact and concourse the feeling that even giants are kneaded of the clay that mothers all mortality. Only when time has raised a screen between the days in which it was theirs to act their part, and subsequent years—when what was a burning issue around which flamed passion and flowered intrigue has grown to be the cherished conviction of the later born—they who in the days of their vigorous manhood were rated and berated partisans are summoned from their graves, exemplars of patriotic devotion, monuments of human greatness. When they and their generation have entered into rest, their fame leaps to the welcoming skies. It is hailed a talisman for the nation—their grave a Mecca, where the faithful seek and find inspiration. The old prophets of Israel had power to break the shackles of death even after their mortality had been laid away in the rock-hewn tomb. This marvellous gift is shared by the memory of the truly glorious.

And herein lies the deeper significance of a day like this. The ancient Greeks fabled about a spring with magic to restore youth to them that courted the embrace of its waters. It is said that as nations grow old their memorial days increase. This is one way of stating the truth. The other is that those nations retain their youth who cherish the memory of their great. This anniversary hour visits us to bestow upon us new strength. It challenges inquiry whether we have proven worthy heirs of the fathers. For every memory is also a monitor. One hundred years have run their circling rounds since the incarnation of Abraham Lincoln—forty and four links of this chain mark the number of solar circuits since his ascension to immortality. What is he for us? What message for us comes on the wing of this centenary?

Lincoln types for us the best and noblest American. The mountain peaks are of one formation with the lower levels. The best that is within us had body and soul in him. America spells opportunity. His life illustrates the verity of this observation. In other lands birth and descent too often decide the place where the late comer shall live his life. Destiny does not signify future; it signifies past. Not so in this blessed country. The upward path to distinction is not closed in by barbed wire. Character and capacity, not coronets, are the credentials which admit to the company of the leaders. . .

. . .Lincoln personalized the grit of the American people. In him came to fullest flower and real presence, that combination of resourcefulness and stubborn pluck which crowned the American conqueror of the prairies' rolling tracts, the primeval forests' tangles, the mountains' rocky ramparts, the rivers' raging wrath. The persistence and perseverance which the nation as a whole applied to the building of the great *emporia*, and the exploitation of mines, and the erection of mills, and the spreading of markets, he energized in making himself.

He himself throughout his rising years which lifted him up from lowliness and set him among the princes—yea, the princes of his people—remained the plain, modest, rugged, strong American. Because the genius of his people had become flesh in him, he never lost contact with the plain folk—after all, the supporting pillar of the great nation's greatness, the Gibraltar of its protection and power. Never did he attempt to put them away from him. He, indeed, was the mountain peak, in its own elevation proclaiming the prowess of the strata out of which it rises to nearer communion with the clouds. This kinship of his with the plain folk comes to gratifying light in that gift of his, in his own lifetime, and still more expressively after his death, the centre of an ever-widening circle of legend. Legend always is tribute paid to genuine greatness

A sheet music cover for a centennial composition by E. T. Paull, 1909.

by neighborhood and posterity conscious of their spiritual affinity to the distinguished and elect, bone of their bone and flesh of their flesh. Around neither the ordinary nor the supercilious, is web of legend spun. In attributing Lincoln the authorship of so many stories, many of which are doubtless apocryphal, the sound sense of the people that has given currency to the anecdotes has for very truth picked out the one quality in the mental equipment of their hero which sets into bold relief his sound Americanism. . .Humor is indigenous to our soil. It is the saving grace of our intense predisposition to practical realism. One might even advance the opinion that humor is the vehicle of expression of our nation's poetry. For such humor as appeals to us has all the elements of true poetic apprehension of great principles. It reads universal facts in the guise of individual occurrence. Our humor is our philosophic vocabulary. Of this humor Lincoln had abundance. It was the patrimony of his profound Americanism. In drawing upon this fund he struck a note which, coming out of the very heart of his people, found its way into the very heart of his people. He knew his power. It served him for a safety valve. With it he laid storms of passion;

Of this humor Lincoln had abundance. It was the patrimony of his profound Americanism.

he disarmed suspicion. Its copious use brought him all the nearer to the affections and respect and confidence of the toilers, the humble mean and women whose sacrifice was all the greater in the years when the hurricane blew, because fame held out no promise of compensation to them— as, indeed, hope of recognition was not the magnet that drew them on.

The typical Americanism of Lincoln is manifested also in his genuine religiosity. For our nation is religious. The solicitude for playing fair, so characteristic of the temper of the American people—what is it, if not the religion of the Golden Rule? That religion was Lincoln's. He was not attached to the externalities of cult. He had little patience for the frills and feathers of the ritual. But he had an abounding childlike faith in Providence. This faith sustained him throughout. He felt his own insufficiency. He knew that human force is limited. In the floodtides and ebbs of human happenings he humbly beheld the working out of a divine plan and purpose. His simple faith asked for no creed. It brooked no cant. Overpowering in their simplicity and inspiring in their honesty and earnestness are the words with which he bade his townsmen of Springfield *adieu* when he set out to take the helm of the Ship of State in the stormy days when the war clouds were thickening: "Without the assistance of that Divine Being who ever attended him [Washington], I cannot succeed. With that assistance, I cannot fail. Trusting in Him who can go with me and remain with you and be everywhere for good, let us confidently hope that all will yet be well." These sentiments were his parting benediction to his neighbors among whom he had "lived for a quarter of a century, passing from a young to an old man." No prophet ever consecrated himself to his duty more reverently than did he in the sad moment of leavetaking, when the shadow of the premonition that he was never to return was, as his words show, even then upon him. . .

. . .When Lincoln made his bow on the stage of public and political life, slavery and its extension into new territory was dividing the people, and keeping the public mind at fever heat. His elevation to the presidency sent the nation into the valley of decision, a valley which at times took on the terrible aspect of the "valley of the shadow of death." Statesman Lincoln had defined his position clearly in the historic debates with Douglas. Not a politician of the modern cast, but on of the old mould, knowing that party is a means to an end and patriotism must sanctify partisanship, he spoke out when silence and ambiguity might have been personally more profitable for him. "A house divided against itself cannot stand"—this prediction cost him the senatorship, but won him the presidency. And yet when the responsibility of the high trust was laid on him, to many he seemed, all of a sudden, to be struck with hesitating indecision. The Abolitionists were not slow to utter their bitter impatience. In his biding his time he displayed his mastership as a statesman. The deliberateness of his executive action reflects the sterling conservatism of his Americanism.

No other man ever ascended throne, or assumed the pilot's chard of the Ship of State, under more disheartening circumstances—the nation cleft into two—the North, not a united band, to support him—the enemy prepared, the Union unequipped! Armies had to be created, navies had to be built, the treasury had to be filled, the finances put on a workable basis, the jealousy of the European nations to be disarmed and thwarted. Lincoln had loyal helpers, men of genius and of eminent power of organization. Yet his was the supreme responsibility. He, the man of tender, sympathetic heart, had to give the word that sent thousands to their death, millions into the furnace of fire. No wonder that his face assumed an expression of deep sadness. It seemed as though in the lines of his brow, in the look of his eyes, were symbolized all the pathos of those four years of doubt and daring, of suffering and striving. Republics are never so well armored for the bloody business of war as are autocracies. Where the king's will is the supreme law, the petty bickerings among the chieftains are soon hushed. Not so in a Republic. Cooperation among the various commanders is much more difficult to secure. With all this and worse, Lincoln had to contend. He bore his cross cheerfully, for he had an abiding faith in the destiny of his nation, a wonderful confidence in the loyalty of the common people. What share he had in directing to final and glorious victory the engine of war, what his part in the financing of the gigantic combat, what inspiration came from him in the work of keeping the European detractors of our liberty at bay, we know better than they that lived through those terrible years of suspense and darkness. Latest memoirs of the chief actors in this stupendous drama have thrown onto the screen the astounding certainty that this country-bred, lank, lean lawyer proved to be a strategist of no mean calibre, a financier of high resourcefulness, a diplomat of wide outlook. He was a statesman who has had and will have, but few peers and no superior in the annals of the onflowing centuries.

We sons of Illinois particularly rejoice that he was ours. We gave him to the Union. Among us he spent his years of preparation. It is significant that the President that saved the nation was a Western man. The issues around which the War was fought had indeed become acute in measure as the West became a factor in the destiny of the nation. Were the new States to be kept clean of the blight of slavery? That was the pith of the dispute. The wheat and corn belt would not pay homage to King Cotton. It seemed to be in the order of things that the leader should hail from the West. Western regiments, in sober truth, composed the elite of the army, as the West had been the most pronounced adversary of State rights and secession. This West was peopled by immigrants. They had pilgrimed with the sun from New England, the classic home of Pilgrim civilization; and then from Germany, lovers of freedom, idealists, and dreamers, yet sturdy farmers and clear thinkers withal; and also from Ireland, carrying with them the hatred of despotism and the flaming courage to dare and to do. These new wheat fields furnished sustenance to the fighting nation. Their wealth made good the deficiency caused by the blockaded shore line of the cotton-raising States, for cotton had been the nation's means of exchange for Europe's advances in money and ammunition. . . .

. . . The President from the West, when the first victories also were those won by the Western army corps under generals from the West, saw the dawn of peace light up the sky with new hope, but then—another Moses, vouchsafed merely a prophetic vision of the realization—he had to lay down his life that the new covenant of love might be firmly sealed by his blood.

When he fell, the world wept. They that buy yesterday had carried the musket for the defense of what they believed to be their rights, the men who wore the battle-tattered gray felt that in him they lost their truest friend. Monarchs shed a tear at his bier. The noblest of rulers had ascended to glory. They knew none to the purple born who bore escutcheon more lustrous than was his, the great commoner's.

But we at this hour must not forget that memory spells also monition. How do we measure up against him? He laid tribute on the graves of those that died that the government of the people, for the people, and by the people might not perish. No enemy from without, indeed, is threatening the permanence of our institutions, the independence of our State, the prosperity of our people. We have been garnering the harvest of the day at Appomattox. Ours is now a world empire. But is ours, for all this, a government of the people? Is it not a government of politicians, for politicians? Serious question, this, inviting searching of the heart. Has increase in wealth tended to undemocratize our manners, our ambitions? Has it obscured our ideals, placed near the altar new, strange deities wrought of gold? Are these the Gods that have led us forth out of Egypt, out of the crucible of trial and distress? Has there been profounder reverence for law among us, the heirs of the men that were giants in those gigantic days?

> *How do we measure up against him? He laid tribute on the graves of those that died that the government of the people, for the people, and by the people might not perish.*

Great men are mountain peaks. As we look up toward the peak named the Martyr-Savior-President, shall the lifted finger, tipped with the gold of glorious sunshine, not be for us sign and symbol that our way shall lead upwards? The mountain range of which he is the highest point embraces many crests. Grant, Seward, Stanton, Sherman, Sheridan, Logan, Schurz, Sumner, Morton, Yates, Curtis, and a host of other names tell their significance. Yet high as they are, their height is worthily crowned and completed in the one that stands out above all in superb majesty—Abraham Lincoln.

Source:

Hirsh, Emil G. "The Great Commoner." In *Abraham Lincoln: The Tribute of a Century, 1809-1909; Commemorative of the Lincoln Centenary and Containing the Principal Speeches Made in Connection Therewith*. Edited by Nathan William MacChesney. Chicago: A. C. McClurg & Co., 1910.

6-4
Centennial Celebration in Chicago, Illinois—A. J. Carey

Reverend A. J. Carey presented the following speech at the celebration held in Chicago at the Seventh Regiment Armory on the evening of February 12, 1909. This observance was sponsored by the Eighth Infantry (Colored), the Colored Citizens' Committee, and the Illinois National Guard.

One hundred years ago to-day, the wilds of Kentucky gave to America an American, rugged as his surroundings in all save his kindliness of spirit, unprepossessing in all save his beauty of soul. The world saw him while he lived, as through a glass, darkly. To-day the vision becomes more distinct, although not altogether clear.

The heroic effort made this week by old America in memory, by new America in prophecy, to find itself, to know itself, is worthy of so noble an occasion. From church, from schoolhouse, from college, and from public hall one and the same strain floats forth: "Lincoln, Liberty, and Love." The quiet of the private home, the noises of the busy mart, are lost in one great anthem, one mighty paean of praise.

That marvel of the twentieth century, the daily press, has labored overtime that none may be ignorant, that even the humblest may know and receive inspiration form Lincoln's life and times. The minor strain, the note of regret, is, that the life then just beginning should have been laid so untimely as a sacrifice on its country's altar, leaving its task unfinished.

The unfinished task, who will assume it? The task of loving the nation—not the sections simply but the nation—into one; the task of throwing himself with God, and counting a majority on the side of the oppressed; the task of doing the right as God gives him to see the right.

If the spirit has interest in this material world, how depressed must be the spirit of Lincoln at the backward swinging of the pendulum, at the retreat of American sentiment from the glory-crowned heights of freedom for all, to the valley of restriction and class legislation. The call of the sixties was for a man of heroic mould, a man who had been "driven many times to his knees by the overwhelming conviction that he had nowhere else to go." Such was the call and Lincoln was its answer.

330

Commemorative lapel pins produced for the centennial.

The call in this, the morning of the twentieth century, is for a character no less true, a soul no less courageous, a spirit no less reliant upon its God—another man who will rise up and say, "The nation cannot live on injustice." Whence next will come the answer? for come it will and come it must. The country still lives upon Lincoln's ideals; still grows because of his sacrifices; and still marches in his spirit to meet and master the problems of to-day, whether social, industrial, or racial.

In him we have found the sources of abiding, conquering character. With him we have seen that to "allow all the governed an equal voice in the government—that, and that alone is self-government." With him we have seen that "in giving freedom to the slave"—physical freedom, intellectual freedom, political freedom—we assure freedom to the free.

Nothing stamped with the Divine image was sent into the world to be trodden on, to be degraded and imbruted by his fellows, and he who denies to the weakest of mankind the right, the privilege, the opportunity of rising to his greatest possibilities, not only displays his own cowardice and weakness but robs posterity of a legacy which a life enriched and glorified might bequeath to coming generations.

It is not Lincoln, the lawyer, nor Lincoln the politician, nor even Lincoln the statesman that will survive; but Abraham Lincoln, the friend of the oppressed, the champion of human rights, the great emancipator. Of him we speak and in his memory are we gathered, and with him we are dedicating ourselves to the great task remaining before us, the task remaining before this nation, the cherished hope of his life, "that government of the people, by the people, for the people, shall not perish from the earth."

Source:

Carey, A. J. "The Unfinished Task." In *Abraham Lincoln: The Tribute of a Century, 1809-1909; Commemorative of the Lincoln Centenary and Containing the Principal Speeches Made in Connection Therewith.* Edited by Nathan William MacChesney. Chicago: A. C. McClurg & Co., 1910.

6-5
Centennial Celebration in Chicago, Illinois—J. W. E. Bowen

Reverend J. W. E. Bowen (1855-1933) was president of the Gammon Theological Seminary in Atlanta, Georgia. He delivered a speech at the celebration held in Chicago at the Seventh Regiment Armory on the evening of February 12, 1909. This observance was sponsored by the Eighth Infantry (Colored), the Colored Citizens' Committee, and the Illinois National Guard. The following excerpts focus on Lincoln's legacy as the Great Emancipator.

Even the schoolboy of to-day may easily interest an audience upon any phase of the life and deeds of Abraham Lincoln. It is not a difficult task, therefore to gain attention, for the life of the man is full, his deeds are permanent, and his character is far-reaching in the superb and dominating elements that are appreciated by all mankind. I take it that the best thing to do on this occasion is to call your attention to some of the fundamental ideas that crystallized into deeds of the immortal Lincoln.

The name of Abraham Lincoln and the Emancipation Proclamation should be spoken with one breath. It is impossible to separate them. But there is more to the Emancipation Proclamation in its essence and truth than the mere removing of the shackles of the slave, and the freeing of man from between the plough handles to enter the battle of life. . . His thought reached beyond the liberation of hand and foot. He who knocks the manacles from the wrists of the slave has done a great thing; but that is only the beginning of the work of emancipation. Utter, complete emancipation, not only of the hand and foot, but of mind and heart, and a complete amalgamation into the body politic as a citizen of the mighty

Republic, is the ultimate hope and the larger result to be looked forward to as the outcome of the emancipation of the slave.

We have come to a period in the discussion of this question when we must regard truth and not sentiment; when we must see fact and logic, and not be driven by whim. No race can be fully set free by shot and shell. Gunpowder cannot liberate a man in the truest and fullest sense of the term. Shot and shell make a beginning; but freedom is not "of the earth, earthy." Abraham Lincoln represented the American nationality—the American nationalism,—a mighty thought. . .

. . .These white men who sit here in the pride of American citizenship are the descendants of an illustrious ancestry. But who am I? Where did I come from?

I dare not step back one foot lest I fall into the pit from which God Almighty, through Abraham Lincoln, digged me. Even now, with the memory of my ancestors illuminating my brain, I can hear the pathetic wail of the bloodhound that tracked them through the South. I have no kings and prophets back of me. No queens illuminate the firmament of my history. No men who wrote constitutions and laid the foundations of a government are back of me.

Who am I? The blue-eyed Saxon had his history written; the black-eyed Hamite will write his. He has been made; I am going to make somebody. "He is a descendant; I am an ancestor!"

This celebration of the hundredth anniversary of the birthday of the great, martyred War President is observed all over the country, and we believe that ultimately we shall have a nation in this country that is united in its faith, in its zeal, in its absolute equality of political prerogatives, in its great purpose to make this the proudest nation on the face of the earth. . .

. . .You must not measure the man by the color of his skin. Great as Abraham Lincoln was, he was not great because he was white. He was great because he had a great soul in him.

The man of backbone has heart and will and courage and skill. The race is yours. Enter the battle. Don't ask to be given a chance. Don't plead for a chance. Enter the race. Make a chance. Take a chance. Fight the battle of life, and the time will come when the gray morn shall usher in that beautiful day when we shall be able to say, "It is daybreak everywhere."

Source:

Bowen, J. W. E. "The Liberation of the Negro." In *Abraham Lincoln: The Tribute of a Century, 1809-1909; Commemorative of the Lincoln Centenary and Containing the Principal Speeches Made in Connection Therewith.* Edited by Nathan William MacChesney. Chicago: A. C. McClurg & Co., 1910.

6-6
Centennial Celebration in Chicago, Illinois—Frederick Dent Grant

Major-General Frederick Dent Grant (1850-1912) was the son of Ulysses S. Grant (see document 5-7). He spoke at the celebration held at the Congress Hotel on February 12, 1909. Below, Grant shares his memories of Lincoln formally commissioning his father to lead the Union Army in 1864.

I feel deeply honored that you have called upon me on this interesting occasion, but I have great modesty in speaking to you here, in the presence of these many distinguished and gifted orators, and while I appreciate the compliment you pay me, I fully realize that it is not myself personally whom you wish to hear, but that I am being welcomed as the son of Ulysses S. Grant, who served his country faithfully, with Abraham Lincoln, and who loyally loved our martyred President, revering his memory throughout his life; it is the descendant of Lincoln's friend and compatriot whom you call upon for a few words.

This hundredth anniversary of the birth of Abraham Lincoln is an occasion which the people of the United States honor themselves in celebrating, and they should, in my opinion, keep forever green the memory of this great American statesman and patriot by making the annual anniversary of his birth a national holiday.

It was my great good fortune to be with my father, close at his side, much of the time during the Civil War, when I had the opportunity of seeing and listening to many of the noble and distinguished men who were loyally serving their country during that great struggle; thus I had the honor and happiness of seeing and meeting our revered and martyred President, Abraham Lincoln.

In looking back to those dark days of the Civil War, I have distinct personal recollections of the first two meetings between President Lincoln and my father, General U. S. Grant. These two occasions seem to my mind the most momentous and memorable in the history of our nation, as these meetings marked the beginning of the end of our great struggle for the existence of our nation.

The principal and determined efforts of President Lincoln's administration were directed to the preservation of the Union, which, naturally, could not be accomplished without the success of the Union armies in the field. Up to the Spring of 1864 the progress of the Civil War had not been satisfactory to the people of the North, and little success had been accomplished except in the victories at Donelson, Vicksburg, and Chattanooga.

After the Campaign of Chattanooga, the President and the people of the United States turned impulsively to General Grant as the leader of the Union Armies, and a bill was introduced in Congress reviving for him the grade of Lieutenant-General, which grade had died with Washington (though Scott had held it by brevet.). The enthusiastic members of the House of Representatives received the bill with applause. They made no concealment of their wishes, and recommended Grant by name for the appointment of Lieutenant-General. The bill passed the House by a two-thirds majority; and the Senate, with only six dissenting votes.

President Lincoln seemed impatient to put Grant in his high grade, and said he desired to do so to relieve himself from the responsibilities of managing the military forces. He sent the nomination to the Senate, and General Grant, who was at Nashville, received an order from the Secretary of War, to report in person to Washington. In compliance with this order, he left Chattanooga on March 5 for Washington, taking with him some members of his staff. My father allowed me to accompany him there, I having been with him during the Vicksburg campaign and at Donelson. We reached Washington in the afternoon of March 7, and went direct to Willard's Hotel. . .

Senator Simon Cameron of Pennsylvania, ex-Secretary of War, soon called at Willard's Hotel for my father, and accompanied him, with his staff, to the White House, where President and Mrs. Lincoln were holding a reception.

As my father entered the drawing-room door at the White House, the other visitors fell back in silence, and President Lincoln received my father most cordially,

*This statue of Lincoln in Grant Park, Chicago,
was completed in 1906 by sculptor Augustus Saint-Gaudens.*

taking both his hands, and saying, "I am most delighted to see you, General." I myself shall never forget the first meeting of Lincoln and Grant. It was an impressive affair, for there stood the Executive of this great nation, welcoming the Commander of its armies. I see them now before me—Lincoln, tall, thin, and impressive, with deeply lined face, and his strong sad eyes—Grant, compact, of good size, but looking small beside the President, with his broad, square head and compressed lips, decisive and resolute. This was a thrilling moment, for in the hands of these two men was the destiny of our country. Their work was in cooperation, for the preservation of our great nation, and for the liberty of men. They remained talking together for a few moments, and then General Grant passed on into the East Room with the crowd which surrounded and cheered him wildly, and all present were eager to press his hand. . .

. . . Soon a messenger reached my father calling him back to the side of Mrs. Lincoln, and with her he made a tour of the reception rooms, followed by President Lincoln, whose noble, rugged faced beamed with pleasure and gratification.

When an opportunity presented itself for them to speak privately, President Lincoln said to my father, "I am to formally present you your commission to-morrow morning at ten o'clock, and knowing, General, your dread of speaking, I have written out what I have to say, and you will read it; it will only be four or five sentences. I would like you to say something in reply which will soothe the feeling of jealousy among the officers, and be encouraging to the nation." Thus spoke this great and noble peacemaker to the general who so heartily coincided with him in sentiments and work for union and peace. . .

Father proceeded to the White House a few minutes before ten o'clock the next morning, permitting me to accompany him. Upon arriving there, General Grant and his staff were ushered into the President's office, which I remember was the room immediately above what is now known as the Red Room of the Executive Mansion. There the President and his Cabinet were assembled, and after a short and informal greeting, all standing, the President faced General Grant, and from a sheet of paper read the following:

> "GENERAL GRANT: The nation's appreciation of that you have done and its reliance upon you for what remains to do in the existing great struggle, are now presented with this commission, constituting you lieutenant-general in the Army of the United States.

337

"With this high honor devolves upon you also a corresponding responsibility. As the country herein trusts you, so, under God, it will sustain you. I scarcely need add, that with what I here speak for the nation, goes my own hearty personal concurrence."

My father, taking from his pocket a sheet of paper containing the words that he had written the night before, read quietly and modestly, to the President and his Cabinet:

"MR. PRESIDENT: I accept the commission with gratitude for the high honor conferred. With the aid of the noble armies that have fought in so many fields for our common country, it will be my earnest endeavor not to disappoint your expectations. I feel the full weight of the responsibilities now devolving upon me, and I know that if they are met, it will be due to those armies, and, above all, to the favor of that Providence which leads both nations and men."

> *"Washington the Father, Lincoln the Saviour, and Grant the Preserver"—emblematic of a great and patriotic trinity.*

President Lincoln seemed profoundly happy, and General Grant deeply gratified. It was a supreme moment when these two patriots shook hands, in confirming the compact that was to finish our terrible Civil War and to save our united country, and to give us a nation without master and without a slave.

From the time of these meetings, the friendship between the President and my father was most close and loyal. President Lincoln seemed to have absolute confidence in General Grant, and my father always spoke of the President with the deepest admiration and affection. This affection and loyal confidence was maintained between them until their lives ended.

I feel deeply grateful to have been present when these two patriots met, on the occasion when they loyally promised one another to preserve the Union at all costs. I preserve always, as a treasure in my home, a large bronze medallion which was designed by a distinguished artist at the request of the loyal citizens of Philadelphia, upon the happy termination of our great Civil War, and which is a beautiful work of art. Upon this bronze medallion are three faces, in relief, with the superscription: "Washington the Father, Lincoln the Saviour, and Grant the Preserver"—emblematic of a great and patriotic trinity.

Source:

Grant, Frederick Dent. "Two Momentous Meetings." In *Abraham Lincoln: The Tribute of a Century, 1809-1909; Commemorative of the Lincoln Centenary and Containing the Principal Speeches Made in Connection Therewith.* Edited by Nathan William MacChesney. Chicago: A. C. McClurg & Co., 1910.

6-7
Centennial Celebration in Springfield, Illinois— Jean Adrian Jusserand

Jean Adrian Jusserand (1855-1932) was a writer and the French ambassador to the United States. He spoke at the centennial celebration in Springfield, Illinois, on the evening of February 12, 1909 at the State Arsenal. The following excerpts from his speech highlight French reaction to Lincoln's assassination and his tribute to the President.

On two tragic occasions, at a century's distance, the fate of this country has trembled in the balance—would it be a free nation? Would it continue to be one nation? A leader was wanted on both occasions, a very different one in each case. This boon from above was granted to the American people, who had a Washington when a Washington was needed, and a Lincoln when a Lincoln could save them. Both had enemies, both had doubters, but both were recognized by all open-minded people, and above all by the nation at large, as the men to shape the nation's destinies. . .

Nearly a century of gradually increasing prosperity had elapsed when came the hour of the nation's second trial. Though it may seem to us a small matter compared with what we have seen since, the development had been considerable; the scattered colonies of yore had become a great nation; yet now it seemed as if all was again in doubt. The nation was young, wealthy, powerful, prosperous; it had immense domains and resources; yet it seemed that her fate was doomed to parallel those of the old empires described by Tacitus, and by Raleigh after him, which, without foes, crumble to pieces under their own weight. Within her own frontiers, elements of destruction or disruption had been growing; hatreds were engendered between people equally brave, bold, and sure of their rights. The edifice raised by Washington was shaking on its base; a catastrophe was at hand. Then it was that in a middle-sized, not yet world-famous town—Chicago by name—the Republican Convention, called there for the first time, met to choose a candidate for the presidency. It has met there again since and has made, each time, a remarkable choice. In 1860 it chose a man whom my predecessor of those days, announcing the news to his Government, described as "a man almost unknown, Mr. Abraham Lincoln." Almost unknown he was indeed, at home as well as abroad, and the news of his election was received with anxiety.

My country, France, was then governed by Napoleon III; all liberals had their eyes fixed on America. Your example was the great example which gave heart to our most progressive men. You had proved that Republican government was possible, by having one. If it broke to pieces, so would the hopes of all those among us who expected that one day we should have done the same. And the partisans of autocracy were loud in their assertion that a Republic was well and good for a country without enemies or neighbors; but that if a storm arose, it would be shattered. A storm had arisen, and the helm had been placed in the hands of that "man almost unknown, Mr. Abraham Lincoln."

> "We still remember," wrote years later the illustrious French writer, Prevost-Paradol, "the uneasiness with which we awaited the first words of that President, then unknown, upon whom a heavy task had fallen, and from whose advent to power might be dated the ruin or regeneration of his country. All we knew was that he had sprung from the humblest walks of life, that his youth had been spent in manual labor; that he had risen by degrees in his town, in his county, and in his State. What was this favorite of the people? Democratic societies are liable to errors which are fatal to them. But as soon as Mr. Lincoln arrived in Washington, as soon as he spoke, all our doubts and fears were dissipated; and it seemed to us that fate itself had pronounced in favor of the good cause, since, in such an emergency, it had given the country an honest man . . ."

Well indeed might people have wondered and felt anxious when they remembered how little training in great affairs the new ruler had had, and the incredible difficulty of the problems he would have to solve—to solve, his heart bleeding at the very thought, for he had to fight—not enemies, but friends. ("We must not be enemies. . .")

His instinct, his good sense, his personal disinterestedness, his warmth of heart for friend or foe, his high aim, led him through the awful years of anguish and bloodshed during which the number of fields decked with tombs ceaselessly increased, and no one knew whether there would be one powerful nation or two weaker ones, the odds were so great. They led him through the worst and through the best hours; and that of triumph found him none other than what he had ever been before, a man of duty, the devoted servant of his country, with deeper furrows on his face and more melancholy in his heart. And so, after having saved the nation, he went to his doom and, as he had long foreseen, fell a victim to the cause for which he had fought.

The emotion caused by the event was immense. Among my compatriots, part were for the South, part for the North. They should not be blamed; it was the same among Americans. But the whole of those who had liberal ideas, the bulk of my nation, considered neither North nor South, and thought only whether the Republic would survive and continue a great Republic, or be shattered to pieces. The efforts of Lincoln to preserve the Union were followed with keen anxiety, and with the fervent hope that he would succeed.

When the catastrophe happened, there were no more differences, and the whole French nation was united in feeling. From the Emperor and the Empress, who telegraphed Mrs. Lincoln, to the humblest workman, the emotion was the same a wave of sympathy covered the country, such a one as was never before seen. A subscription was opened to have a medal struck and a copy in gold presented to Mrs. Lincoln. In order that it might be a truly national offering, it was decided that no one would be permitted to subscribe more than two cents. The necessary money was collected in an instant, and the medal was struck, bearing these memorable words: "Dedicated by French democracy to Lincoln, honest man, who abolished slavery, reestablished the Union, saved the Republic, without unveiling the statue of Liberty."

The French press was unanimous; from the Royalist Gazette de France, to the liberal Journal des Debats, came forth the same expression of admiration and sorrow. "A Christian," said the Gazette de France, "has just ascended before the throne of the Final Judge, accompanied by the souls of four millions of slaves, created like ours in the image of God, and who have been endowed with freedom by a word from him." Prevost-Paradol, a member of the French Academy, and a prominent liberal, wrote:

"The political instinct which made enlightened Frenchmen interested in the maintenance of the American power, more and more necessary to the equilibrium of the world, the desire to see a great democratic State surmount terrible trials and continue to give an example of the most perfect liberty united with the most absolute equality, assured the cause of the North a number of friends among us. . . . Lincoln was indeed an honest man, giving to the word its full meaning, or rather the sublime sense which belongs to it, when honesty was to contend with the severest trials which can agitate States and with events which have an influence on the fate of the world. . . . Mr. Lincoln had but one object in view, from the day of his election to that of his death, namely, the fulfillment of his duty, and his imagination never carried him beyond it. He has fallen at the very foot of the altar, covering it with his blood. But his work was done, and the spectacle of a rescued Republic was what he could look upon with consolation when his eyes were closing in death. Moreover he has not lived for his country alone, since he leaves to everyone in the world to whom liberty and justice are dear, a great remembrance and a pure example."

When, in a log cabin in Kentucky, a hundred years ago this day, that child was born who was named, after his grandfather killed by the Indians—Abraham Lincoln—Napoleon I swayed Europe, Jefferson was President of the United States, and the second War of Independence had not yet come to pass. It seems all very remote, but the memory of the great man whom we try to honor to-day is as fresh as if he had only just left us. "It is," says Plutarch, "the fortune of all good men that their virtue rises in glory after their death, and that the envy which any evil man may have conceived against them never survives the envious." Such was the fate of Lincoln.

Source:

Jussserand, Jean Adrian. "Lincoln as France Saw Him." In *Abraham Lincoln: The Tribute of a Century, 1809-1909; Commemorative of the Lincoln Centenary and Containing the Principal Speeches Made in Connection Therewith.* Edited by Nathan William MacChesney. Chicago: A. C. McClurg & Co., 1910.

Menu

COTUITS

———

Martini Cocktail

MOCK TURTLE——AMERICAN

CELERY   OLIVES   RADISHES

———

Haut Sauternes

CRAB MEAT WITH FRESH MUSHROOMS——ILLINI

———

TENDERLOIN OF BEEF——SANGAMO

Appollinaris

———

DUCHESSE POTATO   GREEN PEAS

———

BREAST OF GUINEA SQUAB——OLD SALEM

Pommard

COMPOTE OF FRUIT   LETTUCE AND ENDIVE SALAD

———

ICE CREAM   ASSORTED CAKES

Pommery aud Greno Sec

———

CREAMED ROQUEFORT CHEESE. IN CELERY

CRACKERS

———

Cordials

COFFEE

APPOLLINARIS   CIGARS   CIGARETTES

A menu for a centennial banquet in Springfield, Illinois.

343

6-8
Centennial Celebration in Peoria, Illinois—Kogoro Takahira

Kogoro Takahira (1854-1926) was the Japanese ambassador to the United States. He delivered the following speech on the evening of February 12, 1909 at the centennial observance in Peoria, Illinois. In the excerpts below, the ambassador pays tribute to Lincoln as a universal example of good statesmanship.

• • • When I began to prepare my speech a few days ago, I found that Lincoln's greatness as a man and as a public servant has been exhaustively described is so many "Lives" and "Biographies" that all patriotic citizens of this country must be fully familiar with it. There is no room for any additional remarks from such a stranger as myself. If, however, I should be required to say what has impressed me most strongly in his life and character, I would mention that the nobleness of this heart and the generosity of this mind, amply verified in every detail by acts and conduct which leave no trace of personal motives in his management of public affairs, but abound in every proof of the sincerity of his desire for the good of his country and fellow-beings, are fully illustrative of the life and character of a statesman idealized by all men of every nationality. Lincoln left in his life a great example of a public man, not only for his own, but for all countries. So it is no wonder that his fame is world-wide and adorns the universal history of the modern age, as one of the greatest men that ever lived.

Another feature of his life which appears particularly interesting and instructive to me as a diplomat, was his method of conducting the foreign affairs of his country. The Civil War did so much to endanger the international position of the United States as to threaten the internal solidity of the Union, and in so great adversity it must have required extraordinary power of foresight and precision, as well as an unusual command of resolution and courage, to handle such intricate questions of foreign affairs as the United States had to face at that time. It is true that Lincoln had a great, able man for his Secretary of State in the person of William H. Seward, but if his biographies which I have read are to be depended on, Mr. Lincoln himself had often to examine important diplomatic documents drawn by Secretary Seward with great skill and care, and to amend them in many particulars in order to communicate to the powers interested, the exact motives and intentions of the American Government in those straightforward and forceful expressions, coupled with a sense of moderation and dignity, which made the American diplomacy so famous at the chancelleries of those Powers. Those who learned to admire his method of diplomatic transaction, called it "Lincoln's diplomacy"—the diplomacy which upheld the dignity and interest of the United States when she still remained in a less important position and under very adverse circumstances. Mr. John Hay, who was once President Lincoln's private secretary, said, in speaking of American diplomacy, "The briefest expression of our rule of conduct is perhaps the Monroe Doctrine and the Golden Rule." The origin of the Monroe Doctrine as the policy to be observed in the affairs of this hemisphere is too well known to everyone to require any explanation. But Mr. Hay's expression of the Golden Rule as the rule of American diplomacy, attracted the great admiration of every student of international affairs when it was announced. The idea was not only plausible in expression, but irresistible in effect, and it was considered most adapted to this country from the point of view of its dignity as well as its interest. I regret I did not ask Mr. Hay, when I had to see him so often, where he obtained that expression. It may be the result of his own conviction of American diplomacy. But it is possible that he conceived such an idea when he was so closely associated with the great President, from his method of handling international dealings with all the powers, the proudest as well as the humblest. . .

. . .I most emphatically declare that so long as the Golden Rule is considered the guiding principle of our diplomacy, we shall be enabled to enjoy the benefits of peace and prosperity; and this must be, I dare say, in accordance with the high ideal forever fixed by Lincoln's diplomacy. . .

Source:

Takahira, Korogo. "Lincoln's Diplomacy." In *Abraham Lincoln: The Tribute of a Century, 1809-1909; Commemorative of the Lincoln Centenary and Containing the Principal Speeches Made in Connection Therewith*. Edited by Nathan William MacChesney. Chicago: A. C. McClurg & Co., 1910.

6-9
Centennial Celebration in Bloomington, Indiana—Adlai E. Stevenson

Adlai E. Stevenson (1835-1914) was vice president under Grover Cleveland from 1893 to 1897; his great-grandson and namesake, Adlai E. Stevenson, unsuccessfully ran for president in 1952 and 1956. Stevenson addressed a gathering in Bloomington, Indiana, on the centennial of Lincoln's birth. The excerpts below pay tribute to some of Lincoln's actions as president.

In the humblest of homes in the wilds of a new and sparsely settled State, Abraham Lincoln was born one hundred years ago this day. The twelfth day of February—like the twenty-second day of the same month—is one of the sacred days in the American calendar. It is well that his day be set apart from ordinary uses, the headlong rush in the crowded mart suspended, the voice of fierce contention in legislative hall be hushed, and that the American people—whether at home, in foreign land, or upon the deep—honor themselves by honoring the memory of the man of whose birth this day is the first centennial.

This coming together is no idle ceremony, no unmeaning observance. For to this man—more than to any other—are we indebted for the supreme fact that ninety millions of the people are at this hour, in the loftiest sense of the expression, fellow citizens of a common country. Some of us through the mists of half a century distinctly recall the earnest tones in which Mr. Lincoln in public speech uttered the words, "My fellow citizens." Truly the magical words "fellow citizens" never fail to touch a responsive chord in the patriotic heart. . .

The fifty-six years that compassed the life of Abraham Lincoln were years of transcendent significance to our country. While yet in his rude cradle, the African slave trade had just terminated by constitutional inhibition. While Lincoln was still in attendance upon "the old field school," Henry Clay—yet to be known as the "Great Pacificator"—was pressing the admission of Missouri into the Union under the first compromise upon the question of slavery since the adoption of the Federal Constitution. From the establishment of the government the question of human slavery was the one perilous question—the one constant menace to national unity, until its final extinction amid the flames of war. Marvellous to man are the purposes of the

Almighty. What seer could have foretold that from this humblest of homes upon the frontier was to spring the man who at the crucial moment should cut the Gordian knot, liberate a race, and give to the ages enlarged and grander conception of the deathless principles of the declaration of human rights?

> "Often do the spirits of great events
> > Stride on before the events,
> > And in to-day already walks to-morrow."

The first inauguration of President Lincoln noted the hour of the "breaking with the past." It was a period of gloom, when the very foundations were shaken, when no man could foretell the happening of the morrow, when strong men trembled at the possibility of the destruction of our government.

Pause a moment, my countrymen, and recall the man who, under the conditions mentioned, on the fourth of March, 1861, entered upon the duties of the great office to which he had been chosen. He came from the common walks of life—from what in other countries would be called the great middle class. His early home was one of the humblest, where he was a stranger to the luxuries, and to many of the ordinary comforts of life. His opportunities for education were only such as were common in the remote habitations of our Western country one century ago.

Under such conditions began a career that in grandeur and achievement has but a single counterpart in our history. And what a splendid commentary this upon our free institutions—upon the sublime underlying principle of popular government! How inspiring to the youth of high aims every incident of the pathway that led from the frontier cabin to the executive mansion—from the humblest position to the most exalted yet attained by man! In no other country than ours could such attainment have been possible for the boy whose hands were inured to toil, whose bread was eaten under the hard conditions that poverty imposes, whose only heritage was brain, integrity, lofty ambition, and indomitable purpose. Let it never be forgotten that the man of whom I speak possessed an integrity that could know no temptation, a purity of life that was never questioned, a patriotism that no sectional lines could limit, and a fixedness of purpose that knew no shadow of turning.

The decade extending from our first treaty of peace with Great Britain to the inauguration of Washington has been truly denominated the critical period of our history. The eloquence of Adams and Henry had precipitated revolution; the unfaltering courage of Washington and his comrades had secured independence; but the more difficult task of garnering up the fruits of victory by stable government was yet to be achieved. The hour for the constructive statesman had arrived, and James Madison and his associates—equal to the emergency—formulated the Federal Constitution.

No less critical was the period that bounded the active life of the man whose memory we honor to-day. One perilous question to national unity—for near three-quarters of a century the subject of repeated compromise by patriotic statesmen, the apple of discord producing sectional antagonism, whose shadow had darkened our national pathway from the beginning—was now for weal or woe to find determination. Angry debate in senate and upon the forum was now hushed, and the supreme question that took hold of national life was to find enduring arbitrament in the dread tribunal of war.

It was well in such an hour—with such tremendous issues in the balance—that a steady hand was at the helm; that a conservative statesman—one whose mission was to save, not to destroy—was in the high place of responsibility and power. It booted little, then, that he was untaught of schools, unskilled in the ways of courts, but it was of supreme moment that he could touch responsive chords in the great American heart; all-important that his very soul yearned for the preservation of the government established through the toil and sacrifice of the generation that had gone. . .

Fortunate, indeed, that the ark of our covenant was then borne by the plain brave man of conciliatory spirit and kind words, and whose heart, as Emerson, said, "Was as large as the world but nowhere had room for the memory of wrong!"

Nobler words have never fallen from human lips than the closing sentences of his First Inaugural in one of the pivotal days of human history—immediately upon taking the oath to preserve, protect, and defend the country:

> "I am loath to close. We are not enemies, but friends. We must not be enemies. Though passion may have strained, it must not break the bonds of affection. The mystic chords of memory, stretching form every battlefield and patriot grave to every living heart and hearthstone all over this broad land, will yet swell the chorus of the Union when again touched, as surely they will be, by the better angels of our nature."

In the light of what we now know so well, nothing is hazarded in saying that the death of no man has been to this country so irreparable a loss—one so grievous to be borne—as that of Abraham Lincoln. When Washington died his work was done, his

This centennial souvenir postcard features the text of a poignant letter of consolation and sympathy Lincoln is widely believed to have written to a Mrs. Bixby, who had lost two sons in the Civil War (not five, as the letter states). Some controversy has surrounded the issue of Lincoln's authorship; the original has not been found.

life well rounded out—save one, the years allotted had been passed. Not so with Lincoln. To him a grander task was yet in waiting—one no other could so well perform. The assassin's pistol proved the veritable Pandora's box from which sprung evils untold—whose consequences have never been measured—to one-third of the States of our Union. But for his untimely death, how the current of history might have been changed—and many a sad chapter remained unwritten! How earnestly he desired a restored Union, and that the blessings of peace and of concord should be the common heritage of every section, is known to all.

When in the loom of time have such words been heard above the din of fierce conflict as his sublime utterances but a brief time before his tragic death:

"With malice toward none, with charity for all, with firmness for the right
as God gives us to see the right, let us strive on to finish the work we are

349

in, to bind up the nation's wounds, to care for him who shall have borne the battle and for his widow and his orphan, to do all which may achieve a lasting peace among ourselves and among all nations."

No fitter occasion than this can ever arise in which to refer to two historical events that at a crucial moment tested to the utmost the safe and far-seeing statesmanship of President Lincoln. The first was the seizure upon the high seas of Mason and Slidell, the accredited representatives from the Southern Confederacy, respectively to the Courts of England and of France. The seizure was in November, 1861, by Capt. Wilkes of our Navy—and the envoys named were taken by him from the Trent, a mail-carrying steamer of the British Government. The act of Capt. Wilkes met with enthusiastic commendation throughout the entire country; he was voted the thanks of Congress and his act publicly approved by the Secretary of the Navy.

The demand by the British government for reparation upon the part of the United States was prompt and explicit. The perils that then environed us were such as rarely shadow the pathway of nations. Save Russia alone, our government had no friend among the crowned heads of Europe. Menaced by the peril of the recognition of the Southern Confederacy by England and France—with the very stars apparently warring against us in their course—the position of the President was in the last degree trying. To surrender the Confederate envoys was in a measure humiliating and in opposition to the popular impulse; their retention, the signal for the probable recognition of the Southern Confederacy by the European powers, and the certain and immediate declaration of war by England.

The good genius of President Lincoln—rather his wise, just, far-seeing statesmanship—stood him well in hand at the critical moment. Had a rash, opinionated, impulsive man then held the executive office, what a sea of troubles might have overwhelmed us—how the entire current of our history might have been changed!

The calm, wise President in his council chamber—aided by his closest official adviser, Secretary Seward—discerned clearly the path of national safety and of honor. None the less was the act of the President one of justice—one that will abide the sure test of time. Upon the real ground that the seizure of the envoys was in violation of the law of nations, they were eventually surrendered; war with England—as well as immediate danger of recognition of the Confederacy—averted. And let it not be forgotten that this very act of President Lincoln was a triumphant vindication of our government in its second war with Great Britain—a war waged as a protest upon our part against British seizure and impressments of American citizens upon the high seas.

The other incident to which I briefly refer was the Proclamation of Emancipation. As a war measure of stupendous significance in the national defense—as well as of justice to the enslaved—such proclamation, immediate in time, and radical in terms, had, to greater or less degree been urged upon the President from the outbreak of the Rebellion. That slavery was to perish amid the great upheaval, became in time the solemn conviction of all thoughtful men. Meanwhile there were divided counsels among the earnest supporters of the President as to the time the masterful act—"that could know no backward steps"—should be taken. Unmoved amid divided counsels—and at times fierce dissensions—the calm, far-seeing Executive upon whom was cast the tremendous responsibility, patiently bided his time. Events that are now the masterful theme of history crowded in rapid succession, the opportune moment arrived, the hour struck, the Proclamation—that has no counterpart—fell upon the ears of the startled world, and as by the interposition of a mightier hand, a race was lifted out of the depths of bondage.

> *At the crucial moment in one of the exalted days of human history, "He sounded forth the trumpet that has never called retreat."*

To the one man at the helm seems to have been given to know "the day and the hour." At the crucial moment in one of the exalted days of human history, "He sounded forth the trumpet that has never called retreat."

My fellow-citizens, the men who knew Abraham Lincoln, who saw him face to face, who heard his voice in public assemblage, have, with few exceptions, passed to the grave. Another generation is upon the busy stage. The book has forever closed upon the dread pageant of civil strife. Sectional animosities, thank God, belong now only to the past. The mantle of peace is over our entire land and prosperity within our borders.

Through the instrumentality—in no small measure—of the man whose memory we now honor, the government established by our fathers, untouched by the finger of Time, has descended to us. The responsibility of its preservation and transmission rests upon the successive generations as they shall come and go. To-day, at this auspicious hour—sacred to the memory of Lincoln—let us, his countrymen, inspired by sublime lessons of his wondrous life, and grateful to God for all He has vouchsafed to our fathers and to us in the past, take courage and turn our faces resolutely, hopefully, trustingly to the future. I know of no words more fitting with which to close this humble tribute to the memory of Abraham Lincoln than those inscribed upon the monument of Moliere: "Nothing was wanting to his glory; he was wanting to ours."

Source:

Stevenson, Adlai E. "Lincoln the Statesman." In *Abraham Lincoln: The Tribute of a Century, 1809-1909; Commemorative of the Lincoln Centenary and Containing the Principal Speeches Made in Connection Therewith*. Edited by Nathan William MacChesney. Chicago: A. C. McClurg & Co., 1910.

6-10
Centennial Celebration in Hodgenville, Kentucky— James Grant Wilson

> *James Grant Wilson (1832-1914) of New York was a writer and a general in the Union Army during the Civil War. He spoke at the centennial commemoration in Hodgenville, Kentucky. The observance took place on February 12, 1909, at the site of Lincoln's birthplace, where President Theodore Roosevelt laid the cornerstone for the birthplace memorial. In the following excerpts, Wilson shares remembrances of Lincoln's presidency and his death.*

With pride and unfeigned pleasure, I appear in this place and in this presence, as the representative of the survivors of almost three millions of Lincoln soldiers and sailors, who served in the army and navy of the United States during what is officially designated as the War of the Rebellion. Of the two million seven hundred and seventy-eight thousand three hundred and four men who, on land and sea, fought for four fateful years that this nation should not perish from the earth, less than one-fourth are now living. In a few decades the last survivor who followed the dear old flag on the fields of Shiloh, Gettysburg, Chattanooga, and Mobile Bay, will have joined our great President in honor of whose gracious memory we are here assembled on this hallowed spot of his birth.

It is among the greatest mysteries of modern history that the child born in *annus mirabilis*, 1809, of illiterate and impoverished parents, in this unpromising place, and without any advantages whatsoever, should through life have been always a leader and master of men. For hundreds of years, scholars have in vain searched for the sources from which Shakespeare drew the inspiration that has placed him first among the sons of men. Lincoln biographers have been equally baffled in similar attempts to discover from whence came the truly wonderful power to control and lead all sorts and conditions of men, that was certainly possessed by the son of "poor whites" of Kentucky who occupied yonder rude log cabin.

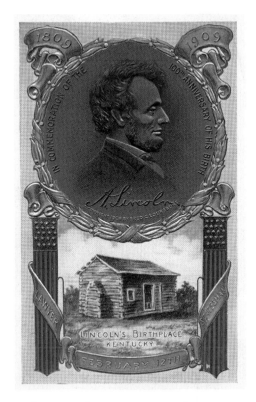

The cover from a centennial program, featuring an illustration of Lincoln's birthplace cabin.

As a youth, Abraham Lincoln's alertness, skill, and strength, easily made him a recognized leader among his rough companions in their amusements and contests, including wrestling. When a company was raised in his County for the Black Hawk War, Lincoln, then but twenty-three years of age, was unanimously elected by his seniors their Captain, which gave him, he asserted, greater happiness than the presidency. At the Illinois bar he was early recognized by his integrity and ready wit, as the superior of his duller associates. As a political debater, Lincoln defeated one of the ablest speakers of the United States Senate, and but a brief period passed as President before the most gifted statesman of his Cabinet unhesitatingly recognized him as their master. Grant praised Lincoln as being in military matters superior to many of his prominent generals, and your speaker heard Sherman say that the President was among the ablest strategists of the War. The beau sabreur Sheridan shared the opinion of his two seniors.

It was my peculiar privilege to hear several of the most famous speeches delivered during and before the Civil War by the great American, who stands second only to Washington. Abraham Lincoln was not only one of the wisest of men, but the English-speaking world is now aware that he was also among its very greatest orators. This fact was not appreciated during his life. The flowers of rhetoric are conspicuous by their absence from his speeches, but it may be doubted if Demosthenes, Burke, or Webster, could have found equally fit words to express the broad philosophy and the exquisite pathos of the Gettysburg Address of November, 1863. . .

I well remember as a youth, the nation's grief over the death of Kentucky's distinguished son, Henry Clay; the widespread mourning occasioned by the departure of New England's majestic Webster, and the sorrow caused by the passing away of famous Farragut, and the illustrious triumvirate, Grant, Sherman, and Sheridan; but never except in the death of Lincoln, did the country witness such sorrow among the plain people and the race that he had liberated, and also such numbers of sailors and soldiers shedding tears for the great Commander whom they never saw. Children were seen crying in our streets. Never before, it has been truthfully said by Lowell, was funeral panegyric so eloquent as the silent look of sympathy which strangers exchanged when they met that day. Their common manhood had lost a kinsman. Grant said to your speaker that the day of Lincoln's death was the saddest of his life. The great War President's was a life that made a vast difference for all Americans; all are better off than if he had not lived; and this betterment is for always, it did not die with him—that is the true estimate of a great life. . .

Source:

Wilson, James Grant. "Abraham Lincoln: Leader and Master of Men." In *Abraham Lincoln: The Tribute of a Century, 1809-1909; Commemorative of the Lincoln Centenary and Containing the Principal Speeches Made in Connection Therewith.* Edited by Nathan William MacChesney. Chicago: A. C. McClurg & Co., 1910.

6-11
Centennial Celebration in New York, New York—
Joseph Hodges Choate

Joseph Hodges Choate (1832-1917) was a lawyer and diplomat. He spoke at the centennial celebration at Cooper Union (Institute) in New York City. In the following excerpts, Choate remembers hearing Lincoln give his famous speech at the same hall nearly 50 years earlier (see document 7-3).

Just forty-nine years ago, in this very month of February, on this very spot, before just such an audience as this, which filled this historic hall to overflowing, I first saw Abraham Lincoln, and heard him deliver that thrilling address which led to his nomination at Chicago three months afterwards and to his triumphant election in November. The impression of that scene and of that speech can never be effaced from my memory.

After his great success in the West, which had excited the keenest expectation, he came to New York to make a political address—as he had supposed at Plymouth Church in Brooklyn, and it was only when he left his hotel that he found he was coming to Cooper Institute. He appeared in every sense of the word like one of the plain people, among whom he always loved to be counted.

At first sight there was nothing impressive or imposing about him. Nothing but his great stature singled him out from the crowd. His clothes hung awkwardly on his gaunt and giant frame. His face was of a dark pallor, without a tinge of color. His seamed and rugged features bore the furrows of hardship and struggle. His deep-set eyes looked sad and anxious. His countenance in repose gave little evidence of that brain-power which had raised him from the lowest to the highest station among his countrymen. As he spoke to me before the meeting opened, he seemed ill at ease, with that sort of apprehension that a young man might feel before facing a new and strange audience whose critical disposition he dreaded. Here were assembled all the noted men of his party—all the learned and cultured men of the city, editors, clergymen, statesmen, lawyers, merchants, critics.

When Mr. Bryant presented him on this platform, a vast sea of eager, upturned faces greeted him, full of intense curiosity to see what this rude son of the people was like.

He was equal to the occasion. When he spoke he was transfigured before us. His eye kindled, his voice rang, his face shone and seemed to light up the whole assembly as by an electric flash. For an hour and more he held his audience in the hollow of his hand. His style of speech and manner of delivery were severely simple. The grand simplicities of the Bible, with which he was so familiar, were distinctly his. With no attempt at ornament or rhetoric, without pretence or parade, he spoke straight to the point. It was marvellous to see how this untutored man, by mere self-discipline and the chastening of his own spirit, had outgrown all meretricious arts and had found his own way to the grandeur and the strength of absolute simplicity.

He spoke upon the theme which he had mastered so thoroughly. He demonstrated with irresistible force, the power and the duty of the Federal Government to exclude slavery from the Territories. In the kindliest spirit he protested against the threat of the Southern States to destroy the Union if a Republican President was elected. He closed with an appeal to his audience, spoken with all the fire of his aroused and inspired conscience, with a full outpouring of his love of justice and liberty, to maintain their political purpose on that lofty issue of right and wrong which alone could justify it, and not to be intimidated from their high resolve and sacred duty, by any threats of destruction to the government or of ruin to themselves. He concluded with that telling sentence which drove the whole argument home to all our hearts, "Let us have faith that right makes might, and in that faith let us to the end dare to do our duty as we understand it."

> *The grand simplicities of the Bible, with which he was so familiar, were distinctly his.*

That night the great hall, and the next day the whole city, rang with delighted applause and congratulation, and he who had come as a stranger, departed with the laurels of a great triumph.

Alas! in five years from that exulting night we saw him again for the last time in this city, borne in his coffin through the draped streets. With tears and lamentations a heartbroken people accompanied him from Washington, the scene of his martyrdom, to his last resting place in the young city of the West, where he had worked his way to fame.

The great events and achievements of those five years, seen through the perspective of the forty that have since elapsed, have fixed his place in history forever. It is the supreme felicity of the American people, in the short period of their existence as a nation, to have furnished to the world the two greatest benefactors, not of their own time only, but of all modern history. Washington created the nation and is known the world over as the Father of his Country. Lincoln came to be its saviour and redeemer—to save it from self-destruction, and to redeem it from the cancer of slavery which has been gnawing upon its vitals from the beginning. If it had been put to the vote of the forty-four nations assembled at the Hague for the first time in the world's history, representing the whole of civilization, Christian and Pagan, to name the two men who in modern times had done the most to promote liberty, justice, civilization, and peace, I am sure that with one voice they would have acclaimed these two greatest Americans. Let their names stand together for all time to come.

Source:

Choate, Joseph Hodges. "Abraham Lincoln at Cooper Institute." In *Abraham Lincoln: The Tribute of a Century, 1809-1909; Commemorative of the Lincoln Centenary and Containing the Principal Speeches Made in Connection Therewith.* Edited by Nathan William MacChesney. Chicago: A. C. McClurg & Co., 1910.

6-12
Centennial Celebration in New York, New York—
Booker T. Washington

Booker T. Washington (1856-1915) was a prominent educator and a former slave; he was still a child when Lincoln was assassinated. He was invited by the Republican Club of New York City, which held an annual banquet on Lincoln's birthday, to deliver the following speech at the centennial celebration of Lincoln's birth at the Waldorf-Astoria Hotel on February 12, 1909.

Mr. Chairman, Ladies and Gentlemen: You ask that which he found a piece of property and turned into a free American citizen to speak to you tonight on Abraham Lincoln. I am not fitted by ancestry or training to be your teacher tonight for, as I have stated, I was born a slave.

My first knowledge of Abraham Lincoln came in this way: I was awakened early one morning before the dawn of day, as I lay wrapped in a bundle of rags on the dirt floor of our slave cabin, by the prayers of my mother, just before leaving for her day's work as she was kneeling over my body earnestly praying that Abraham Lincoln might succeed, and that one day she and her boy might be free. You give me the opportunity here this evening to celebrate with you and the nation the answer to that prayer.

Says the Great Book somewhere, "Though a man die, yet shall he live" [John 11:25]. If this is true of the ordinary man, how much more true is it of the hero of the hour and the hero of the century—Abraham Lincoln! One hundred years of the life and influence of Lincoln is the story of the struggles, the trials, ambitions, and triumphs of the people of our complex American civilization. Interwoven into the warp and woof of the human complexity is the moving story of men and women of nearly every race and color in their progress from slavery to freedom, from poverty to wealth, from weakness to power, from ignorance to intelligence. Knit into the life of Abraham Lincoln is the story and success of the nation in the blending of all tongues, religions, colors, and races into one composite nation, leaving each group and race free to live its own separate social life, and yet all a part of the great whole.

If a man die, shall he live? Answering this question as applied to our martyred President, perhaps you expect me to confine my words of appreciation to the great boon which, through him, was conferred upon my race. My undying gratitude and that of ten millions of my race for this and yet more! To have been the instrument used by Providence through which four millions of slaves, now grown into ten millions of free citizens, were made free would bring eternal fame within itself, but this is not the only claim that Lincoln has upon our sense of gratitude and appreciation.

By the side of [Samuel Chapman] Armstrong, and [William Lloyd] Garrison, Lincoln lives today. In the very highest sense he lives in the present more potently than fifty years ago; for that which is seen is temporal, that which is unseen is eternal. He lives in the 32,000 young men and women of the Negro race learning trades and useful occupations; in the 200,000 farms acquired by those he freed; in the more than 400,000 homes built; in the forty-six banks established and 10,000 stores owned; in the $500,000,000 worth of taxable property in hand; in the 28,000 public schools existing, with 30,000 teachers; in the 170 industrial schools and colleges; in the 23,000 ministers and 26,000 churches.

But, above all this, he lives in the steady and unalterable determination of ten millions of black citizens to continue to climb year by year the ladder of the highest usefulness and to perfect themselves in strong, robust character. For making all this possible, Lincoln lives.

But, again, for a higher reason he lives tonight in every corner of the republic. To set the physical man free is much. To set the spiritual man free is more. So often the keeper is on the inside of the prison bars and the prisoner is on the outside.

As an individual, grateful as I am to Lincoln for freedom of body, my gratitude is still greater for freedom of soul—the liberty which permits one to live up in that atmosphere where he refuses to permit sectional or racial hatred to drag down, to warp and narrow his soul.

The signing of the Emancipation Proclamation was a great event, and yet it was but the symbol of another, still greater and more momentous. We who celebrate this anniversary should not forget that the same pen that gave freedom to four millions of African slaves at the same time struck the shackles from the souls of twenty-seven millions of Americans of another color.

In any country, regardless of what its laws say, wherever people act upon the idea that the disadvantage of one man is the good of another, there slavery exists. Wherever in any country the whole people feel that the happiness of all is dependent upon the happiness of the weakest, there freedom exists.

In abolishing slavery, Lincoln proclaimed the principle that, even in the case of the humblest and weakest of mankind, the welfare of each is still the good of all. In reestablishing in this country the principle that, at bottom, the interests of humanity and of the individual are one, he freed men's souls from spiritual bondage; he freed them to mutual helpfulness. Henceforth no man of any race, either in the North or in the South, need feel constrained to fear or hate his brother.

By the same token that Lincoln made America free, he pushed back the boundaries of freedom everywhere, gave the spirit of liberty a wider influence throughout the world, and reestablished the dignity of man as man.

By the same act that freed my race, he said to the civilized and uncivilized world that man everywhere must be free, and that man everywhere must be enlightened, and the Lincoln spirit of freedom and fair play will never cease to spread and grow in

*This photo was taken at the centennial banquet of the Republican Club
in New York City, held at the Waldorf-Astoria.*

power till throughout the world all men shall know the truth, and the truth shall make them free.

Lincoln in his day was wise enough to recognize that which is true in the present and for all time: that in a state of slavery and ignorance man renders the lowest and most costly form of service to his fellows. In a state of freedom and enlightenment he renders the highest and most helpful form of service.

The world is fast learning that of all forms of slavery there is none that is so harmful and degrading as that form of slavery which tempts one human being to hate another by reason of his race or color. One man cannot hold another man down in the ditch without remaining down in the ditch with him. One who goes through life with his eyes closed against all that is good in another race is weakened and circumscribed, as one who fights in a battle with one hand tied behind him. Lincoln was in the truest sense great because he unfettered himself. He climbed up out of the valley, where his vision was narrowed and weakened by the fog and miasma, onto the mountain top, where in a pure and unclouded atmosphere he could see the truth which enabled him to rate all men at their true worth. Growing out of this anniversary season and atmosphere, may there crystallize a resolve throughout the nation that on such a mountain the American people will strive to live.

We owe, then, to Lincoln physical freedom, moral freedom, and yet this is not all. There is a debt of gratitude which we as individuals, no matter what race or nation, must recognize as due Abraham Lincoln—not for what he did as chief executive of the nation, but for what he did as a man. In his rise from the most abject poverty and ignorance to a position of high usefulness and power, he taught the world one of the greatest of all lessons. In fighting his own battle up from obscurity and squalor, he fought the battle of every other individual and race that is down, and so helped to pull up every other human who was down. People so often forget that by every inch that the lowest man crawls up he makes it easier for every other man to get up. Today, throughout the world, because Lincoln lived, struggled, and triumphed, every boy who is ignorant, is in poverty, is despised or discouraged, hold his head a little higher. His heart beats a little faster, his ambition to do something and be something is a little stronger, because Lincoln blazed the way.

Lincoln was in the truest sense great because he unfettered himself.

To my race, the life of Abraham Lincoln has its special lesson at this point in our career. In so far as his life emphasizes patience, long suffering, sincerity, naturalness, dogged determination, and courage—courage to avoid the superficial, courage to persistently seek the substance instead of the shadow—it points the road for my people to travel.

As a race we are learning. I believe, in an increasing degree that the best way for us to honor the memory of our Emancipator is by seeking to imitate him. Like Lincoln, the Negro race should seek to be simple, without bigotry and without ostentation. There is great power in simplicity. We as a race should, like Lincoln, have moral courage to be what we are, and not pretend to be what we are not. We should keep in mind that no one can degrade us except ourselves; that if we are worthy, no influence can defeat us. Like other races, the Negro will often meet obstacles, often be sorely tried and tempted; but we must keep in mind that freedom, in the broadest and highest sense, has never been a bequest; it has been a conquest.

In the final test, the success of our race will be in proportion to the service that it renders to the world. In the long run, the badge of service is the badge of sovereignty.

With all his other elements of strength, Abraham Lincoln possessed in the highest degree patience and, as I have said, courage. The highest form of courage is not always that exhibited on the battlefield in the midst of the blare of trumpets and the waving of banners. The highest courage is of the Lincoln kind. It is the same kind of courage, made possible by the new life and the new possibilities furnished by Lincoln's Proclamation, displayed by thousands of men and women of my race every year who are going out from Tuskegee and other Negro institutions in the South to lift up their fellows. When they go, often into lonely and secluded districts, with little thought of salary, with little thought of personal welfare, no drums beat, no banners fly, no friends stand by to cheer them on; but these brave young souls who are erecting schoolhouses, creating school systems, prolonging school terms, teaching the people to buy homes, build houses, and live decent lives are fighting the battles of this country just as truly and bravely as any persons who go forth to fight battles against a foreign foe.

In paying my tribute of respect to the Great Emancipator of my race, I desire to say a word here and now in behalf of an element of brave and true white men of the South who, though they saw in Lincoln's policy the ruin of all they believed in and hoped for, have loyally accepted the results of the Civil War, and are today working with a courage few people in the North can understand to uplift the Negro in the South and complete the emancipation that Lincoln began. I am tempted to say that it certainly required as high a degree of courage for men of the type of Robert E. Lee and John B. Gordon to accept the results of the war in the manner and spirit in which they did, as that which [Ulysses S.] Grant and [William T.] Sherman displayed in fighting the physical battles that saved the Union

Lincoln also was a Southern man by birth, but he was one of those white men, of whom there is a large and growing class, who resented the idea that in order to assert and maintain the superiority of the Anglo-Saxon race it was necessary that another group of humanity should be kept in ignorance.

Lincoln was not afraid or ashamed to come into contact with the lowly of all races. His reputation and social position were not of such a transitory and transparent kind that he was afraid that he would lose them by being just and kind, even to a man of dark skin. I always pity from the bottom of my heart any man who feels that some-

362

body else must be kept down or in ignorance in order that he may appear great by comparison. It requires no courage for a strong man to kick a weak one down.

Lincoln lives today because he had the courage which made him refuse to hate the man at the South or the man at the North when they did not agree with him. He had the courage as well as the patience and foresight to suffer in silence, to be misunderstood, to be abused, to refuse to revile when reviled. For he knew that, if he was right, the ridicule of today would be the applause of tomorrow. He knew, too, that at some time in the distant future our nation would repent the folly of cursing our public servants while they live and blessing them only when they die. In this connection I cannot refrain from suggesting the question to the millions of voices raised today in his praise: "Why did you not say it yesterday?" Yesterday, when one word of approval and gratitude would have meant so much to him in strengthening his hand and heart.

As we recall tonight his deeds and words, we can do so with grateful hearts and strong faith in the future for the spread of righteousness. The civilization of the world is going forward, not backward. Here and there for a little season the progress of mankind may seem to halt or tarry by the wayside, or ever appear to slide backward, but the trend is ever onward and upward, and will be until someone can invent and enforce a law to stop the progress of civilization. In goodness and liberality the world moves forward. It goes forward beneficently, but it moves forward relentlessly. In the last analysis the forces of nature are behind the moral progress of the world, and these forces will crush into powder any group of humanity that resists this progress.

> *It requires no courage for a strong man to kick a weak one down.*

As we gather here, brothers all, in common joy and thanksgiving for the life of Lincoln, may I not ask that you, the worthy representatives of seventy millions of white Americans, join heart and hand with the ten millions of black Americans—these ten millions who speak your tongue, profess your religion—who have never lifted their voices or hands except in defense of their country's honor and their country's flag— and swear eternal fealty to the memory and traditions of the sainted Lincoln? I repeat, may we not join with your race, and let all of us here highly resolve that justice, good will, and peace shall be the motto of our lives? If this be true, in the highest sense Lincoln shall not have lived and died in vain.

And, finally, gathering inspiration and encouragement from this hour and Lincoln's life, I pledge to you and to the nation that my race, in so far as I can speak for it, which in the past, whether in ignorance or intelligence, whether in slavery or in freedom, has always been true to the Stars and Stripes and to the highest and best interests of this country, will strive to so deport itself that it shall reflect nothing but the highest credit upon the whole people in the North and in the South.

Source:

Washington, Booker T. "My Tribute to the Great Emancipator." *The Booker T. Washington Papers*. 14 vols. Edited by Louis R. Harlan and Raymond W. Smock. Urbana: University of Illinois Press, 1972-89.

6-13
Centennial Celebration in New York, New York— Chauncey M. Depew

Chauncey M. Depew (1834-1928) was the U.S. senator from New York. He delivered a speech at the evening centennial observance held at the Seventy-first Regiment Armory in New York City. In the following excerpts, Depew recalls his acquaintance with Lincoln and his attendance at the funeral train through New York state.

It is eminently fitting that the birthday of Abraham Lincoln should be celebrated by the Grand Army of the Republic. It was at his call, as President, that the first seventy-five thousand men enlisted to save the Union. Afterward, on other appeals, the cry, "We are coming, Father Abraham, three hundred thousand more," rang through every city, village, and hamlet in the land; and forth from the fields, the workshop, the factory, the store, and the office went these followers of Abraham Lincoln to fight for the preservation of the Union. In every way in which a great ruler can alleviate the horrors of war and care for his soldiers, Abraham Lincoln rendered to them, as a body and individually, all the service in his power. They were ever in that great heart of his, and an appeal on their behalf would cause him to lay aside every duty, no matter how great, to encourage, rescue or save. . .

. . .With the ability to make difficult things plain to the humblest understanding, and to clarify the most murky atmosphere of conflicting testimony, he added humor and a faculty for apt illustration cultivated by his Bible, Bunyan's "Pilgrim's Progress," and Aesop's "Fables," and he possessed an exhaustless fund of anecdotes which nobody could tell so well or apply so happily as Abraham Lincoln. When he left the bar, after twenty-three years of practice, to become President of the United States, he stood among the first of the legal lights of the State of Illinois.

YOU ARE MOST CORDIALLY INVITED TO ATTEND

the

Centennial Celebration

of the birth of

ABRAHAM LINCOLN

FRIDAY, FEBRUARY TWELFTH

EIGHT P. M.

by the

YOUNG MEN'S LINCOLN CLUB

OF FIVE POINTS

New York City

Club Room, 63 Park Street

Prayer . Rev. Elbert H. Todd, Chaplain Y. M. L. C.
Music—Lincoln's Favorite Tune, "Dixie"
Lincoln Fife and Drum Corps
Appreciations of Lincoln . Read by Louis Mazzoni

An invitation to a centennial celebration in New York City.

But it was in riding the circuit during that quarter of a century, that he was preparing unconsciously for the Presidency. He told me that at the County towns when Court was held, the judge, lawyers, litigants, witnesses, and grand and petit jurors would sit up all night at the hotel, telling stories of things which had happened in the lives of an original frontier people, and he said the were better, more to the point, and infinitely stronger for illustration and the enforcement of argument, than all the stories and anecdotes which were ever invented. Human nature is best studied, public questions are more keenly discussed, character is better exhibited, in the forum of the country grocery or drug store than anywhere else. There gather the elders, more or less wise, the lawyers looking for acquaintances, popularity and clients, and the young men listening and absorbing. Lincoln, with his wonderful gift of humor, anecdote, and argument, was for years the idol of that forum. It was there he learned the lesson, invaluable to him when dealing afterwards with mighty problems of state which required for their solution the support of the people, how to so state his ease and make his appeal that it would find a response in the humblest homes in every part of the land. . .

365

Years of diligent study, and this habit, continued form early youth, of expressing his ideas aloud and making speeches alike to trees and to people, made him attractive to the local leaders of his party. His speech when nominated for the Legislature of Illinois, was a model of brevity. It was substantially this: "I am in favor of a protective tariff, a national bank, and internal improvements. If you like my principles, I should be glad to serve you." With the exception of the slavery issue, that speech, made in 1834, seventy-five years ago, has been practically the platform of the Republican party since its formation until to-day.

> *He was superbly prepared, equipped with every art of the orator, resourceful beyond anyone of his time, and unscrupulous in the presentation of his own case and the misrepresentation of that of his opponent.*

Lincoln was of slow growth. There was nothing precocious about him. He matured along fine lines, and each year added to his mental stature. He made little impression during his four terms in the Legislature, except for diligence and intelligence. He served one term in Congress. There he displayed the prevailing characteristic of his political life. He expressed his opinions regardless of consequences. The country was aflame for the Mexican War. The American people are always with the President against a foreign army. He knew that war had been provoked in order to take territory away from Mexico for the extension of slavery. He followed in the lead of Tom Corwin and made a vigorous speech denouncing the policy and purpose of the war. Corwin's speech retired him permanently from public life, and Lincoln was not again a candidate for the House of Representatives. This quality of his mind, and moral courage, were happily illustrated in the famous joint debates between Douglas and himself. Douglas was the most formidable debater, either in the Senate or on the platform, in the country. He was superbly prepared, equipped with every art of the orator, resourceful beyond anyone of his time, and unscrupulous in the presentation of his own case and the misrepresentation of that of his opponent. There was at that period a passionate devotion, among the people, to the Union, but very little sentiment against slavery. The Union was paramount above everything. There was no disposition to interfere with slavery where it was. The only unity on anti-slavery was against its extension into the Territories. Lincoln prepared his first speech in this debate with great care, and then submitted it to the party leaders who had put him forward and who constituted his advisers. When he came to the sentence, "A house divided against itself cannot stand. I believe this Government cannot endure permanently half slave and half free," they unanimously advised him to cut it out. They told him that Douglas would take advantage of it by appealing to the sentiment for the preservation of the Union as paramount to anything else, and that he would charge Lincoln with being in favor of dissolving the Union in order to free the Negroes. Lincoln said: "We are entering upon a great moral campaign of education. I am not advocating Mr. Seward's higher law, but I am advocating the restriction of slavery within its present limits, and the preservation of the new Territories for free labor. That is more than immediate success, and on that question we will ultimately succeed." Douglas did attack Lincoln, making this point, as the advisers thought, his main subject, and it was one of the principal elements in his election. Once more the moral quality and courage of Lincoln came out, when he submitted to his advisers, putting to Douglas the question whether the people of the Territories could exclude slavery by their territorial legislation. Douglas was claiming that it was a great chance for popular sovereignty to repeal the Missouri Compromise of 1820 which prohibited slavery in the Territories, by leaving the question to the people. Lincoln's advisers said, "He will answer, 'Yes.'" "Well," said Lincoln, "by answering 'No,' it will ruin his whole programme. If he answers 'Yes,' that will alienate the South, prevent his nomination for President, and split the Democratic Party." The results were as Lincoln predicted. Douglas was elected Senator. The South bolted the Democratic Convention, the northern half nominating Douglas, the southern half Breckinridge. But what Lincoln did not anticipate, the Republican Party nominated him and he was elected.

None of our Presidents have ever faced such conditions and problems as Lincoln encountered when inaugurated. Five States had already seceded. A Confederate government had been formed, and its whole machinery was in operation with a President, Cabinet, Congress, and Constitution. The arsenals were stripped of arms, the forts of guns, a large number of the ablest army officers were deserting to the Southern Confederacy, but his initial difficulties were with his own household. With the courage born of true greatness, he summoned to his Cabinet, statesmen who had been, for years, national leaders and who were his contestants in the national Convention. As far as possible, he drew them equally from those who had been Whigs and Democrats prior to the formation of the Republican party four years before, and who had come together on the question of the extension of slavery, though they differed upon every other matter of governmental policy. Seward, Chase, and Cameron were household words in the country. The President was hardly known. These strong, cultured, ambitious, and self-centered men, veterans in the public service, regarded with very little respect this homely, uncouth, and almost unknown frontiersman who had, as they thought, become President by accident, when that great honor belonged to each of them. They thought that the President would be a cipher, and the struggle would be only between them as to which, as the stronger, would so dominate the administration as to be practically President of the United States. Lincoln understood this and them perfectly. After a month Mr. Seward presented a written proposition to the President which meant practically that, to unite the country, war should be provoked with England and France, and that he in those difficulties was quite willing to undertake the administration of affairs. There is no President, including Washington, who would not on such a letter have either surrendered or called for the resignation of the Cabinet Minister. But Lincoln's answer was the perfection of confident strength and diplomacy. He wanted the services of the best equipped man in the country for Secretary of State, and the idol of nearly a majority of his party, and so he said, in effect, "The European war will lead to their siding with the South and dissolving the Union. We are to have a civil war, and one is enough at once. You can perform invaluable service in your great department. I have been elected President and will discharge, myself, the duties of that office." He knew that Chase was disparaging him in conversation and trying to prevent his nomination in order to get it for himself, but he ignored these facts and supported Chase until his financial schemes, as Secretary of the Treasury, had given the country credit and money, and then promoted him out of the Cabinet and out of politics by making him Chief Justice of the Supreme Court of the United States.

Seward early recognized the master mind of the President, and that behind an exterior of deference and extreme amiability was the confident judgment and giant grip of a natural leader of men. Thenceforth this most accomplished of the orators, rhetoricians, and dialecticians of his day, as well as one of its greatest statesmen, became the devoted assistant of his chief. . .

Lincoln hated slavery, but his love for the Union was greater. If he could save the Union by freeing all the slaves, or part of them, or none of them, he would so save the Union. I remember the gathering, and then the full force, of the storm against him because he would not free the slaves. Thaddeus Stevens, Horace Greeley, Benjamin

Wade, Henry Winter Davis, and all the old Abolitionists like Wendell Phillips, and William Lloyd Garrison, were the mighty leaders of a formidable and an intelligent assault which few, if any, but him could have resisted. He knew that at least one-half of the Union Army cared nothing about slavery, but were willing to die for the Union. He knew that New York, Connecticut, and New Jersey would be uncertain, if the issue were for slavery. He knew that the hundreds of thousands of soldiers from Kentucky, Tennessee, Maryland, Missouri, and Virginia—who were among the best troops he had—might join the Confederate Army and carry with them their States if he attempted to free the slaves before they saw it was a necessity of war. The folly of these brilliant reformers is best exhibited by an incident which I knew, when they answered this statement by saying it would be a gain to the cause if the border States were all lost and their troops with them. When, however, with knowledge greater than all of them, with a wisdom surer than any of them, with a contact and understanding with the plain people of the country such as none of them possessed, he saw the time had come when the enemy must be deprived of the workers of the field who were supplying the armies, and the servants in their camps who were attending to their wants and relieving their fighting force, he issued the immortal Proclamation of Emancipation and the doom of the Confederacy was sealed.

Justice and mercy were Lincoln's supreme characteristics.

Justice and mercy were Lincoln's supreme characteristics. He bore no enmities, cherished no ill will, and never executed any revenges. While the whole North was raging against those who had rebelled, and millions believed that the destruction of their properties, the devastation of their lands, and the loss of their slaves, which were their main property, was a just punishment for endeavoring to break up the Union, Lincoln appreciated thoroughly the conditions which had impelled them to rebel. In the early days of the War he argued earnestly with his Cabinet and the leaders in Congress for authorization to offer the South four hundred millions of dollars as a compensation for freeing their slaves. To the answer that the country could not stand the expense, he said, "The War is costing four millions a day and it will certainly last one hundred days." After he had visited Richmond when the War was over, and returned to Washington, he again urged this proposition, saying that the South was completely exhausted and this four hundred million would be the best investment the country could make in at once restoring peace and good will between all sections, and furnishing the capital to the

Southern people to restore their homes, recuperate their fortunes and start their industries. But in the bitter passions of the hour the proposition received no support. . .

I first saw Lincoln when he stepped off his car for a few minutes at Peekskill, while on his way to Washington for his inauguration. He was cheerful and light hearted, though he traveled through crowds, many of whom were enemies, part of the time in secret, and all the time in danger of assassination. I met him frequently three years afterwards, when care, anxiety, and overwork had made him look prematurely aged. I was one of the committee in charge of the funeral train which was bearing his body to his home, while on its way through the State of New York. The hostile hosts of four years before were now standing about the roadway with bared heads, weeping. As we sped over the rails at night, the scene was the most pathetic I ever witnessed. At every cross-roads the glare of innumerable torches illumined the whole population, from age to infancy, kneeling on the ground, and their clergymen leading in prayers and hymns. The coffin was placed in the capitol at Albany that the Governor, State Officers, and Legislature might have a farewell look at the great President. The youthful confidence of my first view was gone, also the troubled and worn look of the closing years of his labors, but there rested upon the pallid face and noble brow an expression in death of serenity, peace, and happiness.

We are celebrating within a few months of each other the ter-centenary of Milton and the centenaries of Poe and Darwin. Our current literature of the daily, weekly, and monthly press is full of eulogy of the Puritan poet, of his influence upon English literature and the English language, and of his immortal work, "Paradise Lost." There are not in this vast audience twenty people who have read "Paradise Lost," while there is scarcely a man, woman, or child in the United States who has not read Lincoln's "Speech at Gettysburg." Few gathered to pay tribute to that remarkable genius, Edgar Allan Poe, and yet in every school house in the land to-day the children are reciting or hearing read extracts from the address of Lincoln. Darwin carved out a new era in scientific research and established the truth of one of the most beneficent principles for the progress of growth in the world. Yet Darwin's fame and achievements are for the select few in the higher realms of liberal learning. But for Lincoln—the acclaim goes up to him to-day as one of the few foremost men of all the ages, from statesmen and men of letters in every land, from the halls of Congress and of the Legislatures, from the seats of justice, from colleges and universities, and above and beyond all, from the homes of the plain people of the United States.

Source:

Depew, Chauncey M. "One of the Plain People." In *Abraham Lincoln: The Tribute of a Century, 1809-1909; Commemorative of the Lincoln Centenary and Containing the Principal Speeches Made in Connection Therewith.* Edited by Nathan William MacChesney. Chicago: A. C. McClurg & Co., 1910.

6-14
Centennial Celebration in Washington, D.C.— Joaquim Nabuco

Joaquim Nabuco (1849-1910) was the Brazilian ambassador to the United States. He spoke at the centennial observance at the Masonic Temple in Washington, D.C. Nabuco, who was an abolition leader in Brazil, argued that Lincoln's emancipation of slaves in the United States helped pave the way for emancipation in Brazil in 1888.

It was not without much hesitation that I accepted the invitation to speak by the side of the distinguished men chosen to address you on this great occasion, but when I was told that I would represent here the sentiment of Latin America, I felt that was a call I could not fail to answer.

The presence at this place of any single foreign nation, in the person of its official representative, would be a sufficient acknowledgment that Lincoln belongs to all the world. But there are reasons why the other nations of this continent feel themselves more closely associated with him than the rest of the world, and why they owe him the greater gratitude after that of the United States.

We are bound, indeed, to form with you a political moral unit, and no man, after Washington, has done more than Lincoln to strengthen the magnet that attracts us to you. Washington created the American freedom; Lincoln purified it.

Personally, I owe to Lincoln, not only the choice, but the easy fulfillment of what I consider was my task in life, as it was the task of so many others—the emancipation

371

*The front of this centennial medallion is based on the Lincoln penny,
issued in 1909 in honor of the 100th anniversary of his birth.*

of the slaves. Nobody, indeed, could say what would have been the struggle for abolition in Brazil, if, past the middle of the nineteenth century, a new and powerful
nation had sprung up in America, having for its creed the maintenance and the
expansion of slavery. Through what Lincoln did, owing to the great light he kindled
for all the world with his Proclamation, we could win our cause without a drop of
blood being shed. In fact, we won it in a national embrace—the slave-owners themselves, with the lavishness of their letters of manumission, emulating the action of the
laws of freedom, successively enacted.

Lincoln, like Washington, is one of the few great men in history about whom the
moral sense of mankind is not divided. His record is, throughout, one of inspiration.
His part at the White House was that of the national Fate. To-day, when one looks
from this distance of time to the fields of that terrible Civil War, one sees in them,
not only the shortest cut, but the only possible road, to a common national destiny. I
construe to myself that War as one of those illusions of life, in which men seem to
move of their own free will, projected by a Providence intent on saving their nation
from the course she was pursuing. Nobody can say what would have been the dura-

tion of slavery, if the Southern States had not acted as they did. By seceding, they doomed it to death and saved themselves. In that way the Secession, although a wholly different episode, will have had in the history of the United States the same effect that the secession of the people to the Sacred Mount had in the history of Rome, in the early period of the Republic—that is, that of cementing the national unity and of assuring the destiny of the nation for centuries of ever-widening power.

Lincoln, with the special sense bestowed by the Author of that great Play, upon one entrusted with its leading part, saw distinctly that the South was not a nation, and that it would not think of being one, except during the hallucination of the crisis. If the South had been a nation, the North, with all its strength, would not have subdued it. Neither would the American people care to have a foreign nation attached to its side by conquest; nor would a coerced nation, after such a bloody war, reenter the Union in the spirit of staying forever, as did the South, once the passion spent that moved it to secede.

I believe such was the feeling of General Lee during the whole campaign; only he could not utter it, and the secret died with him. But only such a feeling could have kept his surrender free from all bitterness as if he had only fought a duel of honor for the South. Nothing is so beautiful to me in the celebration of this first centenary of Lincoln, as the tributes of men who represent the noblest spirit of the South.

I came here to say a word—I have said it. With the increased velocity of modern changes, we do not know what the world will be in a hundred years hence. For, surely, the ideals of the generation of the year 2000 will not be the same as those of the generation of the year 1900. Nations will then be governed by currents of political thought which we can no more anticipate than could the seventeenth century anticipate the political currents of the eighteenth, which still in part sway us. But whether the spirit of authority—or that of freedom—increases, Lincoln's story will ever appear more luminous in the amalgamation of centuries, because he supremely incarnated both those spirits. And this veneration for Lincoln's memory, throughout the world, is bound more and more to center in this city—which was the exclusive theatre of his glory, and which alone could reflect the anxieties and the elations of his heart during the whole performance of his great part in history—as holding the great preeminent title of being the place of his martyrdom.

I am proud of having spoken here at his first Centennial in the name of Latin America. We all owe Lincoln the immense debt of having fixed forever the free character of American civilization.

Source:

Nabuco, Joaquim. "Lincoln and the Character of American Civilization." In *Abraham Lincoln: The Tribute of a Century, 1809-1909; Commemorative of the Lincoln Centenary and Containing the Principal Speeches Made in Connection Therewith.* Edited by Nathan William MacChesney. Chicago: A. C. McClurg & Co., 1910.

6-15
Centennial Celebration in Manchester, England—
Church Howe

> *Church Howe (1839-?) was a major in the Union Army. He served as the United States Consul in Manchester, England, where he delivered a speech at the centennial celebration in which he shared memories of Lincoln during the Civil War.*

[I am not here] to deliver a eulogy on the life of Mr. Lincoln. That was for you to do, and grandly you have done it. I am here to thank you for this great interest, for the cordial manner in which you bring back to memory Abraham Lincoln, the great, the commoner, the man of the people, the man who believed in the government 'of the people, for the people, by the people.'

I have been asked to relate some of my experiences as a soldier of the Civil War, and I do so with a great deal of pride. I am proud that I was a soldier under the great Commander-in-chief Abraham Lincoln. You must remember that our army was made up of the boys of the country. In my own regiment, the first regiment that responded to the call, there were not twenty per cent over twenty-two years old. The soldiers of the army were the youth of the country. And they responded as the English boy would respond to-day if he was called upon. The American boy was patriotic, like the English boy. I belonged, as a boy of seventeen years, to the Massachusetts militia, which is similar to your Territorial Force. The War was commenced by the South, not by the North, and Mr. Lincoln, as Commander-in-chief, acted on the defensive. The South, which had enjoyed the fruits of slavery for generations, believing that it was right, that the slave was chattel and property that could be bought and sold, that wife could be separated from husband and children from father and mother, went into the War in the belief that it could conquer. When Lincoln stood in the way, they declared their intention to establish a union of their own. It was then that Mr. Lincoln saw he was in danger. You can realize now how little he thought the War would amount to, when his first call was for only seventy-five thousand troops. Among those troops was the regiment of which I was a member—the old 6th Massachusetts. At six o'clock in the afternoon we received notice to go to the armory. We took off our clothing, put on our uniforms, and at nine o'clock were on our way to Washington.

Upon passing through Maryland, a slave-owning State, on the nineteenth of April, about two o'clock in the afternoon, an assault was made on that regiment and the first blood was shed. We proceeded, and in an hour's time we were at Washington. Lincoln met us. I recollect that as we lined up he came down the line and shook hands with every boy, and thanked us for coming. And then he marched with us to the Senate Chamber, where we stood guard for weeks. After that he was continually coming to us, talking with every one.

Oh, he was a commoner, he was a democrat, he was a man who felt that you were as good as he was. And we all loved him. He was a gaunt, tall man, better than six foot, homely and ungainly. But when you came to listen to his talk, you realized what was in the man.

Source:

Howe, Church. "The Commemoration Abroad: Manchester, England." In *Abraham Lincoln: The Tribute of a Century, 1809-1909; Commemorative of the Lincoln Centenary and Containing the Principal Speeches Made in Connection Therewith*. Edited by Nathan William MacChesney. Chicago: A. C. McClurg & Co., 1910.

6-16
"Lincoln on Pennies" by Carl Sandburg

Poet Carl Sandburg (1878-1967) was a great admirer of Lincoln. Through-
out his career, Sandburg wrote several poems and a two-volume biography
about the president. The selection below, an editorial written for the Milwaukee Daily News *on August 3, 1909, is purported to be Sandburg's first pub-*
lished writing about Lincoln.

The face of Abraham Lincoln on the copper cent seems well and proper. If it were possible to talk with that great, good man, he would probably say that he is perfectly willing that his face is to be placed on the cheapest and most common coin in the country.

The penny is strictly the coin of the common people. At Palm Beach, Newport and Saratoga you will find nothing for sale at one cent. No ice cream cones at a penny apiece there.

Carl Sandburg.

"Keep the change," says the rich man. "How many pennies do I get back?" asks the poor man.

Only the children of the poor know the joy of getting a penny for running around the corner to the grocery.

The penny is the bargain counter coin. Only the common people walk out of their way to get something for 9 cents reduced from 10 cents. The penny is the coin used by those who are not sure of tomorrow, those who know that if they are going to have a dollar next week they must watch the pennies this week.

Follow the travels of a penny and you find it stops at many cottages and few mansions.

The common, homely face of "Honest Abe" will look good on the penny, the coin of the common folk from whom he came and to whom he belongs.

Source:

Sandburg, Carl. "Lincoln on Pennies." Editorial in the *Milwaukee Daily News*, August 3, 1909.

Part 7
A Selection of Lincoln's
Speeches and Writings

Lincoln was a man of many talents, not least of which was his skill as a writer and speaker. His ability to speak directly to people in a clear and forthright manner won him the admiration and respect of many. This section contains text from some of Lincoln's most important speeches and writings. Three pieces are speeches delivered before his presidency: one at Peoria, Illinois; one at Cooper Institute in New York City; and one at Springfield, Illinois, upon his Senate nomination in 1858, better known as the "House Divided" speech. Also included are his first and second inaugural addresses; a famous letter to *New York Tribune* editor Horace Greeley on slavery and preserving the Union; the Gettysburg Address; and the Emancipation and Thanksgiving Proclamations.

7-1
Speech at Peoria, Illinois, October 16, 1854

In the fall of 1854 Lincoln ran for a seat in the Illinois House of Representatives. During this campaign, he delivered a speech in Peoria, Illinois, on October 16, 1854, that an early biographer, Albert J. Beveridge, considered his "first great speech." In the following excerpts from the three-hour oration, Lincoln argues his opposition to slavery and its extension into Nebraska and Kansas, noting its incompatibility with the principles of the Declaration of Independence.

This declared indifference, but, as I must think, covert real zeal, for the spread of slavery, I cannot but hate. I hate it because of the monstrous injustice of slavery itself. I hate it because it deprives our republican example of its just influence in the world; enables the enemies of free institutions with plausibility to taunt us as hypocrites; causes the real friends of freedom to doubt our sincerity; and especially because it forces so many good men among ourselves into an open war with the very fundamental principles of civil liberty, criticizing the Declaration of Independence, and insisting that there is no right principle of action but self-interest. . . .

The doctrine of self-government is right,—absolutely and eternally right,—but it has no just application as here attempted. Or perhaps I should rather say that whether it has such application depends upon whether a negro is not or is a man. If he is not a man, in that case he who is a man may as a matter of self-government do just what he pleases with him.

But if the negro is a man, is it not to that extent a total destruction of self-government to say that he too shall not govern himself. When the white man governs himself, that is self-government; but when he governs himself, and also governs another man, that is more than self-government—that is despotism. . . .

What I do say is that no man is good enough to govern another man without that other's consent. . . .

The master not only governs the slave without his consent, but he governs him by a set of rules altogether different from those which he prescribes for himself. Allow all the governed an equal voice in the government, and that, and that only, is self-government. . . .

381

Lincoln in 1858.

Slavery is founded in the selfishness of man's nature—opposition to it in his love of justice. These principles are an eternal antagonism, and when brought into collision so fiercely as slavery extension brings them, shocks and throes and convulsions must ceaselessly follow. Repeal the Missouri Compromise, repeal all compromises, repeal the Declaration of Independence, repeal all past history, you still cannot repeal human nature. . . .

I particularly object to the new position which the avowed principle of this Nebraska law gives to slavery in the body politic. I object to it because it assumes that there can be moral right in the enslaving of one man by another. I object to it as a dangerous dalliance for a free people—a sad evidence that, feeling prosperity, we forget right; that liberty, as a principle, we have ceased to revere. . . .

Little by little, but steadily as man's march to the grave, we have been giving up the old for the new faith. Near eighty years ago we began by declaring that all men are created equal; but now from that beginning we have run down to the other declaration, that for some men to enslave others is a "sacred right of self-government." These principles cannot stand together. They are as opposite as God and Mammon. . . .

Our republican robe is soiled and trailed in the dust. Let us repurify it. Let us turn and wash it white in the spirit, if not in the blood, of the Revolution. Let us turn slavery from its claims of "moral right" back upon its existing legal rights and its arguments of "necessity." Let us return it to the position our fathers gave it, and there let it rest in peace. Let us readopt the Declaration of Independence, and with it the practices and policy which harmonize with it. Let North and South—let all Americans—let all lovers of liberty everywhere join in the great and good work. If we do this, we shall not only have saved the Union, but we shall have so saved it as to make and to keep it forever worthy of the saving. We shall have so saved it that the succeeding millions of free, happy people, the world over, shall rise up and call us blessed to the latest generations. . . .

Source:

Lincoln, Abraham. Speech at Peoria, Illinois, October 16, 1854. In *Complete Works of Abraham Lincoln*. Vol. 2. Edited by John G. Nicolay and John Hay. New York: Francis D. Tandy Company, 1905.

7-2
"House Divided" Speech at Springfield, Illinois, June 16, 1858

Lincoln delivered the following speech at the Republican State Convention in Springfield, Illinois, on the evening of June 16, 1858, after the Convention had nominated him as their candidate for the United States Senate. In his acceptance address, excerpted below, Lincoln foresees that the nation will decide to be either for or against slavery. He also argues that there is no reason to believe that his opponent Stephen A. Douglas will work toward eventually ending slavery. Lincoln's colleagues considered the speech to be detrimental to his political future, and indeed, he lost the Senate campaign of 1858. But he won the presidency two years later.

Mr. President and Gentlemen of the Convention:

If we could first know where we are, and whither we are tending, we could better judge what to do, and how to do it. We are now far into the fifth year since a policy was initiated with the avowed object and confident promise of putting an end to slavery agitation. Under the operation of that policy, that agitation has not only not ceased but has constantly augmented. In my opinion, it will not cease until a crisis shall have been reached and passed. "A house divided against itself cannot stand." I believe this government cannot endure permanently half slave and half free. I do not expect the Union to be dissolved—I do not expect the house to fall—but I do expect it will cease to be divided. It will become all one thing, or all the other. Either the opponents of slavery will arrest the further spread of it, and place it where the public mind shall rest in the belief that it is in the course of ultimate extinction; or its advocates will push it forward till it shall become alike lawful in all the States, old as well as new, North as well as South.

Have we no tendency to the latter condition?

Let any one who doubts carefully contemplate that now almost complete legal combination—piece of machinery, so to speak—compounded of the Nebraska doctrine and the Dred Scott decision. Let him consider not only what work the machinery is adapted to do, and how well adapted; but also let him study the history of the construction, and trace, if he can, or rather fail, if he can, to trace the evidences of design and concert of action among its chief architects, from the beginning.

The new year of 1854 found slavery excluded from more than half the States by State constitutions, and from most of the national territory by congressional prohibition. Four days later commenced the struggle which ended in repealing that congressional prohibition. This opened all the national territory to slavery, and was the first point gained.

But, so far, Congress only had acted; and an indorsement by the people, real or apparent, was indispensable to save the point already gained and give chance for more.

This necessity had not been overlooked, but had been provided for, as well as might be, in the notable argument of "squatter sovereignty," otherwise called "sacred right of self-government," which latter phrase, though expressive of the only rightful basis of any government, was so perverted in this attempted use of it as to amount to just this: That if any one man choose to enslave another, no third man shall be allowed to object. That argument was incorporated into the Nebraska bill itself, in the language which follows: "It being the true intent and meaning of this act not to legislate slavery into any Territory or State, nor to exclude it therefrom; but to leave the people thereof perfectly free to form and regulate their domestic institutions in their own way, subject only to the Constitution of the United States." Then opened the roar of loose declamation in favor of "squatter sovereignty" and "sacred right of self-government." "But," said opposition members, "let us amend the bill so as to expressly declare that the people of the Territory may exclude slavery." "Not we," said the friends of the measure; and down they voted the amendment.

While the Nebraska bill was passing through Congress, a law case involving the question of a negro's freedom, by reason of his owner having voluntarily taken him first into a free State and then into a Territory covered by the congressional prohibition, and held him as a slave for a long time in each, was passing through the United States Circuit Court for the District of Missouri; and both Nebraska bill and lawsuit were brought to a decision in the same month of May, 1854. The negro's name was Dred Scott, which name now designates the decision finally made in the case. Before the then next presidential election, the law case came to and was argued in the Supreme Court of the United States; but the decision of it was deferred until after the election. Still, before the election, Senator Trumbull, on the floor of the Senate, requested the leading advocate of the Nebraska bill to state his opinion whether the people of a Territory can constitutionally exclude slavery from their limits; and the latter answered: "That is a question for the Supreme Court."

The election came. Mr. [James] Buchanan was elected, and the indorsement, such as it was, secured. That was the second point gained. The indorsement, however, fell short of a clear popular majority by nearly four hundred thousand votes, and so, perhaps, was not overwhelmingly reliable and satisfactory. The outgoing President, in his last annual message, as impressively as possible echoed back upon the people the weight and authority of the indorsement. The Supreme Court met again; did not announce their decision, but ordered a reargument. The presidential inauguration came, and still no decision of the court; but the incoming President in his inaugural address, fervently exhorted the people to abide by the forthcoming decision, whatever it might be. Then, in a few days, came the decision.

The reputed author of the Nebraska bill finds an early occasion to make a speech at this capital indorsing the Dred Scott decision, and vehemently denouncing all opposition to it. The new President, too, seizes the early occasion of the Silliman letter to indorse and strongly construe that decision, and to express his astonishment that any different view had ever been entertained!

At length a squabble springs up between the President and the author of the Nebraska bill, on the mere question of fact, whether the Lecompton constitution was or was not, in any just sense, made by the people of Kansas; and in that quarrel the latter declares that all he wants is a fair vote for the people, and that he cares not whether slavery be voted down or voted up. I do not understand his declaration that he cares not whether slavery be voted down or voted up to be intended by him other than as an apt definition of the policy he would impress upon the public mind—the principle for which he declares he has suffered so much, and is ready to suffer to the end. And well may he cling to that principle. If he has any parental feeling, well may he cling to it. That principle is the only shred left of his original Nebraska doctrine. Under the Dred Scott decision "squatter sovereignty" squatted out of existence, tumbled down like temporary scaffolding,—like the mold at the foundry, served through one blast and fell back into loose sand,—helped to carry an election, and then was kicked to the winds. His late joint struggle with the Republicans against the Lecompton constitution involves nothing of the original Nebraska doctrine. That struggle was made on a point—the right of a people to make their own constitution—upon which he and the Republicans have never differed.

The several points of the Dred Scott decision, in connection with Senator [Stephen A.] Douglas's "care not" policy, constitute the piece of machinery in its present state of advancement. This was the third point gained. The working points of that machinery are:

(1) That no negro slave, imported as such from Africa, and no descendant of such slave, can ever be a citizen of any State, in the sense of that term as used in the Constitution of the United States. This point is made in order to deprive the negro in every possible event of the benefit of that provision of the United States Constitution which declares that "the citizens of each State shall be entitled to all the privileges and immunities of citizens in the several States."

Under the Dred Scott decision "squatter sovereignty" squatted out of existence, tumbled down like temporary scaffolding,—like the mold at the foundry, served through one blast and fell back into loose sand,— helped to carry an election, and then was kicked to the winds.

(2) That, "subject to the Constitution of the United States," neither Congress nor a territorial legislature can exclude slavery from any United States Territory. This point is made in order that individual men may fill up the Territories with slaves, without danger of losing them as property and thus to enhance the chances of permanency to the institution through all the future.

(3) That whether the holding a negro in actual slavery in a free State makes him free as against the holder, the United States courts will not decide, but will leave to be decided by the courts of any slave State the negro may be forced into by the master. This point is made not to be pressed immediately, but, if acquiesced in for a while, and apparently indorsed by the people at an election, then to sustain the logical conclusion that what Dred Scott's master might lawfully do with Dred Scott in the free State of Illinois, every other master may lawfully do with any other one or one thousand slaves in Illinois or in any other free State.

Auxiliary to all this, and working hand in hand with it, the Nebraska doctrine, or what is left of it, is to educate and mold public opinion, at least Northern public opinion, not to care whether slavery is voted down or voted up. This shows exactly where we now are, and partially, also, whither we are tending.

It will throw additional light on the latter, to go back and run the mind over the string of historical facts already stated. Several things will now appear less dark and mysterious than they did when they were transpiring. The people were to be left "perfectly free," "subject only to the Constitution." What the Constitution had to do with it outsiders could not then see. Plainly enough now, it was an exactly fitted niche for the Dred Scott decision to afterward come in, and declare the perfect freedom of the people to be just no freedom at all. Why was the amendment expressly declaring the right of the people voted down? Plainly enough now, the adoption of it would have spoiled the niche for the Dred Scott decision. Why was the court decision held up? Why even a senator's individual opinion withheld till after the presidential election? Plainly enough now, the speaking out then would have damaged the "perfectly free" argument upon which the election was to be carried. Why the outgoing President's felicitation on the indorsement? Why the delay of a reargument? Why the incoming President's advance exhortation in favor of the decision? These things look like the cautious patting and petting of a spirited horse preparatory to mounting him, when it is dreaded that he may give the rider a fall. And why the hasty after-indorsement of the decision by the President and others?

We cannot absolutely know that all these exact adaptations are the result of pre-concert. But when we see a lot of framed timbers, different portions of which we know have been gotten out at different times and places and by different work-men,—Stephen, Franklin, Roger, and James, for instance,—and when we see these timbers joined together, and see they exactly make the frame of a house or a mill, all the tenons and mortises exactly fitting, and all the lengths and propor-tions of the different pieces exactly adapted to their respective places, and not a piece too many or too few, not omitting even scaffolding—or, if a single piece be lacking, we see the place in the frame exactly fitted and prepared yet to bring such piece in—in such a case we find it impossible not to believe that Stephen and Franklin and Roger and James all understood one another from the begin-ning, and all worked upon a common plan or draft drawn up before the first blow was struck.

It should not be overlooked that, by the Nebraska bill, the people of a State as well as Territory were to be left "perfectly free," "subject only to the Constitution." Why mention a State? They were legislating for Territories, and not for or about States. Certainly the people of a State are and ought to be subject to the Constitution of the United States; but why is mention of this lugged into this merely territorial law? Why are the people of a Territory and the people of a State therein lumped together, and their relation to the Constitution therein treated as being precisely the same? While the opinion of the court, by Chief Justice Taney, in the Dred Scott case, and the separate opinions of all the concurring judges, expressly declare that the Constitution of the United States neither permits Congress nor a territorial legislature to exclude slavery from any United States Territory, they all omit to declare whether or not the same Constitution permits a State, or the people of a State, to exclude it. Possibly, this is a mere omission; but who can be quite sure, if McLean or Curtis had sought to get into the opinion a declaration of unlimited power in the people of a State to exclude slavery from their limits, just as Chase and Mace sought to get such declaration, in behalf of the people of a Territory, into the Nebraska bill—I ask, who can be quite sure that it would not have been voted down in the one case as it had been in the other? The nearest approach to the point of declaring the power of a State over slavery is made by Judge Nelson. He approaches it more than once, using the precise idea, and almost the language too, of the Nebraska act. On one occasion, his exact language is, "Except in cases where the power is restrained by the Constitution of the United States, the law of the State is supreme over the subject of slavery within its jurisdiction." In what cases the power of the States is so restrained by the United States Constitution is left an open question, precisely as the same question as to the restraint on the power of the Territories was left open in the Nebraska act. Put this and that together, and we have another nice little niche, which we may, ere long, see filled with another Supreme Court decision declaring that the Constitution of the United States does not permit a State to exclude slavery from its limits. And this may especially be expected if the doctrine of "care not whether slavery be voted down or voted up" shall gain upon the public mind sufficiently to give promise that such a decision can be maintained when made.

Such a decision is all that slavery now lacks of being alike lawful in all the States. Welcome, or unwelcome, such decision is probably coming, and will soon be upon us, unless the power of the present political dynasty shall be met and overthrown. We shall lie down pleasantly dreaming that the people of Missouri are on the verge of making their State free, and we shall awake to the reality instead that the Supreme

Court has made Illinois a slave State. To meet and overthrow the power of that dynasty is the work now before all those who would prevent that consummation. That is what we have to do. How can we best do it?

There are those who denounce us openly to their own friends, and yet whisper us softly, that Senator Douglas is the aptest instrument there is with which to effect that object. They wish us to infer all from the fact that he now has a little quarrel with the present head of the dynasty; and that he has regularly voted with us on a single point upon which he and we have never differed. They remind us that he is a great man, and that the largest of us are very small ones. Let this be granted. But "a living dog is better than a dead lion." Judge Douglas, if not a dead lion for this work, is at least a caged and toothless one. How can he oppose the advances of slavery? He don't care anything about it. His avowed mission is impressing the "public heart" to care nothing about it. A leading Douglas Democratic newspaper thinks Douglas's superior talent will be needed to resist the revival of the African slave-trade. Does Douglas believe an effort to revive that trade is approaching? He has not said so. Does he really think so? But if it is, how can he resist it? For years he has labored to prove it a sacred right of white men to take negro slaves into the new Territories. Can he possibly show that it is less a sacred right to buy them where they can be bought cheapest? And unquestionably they can be bought cheaper in Africa than in Virginia. He has done all in his power to reduce the whole question of slavery to one of a mere right of property; and as such, how can he oppose the foreign slave-trade? How can he refuse that trade in that "property" shall be "perfectly free," unless he does it as a protection to the home production? And as the home producers will probably not ask the protection, he will be wholly without a ground of opposition.

> *We shall lie down pleasantly dreaming that the people of Missouri are on the verge of making their State free, and we shall awake to the reality instead that the Supreme Court has made Illinois a slave State.*

Senator Douglas holds, we know, that a man may rightfully be wiser to-day than he was yesterday—that he may rightfully change when he finds himself wrong. But can we, for that reason, run ahead, and infer that he will make any particular change of which he, himself, has given no intimation? Can we safely base our action upon any such vague inference? Now, as ever, I wish not to misrepresent Judge Douglas's position, question his motives, or do aught that can be personally offensive to him. Whenever, if ever, he and we can come together on principle so that our great cause may have assistance from his great ability, I hope to have interposed no adventitious obstacle. But clearly, he is not now with us—he does not pretend to be—he does not promise ever to be.

Our cause, then, must be intrusted to, and conducted by, its own undoubted friends—those whose hands are free, whose hearts are in the work, who do care for the result. Two years ago the Republicans of the nation mustered over thirteen hundred thousand strong. We did this under the single impulse of resistance to a common danger, with every external circumstance against us. Of strange, discordant, and even hostile elements, we gathered from the four winds, and formed and fought the battle through, under the constant hot fire of a disciplined, proud, and pampered enemy. Did we brave all then to falter now?—now, when that same enemy is wavering, dissevered, and belligerent? The result is not doubtful. We shall not fail—if we stand firm, we shall not fail. Wise counsels may accelerate or mistakes delay it, but, sooner or later, the victory is sure to come.

Source:

Lincoln, Abraham. "Speech Delivered at Springfield, Illinois, at the Close of the Republican State Convention by which Mr. Lincoln Had Been Named as Their Candidate for United States Senator, June 16, 1858." In *Complete Works of Abraham Lincoln*. Vol. 3. Edited by John G. Nicolay and John Hay. N.P.: Lincoln Memorial University, 1894.

7-3
Speech at Cooper Institute, New York, February 27, 1860

On February 27, 1860, Lincoln gave a lecture at Cooper Institute, a new educational facility in New York City. It was his first public appearance before an Eastern audience, and it was a huge success. The speech was reprinted in several newspapers, published in pamphlet form, and helped propel Lincoln to the Republican candidacy for president. Lincoln argued convincingly that the Founding Fathers intended to regulate the spread of slavery in the territories. The following excerpts highlight his argument and its famous conclusion.

I defy any one to show that any living man in the whole world ever did, prior to the beginning of the present century (and I might almost say prior to the beginning of the last half of the present century), declare that, in his understanding, any proper division of local from Federal authority, or any part of the Constitution, forbade the Federal Government to control as to slavery in the Federal Territories. To those who now so declare I give not only "our fathers who framed the government under which we live," but with them all other living men within the century in which it was framed, among whom to search, and they shall not be able to find the evidence of a single man agreeing with them. . . .

I do not mean to say we are bound to follow implicitly in whatever our fathers did. To do so would be to discard all the lights of current experience—to reject all progress, all improvement. What I do say is that if we would supplant the opinions and policy of our fathers in any case, we should do so upon evidence so conclusive, and argument so clear, that even their great authority, fairly considered and weighed, cannot stand; and most surely not in a case whereof we ourselves declare they understood the question better than we. . . .

Let all who believe that "our fathers who framed the government under which we live understood this question just as well, and even better, than we do now," speak as they spoke, and act as they acted upon it. . . .

It is exceedingly desirable that all parts of this great Confederacy shall be at peace, and in harmony one with another. Let us Republicans do our part to have it so. Even though much provoked, let us do nothing through passion and ill temper. Even

*This photo of Lincoln was taken before he delivered his
speech at Cooper Institute on February 27, 1860.*

though the Southern people will not so much as listen to us, let us calmly consider their demands, and yield to them if, in our deliberate view of our duty, we possibly can. Judging by all they say and do, and by the subject and nature of their controversy with us, let us determine if we can, what will satisfy them. . . .

Wrong as we think slavery is, we can yet afford to let it alone where it is, because that much is due to the necessity arising from its actual presence in the nation; but can we, while our votes will prevent it, allow it to spread into the national Territories, and to overrun us here in these free States? If our sense of duty forbids this, then let us stand by our duty fearlessly and effectively. Let us be diverted by none of those sophistical contrivances wherewith we are so industriously plied and belabored— contrivances such as groping for some middle ground between the right and wrong: vain as the search for a man who should be neither a living man nor a dead man; such as a policy of "don't care" on a question about which all true men do care; such as Union appeals beseeching true Union men to yield to Disunionists, reversing the divine rule, and calling, not the sinners, but the righteous to repentance; such as invocations to Washington, imploring men to unsay what Washington said and undo what Washington did. . . .

Let us have faith that right makes might, and in that faith let us to the end dare to do our duty as we understand it.

Source:

Lincoln, Abraham. Speech at Cooper Institute, February 27, 1860. In *Complete Works of Abraham Lincoln*. Vol. 5. Edited by John G. Nicolay and John Hay. New York: Francis D. Tandy Company, 1905.

7-4
First Inaugural Address, March 4, 1861

Lincoln was sworn in as president on March 4, 1861, and delivered the following inaugural address. The United States was on the verge of Civil War, and Lincoln endeavored to calm Southerners' fears and keep the nation united.

*F*ellow-Citizens of the United States: In compliance with a custom as old as the Government itself, I appear before you to address you briefly, and to take in your presence the oath prescribed by the Constitution of the United States to be taken by the President "before he enters on the execution of his office."

I do not consider it necessary at present for me to discuss those matters of administration about which there is no special anxiety or excitement.

Apprehension seems to exist among the people of the Southern States that by the accession of a Republican Administration their property and their peace and personal security are to be endangered. There has never been any reasonable cause for such apprehension. Indeed, the most ample evidence to the contrary has all the while existed and been open to their inspection. It is found in nearly all the published speeches of him who now addresses you. I do but quote from one of those speeches when I declare that "I have no purpose, directly or indirectly, to interfere with the institution of slavery in the States where it exists. I believe I have no lawful right to do so, and I have no inclination to do so." Those who nominated and elected me did so with full knowledge that I had made this and many similar declarations, and had never recanted them. And, more than this, they placed in the platform for my acceptance, and as a law to themselves and to me, the clear and emphatic resolution which I now read:

"*Resolved,* That the maintenance inviolate of the rights of the States, and especially the right of each State to order and control its own domestic institution, according to its own judgment exclusively, is essential to that balance of power on which the perfection and endurance of our political fabric depend, and we denounce the lawless invasion by armed force of the soil of any State or Territory, no matter under what pretext, as among the gravest of crimes."

I now reiterate these sentiments; and, in doing so, I only press upon the public attention the most conclusive evidence of which the case is susceptible, that the property, peace, and security of no section are to be in any wise endangered by the now incoming Administration. I add, too, that all the protection which, consistently with the Constitution and the laws, can be given, will be cheerfully given to all the States when lawfully demanded, for whatever cause—as cheerfully to one section, as to another.

There is much controversy about the delivering up of fugitives from service or labor. The clause I now read is as plainly written in the Constitution as any other of its provisions:

"No person held to service or labor in one State, under the laws thereof, escaping into another, shall in consequence of any law or regulation therein be discharged from such service or labor, but shall be delivered up on claim of the party to whom such service or labor may be due."

It is scarcely questioned that this provision was intended by those who made it for the reclaiming of what we call fugitive slaves; and the intention of the lawgiver is the law. All Members of Congress swear their support to the whole Constitution—to this provision as much as to any other. To the proposition, then, that slaves whose cases come within the terms of this clause, "shall be delivered up," their oaths are unanimous. Now, if they would make the effort in good temper, could they not with nearly equal unanimity frame and pass a law by means of which to keep good that unanimous oath?

There is some difference of opinion whether this clause should be enforced by national or by State authority; but surely that difference is not a very material one. If the slave is to be surrendered, it can be of but little consequence to him, or to others, by which authority it is done. And should any one, in any case, be content that his oath shall go unkept, on a merely unsubstantial controversy as to *how* it shall be kept?

Again, in any law upon this subject, ought not all the safeguards of liberty known in civilized and humane jurisprudence to be introduced so that a free man be not, in any case, surrendered as a slave? And might it not be well at the same time to provide by law for the enforcement of that clause in the Constitution which guarantees that "the citizens of each State shall be entitled to all privileges and immunities of citizens in the several States"?

I take the official oath to-day with no mental reservations and with no purpose to construe the Constitution or laws by any hypercritical rules. And while I do not choose now to specify particular acts of Congress as proper to be enforced, I do suggest that it will be much safer for all, both in official and private stations, to conform to and abide by all those acts which stand unrepealed, than to violate any of them trusting to find impunity in having them held to be unconstitutional.

It is seventy-two years since the first inauguration of a President under our National Constitution. During that period fifteen different and greatly distinguished citizens have, in succession, administered the Executive branch of the Government. They have conducted it through many perils, and generally with great success. Yet, with all this scope of precedent, I now enter upon the same task for the brief constitutional term of four years under great and peculiar difficulty. A disruption of the Federal Union, heretofore only menaced, is now formidably attempted.

I hold that, in contemplation of universal law and of the Constitution, the Union of these is perpetual. Perpetuity is implied, if not expressed, in the fundamental law of all national governments. It is safe to assert that no government proper ever had a provision in its organic law for its own termination. Continue to execute all the express provisions of our National Constitution, and the Union will endure forever—it being impossible to destroy it except by some action not provided for in the instrument itself.

Again, if the United States be not a Government proper, but an association of States in the nature of contract merely, can it, as a contract, be peaceably unmade by less than all the parties who made it? One party to a contract may violate it—break it, so to speak, but does it not require all to lawfully rescind it?

Descending from these general principles, we find the proposition that, in legal contemplation, the Union is perpetual, confirmed by the history of the Union itself. The Union is much older than the Constitution. It was formed, in fact, by the Articles of Association in 1774. It was matured and continued by the Declaration of Independence in 1776. It was further, matured, and the faith of all the then thirteen States expressly plighted and engaged that it should be perpetual, by the Articles of Confederation in 1778. And, finally, in 1787, one of the declared objects for ordaining and establishing the Constitution was, *"to form a more perfect Union."*

But if the destruction of the Union by one, or by a part only, of the States be lawfully possible, the Union is *less* perfect than before the Constitution, having lost the vital element of perpetuity.

It follows from these views that no State, upon its own mere motion, can lawfully get out of the Union; that *resolves* and *ordinances* to that effect are legally void; and that acts of violence, within any State or States, against the authority of the United States, are insurrectionary or revolutionary, according to circumstances.

> *It follows from these views that no State, upon its own mere motion, can lawfully get out of the Union; that resolves and ordinances to that effect are legally void; and that acts of violence, within any State or States, against the authority of the United States, are insurrectionary or revolutionary, according to circumstances.*

I therefore consider that, in view of the Constitution and the laws, the Union is unbroken; and to the extent of my ability I shall take care, as the Constitution itself expressly enjoins upon me, that the laws of the Union be faithfully executed in all of the States. Doing this I deem to be only a simple duty on my part; and I shall perform it, so far as practicable, unless my rightful masters, the American people, shall withhold the requisite means, or in some Authoritative manner direct the contrary. I trust this will not be regarded as a menace, but only as the declared purpose of the Union that it will constitutionally defend and maintain itself.

In doing this there needs to be no bloodshed or violence; and there shall be none, unless it be forced upon the national authority. The power confided to me will be used to hold, occupy, and possess the property and places belonging to the Government, and to collect the duties and imposts; but beyond what may be necessary for these objects, there will be no invasion, no using of force against or among the people anywhere. Where hostility to the United States, in any interior locality, shall be so great and universal as to prevent competent resident citizens from holding the Federal offices, there will be no attempt to force obnoxious strangers among the people for that object. While the strict legal right may exist in the Government to enforce the exercise of these offices, the attempt to do so would be so irritating, and so nearly impracticable withal, that I deem it better to forego for the time the uses of such offices.

The mails, unless repelled, will continue to be furnished in all parts of the Union. So far as possible, the people everywhere shall have that sense of perfect security which is most favorable to calm thought and reflection. The course here indicated will be followed unless current events and experience shall show a modification or change to be proper, and in every case and exigency my best discretion will be exercised according to circumstances actually existing, and with a view and a hope of a peaceful solution of the national troubles, and the restoration of fraternal sympathies and affections.

That there are persons in one section or another who seek to destroy the Union at all events, and are glad of any pretext to do it, I will neither affirm nor deny; but if there be such, I need address no word to them. To those, however, who really love the Union may I not speak?

Before entering upon so grave a matter as the destruction of our national fabric, with all its benefits, its memories, and its hopes, would it not be wise to ascertain precisely why we do it? Will you hazard so desperate a step while there is any possibility that any portion of the ills you fly from have no real existence? Will you, while the certain ills you fly to are greater than all the real ones you fly from—will you risk the commission of so fearful a mistake?

All profess to be content in the Union, if all constitutional rights can be maintained. Is it true, then, that any right, plainly written in the Constitution, has been denied? I think not. Happily the human mind is so constituted, that no party can reach to the audacity of doing this. Think, if you can, of a single instance in which a plainly written provision of the Constitution has ever been denied. If by the mere force of numbers a majority should deprive a minority in any clearly written constitutional right, it might, in a moral point of view, justify revolution—certainly would if such a right were a vital one. But such is not our case. All the vital rights of minorities and of individuals are so plainly assured to them by affirmations and negations, guaranties and prohibitions, in the Constitution, that controversies never arise concerning them. But no organic law can ever be framed with a provision specifically applicable to every question which may occur in practical administration. No foresight can anticipate, nor any document of reasonable length contain, express provisions for all possible questions. Shall fugitives from labor be surrendered by national or by State authority? The Constitution does not expressly say. *May* Congress prohibit slavery in the Territories? The Constitution does not expressly say. *Must* Congress protect slavery in the Territories? The Constitution does not expressly say.

From questions of this class spring all our constitutional controversies, and we divide upon them into majorities and minorities. If the minority will not acquiesce, the majority must, or the Government must cease. There is no other alternative; for continuing the Government is acquiescence on one side or the other.

If a minority in such case will secede rather than acquiesce, they make a precedent which in turn will divide and ruin them; for a minority of their own will secede from them whenever a majority refuses to be controlled by such minority. For instance, why may not any portion of a new confederacy a year or two hence arbitrarily secede again, precisely as portions of the present Union now claim to secede from it? All who cherish disunion sentiments are now being educated to the exact temper of doing this.

Is there such perfect identity of interests among the States to compose a new Union as to produce harmony only, and prevent renewed secession?

Plainly, the central idea of secession is the essence of anarchy. A majority held in restraint by constitutional checks and limitations, and always changing easily with deliberate changes of popular opinions and sentiments, is the only true sovereign of a free people. Whoever rejects it does, of necessity, fly to anarchy or to despotism. Unanimity is impossible; the rule of a minority, as a permanent arrangement, is wholly inadmissible; so that, rejecting the majority principle, anarchy or despotism in some form is all that is left.

I do not forget the position, assumed by some, that constitutional questions are to be decided by the Supreme Court; nor do I deny that such decisions must be binding, in any case, upon the parties to a suit, as to the object of that suit, while they are also entitled to very high respect and consideration in all parallel cases by all other departments of the Government. And while it is obviously possible that such decision may be erroneous in any given case, still the evil effect following it, being limited to that particular case, with the chance that it may be overruled and never become a precedent for other cases, can better be borne than could the evils of a different practice. At the same time, the candid citizen must confess that if the policy of the Government, upon vital questions affecting the whole people, is to be irrevocably fixed by decisions of the Supreme Court, the instant they are made, in ordinary litigation between parties in personal actions, the people will have ceased to be their own rulers, having to that extent practically resigned their government into the hands of that eminent tribunal. Nor is there in this view any assault upon the court or the judges. It is a duty from which they may not shrink to decide cases properly brought before them, and it is no fault of theirs if others seek to turn their decisions to political purposes.

One section of our country believes slavery is *right,* and ought to be extended, while the other believes it is *wrong,* and ought not to be extended. This is the only substantial dispute. The fugitive-slave clause of the Constitution, and the law for the suppression of the foreign slave trade, are each as well enforced, perhaps, as any law can ever be in a community where the moral sense of the people imperfectly supports the law itself. The great body of the people abide by the dry legal obligation in both cases, and a few break over in each. This, I think, cannot be perfectly cured; and it would be worse in both cases *after* the separation of the sections, than before. The foreign slave trade, now imperfectly suppressed, would be ultimately revived without restriction, in one section; while fugitive slaves, now only partially surrendered, would not be surrendered at all by the other.

Physically speaking, we cannot separate. We cannot remove our respective sections from each other, nor build an impassable wall between them. A husband and wife may be divorced, and go out of the presence and beyond the reach of each other; but the different parts of our country cannot do this. They cannot but remain face to face, and intercourse, either amicable or hostile, must continue between them. Is it possible, then, to make that intercourse more advantageous or more satisfactory *after* separation than *before?* Can aliens make treaties easier than friends can make laws? Can treaties be more faithfully enforced between aliens than laws can among friends? Suppose you go to war, you cannot fight always; and when, after much loss on both sides, and no gain on either, you cease fighting, the identical old questions as to terms of intercourse are again upon you.

> One section of our country believes slavery is right, and ought to be extended, while the other believes it is wrong, and ought not to be extended.

This country, with its institutions, belongs to the people who inhabit it. Whenever they shall grow weary of the existing Government, they can exercise their *constitutional* right of amending it, or their *revolutionary* right to dismember or overthrow it. I cannot be ignorant of the fact that many worthy and patriotic citizens are desirous of having the National Constitution amended. While I make no recommendation of amendments, I fully recognize the rightful authority of the people over the whole subject, to be exercised in either of the modes prescribed in the instrument itself; and I should, under existing circumstances, favor rather than oppose, a fair opportunity

401

being afforded the people to act upon it. I will venture to add that to me the convention mode seems preferable, in that it allows amendments to originate with the people themselves, instead of only permitting them to take or reject propositions originated by others, not especially chosen for the purpose, and which might not be precisely such as they would wish to either accept or refuse. I understand a proposed amendment to the Constitution—which amendment, however, I have not seen—has passed Congress, to the effect that the Federal Government shall never interfere with the domestic institutions of the States, including that of persons held to service. To avoid misconstruction of what I have said, I depart from my purpose, not to speak of particular amendments, so far as to say that, holding such a provision to now be implied constitutional law, I have no objection to its being made express and irrevocable.

The Chief Magistrate derives all his authority from the people, and they have conferred none upon him to fix terms for the separation of the States. The people themselves can do this also if they choose; but the Executive, as such, has nothing to do with it. His duty is to administer the present Government, as it came to his hands, and to transmit it, unimpaired by him, to his successor.

Why should there not be a patient confidence in the ultimate justice of the people? Is there any better or equal hope in the world? In our present differences is either party without faith of being in the right? If the Almighty Ruler of Nations, with his eternal truth and justice, be on your side of the North, or on yours of the South, that truth and that justice will surely prevail by the judgment of this great tribunal of the American people.

By the frame of the Government under which we live, this same people have wisely given their public servants but little power for mischief; and have, with equal wisdom, provided for the return of that little, to their own hands at very short intervals. While the people retain their virtue and vigilance, no administration, by any extreme of wickedness or folly, can very seriously injure the government in the short space of four years.

My countrymen, one and all, think calmly and *well* upon this whole subject. Nothing valuable can be lost by taking time. If there be an object to *hurry* any of you in hot haste to a step which you would never take *deliberately,* that object will be frustrated by taking time; but no good object can be frustrated by it. Such of you as are now dissatisfied, still have the old Constitution unimpaired, and, on the sensitive point, the laws of your own framing under it; while the new Administration will have no immediate power, if it would, to change either. If it were admitted that you who are dissatisfied hold the right side in the dispute, there still is no single good reason for precipitate action. Intelligence, patriotism, Christianity, and a firm reliance on Him who has never yet forsaken this favored land are still competent to adjust, in the best way, all our present difficulty.

In *your* hands, my dissatisfied fellow-countrymen, and not in *mine,* is the momentous issue of civil war. The Government will not assail *you.* You can have no conflict without being yourselves the aggressors. *You* have no oath registered in Heaven to destroy the Government, while I shall have the most solemn one to "preserve, protect, and defend it."

I am loathe to close. We are not enemies, but friends. We must not be enemies. Though passion may have strained, it must not break our bonds of affection. The mystic chords of memory, stretching from every battle-field and patriot grave to every living heart and hearthstone all over this broad land, will yet swell the chorus of the Union, when again touched, as surely they will be, by the better angels of our nature.

Source:

Lincoln, Abraham. "First Inaugural Address, March 4, 1861." In *American Historical Documents, 1000-1904.* Vol. XLIII. The Harvard Classics. Edited by Charles W. Eliot. New York: P. F. Collier & Son, 1909-14.

7-5
Letter to Horace Greeley, August 22, 1862

Lincoln wrote the letter below in response to a New York Tribune *editorial of August 19, 1862, in which editor Horace Greeley called for immediate emancipation of the slaves. Lincoln's letter was published in the* Tribune; *it is a clear expression of what he considered his constitutional duty as president of the United States: to preserve the Union.*

EXECUTIVE MANSION, WASHINGTON,
AUGUST 22, 1862.

HON. HORACE GREELEY.

Dear Sir: I have just read yours in the 19th, addressed to myself through the New York Tribune. If there be in it any statements or assumptions of fact which I may know to be erroneous, I do not now and here controvert them. If there be in it any inferences which I may believe to be falsely drawn, I do not now and here argue against them. If there be perceptible in titan impatient and dictatorial tone, I waive it in deference to an old friend, whose heart I have always supposed to be right. As to the policy I "seem to be pursuing," as you say, I have not meant to leave any one in doubt.

I would save the Union. I would save it in the shortest way under the Constitution. The sooner the National authority can be restored, the nearer the Union will be "The Union as it was." If there be those who would not save the Union unless they could at the same time destroy slavery, I do not agree with them. My paramount object in this struggle is to save the Union and is not either to save or destroy Slavery. If I could save the Union without freeing any slave, I would do it; and if I could save it by freeing all the slaves, I would do it; and if I could do it by freeing some and leaving others alone, I would also do that. What I do about Slavery and the colored race, I do because I believe it helps to save this Union; and what I forbear, I forbear because I do not believe it would help to save the Union. I shall do less, whenever I shall believe what I am doing hurts the cause; and I shall do more, whenever I shall believe doing more will help the cause. I shall try to correct errors when shown to be errors; and I shall adopt new views so fast as they shall appear to be true views. I have here stated my purpose according to my view of official duty, and I intend no modification of my oft-expressed personal wish that all men, everywhere, could be free.

Yours,
A. Lincoln.

Source:

Lincoln, Abraham. Letter to Horace Greeley, August 22, 1862. Available online at Abraham Lincoln Papers at the Library of Congress. http://memory.loc.gov/ammem/alhtml/malhome.html.

7-6
Emancipation Proclamation, January 1, 1863

Lincoln issued the Emancipation Proclamation on January 1, 1863. It came 100 days after a preliminary proclamation, dated September 22, 1862, stated his intention to declare slaves free by the first of the year 1863 if the Confederacy had not surrendered. The Emancipation Proclamation did not apply to all slaves—only those in Confederate states—and it could not be enforced until those areas came under Union control. But it signaled the president's intention that all should be free and made that freedom the goal of winning the Civil War.

By the President of the United States of America:

A Proclamation.

Whereas, on the twenty-second day of September, in the year of our Lord one thousand eight hundred and sixty-two, a proclamation was issued by the President of the United States, containing, among other things, the following, to wit:

"That on the first day of January, in the year of our Lord one thousand eight hundred and sixty-three, all persons held as slaves within any State or designated part of a State, the people whereof shall then be in rebellion against the United States, shall be then, thenceforward, and forever free; and the Executive Government of the United States, including the military and naval authority thereof, will recognize and maintain the freedom of such persons, and will do no act or acts to repress such persons, or any of them, in any efforts they may make for their actual freedom.

"That the Executive will, on the first day of January aforesaid, by proclamation, designate the States and parts of States, if any, in which the people thereof, respectively, shall then be in rebellion against the United States; and the fact that any State, or the people thereof, shall on that day be, in good faith, represented in the Congress of the United States by members chosen thereto at elections wherein a majority of the qualified voters of such State shall have participated, shall, in the absence of strong countervailing testimony, be deemed conclusive evidence that such State, and the people thereof, are not then in rebellion against the United States."

This print honoring Lincoln's Emancipation Proclamation was published in 1888.

Now, therefore I, Abraham Lincoln, President of the United States, by virtue of the power in me vested as Commander-in-Chief, of the Army and Navy of the United States in time of actual armed rebellion against the authority and government of the United States, and as a fit and necessary war measure for suppressing said rebellion, do, on this first day of January, in the year of our Lord one thousand eight hundred and sixty-three, and in accordance with my purpose so to do publicly proclaimed for the full period of one hundred days, from the day first above mentioned, order and designate as the States and parts of States wherein the people thereof respectively, are this day in rebellion against the United States, the following, to wit:

Arkansas, Texas, Louisiana, (except the Parishes of St. Bernard, Plaquemines, Jefferson, St. John, St. Charles, St. James Ascension, Assumption, Terrebonne, Lafourche, St. Mary, St. Martin, and Orleans, including the City of New Orleans) Mississippi, Alabama, Florida, Georgia, South Carolina, North Carolina, and Virginia, (except the forty-eight counties designated as West Virginia, and also the counties of Berkley, Accomac, Northampton, Elizabeth City, York, Princess Ann, and Norfolk, including the cities of Norfolk and Portsmouth, and which excepted parts, are for the present, left precisely as if this proclamation were not issued.

And by virtue of the power, and for the purpose aforesaid, I do order and declare that all persons held as slaves within said designated States, and parts of States, are, and henceforward shall be free; and that the Executive government of the United States, including the military and naval authorities thereof, will recognize and maintain the freedom of said persons.

And I hereby enjoin upon the people so declared to be free to abstain from all violence, unless in necessary self-defence; and I recommend to them that, in all cases when allowed, they labor faithfully for reasonable wages.

And I further declare and make known, that such persons of suitable condition, will be received into the armed service of the United States to garrison forts, positions, stations, and other places, and to man vessels of all sorts in said service.

And upon this act, sincerely believed to be an act of justice, warranted by the Constitution, upon military necessity, I invoke the considerate judgment of mankind, and the gracious favor of Almighty God.

In witness whereof, I have hereunto set my hand and caused the seal of the United States to be affixed.

Done at the City of Washington, this first day of January, in the year of our Lord one thousand eight hundred and sixty three, and of the Independence of the United States of America the eighty-seventh.

By the President: ABRAHAM LINCOLN
WILLIAM H. SEWARD, Secretary of State.

Source:

Lincoln, Abraham. Emancipation Proclamation, January 1, 1863. Available online at National Archives and Records Administration, 100 Milestone Documents. http://www.ourdocuments.gov.

7-7
Thanksgiving Proclamation, October 3, 1863

On October 3, 1863, Lincoln issued a presidential proclamation designating the last Thursday of November "a Day of Thanksgiving and Praise to our beneficient Father who dwelleth in the heavens." Lincoln proclaimed the holiday in response to numerous appeals by Sarah Josepha Hale, editor of a popular women's magazine, Lady's Book, and an advocate for a national Thanksgiving holiday since 1827.

The year that is drawing toward its close has been filled with blessing of fruitful fields and healthful skies. To these bounties, which are so constantly enjoyed that we are prone to forget the source from which they come, others have been added, which are of so extraordinary a nature that they cannot fail to penetrate and soften the heart which is habitually insensible to the ever-watchful Providence of Almighty God.

In the midst of a civil war of unequaled magnitude and severity, which has sometimes seemed to foreign states to invite and provoke their aggressions, peace has been preserved with all nations, order has been maintained, the laws have been respected and obeyed, and harmony has prevailed everywhere, except in the theatre of military conflict; while that theatre has been greatly contracted by the advancing armies and navies of the Union.

Needful diversions of wealth and strength from the fields of peaceful industry to the national defense have not arrested the plow, the shuttle, or the ship; the axe has enlarged the borders of our settlements, and the mines, as well of iron and coal as of the precious metals, have yielded even more abundantly than heretofore. Population has steadily increased, notwithstanding the waste that has been made by the camp, the siege, and the battle-field, and the country, rejoicing in the consciousness of augmented strength and vigor, is permitted to expect continuance of years with large increase of freedom.

No human council hath devised, nor hath any mortal hand worked out these great things. They are the gracious gifts of the Most High God, who, while dealing with us in anger for our sins, hath nevertheless remembered mercy.

It has seemed to me fit and proper that they should be solemnly, reverentially, and gratefully acknowledged as with one heart and voice by the whole American people. I do, therefore, invite my fellow-citizens in every part of the United States, and also those who are at sea and those who are sojourning in foreign lands, to set apart and observe the last Thursday of November next as a Day of Thanksgiving and Praise to our beneficent Father who dwelleth in the heavens. And I recommend to them that, while offering up the ascriptions justly due to Him for such singular deliverances and blessings, they do also, with humble penitence for our national perverseness and disobedience, commend to His tender care all those who have become widows, orphans, mourners, or sufferers in the lamentable civil strife in which we are unavoidably engaged, and fervently implore the interposition of the Almighty hand to heal the wounds of the nation, and to restore it, as soon as may be consistent with the Divine purposes, to the full enjoyment of peace, harmony, tranquility, and union.

In testimony whereof, I have hereunto set my hand, and caused the seal of the United States to be affixed.

Done at the city of Washington, this third day of October, in the year of our Lord one thousand eight hundred and sixty-three, and of the Independence of the United States the eighty-eighth.

Abraham Lincoln.
By the President:
William H. Seward, Secretary of State

Source:

Lincoln, Abraham. Thanksgiving Proclamation, October 3, 1863. Available online at Library of Congress, American Memory Project. http://memory.loc.gov/ammem/today/nov25.html.

7-8
Gettysburg Address, November 19, 1863

One of the most horrific battles of the Civil War took place at Gettysburg, Pennsylvania. The battle took place July 1-3, 1863, and claimed the lives of more than 50,000 Union and Confederate troops. Lincoln delivered what is perhaps his most famous speech at the Gettysburg battlefield when it was dedicated as a national cemetery on November 19, 1863. (For remembrances of people who attended the dedication, see documents 2-12, 2-13, and 2-14.)

Four score and seven years ago our fathers brought forth on this continent a new nation, conceived in Liberty, and dedicated to the proposition that all men are created equal.

 Now we are engaged in a great civil war, testing whether that nation or any nation so conceived and so dedicated, can long endure. We are met on a great battlefield of that war. We have come to dedicate a portion of that field, as a final resting place for those who here gave their lives that that nation might live. It is altogether fitting and proper that we should do this.

But in a larger sense we cannot dedicate—we cannot consecrate—we cannot hallow—this ground. The brave men, living and dead, who struggled here, have consecrated it, far above our poor power to add or detract. The world will little note, nor long remember what we say here, but it can never forget what they did here. It is for us the living, rather, to be dedicated here to the unfinished work which they who fought here have thus far so nobly advanced. It is rather for us to be here dedicated to the great task remaining before us—that from these honored dead we take increased devotion to that cause for which they gave the last full measure of devotion—that we

THE GETTYSBURG ADDRESS

DELIVERED BY ABRAHAM LINCOLN NOV. 19 1863

AT THE DEDICATION SERVICES ON THE BATTLE FIELD

Fourscore and seven years ago our fathers brought forth on this continent a new nation, conceived in liberty, and dedicated to the proposition that all men are created equal. ★★★ Now we are engaged in a great civil war, testing whether that nation, or any nation so conceived and so dedicated, can long endure. ★ ★ We are met on a great battle-field of that war. ★ We have come to dedicate a portion of that field as a final resting place for those who here gave their lives that that nation might live. ★ ★ It is altogether fitting and proper that we should do this. ★ ★ But in a larger sense we cannot dedicate, we cannot consecrate, we cannot hallow this ground. ★ The brave men, living and dead, who struggled here, have consecrated it far above our poor power to add or detract. The world will little note, nor long remember, what we say here, but it can never forget what they did here. ★★ It is for us, the living, rather to be dedicated here to the unfinished work which they who fought here have thus far so nobly advanced It is rather for us to be here dedicated to the great task remaining before us, that from these honored dead we take increased devotion to that cause for which they gave the last full measure of devotion; ★ that we here highly resolve that these dead shall not have died in vain; that this nation, under God, shall have a new birth of freedom, and that the government of the people, by the people, and for the people, shall not perish from the earth

This print displaying the Gettysburg Address was published in 1909.

here highly resolve that these dead shall not have died in vain; that this nation, under God, shall have a new birth of freedom—and that government of the people, by the people, for the people, shall not perish from the earth.

Source:

Lincoln, Abraham. The Gettysburg Address Drafts. Transcription of the version of the Gettysburg Address inscribed on the walls at the Lincoln Memorial in Washington, D.C. Available online at Library of Congress Exhibition. http://www.loc.gov/exhibits/gadd/gadrft.html.

7-9
Second Inaugural Address, March 4, 1865

Lincoln ran for a second term as president and was reelected in 1864. At his inauguration on March 4, 1865, he delivered the following speech. At 703 words, it was the briefest inaugural address of any president; many also consider it perhaps the most sublime. Lincoln thought it would "wear as well as— perhaps better than—any thing I have produced."

Fellow Countrymen

At this second appearing to take the oath of the presidential office, there is less occasion for an extended address than there was at the first. Then a statement, somewhat in detail, of a course to be pursued, seemed fitting and proper. Now, at the expiration of four years, during which public declarations have been constantly called forth on every point and phase of the great contest which still absorbs the attention, and engrosses the energies of the nation, little that is new could be presented. The progress of our arms, upon which all else chiefly depends, is as well known to the public as to myself; and it is, I trust, reasonably satisfactory and encouraging to all. With high hope for the future, no prediction in regard to it is ventured.

On the occasion corresponding to this four years ago, all thoughts were anxiously directed to an impending civil-war. All dreaded it—all sought to avert it. While the inaugural address was being delivered from this place, devoted altogether to saving the Union without war, insurgent agents were in the city seeking to destroy it without war—seeking to dissolve the Union, and divide effects, by negotiation. Both parties deprecated war; but one of them would make war rather than let the nation survive; and the other would accept war rather than let it perish. And the war came.

One eighth of the whole population were colored slaves, not distributed generally over the Union, but localized in the Southern ~~half~~ part of it. These slaves constituted a peculiar and powerful interest. All knew that this interest was, somehow, the cause of the war. To strengthen, perpetuate, and extend this interest was the object for which the insurgents would rend the Union, even by war; while the government claimed no right to do more than to restrict the territorial enlargement of it. Neither party expected for the war, the magnitude, or the duration, which it has already attained. Neither anticipated that the cause of the conflict might cease with, or even before, the conflict itself should cease. Each looked for an easier triumph, and a result less fundamental and astounding. Both read the same Bible, and pray to the same God; and each invokes His aid against the other. It may seem strange that any men should dare to ask a just God's assistance in wringing their bread from the sweat of other men's faces; but let us judge not that we be not judged. The prayers of both could not be answered; that of neither has been answered fully. The Almighty has His own purposes. "Woe unto the world because of offences! for it must needs be that offences come; but woe to that man by whom the offence cometh!" If we shall suppose that American Slavery is one of those offences which, in the providence of God, must needs come, but which, having continued through His appointed time, He now wills to remove, and that He gives to both North and South, this terrible war, as the woe due to those by whom the offence came, shall we discern therein any departure from those divine attributes which the believers in a Living God always ascribe to Him? Fondly do we hope—fervently do we pray—that this mighty scourge of war may speedily pass away. Yet, if God wills that it continue, until all the wealth piled by the bond-man's two hundred and fifty years of unrequited toil shall be sunk, and until every drop of blood drawn with the lash, shall be paid by another drawn with the sword, as was said f[~~our~~] three thousand years ago, so still it must be said "the judgments of the Lord, are true and righteous altogether"

With malice toward none; with charity for all; with firmness in the right, as God gives us to see the right, let us strive on to finish the work we are in; to bind up the nation's wounds; to care for him who shall have borne the battle, and for his widow, and his orphan—~~to achieve and cherish a lasting peace among ourselves and with the~~

LINCOLN TAKING THE OATH AT HIS SECOND INAUGURATION, MARCH 4, 1865.—PHOTOGRAPHED BY GARDNER, WASHINGTON.—[SE

This illustration of Lincoln taking the oath of office at his second inauguration was published in Harper's Weekly *on March 18, 1865.*

world. to do all which may achieve and cherish a just, and a lasting peace, among ourselves, and with ~~the world.~~ all nations.

[Endorsed by Lincoln:]

Original manuscript of second Inaugural presented to Major John Hay.
A. Lincoln
April 10, 1865

Source:

Lincoln, Abraham. Second Inaugural Address; endorsed by Lincoln, April 10, 1865. Transcribed and annotated by the Lincoln Studies Center, Knox College, Galesburg, Illinois. Available online at Abraham Lincoln Papers at the Library of Congress, Manuscript Division, American Memory Project. http://memory.loc.gov/ammem/alhtml/malhome.html.

Photo and Illustration Credits

Photo and Illustration Credits

Cover photo: American Patriotism © 2000 Comstock Inc.

Part 1 – Early Life and Career

Part 2 – The 16th President: Great Emancipator and Commander-in-Chief

Part 3 – The Man Behind the Legend

Part 4 – The Death of Lincoln

Page 185:   Prints and Photographs Division, Library of Congress, LC-USZ62-8812
Page 191:   Civil War Glass Negative Collection, Library of Congress, LC-DIG-cwpb-02962
Page 196:   Detroit Publishing Company Photograph Collection, Library of Congress, LC-D4-13021
Page 200:   Rare Book and Special Collections Division, Library of Congress, LC-USZC4-5341
Page 207:   Prints and Photographs Division, Library of Congress, LC-USZ62-98750
Page 214:   Feinberg-Whitman Collection, Library of Congress, LC-USZ62-98114
Page 225:   Prints and Photographs Division, Library of Congress, LC-USZC4-1847
Page 230:   Prints and Photographs Division, Library of Congress, LC-USZ62-14065
Page 236:   Prints and Photographs Division, Library of Congress, LC-USZ62-7591
Page 241:   Brady-Handy Photograph Collection, Library of Congress, LC-DIG-cwpbh-00752

Part 5 – Tributes and Legacy

Page 256:   Daguerreotype Collection, Library Collection, LC-USZC4-6189
Page 261:   Prints and Photographs Division, Library of Congress, LC-USZ62-044
Page 269:   Alfred Whital Stern Collection of Lincolniana, Rare Book and Special Collections Division, Library of Congress, LC-scsm-0040
Page 275:   Brady-Handy Photograph Collection, Library of Congress, LC-DIG-cwpbh-05089
Page 278:   Prints and Photographs Division, Library of Congress, LC-USZ62-1770
Page 285:   Prints and Photographs Division, Library of Congress, LC-USZ62-5446
Page 291:   Prints and Photographs Division, Library of Congress, LC-USZ62-60898
Page 296:   Prints and Photographs Division, Library of Congress, LC-USZ62-2573
Page 304:   Prints and Photographs Division, Library of Congress, LC-USZ62-28851
Page 308:   Prints and Photographs Division, Library of Congress, LC-D4-9090

Part 6 – Centennial Celebrations

Page 316:   Abraham Lincoln Presidential Library
Page 320:   Courtesy of the Plymouth Historical Museum, Plymouth, MI
Page 325:   Alfred Whital Stern Collection of Lincolniana, Rare Book and Special Collections Division, Library of Congress, LC-scsm-0133
Page 331:   Abraham Lincoln Presidential Library
Page 336:   Prints and Photographs Division, Library of Congress, LC-USZ62-58396
Page 343:   Abraham Lincoln Presidential Library
Page 349:   Courtesy of the Plymouth Historical Museum, Plymouth, MI
Page 353:   Courtesy of the Lincoln Museum, Fort Wayne, IN (#4628)
Page 360:   Prints and Photographs Division, Library of Congress, LC-USZ62-115700
Page 365:   Courtesy of the Lincoln Museum, Fort Wayne, IN (#4627)
Page 372:   Prints and Photographs Division, Library of Congress, LC-USZ62-58312
Page 376:   FSA/OWI Collection, Library of Congress, LC-USE6-D-001429

Part 7 – A Selection of Lincoln's Speeches and Writings

Page 382:   Prints and Photographs Division, Library of Congress, LC-USZ62-132820
Page 393:   Prints and Photographs Division, Library of Congress, LC-USZ62-5803
Page 406:   Prints and Photographs Division, Library of Congress, LC-USZC4-1526
Page 411:   Prints and Photographs Division, Library of Congress, LC-USZ62-5438
Page 414:   Prints and Photographs Division, Library of Congress, LC-USZ62-2578

Chronology

Chronology

1809

February 12 – Abraham Lincoln is born near Hodgenville in Hardin (now LaRue) County, Kentucky.

1811

The Lincolns move to a farm on Knob Creek, northeast of Hodgenville.

1812

Lincoln's younger brother Thomas dies as a baby.

1815

Autumn – Lincoln and his sister Sarah attend school for a short time.

1816

Autumn – Lincoln and his sister Sarah attend school for a short time.

December – Lincoln family moves to Perry County (now Spencer County), Indiana; it takes about five days to travel the 91 miles.

1818

October 5 – Mother Nancy Hanks Lincoln dies of milk sickness.

1819

December 2 – Father Thomas marries Sarah Bush Johnston.

1820

Lincoln attends school for about three months.

1821

Lincoln attends school for about six months.

June 14 – Stepsister Elizabeth marries Dennis Hanks, his mother's cousin.

1826

August 2 – Lincoln's older sister Sarah marries Aaron Grigsby.

1828

January 20 – Sister Sarah dies in childbirth.

April – Lincoln and Allen Gentry deliver goods for Gentry's father James to New Orleans on a flatboat Lincoln built.

1830

March 1 – Lincoln family leaves Indiana and moves to Illinois.

March 15 – Lincoln family settles in Macon County, Illinois, outside Decatur, where Abraham and his father build a log cabin.

1831

March – Lincoln, his cousin John Hanks, and his stepbrother John D. Johnston are hired to build and drive a flatboat of goods to New Orleans.

April 8 – Lincoln and others leave on boat trip to New Orleans.

July – Lincoln returns to New Salem, Illinois, from trip, and settles there.

September – Lincoln begins a job as a store clerk.

1832

April 21 – Lincoln is elected captain of the Thirty-first Regiment of Illinois to serve in the Black Hawk War.

July 26 – Lincoln is honorably discharged from military service.

Summer – Lincoln campaigns for a seat on the Illinois State Legislature.

August 6 – Lincoln is not elected.

1833

January 15 – Lincoln and a partner, William F. Berry, buy a store in New Salem.

May 7 – Lincoln becomes postmaster at New Salem.

Lincoln becomes a deputy surveyor of Sangamon County.

1834

July – Lincoln begins studying law books at the recommendation of John T. Stuart.

August 4 – Lincoln is elected state representative in Illinois.

1836

May 30 – Lincoln's job as postmaster ends when New Salem Post Office is closed down.

August 1 – Lincoln is reelected to Illinois House of Representatives.

September 9 – Lincoln receives license to practice law in the state of Illinois.

November 17 – Lincoln conducts his last land survey, a side job since 1833.

1837

April 15 – Lincoln moves to Springfield, Illinois, where he meets and rooms with lifelong friend Joshua Speed and enters John T. Stuart's law practice as a partner.

1838

Spring – Mary Owens turns down Lincoln's marriage proposal.

August 6 – Lincoln is reelected to the Illinois House of Representatives.

1839

Lincoln meets Mary Todd.

1840

August 3 – Lincoln is reelected to Illinois House of Representatives.

December – Lincoln becomes engaged to Mary Todd.

1841

April 14 – Lincoln leaves Stuart's law practice and joins Stephen T. Logan's practice.

1842

November 4 – Lincoln marries Mary Todd at the home of her sister Elizabeth and brother-in-law Ninian W. Edwards.

November 5 – The Lincolns lease a room at the Globe Tavern in Springfield, Illinois.

1843

August 1 – Son Robert Todd is born in the Lincolns' apartment at the Globe Tavern.

1844

January 16 – The Lincolns buy their first, and only, house, located on the corner of Eighth and Jackson Streets in Springfield.

May 1 – The Lincolns move into their new home.

Autumn – Lincoln and Logan end their joint law practice, and Lincoln begins a new law partnership with William H. Herndon.

1846

January – Lincoln decides to run for U.S. House of Representatives.

March 10 – Son Edward Baker born.

August 3 – Lincoln is elected to the U.S. House of Representatives.

1847

October 25 – The Lincolns leave Springfield for Washington, D.C., stopping for a visit in Lexington, Kentucky.

December 2 – The Lincolns arrive in Washington, D.C.

December 6 – Lincoln is sworn into office, along with other elected representatives.

1849

March 4 – Lincoln's term as U.S. Representative from Illinois ends, and the Lincolns return to Springfield.

May 22 – Lincoln receives a patent for invention of device to raise boats over low waters.

September 21 – U.S. Interior Secretary Thomas Ewing offers Lincoln the governorship of the Territory of Oregon; Lincoln declines.

1850

February 1 – Son Edward Baker dies, probably of tuberculosis.

December 21 – Son William Wallace (Willie) is born.

1851

January 17 – Father Thomas dies.

1853

February 12 – The U.S. Senate approves the new town of Lincoln, Illinois—the first place named after Lincoln—to become the county seat of Logan County; the U.S. House of Representatives voted in favor the day before.

April 4 – Son Thomas (Tad) is born.

1854

May 30 – Lincoln decides to reenter politics when the Kansas-Nebraska Act passes, which makes it easier for slavery to spread into the territories.

October 16 – Lincoln delivers speech at Peoria, Illinois.

November 7 – Lincoln is elected to the Illinois House of Representatives.

November 25 – Lincoln writes letter to clerk of Sangamon Circuit Court to withdraw from elected office in order to run for the U.S. Senate.

December 23 – Special election is held to decide Lincoln's replacement in the Illinois House of Representatives.

1855

February 8 – Illinois Legislature elects Lyman Trumbull to U.S. Senate instead of Lincoln.

1856

June 19 – Republican convention at Bloomington, Indiana, nominates Lincoln for vice president.

1858

June 16 – Illinois Republican Party nominates Lincoln for U.S. Senate, and he delivers his "House Divided" speech.

July 24 – Lincoln challenges Stephen A. Douglas, incumbent U.S. Senator from Illinois, to a series of debates.

July 28 – Douglas accepts challenge.

August 21 – First debate between Lincoln and Douglas takes place in Ottawa, Illinois; audience estimated to be at least 10,000.

August 27 – Second debate between Lincoln and Douglas in Freeport, Illinois.

September 15 – Third Lincoln-Douglas debate at Jonesboro, Illinois.

September 18 – Fourth Lincoln-Douglas debate at Charleston, Illinois.

October 7 – Fifth Lincoln-Douglas debate at Galesburg, Illinois.

October 13 – Sixth Lincoln-Douglas debate at Quincy, Illinois.

October 15 – Seventh Lincoln-Douglas debate at Alton, Illinois.

November 2 – Douglas defeats Lincoln in U.S. Senate election.

November 6 – Lincoln returns to his law practice with Herndon in Springfield.

1860

February 27 – Lincoln delivers speech at Cooper Institute in New York City.

March – Lincoln gives sittings for sculptor Leonard Wells Volk.

May 18 –Republican National Convention nominates Lincoln for president.

October – Grace Bedell, an 11 year old in Westfield, New York, writes Lincoln and suggests he grow a beard.

November 6 – Lincoln is elected President of the United States.

December 20 – South Carolina votes to secede from the Union.

1861

January 9 – Mississippi secedes from the Union.

January 10 – Florida secedes from the Union.

January 11 – Alabama secedes from the Union.

January 19 – Georgia secedes from the Union.

January 20 – Louisiana secedes from the Union.

January 31 – Lincoln visits his stepmother in Coles County.

February 4 – Seceded states form the Confederate States of America.

February 11 – Lincoln leaves Springfield for Washington, D.C.; his train trip includes stops at many cities along the way.

February 16 – Lincoln meets Grace Bedell at train stop in Westfield, New York.

February 23 – Lincoln arrives in Washington, D.C.; Texas secedes from the Union.

March 4 – Lincoln is sworn in as president.

April 12 – Civil War begins when South Carolina troops attack Fort Sumter.

May 6 – Arkansas secedes from the Union.

May 20 – North Carolina secedes from the Union.

June 8 – Tennessee secedes from the Union.

1862

February 20 – Son Willie dies of typhoid fever.

March – Writer Nathaniel Hawthorne meets Lincoln.

July 1 – Issues call for 300,000 volunteer troops.

July 16 – Poem about Lincoln's call for troops appears in the *New York Evening Post* and quickly becomes a popular song.

July 22 – Lincoln reads his cabinet a draft of the Emancipation Proclamation.

August 22 – Lincoln writes letter to Horace Greeley on slavery and preserving the Union.

September 22 – Lincoln issues the preliminary Emancipation Proclamation, giving the South until January 1, 1863, to rejoin the Union.

November – Writer Harriet Beecher Stowe meets Lincoln.

1863

January 1 – Lincoln issues the Emancipation Proclamation, declaring freedom of slaves in Confederate territories.

July 1-3 – Battle of Gettysburg, Pennsylvania, is fought. Union troops under General Meade defeat Confederate General Robert E. Lee's attempted invasion of Pennsylvania.

October 3 – Lincoln issues a proclamation designating a day of national thanksgiving to be observed on the last Thursday in November.

November 19 – Lincoln delivers Gettysburg Address at dedication of national cemetery.

1864

February - July – Artist Francis B. Carpenter spends time at White House painting Lincoln presenting his cabinet with the Emancipation Proclamation.

March 10 – Lincoln commissions General Ulysses S. Grant to command the Union Army.

June 8 – The National Union Party (temporary name for the Republican Party) nominates Lincoln for President.

September 1 – General William T. Sherman's troops capture Atlanta, Georgia.

October 29 – Abolitionist Sojourner Truth meets Lincoln.

November 8 – Lincoln is reelected President.

November 16 - December 22 – General Sherman's March to the Sea through Georgia; captures Savannah on the 22nd.

1865

February 1 – Lincoln approves the 13th Amendment to the Constitution, making slavery illegal.

February 11 – Son Robert, after graduating from Harvard, begins military service as a member of General Ulysses S. Grant's staff.

February 23 – Friend Joshua Speed visits Lincoln for second-to-last time.

March 4 – Lincoln's second inauguration.

March 23 - April 8 – Lincoln travels to Virginia to meet General Grant at City Point; visits Richmond on April 4, the day after General Weitzel's troops had captured the city.

April 9 – Civil War ends when Confederate General Robert E. Lee surrenders at Appomattox Court House, Virginia.

April 14 – Lincoln is shot by John Wilkes Booth while attending a performance of *Our American Cousin* at Ford's Theatre in Washington, D.C.

April 15 – Lincoln dies at about 7:22 A.M.

April 19 – Funeral service at the White House. Ralph Waldo Emerson delivers eulogy in Concord, Massachusetts.

April 21 – Funeral train leaves from Washington, D.C., for Springfield, Illinois, where Lincoln will be buried; it stops at Baltimore, Maryland, and York, Pennsylvania, before halting for the night at Harrisburg, Pennsylvania.

April 22 – Funeral train stops at Philadelphia and Lincoln's body lies in Independence Hall.

April 23 – Phillips Brooks delivers eulogy in Philadelphia; Henry Ward Beecher delivers eulogy in Brooklyn, New York; Seth Sweetser delivers eulogy in Worcester, Massachusetts.

April 24 – Funeral train leaves Philadelphia and arrives in New York City; Lincoln's body lies in city hall.

April 25 – Funeral train leaves New York City and stops at Albany, where Lincoln's body lies at the Capitol.

April 26 –John Wilkes Booth is apprehended and killed near Bowling Green, Virginia.

April 27 – Funeral train stops in Buffalo, New York.

April 28 – Funeral train stops in Cleveland, Ohio.

April 29 – Funeral train stops in Columbus, Ohio.

April 30 – Funeral train stops in Indianapolis, Indiana

May 1 – Funeral train stops in Chicago, Illinois.

May 3 – Funeral train arrives in Springfield; Lincoln's body lies in the statehouse.

May 4 – Lincoln's body is buried at Oak Ridge Cemetery, Springfield, Illinois; Matthew Simpson delivers the eulogy.

July 26 – Memorial service is held at Harvard University, where James Russell Lowell presents a poem.

1869

July 1 – Soldiers' Monument is dedicated at Gettysburg National Cemetery.

1876

April 14 – Freedmen's Monument is unveiled in Washington, D.C.; Frederick Douglass delivers speech.

1878

February 12 – Francis B. Carpenter's painting, *The First Reading of the Emancipation Proclamation,* is presented to the U.S. Congress; James A. Garfield delivers speech.

1888

February 12 – Frederick Douglass delivers speech at birthday commemoration in Washington, D.C.

1890

February 12 – Senator Shelby M. Collum delivers speech at the Republican Club of New York City.

1900

February 12 – Edwin Markham's poem, "Lincoln, The Man of the People," is recited at birthday commemoration at the Republican Club of New York City; James Weldon Johnson and John Rosamond Johnson's hymn, "Lift Ev'ry Voice and Sing," is sung at birthday commemoration at Stanton School, Jacksonville, Florida.

1905

February 12 – Senator Jonathan Dolliver delivers speech at the Republican Club of New York City.

1907

January 13 – Mark Twain writes an editorial advocating that Lincoln's birthplace be made a national monument.

1909

February – Centennial celebrations take place around the nation and the world on and around Lincoln's birthday on the 12th.

August 2 – Lincoln penny is issued.

Bibliography

Bibliography

This bibliography lists all sources consulted as well as suggestions for further reading. Sources are organized under the following headings: Reference; Biographies; Lincoln's Presidency; Lincoln's Speeches and Writings; Lincoln's Image and Legacy; Commemorative Works—Reminiscences, Speeches, Poems, and Tributes; Young Adult Titles; and Journals.

Reference

Burkhimer, Michael. *100 Essential Lincoln Books*. Nashville, TN: Cumberland House, 2003.

Herndon-Weik Collection, Manuscript Division, Library of Congress, Washington, DC.

Lincoln Sesquicentennial Commission in cooperation with the Abraham Lincoln Association. *The Lincoln Log: A Daily Chronology of the Life of Abraham Lincoln*. Washington, DC: Government Printing Office, 1960. Online version sponsored by the Illinois Historic Preservation Agency and the Abraham Lincoln Presidential Library and Museum at http://www.stg.brown.edu/projects/lincoln.

Meirs, Earl S., ed. *Lincoln Day by Day: A Chronology, 1809-1865*. Dayton, OH: Morningside House, 1991.

Neely, Mark E., Jr. *The Abraham Lincoln Encyclopedia*. New York: Da Capo Press, 1982.

Shaw, Archer H., ed. *The Lincoln Encyclopedia: The Spoken and Written Words of A. Lincoln Arranged for Ready Reference*. New York: The Macmillan Company, 1950.

Biographies

Angle, Paul M. *The Lincoln Reader*. New Brunswick, NJ: Rutgers University Press, 1947.

Beveridge, Albert J. *Abraham Lincoln, 1809-1858.* 2 vols. Boston: Houghton Mifflin Company, 1928.

Brooks, Noah. *Abraham Lincoln: The Nation's Leader in the Great Struggle through which was Maintained the Existence of the United States.* Washington, DC: National Tribune, 1888.

Donald, David Herbert. *Lincoln.* New York: Simon & Schuster, 1995.

———. *"We Are Lincoln Men": Abraham Lincoln and His Friends.* New York: Simon & Schuster, 2003.

Guelzo, Allen C. *Abraham Lincoln: Redeemer President.* Grand Rapids, MI: William R. Eerdmans, 1999.

Harris, William C. *Lincoln's Last Months.* Cambridge, MA: Harvard University Press, 2004.

Herndon, William H., and Jesse W. Weik. *Herndon's Life of Lincoln: The History and Personal Recollections of Abraham Lincoln as Originally Written by William H. Herndon and Jesse W. Weik, with Introduction and Notes by Paul M. Angle.* New introduction by Henry Steele Commager. New York: Da Capo Press, 1983.

Holland, Josiah Gilbert. *Holland's Life of Abraham Lincoln.* Introduction by Allen C. Guelzo. Lincoln: University of Nebraska Press, 1998.

Kunhardt, Philip B., Jr., et al. *Lincoln: An Illustrated Biography.* New York: Random House, 1992.

Miller, William Lee. *Lincoln's Virtues: An Ethical Biography.* New York: Vintage Books, 2002.

Neeley, Mark E. Jr., and Harold Holzer. *The Lincoln Family Album.* New York: Doubleday, 1990.

Nicolay, John G., and John Hay. *Abraham Lincoln: A History.* 10 vols. New York: Century, 1890.

Oates, Stephen B. *With Malice Toward None: The Life of Abraham Lincoln.* New York: New American Library, 1977.

Sandburg, Carl. *Abraham Lincoln, The Prairie Years.* 2 vols. New York: Harcourt Brace and Co., 1926.

————. *Abraham Lincoln: The War Years.* 4 vols. New York: Harcourt Brace and Co., 1939.

Tarbell, Ida M. *The Life of Abraham Lincoln.* 2 vols. New York: Doubleday & McClure Company, 1900.

Thomas, Benjamin P. *Abraham Lincoln: A Biography.* New York: Knopf, 1952.

————. *"Lincoln's Humor" and Other Essays.* Edited by Michael Burlingame. Urbana: University of Illinois Press, 2002.

Weik, Jesse W. *The Real Lincoln: A Portrait.* Boston: Houghton Mifflin, 1922.

Wilson, Douglas L. *Honor's Voice: The Transformation of Abraham Lincoln.* New York: Knopf, 1998.

Lincoln's Presidency

David, William C. *Lincoln's Men: How President Lincoln Became Father to an Army and a Nation.* New York: Touchstone/Simon & Schuster, 1999.

Franklin, John Hope. *The Emancipation Proclamation.* Garden City, NY: Doubleday, 1963.

Gienapp, William E. *This Fiery Trial: The Speeches and Writings of Abraham Lincoln.* New York: Oxford University Press, 2002.

Goodwin, Doris Kearns. *Team of Rivals: The Political Genius of Abraham Lincoln.* New York: Simon & Schuster, 2005.

Guelzo, Allen C. *Lincoln's Emancipation Proclamation: The End of Slavery in America.* New York: Simon & Schuster, 2004.

McPherson, James M. *Abraham Lincoln and the Second American Revolution.* New York: Oxford University Press, 1990.

Neely, Mark E., Jr. *The Last Best Hope of Earth: Abraham Lincoln and the Promise of America.* Cambridge: Harvard University Press, 1993.

Paludan, Philip Shaw. *The Presidency of Abraham Lincoln.* Lawrence: University of Kansas Press, 1994.

Quarles, Benjamin. *Lincoln and the Negro.* New York: Oxford University Press, 1962.

White, Ronald C., Jr. *The Eloquent President: A Portrait of Lincoln through His Words.* New York: Random House, 2005.

———. *Lincoln's Greatest Speech: The Second Inaugural.* New York: Simon & Schuster, 2002.

Wills, Garry. *Lincoln at Gettysburg: The Words That Remade America.* New York: Touchstone/Simon & Schuster, 1992.

Lincoln's Speeches and Writings

Abraham Lincoln Papers, Library of Congress. http://memory.loc.gov/ammem/alhtml/malhome.html

Basler, Roy P., ed. *The Collected Works of Abraham Lincoln.* 8 vols. New Brunswick, NJ: Rutgers University Press, 1953-55. Online version sponsored by the Abraham Lincoln Association at http://www.hti.umich.edu/l/lincoln.

Delbanco, Andrew, ed. *The Portable Abraham Lincoln.* New York: Penguin Books, 1992.

Holzer, Harold, ed. *The Lincoln-Douglas Debates: The First Complete, Unexpurgated Text.* New York: HarperCollins, 1993.

Lincoln, Abraham. First Inaugural Address, March 4, 1861. In *American Historical Documents, 1000-1904.* Vol. XLIII. The Harvard Classics. Edited by Charles W. Eliot. New York: P. F. Collier & Son, 1909-14.

Nicolay, John G., and John Hay, eds. *Complete Works of Abraham Lincoln.* 12 vols. F. D. Tandy Company, 1905.

Nicolay, John G., and John Hay, eds. *Complete Works of Abraham Lincoln.* 12 vols. N.P.: Lincoln Memorial University, 1894.

Lincoln's Image and Legacy

Boritt, Gabor, ed. *The Lincoln Enigma: The Changing Faces of an American Icon.* New York: Oxford University Press, 2001.

Hamilton, Charles, and Lloyd Ostendorf. *Lincoln in Photographs: An Album of Every Known Pose.* Norman: University of Oklahoma Press, 1963.

Hanchett, William. *The Lincoln Murder Conspiracies.* Urbana: University of Illinois Press, 1983.

Holzer, Harold. *Lincoln at Cooper Union: The Speech that Made Abraham Lincoln President.* New York: Simon & Schuster, 2004.

———. *Lincoln Seen & Heard.* Lawrence: University Press of Kansas, 2000.

Holzer, Harold, Gabor S. Boritt, and Mark E. Neely Jr., eds. *The Lincoln Image: Abraham Lincoln and the Popular Print.* New York: Charles Scribner's Sons, 1984.

Oates, Stephen B. *Abraham Lincoln: The Man Behind the Myths.* New York: Harper & Row, 1984.

Ostendorf, Lloyd. *Lincoln's Photographs: A Complete Album.* Dayton, OH: Rockywood Press, 1998.

Peterson, Merrill D. *Lincoln in American Memory.* New York: Oxford University Press, 1994.

Schwartz, Barry. *Abraham Lincoln and the Forge of National Memory.* Chicago: University of Chicago Press, 2000.

Williams, Frank J. *Judging Lincoln.* Carbondale: Southern Illinois University Press, 2002.

Zall, Paul M. *Lincoln's Legacy: The Emancipation Proclamation & the Gettysburg Address.* San Marino, CA: Huntington Library, 1994.

Commemorative Works — Reminiscences, Speeches, Poems, and Tributes

Addams, Jane. "Influence of Lincoln." In her *Twenty Years at Hull-House.* New York: Macmillan Co., 1910.

Addresses Delivered at the Lincoln Dinners of Republican Club of the City of New York in Response to the Toast: Abraham Lincoln, 1887-1909. New York: Republican Club of the City of New York, 1909.

Ambrose, James C. "Choosing 'Abe' Captain." *Menasha (WI) Daily Twin City News.* July 2, 1882.

Bates, David Homer. *Lincoln in the Telegraph Office: Recollections of the United States Military Telegraph Corps during the Civil War.* New York: Century Co., 1907.

Betts, William W., Jr., ed. *Lincoln and the Poets.* Pittsburgh: University of Pittsburgh Press, 1965.

Braden, Waldo W., ed. *Building the Myth: Selected Speeches Memorializing Abraham Lincoln.* Urbana: University of Illinois Press, 1990.

Brooks, Noah. "Personal Reminiscences of Lincoln." *Scribner's Monthly Magazine,* February-March 1878.

Brooks, Phillips. *The Life and Death of Abraham Lincoln. A Sermon Preached at the Church of the Holy Trinity, Philadelphia, Sunday Morning, April 23, 1865.* Philadelphia: Henry B. Ashmead, 1865.

Bryant, William Cullen. *The Poetical Works of William Cullen Bryant: Roslyn Edition: With Chronologies of Bryant's Life and Poems and a Bibliography of His Writings By Henry C. Sturges: And a Memoir of His Life By Richard Henry Stoddard.* New York: D. Appleton and Company, 1903.

Burlingame, Michael, ed. *An Oral History of Abraham Lincoln: John G. Nicolay's Interviews and Essays.* Carbondale: Southern Illinois University Press, 1996.

Carman, Bliss. "The Man of Peace." In *The Rough Rider and Other Poems.* New York: Mitchell Kennerley, 1909.

Carpenter, Francis B. *The Inner Life of Abraham Lincoln. Six Months at the White House.* New York: Hurd and Houghton, 1868.

Cheseborough, David B. *"No Sorrow Like Our Sorrow": Northern Protestant Ministers and the Assassination of Lincoln.* Kent, OH: Kent State University Press, 1994.

Crook, William H. *Through Five Administrations: Reminiscences of Colonel William H. Crook, Body-Guard to President Lincoln.* Compiled and edited by Margarita Spalding Gerry. New York: Harper & Brothers Publishers, 1910.

Cullom, Shelby M. *Addresses Delivered at the Lincoln Dinners of Republican Club of the City of New York in Response to the Toast: Abraham Lincoln, 1887-1909.* New York: Republican Club of the City of New York, 1909.

Douglass, Frederick. *Oration by Frederick Douglass Delivered on the Occasion of the Unveiling of the Freedmen's Monument in Memory of Abraham Lincoln in Lincoln Park, Washington, D.C., April 14, 1876.* Washington, DC: Gibson Brothers, 1876.

Dunbar, Paul Laurence. *Lyrics of Love & Laughter.* New York: Dodd, Mead and Company, 1903.

Emerson, Ralph Waldo. "Abraham Lincoln: Remarks at the Funeral Services Held in Concord, April 19, 1865." *Miscellanies.* Vol. 11, *Emerson's Complete Works.* Boston: Houghton, Mifflin and Company; Cambridge, MA: The Riverside Press, 1885.

Field, Maunsell B. "Last Moments of the President." *New York Times*, April 17, 1865.

Garfield, James Abram. "Lincoln and Emancipation: Address Delivered in the Hall of the House of Representatives, February 12, 1878." In *The Works of James Abram Garfield.* Vol. 2. Edited by Burke A. Hinsdale. Boston: James R. Osgood and Company, 1883.

Gibbons, James Sloan. "We are coming Father Abraham, or, Three hundred thousand more: inscribed to our volunteers." *New York Evening Post*, July 16, 1862. Sheet music available online at the Alfred Whital Stern Collection of Lincolniana, Library of Congress. http://memory.loc.gov/ammem/scsmhtml/scsmhome.html.

Gilder, Richard Watson. "On the Life-Mask of Abraham Lincoln." *The Century Illustrated Monthly Magazine*, November 1886-April 1887.

Greeley, Horace. *Greeley on Lincoln, with Mr. Greeley's Letters to Charles A. Dana and a Lady Friend to which Are Added Reminiscences of Horace Greeley.* Edited by Joel Benton. New York: The Baker & Taylor Co., 1893.

Hallowell, Anna Davis, ed. *James and Lucretia Mott. Life and Letters.* Boston: Houghton, Mifflin and Company, 1884.

Hawthorne, Nathaniel. "Chiefly About War Matters." *Atlantic Monthly*, July 1862. Reprinted in *Tales, Sketches, and Other Papers.* Vol. 12. *The Complete Works of Nathaniel Hawthorne.* Edited by George Parsons Lathrop. Boston: Houghton Mifflin Company, 1883.

Hoke, Jacob. *The Great Invasion of 1863; or, General Lee in Pennsylvania.* Dayton, OH: W. J. Shuey, 1887.

Holzer, Harold, ed. *Dear Mr. Lincoln: Letters to the President.* Reading, MA: Addison-Wesley Publishing Co., 1993.

———. *Lincoln as I Knew Him: Gossip, Tributes, and Revelations from His Best Friends and Worst Enemies.* Chapel Hill, NC: Algonquin Books of Chapel Hill, 1999.

———. *The Lincoln Mailbag: America Writes to the President, 1861-1865.* Carbondale: Southern Illinois University Press, 1998.

Johnson, James Weldon, and J. Rosamond Johnson. "Lift Every Voice and Sing." New York: National Association for the Advancement of Colored People, ca. 1920. Available online at University of South Carolina, Department of Rare Books and Special Collections. http://www.sc.edu/library/spcoll/amlit/johnson/johnson2.html.

Keckley, Elizabeth. *Behind the Scenes. Or, Thirty Years a Slave, and Four Years in the White House.* New York: G. W. Carlton, 1868.

Knox, William. *Oh, Why Should the Spirit of Mortal Be Proud?* Boston: Lee and Shepard, 1883.

Kunhardt, Dorothy Meserve, and Philip B. Kunhardt Jr. *Twenty Days: A Narrative in Text and Pictures of the Assassination of Abraham Lincoln and the Twenty Days and Nights that followed – The Nation in Mourning, the Long Trip Home to Springfield.* New York: Harper & Row, 1965.

Lowell, James Russell. "Ode Recited at the Harvard Commemoration." In *The Harvard Classics.* Edited by Charles W. Eliot. Vol. 42: *English Poetry III: From Tennyson to Whitman.* New York: P. F. Collier & Son, 1909-14.

———. *My Study Windows.* Boston: Houghton, Mifflin & Company, 1871.

Mabie, Hamilton Wright. "Abraham Lincoln." In *A Library of the World's Best Literature, Ancient and Modern.* Vol. 23. Edited by Charles Dudley Warner. New York: The International Society, 1897.

MacChesney, Nathan William, ed. *Abraham Lincoln: The Tribute of a Century, 1809-1909; Commemorative of the Lincoln Centenary and Containing the Principal Speeches Made in Connection Therewith.* Chicago: A. C. McClurg & Company, 1910.

McClure, Alexander K. *"Abe" Lincoln's Yarns and Stories: A Complete Collection of the Funny and Witty Anecdotes That Made Lincoln Famous as America's Greatest Story Teller.* Chicago: The Educational Company, 1904.

Markham, Edwin. *Lincoln & Other Poems.* New York: McClure, Phillips & Company, 1901.

Mitgang, Herbert. *Abraham Lincoln, A Press Portrait: His Life and Times from the Original Newspaper Documents of the Union, the Confederacy, and Europe.* New York: Fordham University Press, 2000.

Oldroyd, Osborn H., ed. *The Lincoln Memorial: Album-Immortelles. Original Life Pictures, with Autographs, from the Hands and Hearts of Eminent Americans and Europeans, Contemporaries of the Great Martyr to Liberty, Abraham Lincoln. Together with Extracts from His Speeches, Letters and Sayings.* Springfield, IL: Lincoln Publishing Company, 1890.

Oldroyd, Osborn H., comp. *Words of Lincoln, Including Several Hundred Opinions of his Life and Character by Eminent Persons of this and other Lands.* Washington, DC: O. H. Oldroyd, 1895.

Our Martyr President, Abraham Lincoln. Voices from the Pulpit of New York and Brooklyn. New York: Tibbals and Whiting, 1865.

Rice, Allen Thorndike, ed. *Reminiscences of Abraham Lincoln by Distinguished Men of His Time.* New York: North American Publishing Company, 1886.

Richards, Caroline Cowles. *Village Life in America, 1852-1872, Including the Period of the American Civil War as Told in the Diary of a School-Girl.* New York: Henry Holt and Company, 1913.

Sandburg, Carl. "Lincoln on Pennies." *Milwaukee Daily News*, August 3, 1909.

Schauffler, Robert Haven, ed. *Lincoln's Birthday: A Comprehensive View of Lincoln as Given in the Most Noteworthy Essays, Orations and Poems, in Fiction and in Lincoln's Own Writings.* New York: Dodd, Mead and Company, 1909.

Segal, Charles M., ed. *Conversations with Lincoln.* Introduction by David Donald. New Brunswick, NJ: Transaction Publishers, 2002.

Services Commemorative of the Seventy-Ninth Anniversary of the Birth of Abraham Lincoln by the Republican National League, at the League House, 1401 Massachusetts

Avenue, Washington, D.C., February 12, 1888. Washington, DC: Gibson Bros., 1888.

"The Sorrow of the People." *Chicago Tribune*, April 17, 1865.

Stanton, Edwin M. "President Lincoln Shot by an Assassin." *New York Times*, April 15, 1865.

Stoddard, William O. *Inside the White House in War Times: Memoirs and Reports of Lincoln's Secretary.* Edited by Michael Burlingame. Lincoln: University of Nebraska Press, 2000.

Stowe, Harriet Beecher. "Abraham Lincoln." *Littell's Living Age*, February 6, 1864.

Sumner, Charles. *The Promises of the Declaration of Independence. Eulogy on Abraham Lincoln, Delivered before the Municipal Authorities of the City of Boston, June 1, 1865.* Boston: Ticknor & Fields, 1865.

Taylor, Bayard. "The Gettysburg Ode." *Home Pastorals, Ballads and Lyrics.* Boston: J. R. Osgood and Co., 1875.

Truth, Sojourner. *Narrative of Sojourner Truth; A Bondswoman of Olden Time, With a History of Her Labors and Correspondence Drawn from Her "Book of Life."* Edited by Olive Gilbert. Battle Creek, MI: The Author, 1878.

Twain, Mark. "A Lincoln Memorial: A Plea by Mark Twain for the Setting Apart of His Birthplace." *New York Times*, January 13, 1907.

Villard, Henry. *Memoirs of Henry Villard, Journalist and Financier, 1835-1900.* 2 vols. Boston: Houghton, Mifflin & Co., 1904.

Volk, Leonard Wells. "The Lincoln Life-Mask and How It Was Made." *Century Magazine*, December 1881.

Washington, Booker T. "My Tribute to the Great Emancipator." *The Booker T. Washington Papers.* 14 vols. Edited by Louis R. Harlan and Raymond W. Smock. Urbana: University of Illinois Press, 1972-89.

Whitman, Walt. *Leaves of Grass.* Philadelphia: David McKay, 1900.

———. *Prose Works.* Vol. 2. Philadelphia: David McKay, 1892.

Whitney, Henry Clay. *Life on the Circuit with Lincoln.* Boston: Estes and Lauriat, 1892.

Whittier, John Greenleaf. *Anti-Slavery Poems: Songs of Labor and Reform*. New York: Houghton, Mifflin & Co., 1888.

Wilson, Douglas L., and Rodney O. Davis, ed. *Herndon's Informants: Letters, Interviews, and Statements about Abraham Lincoln*. Urbana: University of Illinois Press, 1998.

Wilson, Rufus Rockwell, ed. *Intimate Memories of Lincoln*. Elmira, NY: Primavera Press, 1945.

Zall, P. M., ed. *Abe Lincoln Laughing: Humorous Anecdotes from Original Sources by and about Abraham Lincoln*. Foreword by Ray Allen Billington. Knoxville: University of Tennessee Press, 1995.

Young Adult Titles

Burchard, Peter. *Lincoln and Slavery*. New York: Atheneum Books for Young Adults, 1999.

Collier, James Lincoln. *The Abraham Lincoln You Never Knew*. New York: Children's Press, 2003.

Freedman, Russell. *Lincoln: A Photobiography*. New York: Clarion Books, 1987.

Marrin, Albert. *Commander in Chief: Abraham Lincoln and the Civil War*. New York: Dutton Children's Books, 1997.

Meltzer, Milton. *Lincoln: In His Own Words*. New York: Harcourt Brace and Co., 1993.

Sullivan, George. *Picturing Lincoln: Famous Photographs that Popularized the President*. New York: Clarion Books, 2000.

Journals

Abraham Lincoln Quarterly. Springfield, IL: Abraham Lincoln Association, 1940-52. http://www.alincolnassoc.com.

Journal of the Abraham Lincoln Association. Springfield, IL: Abraham Lincoln Association, 1987- (continued the *Papers of the Abraham Lincoln Association*, 1970-87). http://www.alincolnassoc.com.

Lincoln Centennial Association Bulletin. Springfield, IL: Lincoln Centennial Association (later Abraham Lincoln Association), 1923-39. http://www.alincolnassoc.com.

Lincoln Centennial Association Papers. Springfield, IL: Lincoln Centennial Association (later Abraham Lincoln Association), 1924-38. http://www.alincolnassoc.com.

Lincoln Herald. Harrogate, TN: Lincoln Memorial University Press, 1899- . http://www.lincolnherald.com.

Lincoln Lore. Fort Wayne, IN: The Lincoln Museum, 1929- . http://www.thelincolnmuseum.org/new/publications/index.html.

Contact Information for Lincoln Groups

Contact Information for Lincoln Groups: Associations, Educational Institutes, Landmarks and Historic Sites, Libraries, Museums, and Other Web Resources Related to Abraham Lincoln

This appendix contains a wide variety of institutions that would be helpful to those interested in further information on Abraham Lincoln. Each listing includes, wherever possible, the group's name, address, phone, web site, and a brief description. The list below is broken down into the following sections:

Associations
Educational Institutes
Landmarks and Historic Sites
Libraries
Museums
Other Web Resources

Associations

Abraham Lincoln Association
#1 Old State Capitol Plaza
Springfield, IL 62701
866-865-8500
http://www.alincolnassoc.com

> Founded in 1908 as the Lincoln Centennial Association. Publishes the *Journal of the Abraham Lincoln Association* (formerly *Papers of the Abraham Lincoln Association*) and a newsletter, *For the People*. Other projects include supporting online access to the *Collected Works of Abraham Lincoln* and *The Lincoln Log: A Daily Chronology of the Life of Abraham Lincoln*, and hosting an annual symposium banquet on Lincoln's birthday.

Abraham Lincoln Bicentennial Commission
Library of Congress
101 Independence Avenue, S.E.
Washington, DC 20540-4015
202-707-6998; fax: 202-707-6995
http://www.lincolnbicentennial.gov

> Created by U.S. Congress in 2000 to encourage observances of Lincoln's 200th birthday in 2009.

Abraham Lincoln Institute
P.O. Box 281
Riverdale, MD 20738-0281
202-572-0769; fax: 202-478-2790
http://www.lincoln-institute.org

> Founded in 1997. Publishes a newsletter, *Lincoln News National,* and sponsors an annual symposium.

Association of Lincoln Presenters
266 Compton Ridge Drive
Cincinnati, OH 45215-4120
http://www.lincolnpresenters.org

> Founded in 1990. Nearly 300 men and women present themselves as Abraham and Mary Lincoln in educational appearances. Publishes a newsletter, *Lincarnations,* and sponsors conventions.

Lincoln Association of Jersey City
111 Gifford Avenue
Jersey City, NJ 07304
http://thelincolnassociationofjerseycity.com/index.html

> Founded in 1867. Sponsors annual celebration on Lincoln's birthday.

Lincoln-Douglas Society of Freeport, Illinois
2236 Chelsea Avenue

Freeport, IL 61032

http://www.lincoln-douglas.org

> Originally founded in 1929 to commemorate the debate between Lincoln and Stephen A. Douglas in Freeport in 1858. Sponsors lectures and publishes a newsletter, *The Stump*.

Lincoln Fellowship of Pennsylvania

P.O. Box 3372

Gettysburg, PA 17325

http://www.gettysburg.edu/civilwar/institute/lincoln_fellowship_/index.dot

> Participates in annual commemoration of Lincoln's Gettysburg Address at Gettysburg National Cemetery.

Lincoln Forum

6009 Queenston Street

Springfield, VA 22152-1723

http://www.thelincolnforum.org

> Founded in 1996. Sponsors symposia, publishes a newsletter, *The Lincoln Forum Bulletin*, and advocates restoration of Lincoln's summer residence at Anderson Cottage.

Lincoln Group of the District of Columbia

P.O. Box 5676

Washington, DC 20016

http://www.lincolngroup.org

> Founded in 1935. Sponsors events, publishes a newsletter, *The Lincolnian*, and supports Lincoln scholarship and historic site preservation.

Lincoln Group of New York

P.O. Box 220

Newton, NJ 07860

973-383-9304

http://www.lincolngroupny.org

Founded in 1978. Promotes Lincoln studies, holds quarterly meetings, and publishes a newsletter, *The Wide Awake.*

Lincoln Society Forum
P.O. Box 1-31
Hwakang, Taipei 11114
Taiwan, Republic of China

Founded in 1984. Sponsors speech and essay contests and annual dinner.

Educational Institutes

Lincoln Institute
Gilder Lehrman Institute of American History
One Fawcett Place, Suite 130
Greenwich, CT 06830-6581
http://www.abrahamlincoln.org/about/index.html

Lincoln Studies Center
Campus Box K-241
Knox College
Galesburg, IL 61401-4999
309-341-7158 or 309-341-7173
http://www.knox.edu/lincolnstudies.xml

Landmarks and Historic Sites

Abraham Lincoln National Cemetery
27034 South Diagonal Road
Elwood, IL 60421
815-423-9958; fax: 815-423-5824
http://www.cem.va.gov/CEM/cems/nchp/abrahamlincoln.asp

Ford's Theatre National Historic Site
511 Tenth Street, N.W.
Washington, DC 20004
202-426-6924; fax: 202-426-1845
http://www.nps.gov/foth

Gettysburg National Military Park and Cemetery
97 Taneytown Road
Gettysburg, PA 17325-2804
717-334-1124; fax: 717-334-1891
http://www.nps.gov/gett

Knob Creek Farm
7120 Bardstown Road
Hodgenville, KY 42748
502-549-3741
http://www.nps.gov/abli

Lincoln Birthplace National Historic Site (Sinking Spring Farm)
2995 Lincoln Farm Road
Hodgenville, KY 42748
270-358-3137; fax: 270-358-3874
http://www.nps.gov/abli

Lincoln Boyhood National Memorial
P.O. Box 1816
Lincoln City, IN 47552-1816
812-937-4541; fax: 812-937-9929
http://www.nps.gov/libo

Lincoln Depot
10th and Monroe
Springfield, IL 62701-1905
http://www.nps.gov/liho/depot/depot.htm

Lincoln-Herndon Law Offices State Historic Site
6th and Adams Streets
Springfield, IL 62701
217-785-7289
http://www.illinoishistory.gov/hs/lincoln_herndon.htm

Lincoln Home National Historic Site
431 South Eighth Street
Springfield, IL 62701-1905
217-492-4241; fax: 217-492-4673
http://www.nps.gov/liho

Lincoln Homestead State Park
5079 Lincoln Park Road
Springfield, KY 40069-9504
859-336-7461
http://parks.ky.gov/stateparks/lh

Lincoln Memorial
900 Ohio Drive, S.W.
Washington, DC 20024
202-485-9880
http://www.nps.gov/linc

Lincoln Memorial Shrine
125 West Vine Street
Redlands, CA 92373
909-798-7632
http://www.lincolnshrine.org

Lincoln Monument
Lafayette and Oakland Avenue
Council Bluffs, IA
800-228-6878

Lincoln Monument
Sherman Hill
Laramie, WY
800-445-5305

Lincoln Tomb State Historic Site
Oak Ridge Cemetery
1500 Monument Avenue
Springfield, IL 62702
217-782-2717
http://www.illinoishistory.gov/hs/lincoln_tomb.htm

Lincoln Trail Homestead State Memorial
705 Spitler Park Drive
Mt. Zion, IL 62549
217-864-3121
http://dnr.state.il.us/lands/landmgt/PARKS/R3/Linctrl.htm

Lincoln's New Salem State Historic Site
15588 History Lane
Petersburg, IL 62675
217-632-4000; fax: 217-632-4010
http://www.lincolnsnewsalem.com

Metamora Courthouse
113 East Partridge
Metamora, IL 61548
309-367-4470
http://www.illinoishistory.gov/hs/metamora_courthouse.htm

Mount Pulaski Courthouse State Historic Site
P.O. Box 355
Lincoln, IL 62656
217-792-3919
http://www.illinoishistory.gov/hs/mount_pulaski.htm

Mount Rushmore National Memorial
13000 Highway 244
Building 31, Suite 1
Keystone, SD 57751-0268
605-574-2523; fax: 605-574-2307
http://www.nps.gov/moru

Old State Capitol State Historic Site
5th and Adams Street
Springfield, IL 62701
217-785-7960
http://www.illinoishistory.gov/hs/old_capitol.htm

Postville Courthouse
Greenfield Village
20900 Oakwood Boulevard
Dearborn, MI 48124-4088
313-982-6100; TDD: 313-271-2455
http://www.hfmgv.org/village/mainstreet/logancounty/default.asp

Postville Courthouse State Historic Site (replica)
914 Fifth Street
Lincoln, IL 62656
217-732-8930
http://www.illinoishistory.gov/hs/postville_courthouse.htm

President Lincoln and Soldiers' Home National Monument
Lincoln Cottage
AFRH-W Box 1315
3700 North Capitol Street, N.W.
Washington, DC 20011-8400
202-829-0436; fax: 202-829-0437
http://www.lincolncottage.org

Libraries

Abraham Lincoln Collection
Department of Special Collections
Green Library
Stanford University Libraries
Stanford, CA 94305-6004
650-725-1022
http://content.cdlib.org/view?docId=tf8g5006hw

Abraham Lincoln Collection
Howard Gotlieb Archival Research Center
Mugar Memorial Library
Boston University
771 Commonwealth Avenue
Boston, MA 02215
617-353-3696; fax: 617-353-2838
http://www.bu.edu/archives/holdings/historical/lincoln.html

Abraham Lincoln Documents
Illinois State Archives
Margaret Cross Norton Building
Capitol Complex
Springfield, IL 62756
217-782-4682; fax: 217-524-3930
http://www.sos.state.il.us/departments/archives/lincoln.html

Abraham Lincoln Library and Museum
Lincoln Memorial University
Cumberland Gap Parkway
Harrogate, TN 37752-2006
423-869-6235; fax: 423-869-6350
http://www.lmunet.edu/museum/index.html

Abraham Lincoln Presidential Library and Museum
112 North Sixth Street

Springfield, IL 62701
800-610-2094 or 217-782-5764
http://www.alplm.org/home.html

Bissett-Witherspoon Lincoln Collection
Washington State University Libraries
Manuscripts, Archives, and Special Collections
Pullman, WA 99164-5610
509-335-6691
http://www.wsulibs.wsu.edu/holland/masc/finders/cg174.htm

llinois State Library
Gwendolyn Brooks Building
300 South 2nd Street
Springfield, IL 62701-1796
217-785-5600
http://www.cyberdriveillinois.com/departments/library/home.html

International Lincoln Center Library
International Lincoln Center for American Studies
Louisiana State University in Shreveport
323 Bronson Hall
One University Place
Shreveport, LA 71115-2301
318-797-5138; fax: 318-795-4203
http://www.lsus.edu/lincoln/library.asp

James Wills Bollinger Collection of Lincolniana
Special Collections Department
University of Iowa Libraries
Iowa City, IA 52242-1420
319-335-5921; fax: 319-335-5900
http://www.lib.uiowa.edu/spec-coll/MSC/ToMsc100/MsC36/MsC36_bollinger.html

Jones Lincoln Collection
West Virginia Wesleyan College

59 College Avenue
Buckhannon, WV 26201
304-473-8013; fax: 304-473-8888
http://www.wvwc.edu/lib/serv-lincoln.htm

Joseph N. Nathanson Collection of Lincolniana
McGill University Libraries
3459 McTavish Street
Montreal, Quebec H3A 1Y1 Canada
514-398-4711; fax: 514-398-5143
http://digital.library.mcgill.ca/lincoln/intro/cover1a.html

Lincoln Collection
Special Collections
University of Delaware Library
Newark, DE 19717-5267
302-831-2229
http://www.lib.udel.edu/ud/spec/exhibits/lincoln/index.htm

Lincoln Collection
Special Collections/Archives
Clement C. Maxwell Library
10 Shaw Road
Bridgewater State College
Bridgewater, MA 02325
508-531-1033
http://www.bridgew.edu/Library/speccoll.cfm

Lincoln Collection
Lawrence Lee Pelletier Library
Allegheny College
Meadville, PA 16335
814-332-3769
http://library.allegheny.edu/Special/OtherCollections.htm

Lincoln Collection Harold K. Sage
Milner Library
Illinois State University
Normal, IL 61790-8900
309-438-7450 or 309-438-2871
http://www.mlb.ilstu.edu/ressubj/speccol/lincoln.htm

Lincoln Digital Collections
William Henry Smith Memorial Library
Indiana Historical Society
450 West Ohio Street
Indianapolis, IN 46202
317-232-1882
http://www.indianahistory.org/library/digital_image/digitalpics.html

Lincoln Room
Lilly Library
Indiana University
1200 East Seventh Street
Bloomington, IN 47405-5500
812-855-2452; fax: 812-855-3143
http://www.indiana.edu/~liblilly/index.html

Lincoln Room Manuscript Collections
University of Illinois
422 Library
1408 West Gregory Drive
Urbana, IL 61801
217-333-1777; 217-333-2214
http://www.library.uiuc.edu/ihx

McClellan-Lincoln Collection
John Hay Library
Brown University
Box A
20 Prospect Street

Providence, RI 02912
401-863-3723; fax: 401-863-2093
http://www.brown.edu/Facilities/University_Library/libs/hay/collections/index.htm

Mr. Lincoln's Virtual Library
Library of Congress
101 Independence Avenue, S.E.
Washington, DC 20540
202-707-5000
http://lcweb2.loc.gov/ammem/alhtml/alhome.html

National Archives and Records Administration
8601 Adelphi Road
College Park, MD 20740-6001
866-272-6272; fax: 301-837-0483
http://www.archives.gov

W. W. Griest Collection of Lincolniana
Archives and Special Collections Department
Shadek-Fackenthal Library
Franklin & Marshall College
P.O. Box 3003
Lancaster, PA 17604-3003
717-291-4225 or 717-358-4433; fax: 717-291-4160
http://www.library.fandm.edu/archives/mscoll/griest.html

Waldo-Lincoln Collection
Department of Special Collections
Waldo Library
Rare Book Rm. #3015
Western Michigan University
1903 West Michigan Avenue
Kalamazoo, MI 49008-5353
269-387-5221
http://www.wmich.edu/library/special/collections/waldo-lincoln.php

William E. Barton Collection of Lincolniana
Special Collections Research Center
University of Chicago Library
1100 E. 57th Street
Chicago, IL 60637
773-702-8705; fax: 773-702-3728
http://www.lib.uchicago.edu/e/spcl/barton.html

Museums

Abraham Lincoln Library and Museum
Lincoln Memorial University
Cumberland Gap Parkway
Harrogate, TN 37752-2006
423-869-6235; fax: 423-869-6350
http://www.lmunet.edu/museum/index.html

Abraham Lincoln Presidential Library and Museum
112 North Sixth Street
Springfield, IL 62701
800-610-2094 or 217-782-5764
http://www.alplm.org/home.html

Captain Forbes House Museum
Lincoln Collection and Log Cabin Replica
215 Adams Street
Milton, MA 02186
617-696-1815
http://www.forbeshousemuseum.org

Lincoln College Museum
300 Keokuk Street

Lincoln, IL 62656
217-735-5050
http://www.lincolncollege.edu/museum/index.htm

Lincoln-Douglas Debate Museum
416 West Madison Avenue
Charleston, IL 61920
217-348-0430
http://www.charlestontourism.org

Lincoln Highway National Museum & Archives
102 Old Lincoln Way West
Galion, OH 44833
419-462-2212; fax: 419-462-2214
http://www.lincoln-highway-museum.org

Lincoln Museum
200 East Berry Street
Fort Wayne, IN 46802
260-455-3864; fax: 260-455-6922
http://www.thelincolnmuseum.org

Lincoln Museum
66 Lincoln Square
Hodgenville, KY 42748
270-358-3163
http://www.noinkmedia.com/lincolnmuseum/index.htm

Lincoln Photo Essay
Chicago Historical Society
Clark Street at North Avenue
Chicago, IL 60614-6071
312-642-4600; fax: 312-266-2077
http://www.chicagohistory.org/lincolnphotoessay.html

Weldon Petz Abraham Lincoln Collection
Plymouth Historical Society Museum
155 South Main Street
Plymouth, MI 48170-1635
734-455-8940; fax: 734-455-7797
http://www.plymouthhistory.org

Other Web Resources

A House Divided: America in the Age of Lincoln
http://www.digitalhistory.uh.edu/ahd/index.html

> An online exhibit sponsored by the Gilder Lehrman Institute of American History.

Looking for Lincoln Heritage Consortium
209 South Sixth Street
Springfield, IL 62701
217-782-6817
http://www.lookingforlincoln.com

> An online guide to sites associated with Lincoln in central Illinois.

Mr. Lincoln
Lincoln Institute
Gilder Lehrman Institute of American History
One Fausett Place, Suite 130
Greenwich, CT 06830-6581
http://www.mrlincolnandthefounders.org
http://www.mrlincolnandfreedom.org
http://www.mrlincolnandfriends.org
http://www.mrlincolnandnewyork.org
http://www.mrlincolnswhitehouse.org

A series of web sites that provide commentary and background on Lincoln and several topics related to his life and presidency: the founders, freedom, friends, New York, and the White House.

The Papers of Abraham Lincoln
#1 Old State Capitol Place
Springfield, IL 62701-1507
217-785-9130; fax: 217-524-6973
http://www.papersofabrahamlincoln.org

A project of the Illinois Historic Preservation Agency and the Abraham Lincoln Presidential Library and Museum.

The Time of the Lincolns
http://www.pbs.org/wgbh/amex/lincolns

An online companion to the PBS film *Abraham and Mary Lincoln: A House Divided.*

Author Index

Author Index

The following index includes all the authors and speakers whose works appear in *The Abraham Lincoln Companion.*

Subject Index

Subject Index

The following index includes the people, places, and events discussed in the documents in *The Abraham Lincoln Companion.*